¡Marcha!

**LATINOS IN CHICAGO
AND THE MIDWEST**

Series Editors
Frances R. Aparicio,
University of Illinois at Chicago
Pedro Cabán,
State University of New York
Juan Mora-Torres,
De Paul University
Maria de los Angeles Torres,
University of Illinois at Chicago

*A list of books in the series appears
at the end of this book.*

¡Marcha!

Latino Chicago and the Immigrant Rights Movement

Edited by
**AMALIA PALLARES AND
NILDA FLORES-GONZÁLEZ**

UNIVERSITY OF ILLINOIS PRESS
Urbana, Chicago, and Springfield

Library of Congress Cataloging-in-Publication Data
Marcha! : Latino Chicago and the immigrant rights movement /
edited by Amalia Pallares and Nilda Flores-Gonzalez.
p.   cm. — (Latinos in Chicago and the Midwest)
Includes bibliographical references and index.
ISBN 978-0-252-03529-6 (cloth : alk. paper)
ISBN 978-0-252-07716-6 (pbk. : alk. paper)
1. Hispanic Americans—Illinois—Chicago. 2. Immigrants—Illinois—
Chicago. 3. Immigrants—Civil rights—United States—Case studies.
4. Immigrants—Government policy—United States—Case studies.
5. Social integration—Government policy—United States—
Case studies. 6. Social action—United States—Case studies.
I. Pallares, Amalia, 1965– II. Flores-Gonzalez, Nilda.
F548.9.S75M37   2010
973'.0468—dc22   2010012544

This book is dedicated
to all our undocumented
sisters and brothers who
struggle every day for
dignity and respect

And to the memory of
Rudy Lozano and all those
who followed his example

No somos uno, no somos cien; somos un chingo, cuéntanos bien!
(We are not one, we are not one hundred; we are loads, count us well!)

—Chant repeated during May 1, 2006, Chicago march

Contents

Acknowledgments   ix

Timeline of Immigrant Mobilization   xi

Introduction   xv

Part 1. Political and Historical Context

1. Taking the Public Square:
   The National Struggle for Immigrant Rights   3
   Nilda Flores-González and Elena R. Gutiérrez

2. The Chicago Context   37
   Amalia Pallares

Part 2. Institutions

3. Competing Narratives on the March: The Challenges
   of News Media Representations in Chicago   65
   Frances R. Aparicio

4. The Role of the Catholic Church in the Chicago
   Immigrant Mobilization   79
   *Stephen P. Davis, Juan R. Martinez,
   and R. Stephen Warner*

5. Hoy Marchamos, Mañana Votamos:
   It's All Part of the Curriculum   97
   Irma M. Olmedo

6. Labor Joins la Marcha: How New Immigrant
   Activists Restored the Meaning of May Day   109
   Leon Fink

Part 3. Agency

7. Marchando al Futuro: Latino Immigrant Rights
   Leadership in Chicago   123
   Leonard G. Ramírez, José Perales-Ramos,
   and José Antonio Arellano

8. Mexican Hometown Associations in Chicago:
   The Newest Agents of Civic Participation   146
   Xóchitl Bada

9. Permission to March? High School Youth Participation
   in the Immigrant Rights Movement   163
   Sonia Oliva

Part 4. Subjectivities

10. Minutemen and the Subject of Democracy   179
    David Bleeden, Caroline Gottschalk-Druschke,
    and Ralph Cintrón

11. Immigrants, Citizens, or Both? The Second Generation
    in the Immigrant Rights Marches   198
    Nilda Flores-González

12. Representing "La Familia": Family Separation and
    Immigrant Activism   215
    Amalia Pallares

13. Grappling with *Latinidad*: Puerto Rican Activism in
    Chicago's Pro–Immigrant Rights Movement   237
    Michael Rodríguez Muñiz

List of Contributors   259

Index   263

Illustrations follow page 62

Acknowledgments

When we embarked on this journey three years ago, we sought to document and analyze an extraordinarily important moment in U.S. social movement and Latino history. As scholars who not only were based in Chicago but understood it as a rich site of community, immigrant, and labor activism, we believed that the city was an ideal case study that could teach us about the causes and consequences of the marches, the subjectivities of its participants, and the impact of these events on immigrant activism and public policy.

What we could not anticipate was that our commitment to this project would be shared so passionately by so many people inside and outside of the university who also wanted the Chicago story to be told. While we compensated some, many more of them generously volunteered their time and energy to ensure that this project would come to fruition. We have been sustained and inspired through the project's most challenging moments by our memories of dozens of students who joined our survey teams though we could offer no pay or academic credit; of graduate students hopping on trains and buses to observe multiple meetings and rallies; and of activists generously allowing us to shadow them.

We would like to thank our undergraduate researchers and especially Nadia Hussein Abdulhamid, Rudy Aguilar, Juan Gerardo Arroyo, Gerardo de Anda, Kimberly Manzanares, Joanna Maravilla, Winne Monu, Emma Olivera, Gisselle Rodriguez, Mauricio Román, Daniela Ruíz, Jodene Velázquez, and Marisol Velásquez. The graduate students who worked arduously on logistics, participant observation, data collection and analysis, and copyediting include Victoria Badillo, Jillian Baez, Amber Cooper, Stephen Davis, Ruth Gomberg, Maria Elena Gutiérrez-Ospitia, Vanessa Guridy, Loren Henderson, Yu-Li Hsieh, Diógenes Lamarche, Della Leavitt, Nawojka Lesinsiki, Juan Martinez, Sonia Oliva, Melissa Rivera Santana, Michael Rodríguez Muñiz, and Luisa Rollins.

We also express our gratitude to the colleagues who have helped us to conceptualize the project and make it more precise: Jonathan Fox, Cedric Herring, Maria Krysan, Aldo Lauria-Santiago, Isabel Molina, and Otto Santa Ana. We also collectively thank our colleagues in Latin American and Latino studies, sociology, and political science who were not part of the project but supported us in many different ways. University of Illinois at Chicago staff and academic professionals who have been extraordinarily helpful include Marta Ayala, Ebony Brooks, Debbie Farrier, Rosa Ortiz Lorenzana, Olga Padilla, Amanda Stewart, and Teri Williams. Two journalists who were especially helpful are Leticia Espinosa and Tania Unzueta. We also thank photographers Crystal Barrios, Sandro Corona, Victor Espinosa, Hector Gonzalez, Jhonathan Gomez, and Anka Karewicz.

The immigrant mobilization project could not have sustained itself without financial support from the following University of Illinois at Chicago academic and research units: the College of Liberal Arts and Sciences, the Great Cities Institute, the Department of Political Science, the Department of Sociology, the Institute for Research on Race and Public Policy, the Institute of Governmental and Public Affairs, the Latin American and Latino Studies Program, and the Office for Social Science Research. More specifically, we thank the people who made this support happen: John Betancur, Bill Bridges, Christopher Comer, Francesca Gaiba, David Perry, Barbara Risman, Dick Simpson, Jeremy Teitelbaum, and Maria de los Angeles Torres. We also appreciate the Mexican American Student Association's assistance in planning our 2007 conference.

We thank Joan Catapano and Rebecca McNulty of the University of Illinois Press for believing in this project from the start. We are also indebted to Rodolfo García Zamora, Raúl Delgado Wise, and Editorial Porrúa for their translation and publication of the book in Spanish.

Both of us owe enormous debts to our families for supporting us throughout the process and forgiving our long absences as we followed activists throughout the United States and in Mexico. Amalia thanks her parents, Victor and Carlota, and her siblings, Victor, Jerry, and Carla, with whom she shares four decades of immigrant experience. She is also grateful to her sons, Antonio and Pablo, for reminding her of the importance of playtime. Nilda appreciates the unconditional love, understanding, and support of her husband, Joel Palka, and their children, Elena, Diana, and Julian. She thanks her mother, Eva, and late father, Erving, for teaching her compassion and commitment to the less fortunate. She also appreciates the support of her siblings, Evi, Naydi, Machin, and Diani, and especially the encouragement and "cheerleading" of her sister Angie.

Finally, we give a very special thanks to all the activists who made this work possible, some of whom are mentioned in this book and some of whom are not. They continue to inform, move, and inspire us through their struggle. This book is dedicated to them.

Timeline of Immigrant Mobilization

2005

July 1: March in Chicago's Back of the Yards neighborhood; approximately fifty thousand people attend.

2006

March 10: First megamarch, between one hundred thousand and three hundred thousand people march from Union Park to Federal Plaza.

March 29: The City of Chicago alters its municipal code to prohibit city public officials, including police, from collecting information on residents' legal status unless they are charged with a criminal violation; this "sanctuary" policy complements executive decrees in place since 1986.

April 19: Nearly twelve hundred IFCO workers are detained in immigration raids nationwide, including sixty in Chicago.

May 1: Between 400,000 and 750,000 people march from Union Park to Grant Park, the largest march in Chicago history.

May 10–June 1: Elvira Arellano (a Sin Fronteras activist and undocumented immigrant) and Flor Crisóstomo (one of the arrested IFCO workers) stage a hunger strike in Pilsen until a federal judge delays the IFCO workers' court appearances for a year.

July 19: Centro sin Fronteras organizes a march to stop deportations and raids; approximately thirty thousand people attend.

August 11–13: The National Convention of Immigrants takes place in Hillside, Illinois.

August 15: Elvira Arellano seeks sanctuary in the Adalberto Unido Church.

September 1–4: The March 10 Coalition organizes a three-day march to Batavia, Illinois.

2007

March 22: Democratic representative Luis Gutiérrez of Illinois and Republican representative Jeff Flake of Arizona introduce the STRIVE Act.

April 24: U.S. Immigration and Customs Enforcement conducts a raid at the Little Village Mall, arresting twelve people for identity theft.

May 1: Approximately three hundred thousand people march from Union Park to Grant Park in the country's largest rally held that day.

May: The Secure Borders, Economic Opportunity, and Immigration Reform Act of 2007 (S. 1348), known as the Comprehensive Immigration Reform Act, is introduced.

June 5: Cook County becomes the first sanctuary county in the nation, prohibiting officials from collecting information on immigrants' legal status.

July–August: The Waukegan City Council investigates the possibility of training local police officers as immigration enforcement agents under Section 287(g) of the Illegal Immigration Reform and Immigrant Responsibility Act; three thousand people rally against the idea on July 21; the Labor Council for Latin American Advancement and Centro sin Fronteras help to organize a consumer boycott of all businesses that do not oppose the plan.

August 19: Elvira Arellano, who has left her sanctuary at the Adalberto Unido Church, is arrested in Los Angeles and deported to Tijuana, Mexico.

November 16–17: The Mexican Parliament hosts a two-day summit with hundreds of representatives of Mexican immigrant organizations from the United States in an effort to create an autonomous Mexican Parliament in the United States.

2008

January 23: Flor Crisóstomo seeks sanctuary at the Adalberto Unido Church.

March 8: The March 10 Coalition hosts a conference to develop coalitions with organizers in other midwestern states.

May 1: Between twenty and twenty-five thousand participants march from Union Square to Federal Plaza under the banner "This is America's new majority."

May 12: U.S. Immigration and Customs Enforcement, the Department of Labor, and the Department of Justice raid a meat processor in Postville, Iowa, arresting 398 people, mostly Guatemalans, on charges of identity theft; those arrested are offered a deal in exchange for a guilty plea.

July 12: Mexican immigrant Luis Ramírez is murdered by four teenagers in Shenandoah, Pennsylvania, mobilizing activists in different parts of the country, who use it as an example of intense anti-immigrant sentiment.

August 5: The Chicago City Council holds a public hearing on complaints that the city's police department is violating a municipal ordinance by providing U.S. Immigration and Customs Enforcement with information about undocumented citizens detained for traffic violations.

October 8: The Chicago City Council adopts a resolution in favor of a moratorium on all raids and deportations, subsequently calling on all Illinois state and national public officials to support the idea.

November 4: Barack Obama is elected U.S. president, raising expectations that comprehensive immigration reform will be addressed during his term in office.

November 15: Luis Gutiérrez and the Ya Basta Coalition hold a massive meeting in the St. Pius Church to collect petitions of citizen support for undocumented family and friends to present to Obama; the event is repeated at other Chicago churches, and the Congressional Hispanic Caucus eventually takes on sponsorship of what becomes known as the Familias Unidas Campaign.

2009

January 20: Barack Obama is inaugurated as U.S. president.

January 21: Rallies are held in Washington, D.C., and other cities to demand a moratorium on raids and deportations.

March 26: The DREAM Act is reintroduced in the U.S. House of Representatives.

March–May: The Congressional Hispanic Caucus holds Familias Unidas events in more than twenty cities, culminating in a Mother's Day event in Chicago.

May 1: Between two thousand and five thousand people march from Union Park to Federal Plaza.

June 24: Senator Charles Schumer announces the principles for the comprehensive immigration reform bill he plans to introduce.

August 20: President Obama and homeland security secretary Janet Napolitano meet with immigration activists and reaffirm their commitment to immigration reform.

September 7: Hundreds march from Union Park to Federal Plaza on Labor Day to protest the lack of movement on immigration reform.

October 13: A national immigration rally is held in Washington, D.C.; more than three thousand demonstrators from seventeen states attend as Congressman Luis Gutiérrez introduces the principles for his bill.

October 18: Flor Crisóstomo leaves sanctuary for an undisclosed location.

Introduction

In 2006, hundreds of thousands of people took to the streets to protest a congressional bill that would have criminalized undocumented immigrants and those who assisted them. More than 250 massive marches, or megamarches, as they were popularly called, were held throughout the country in cities large and small during March and April, culminating in simultaneous marches on May 1 that drew an estimated 3.5 to 5 million people (Bada, Fox, and Selee 2006, 36). In Chicago, more than 100,000 people marched for immigrant rights on March 10; on May 1, over 400,000 marched from Union Park to Grant Park, the largest such demonstration in the city's history.[1] Although the cumulative impact of all these marches cannot yet be fully determined, what became known as the Spring of the Immigrant has had a number of immediate effects—most noticeably, stopping the Senate from enacting the Sensenbrenner Bill, rendering the struggles of undocumented immigrants and their families more visible, and mobilizing thousands of people more systematically to organize for immigrant rights.

These massive mobilizations surprised even the lifelong activists who coordinated the marches. At the University of Illinois at Chicago (UIC), more than a dozen faculty and graduate students met after the March 10 rally to discuss the urgent need to learn more. As the marches unfolded, academics, journalists, and observers began to ask themselves what had made possible these marches, who the marchers were, how a population that analysts had considered a sleeping giant (demographically strong but politically weak) had awakened, why people had become so galvanized, and what the marches meant. (For more on the sleeping giant metaphor, see Monforti 2008.)

To address some of these questions, this group of UIC faculty and students decided to create a collective research project in which each researcher or group of researchers would pursue a discrete but interrelated project from a different perspective and disciplinary approach. Together, we created the Immigrant Mobilization Project (IMP), codirected by Nilda Flores-González and Amalia Pallares, and decided to create a common base of knowledge by conducting a survey of the May 1 marchers to supplement the individual projects.

The IMP randomly surveyed 410 marchers, asking who they were, why they were marching, and what their general patterns of civic and political engagement were. A team of more than seventy faculty members and graduate and undergraduate students surveyed participants in Spanish and English, approaching most of them either in Union Park before the march started or in Grant Park while people were listening to speakers on the stage, eating, or preparing to leave.[2]

Who were the marchers? Perhaps our most important finding was that 74 percent of our respondents were citizens (figure I.1). These initial findings showed a broad support for immigrant rights among the native-born as well as naturalized citizens that runs counter to the image of the marchers as comprised mostly or mainly of undocumented immigrants.[3]

Most of the marchers were Latinos, but other groups were represented (figure I.2). Among participants who were born outside of the United States, 81 percent were Mexican and 10 percent were from other Latin American countries (figure I.3). Participation was fairly evenly distributed between men and women, and 51 percent of the marchers we interviewed were between fifteen and twenty-eight years old. We also found an even distribution of education levels among the marchers as well as a relatively diverse distribution of incomes (figures I.4 and I.5).

Figure I.1. Citizenship of Marchers, 2006 and 2007

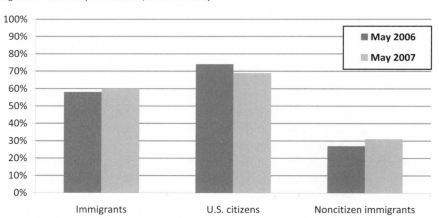

Data for figures in the introduction are from the 2006 report by Nilda Flores-González, Amalia Pallares, Cedric Herring, and Maria Krysan, 2006, "UIC Immigrant Mobilization Project: General Survey Findings." Available at: http://www.wilsoncenter.org/news/docs/uicstudy.pdf.

Figure I.2. Ethnicity of Marchers, 2006 and 2007

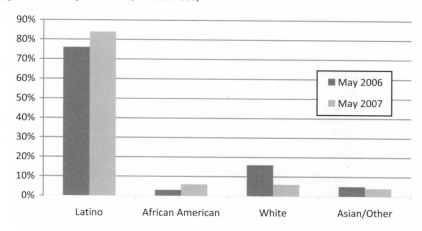

Figure I.3. Nationality of Marchers, 2006 and 2007

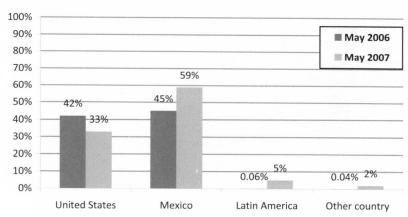

Figure I.4. Age of Marchers, 2006

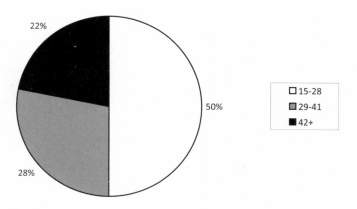

Figure I.5. Household Income of Marchers, 2006

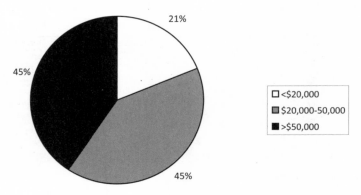

□ <$20,000
▨ $20,000-50,000
■ >$50,000

Why were people marching? Forty-four percent of respondents stated that they were marching to support immigrants. More specific reasons included supporting legalization, defending rights in general, and showing unity (figure I.6). When asked what they hoped the marches would accomplish, the most common response was legalization of undocumented people—that is, policy change—followed by more general concerns about civil rights and justice (figure I.7).

What were the marchers' broader patterns of civic and political engagement? Thirty-six million strong and growing, the Latino population has long been considered demographically important but with a relatively low level of political power that does not yet match its numbers. Our survey revealed that although many marchers had not previously been politically engaged, many other par-

Figure I.6. Important Reasons for Marching, 2006 and 2007

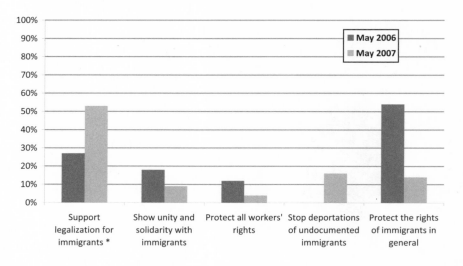

Figure I.7. Goals of Marchers, 2006

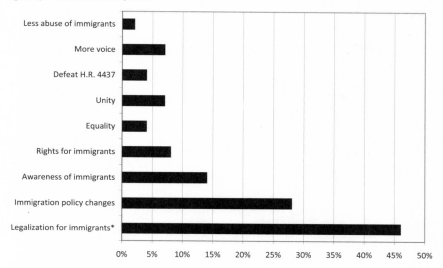

* Marchers were asked, "What do you think this march will accomplish?" Many had more than one reason. These numbers reflect the most popular reasons.

ticipants had engaged in earlier political activity. Sixty-nine percent of those eligible had voted in past elections, and many had attended public meetings, signed petitions, or engaged in other activities (figure I.8). An overwhelming majority of the marchers expressed positive feelings about the United States, with 91 percent expressing strong love for the country (figure I.9).

This quick synopsis of a more extensive survey project provides only a brief glimpse of the marchers and their motivations. (For a more extensive statistical summary of the 2006 march, see Flores-González et al. 2006.) However, this summary points to a broader and more complicated story than the one conveyed by press reports that often portrayed the event as a "march of illegals." While many undocumented people marched, they were clearly outnumbered by citizens. Further, although most marchers were immigrants, others were not. Legalization was a main concern, but the immigrant rights agenda shared by marchers conveyed a much broader set of concerns about civil rights, workers' rights, social justice, and democracy.

Hence, while the survey provided some initial insights, we realized that further learning about this movement required more in-depth research and the use of multiple methodologies to analyze the set of political and historical forces that led to the Chicago marches as well as their meaning and impact. We presented our initial findings at a February 2007 conference held at UIC that brought together academics and activists. We subsequently held a workshop where all of the authors received extensive comments.

Figure I.8. Previous Civic Participation of Marchers, 2006 and 2007

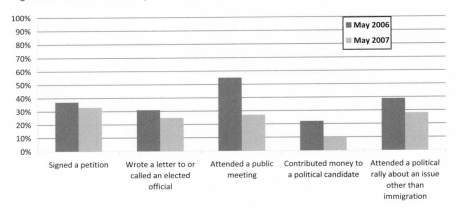

Figure I.9. Percentage Distribution of Patriotism and Love for the United States by Citizenship Status of Marchers, 2006

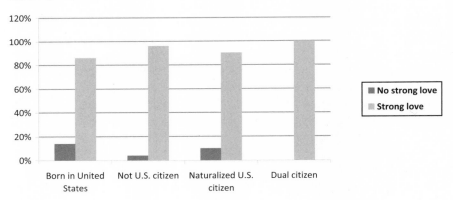

On May 1, 2007, another immigrant rights march took place in Chicago, and we again surveyed participants, reaching the same general conclusions as we found the preceding year. Both marches were majority Latino, but the 2007 march showed slight increases in Latino and African American participation and a significant decline in white participation (figure I.2). The 2007 march also had higher percentages of immigrants and noncitizens (figure I.1). The 2007 marchers were also more likely to come from outside the United States (figure I.3).

People's reasons for participating also changed significantly between 2006 and 2007 as a consequence of the changes that had occurred over that time (figure I.6). In 2006, most survey respondents stated that the most important reason for marching was to protect the rights of immigrants in general, followed by support for legalization of immigrants. In 2007, respondents were more focused on policy, marching to support legalization or to stop deportations.

The most dramatic difference between the marches is the 2007 marchers' somewhat lower reports of civic engagement (figure I.8). Nevertheless, the 2007 rates reflect the national average for the general Latino population, providing support for the claim that marchers are just as likely to participate in political behaviors as other Latinos. In fact, a comparison of the voting rates and civic engagement of 2006 and 2007 marchers with the Pew Hispanic averages shows that the marchers displayed rates of participation at least equal to those of registered Latinos in two categories (writing to elected officials and attending public meetings) but were less likely to contribute money to politicians (figure I.10). Thus, at least among Chicago's Latinos, no strict dichotomy necessarily exists between the use of conventional strategies and mass mobilization.

This volume provides an in-depth and multidisciplinary analysis of the immigrant rights movement in Chicago and its relationship to the national movement. Focusing on Chicago as a case study enables us to provide a more complete examination of the different types of organizations, institutions, and social actors that have shaped the contemporary immigrant rights movement. Chicago has a long-standing and complex history of immigrant activism and has been at the forefront of contemporary activism: it was the second city to hold a massive march in 2006; it is a major center of hometown association national and international organizing (Chicago hometown association leaders helped organize the Latin American Migrant Community Summit in Morelia in May 2007); it is home to the first church to provide sanctuary to an undocumented immigrant

Figure I.10. Civic Participation of Citizen Latino Marchers (2007) versus General Citizen Latino Population

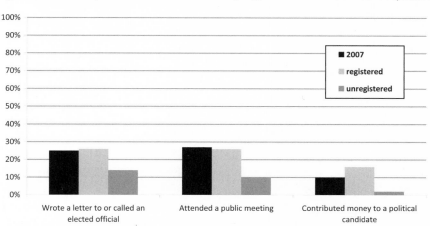

Source: Pew Hispanic Center 2004.

facing deportation (Elvira Arellano); and it staged the largest immigrant rights marches in the country in 2007 and 2008. It is, therefore, a microcosm of the immigrant rights activism that has enveloped the nation and can provide important lessons for the study of the immigrant rights movement as a whole.

The Chicago case has taught us that at least three characteristics distinguish this movement from the Mexican and Puerto Rican civil rights movements of the 1970s. First, while the previous movements had an explicit civil rights agenda, arguing for education, urban justice, and land rights and against police brutality and racism, immigrant rights were often included implicitly but not as a central platform. The current movement is characterized by an agenda that centers on immigrant rights but also relies on them as a platform for engaging questions of human rights, civil rights, and workers' rights that concern most Latinos and all working-class communities of color. Thus, although the two generations of struggle are distinct, they should not be seen as unrelated. In fact, while many of the participants are young, several of the organizers were first active in the 1970s in CASA, the Raza Unida Party, and community organizations; others became involved in immigrant rights as a result of the 1986 amnesty.[4]

The focus on the rights of the undocumented marks a second important characteristic of this movement—a departure from six decades of Mexican activism divided between those who sought to emphasize the struggle for undocumented immigrants and those who sought to deemphasize it or even undermine it. In his important book, *Walls and Mirrors* (1995), David Gutiérrez explains that for many Mexican Americans trying to organize collectively to get ahead, integration into the United States required separating themselves from any association with undocumented immigrants and emphasizing "Americanness."[5] In addition, many Mexican American workers felt that they competed directly with undocumented labor and rejected a more inclusive agenda. Those organizations that spoke for the rights of the undocumented, such as the Congress of Spanish-Speaking Peoples, were in the minority. While Chicano movement activists in the 1970s rejected this assimilationist model and sought to critique the system that excluded them, they focused primarily on their status as second-class citizens, not on the rights of people formally excluded from the category (see Haney-López 2003; Muñoz 2007; Oropeza 2005).

We are increasingly looking at a very different picture. A recent survey by the Pew Hispanic Center reveals that most Latinos oppose the intensification of the campaign against undocumented immigrants: 81 percent of Hispanics say that immigration enforcement should be left mainly to the federal authorities rather than the local police; 76 percent disapprove of workplace raids; 73 percent disapprove of the criminal prosecution of undocumented immigrants; and 70 percent disapprove of the criminal prosecution of employers who hire undocumented immigrants. Moreover, the survey found that a majority of Latinos worry about deportation: 40 percent worry about it a lot, while an additional 17 percent worry about it some (López and Minushkin 2008). These concerns appear to affect Latino voting patterns. A poll conducted by the National Council of La Raza just before the 2006 elections found that 51 percent of Latino registered and likely voters in twenty-three states said that immigration was an important issue, and a Pew Hispanic Center poll in June and July 2008 showed that 75 percent of Latino registered voters viewed the immigration issue as "extremely important" or "very important" (Immigration Policy Center 2008). These findings suggest that while not all Latinos support the rights of the undocumented, the majority of the 46 million Latinos in this country are troubled by current immigration policy and the treatment of the undocumented.

While some of these findings can be explained by the fact that many naturalized Latinos have undocumented immigrants in their immediate or extended families, several of the authors in this volume have determined that this support is also explained by other factors, including political and ideological forms of solidarity in a period of perceived persecution, cultural and transnational affinities in an increasingly globalized world, and second-generation immigrant identification. Several of the citizen-activists we study draw connections between their civil rights struggle against what they perceive as their status as second-class citizens and the exclusion of the undocumented from formal citizenship. Unlike earlier Latino assimilationist views, the struggles of the undocumented do not impede the ascent of new Americans; rather, social justice and dignity for naturalized Latinos and their descendents rests on the inclusion of the undocumented. And, some activists ask, don't those who have formal citizenship status have a responsibility to serve as the voice for those not recognized as legitimate spokespersons for their cause? Hence, this movement is a hybrid one, in which the principal actors are both legal and undocumented and the former's struggle for equal citizenship and the latter's struggle for formal citizenship are deeply intertwined.

The third distinct characteristic of this movement is that it is a panethnic and pan-Latino movement. While other national origin groups were involved in the Chicano and Puerto Rican struggles of the 1970s, those involved in the twenty-first-century movement describe it as a panethnic Latino mobilization. While most of the marchers are Mexican, others are Puerto Rican, Dominican, and Central and South American; in addition, the growing numbers of children of interethnic marriages have participated as organizers, mobilizers, and marchers. The movement also includes immigrants from other groups—in Chicago, Korean, Chinese, Irish, Muslim, and Polish activists have been involved, as have others.

This movement thus simultaneously involves many factors. It clearly involves legalization for undocumented immigrants, but it also a panethnic, transnational, Latino rights, civil rights, human rights, and citizenship rights movement.

To shed light on the movement's complexity and main actors and networks, we divide the book into four parts: Political and Historical Context, Institutions, Agency, and Subjectivities.

Part 1, "Political and Historical Context," introduces the national and local developments and conditions that caused the marches. Chapter 1 provides an overview of the movement's contemporary historical and political context. Starting with the 1986 Immigration and Reform Control Act and ending with the 2008 immigrant marches, Nilda Flores-González and Elena R. Gutiérrez trace the complicated relationships among restrictions on immigration, policy change, and immigrant rights activism that led to the national marches, which did not come out of nowhere. For more than two decades, Latinos have been organizing at the grassroots, state, and national levels to challenge trends in restrictions and enforcement, both internal and on the border, and to struggle for legalization. Although the immigrant rights movement has not always been victorious, it has created an infrastructure and a set of networks that facilitated the massive resistance that arose when draconian policies were proposed in 2006.

Chapter 2 situates the marches in the Chicago Latino context. Amalia Pallares describes the city's history as a center of community and immigrant rights activism, provides some background on the political activism that preceded and informed the marches, describes the main actors and events between the July 2005 and May 2008 marches, and outlines some of the local movement's goals and strategies. Latino community activism began during the late 1960s in Chicago and was followed by a growing number of immigrant-serving organizations and a dense network of community organizing during the 1980s and 1990s. This community activism, however, has a complicated relationship with local politics, as the persistence of the Chicago electoral machine has led to increased Latino political representation but very restricted independent Latino political power. The chapter concludes with an analysis of local activists' ongoing debates regarding mobilization versus organization, grassroots versus national advocacy, and support for party politicians versus political independence, all of which have parallels in other parts of the country.

Part 2, "Institutions," highlights the ways in which the immigrant movement is deeply shaped by and permeates institutions that lie formally outside of but are deeply intertwined with social movement organizations. All three of the institutions examined in this section—the media, the church, and schools—affect the relationship and connections between the marches and Latino communities but do so in an explicitly nonneutral or invested manner.

In chapter 3, Frances R. Aparicio analyzes the differences between the reporting of the marches in Spanish-language and English-language media, finding that Spanish-language outlets are more likely to portray Latinos as voices of authority as well as embodied political subjects. Although Latino reporters for

English-language press provide more balanced representations than do Anglo reporters in the English-language media, the differences between Spanish- and English-language media are difficult to overcome, given the newspapers' different audiences and markets.

In chapter 4, Stephen P. Davis, Juan R. Martinez, and R. Stephen Warner argue that some Catholic parishes have carried out extensive work in politicizing immigrant communities so that members will exercise their economic, social, and political rights. This work predates and extends into the marches and involves what the authors call training in "substantive citizenship"—that is, encouraging immigrants (even those who may not have access to formal citizenship) to act as citizens by assuming new rights and responsibilities. Despite the demographic shifts that may explain this trend, this church activism cannot be taken for granted, as important historical and political conditions may facilitate or impede this type of organizing.

In chapter 5, Irma M. Olmedo enters the classroom to show how some teachers helped make the marches intelligible and meaningful to young Latino students, often within the confines of a predetermined curriculum. These self-selected teachers decided that the normal classroom lesson was insufficient for students in communities active in the marches and decided to integrate the students' life experiences into classroom lessons. Doing so required teachers to take on various tasks and roles in a creative attempt to learn from and use what students already know and to rearticulate it in meaningful and affirmative ways in a pedagogical setting.

Part 3, "Agency," analyzes issues of direct political agency by focusing concretely on the people who organized, mobilized, or participated in the marches. This section highlights the processes by which activists were engaged, addressing concrete visions, goals, strategies, and tactics. Some of these activists were newcomers to the immigrant rights movement, while others had much longer trajectories and still others were shifting gears and creating new priorities.

In chapter 6, Leon Fink examines why labor shifted from opposing to supporting the legalization of undocumented immigrants. First, he argues that unions as political actors experienced an important demographic shift in their rank and file, causing leaders to revisit some of their previous assumptions about the contradictions between the rights of the undocumented and workers' rights. Second, he introduces the voices of local immigrant workers who struggled both within and outside of unions to create an agenda that underscored the congruences between immigrant and workers' rights.

In chapter 7, Leonard G. Ramírez, José Perales-Ramos, and José Antonio Arellano directly address the puzzle of why the immigrant movement lacks one great leader. The movement does not lack leadership but in fact is following a very different model based on a loose coalition of networks and an organizing style that privileges open deliberation and the inclusion of multiple voices. This leadership model enables joint coordination of the marches among very different groups, but it may also impede a more coherent agenda.

In chapter 8, Xóchitl Bada examines the role of hometown associations in the Chicago marches and explains the complex and at times mutually reinforcing relationship between their new role in immigrant activism in the United States and their political activism in Mexico. While hometown associations are better known for their community development work in Mexico, they were active as participants and organizers in the marches. The roots of this activism lie in earlier struggles (directed at governments of both countries) for the rights of Mexican citizens in the United States. The marches have charted new terrain for these associations and provided them with political capital that offers new opportunities for them in U.S. national and local politics.

In chapter 9, Sonia Oliva explains how students participated in the marches despite being prohibited from doing so by the Chicago Public Schools. Students as well as some teachers, staff, and administrators creatively circumvented the school system's directives by individually or collectively identifying tactics that would enable students to attend the march without openly defying regulations, skillfully navigating between acquiescence and contestation. Taking seriously the agency of high school students enables us to move beyond limited views that posit teens as politically passive or potential criminals, a dichotomy that these students' activism directly refutes.

The authors whose chapters are included in part 4, "Subjectivities," examine how groups of people (whether pro-immigrant or restrictionist) articulate their worldview, defend their political positions, and justify their actions. All the chapters part from the premise that political activism does not arise solely from the existence of certain objective conditions. Instead, it is intimately connected to people's subjective interpretations of their social realities, as they select those conditions and "facts" that they find most meaningful. Consequently, debates regarding immigrant rights are never really resolved despite the constant production of data designed to persuade "neutral" citizen-readers to support one particular argument.

In chapter 10, David Bleeden, Caroline Gottschalk-Druschke, and Ralph Cintrón offer a provocative discussion of the rhetoric of the Minutemen, focusing specifically on the views of the Illinois Minutemen whom the authors observed and interviewed. The authors claim that instead of dismissing the Minutemen as mere racists, it is imperative to understand the main premises and assumptions that inform their political positions. Focusing on the Minutemen's topoi (main themes) concerning taxes and the historical foundation of the United States, the authors argue that the Minutemen base their claims on their understanding of democracy as something that they directly own and that is being usurped by a corrupt state and undocumented immigrants, whom they view as cheating or robbing them of their democracy. While the Minutemen exemplify a "limit form" of the democratic subject, they are indeed using the language of democracy to justify their activism and are therefore also a product of liberal democracy.

In chapter 11, Nilda Flores-González examines the participation of U.S.-born, second-generation youth in the immigrant marches, challenging assimilationist views that question citizens' participation in a march for immigrant rights. Second-generation youth identify both as immigrants and as citizens. Paradoxically, their affinity for immigrant communities as a consequence of familial, community, and emotional attachments has led them to realize and exercise their rights as citizens. Frequently underexposed to citizenship education and political participation opportunities in schools, these youth learn substantive citizenship from their more experienced peers as well as youth organizations. Regardless of their level of political experience, most of the youth interviewed expressed an emotional connection to immigrants as well as a deep-seated responsibility to use their citizenship to become a voice for the undocumented.

In chapter 12, Amalia Pallares examines the activism of undocumented immigrants and their family members, who face the possibility of deportation. Using the case study of a campaign founded by a group of families, La Familia Latina Unida, housed in Centro sin Fronteras, she analyzes the forms of participation in which they engage; the identities they construct as tax-paying, law-abiding, moral families; and the ways in which they frame their struggle to appeal to a broader public. The group's president, Elvira Arellano, sought sanctuary in a Methodist church for a year, bringing constantly into question both her agency as an undocumented activist and her fitness as a mother. This case in particular raises important questions about the political subjectivity and representativity of the undocumented among the immigrant movement as well as the general public.

Finally, in chapter 13, Michael Rodríguez Muñiz addresses a question that many observers of the Chicago movement have asked: Why would Puerto Ricans, who are born U.S. citizens, be so active in the immigrant rights movement? Reviewing the existing literature on panethnicity, he emphasizes the need to understand Latino subjectivities as they are transformed over time and not only as "objective" shared historical or cultural conditions. In-depth interviews of activists from the Puerto Rican Cultural Center and a Puerto Rican youth group, Batey Urbano, both of which were extremely active in the movement, show that the sense of solidarity with the immigrant rights movement is explained by anticolonial ideologies, strategic or instrumental visions of mutual exchange, and a sense of shared history of political struggle. Puerto Ricans make the immigrant rights struggle their own not by claiming that they are equal to or like Mexicans but by arguing that they are similar but different. Further, Puerto Ricans view their formal citizenship as a crucial resource in the struggle.

It is our sincere hope that this book will provide a venue for discussion of immigrant rights and Latino politics specifically, and of the health of our democracy more generally. The Chicago case study provides a window into the complexities of the wide range of issues, processes, actors, and relationships that inform the movement and cannot be easily condensed into the metaphor of a sleeping giant's body. The marches were extremely important expressions of the movement for immigrant rights but are not its sole manifestations. Many of the chapters underscore the ways in which this movement is more like a steeple-chase than a marathon, with activists consistently and doggedly working their way over obstacles that at times seem insurmountable.

Seen in a national context, the marches also provide the perfect occasion to question the metaphor of the sleeping giant since they represent the culmination of more than a decade of advocacy and resistance in a context of exclusion, nativism, hatred, and persecution—and a more recent conflation with terrorism. We hope that many other case studies will follow, documenting and analyzing immigrant rights struggles throughout the United States and thus providing a more complete understanding of the modes and types of Latino resistance that include but go beyond electoral engagement.

Notes

1. Bada, Fox, and Selee 2006 calculated this estimate based on the minimums reported by leading English-language daily newspapers. For more, see Mexico Institute 2009.

2. The survey used a multistage block sampling technique to give respondents an equal chance of being selected for the study. Interviewers were assigned "block numbers" within Union Park and Grant Park. Within those blocks, they were instructed to approach every tenth person as a potential respondent for the survey. Because of Institutional Review Board restrictions, interviewers were instructed only to approach people who were clearly over age sixteen.

3. Because we did not ask noncitizens to specify their legal status in the United States, we do not know for certain how many were undocumented immigrants.

4. In addition to Casa Aztlán, the Puerto Rican Cultural Center, and the Centro sin Fronteras, other organizations with more than a twenty-year history of organizing for immigrant rights include the Illinois Coalition for Immigrant and Refugee Rights (founded in 1986), the American Friends Service Committee, and the Association of Community Organizations for Reform Now.

5. For other examples of how the Mexican American generation (from the 1930s through the 1950s) tried to assimilate through membership in ethnic organizations, see Marquez 1993. For a discussion of enlistment in the military as a route to assimilation, see Oropeza 2005.

References

Bada, Xótchil, Jonathan Fox, and Andrew Selee, eds. 2006. *Invisible No More: Mexican Migrant Civic Participation in the United States*. Washington, D.C.: Woodrow Wilson International Center for Scholars. www.wilsoncenter.org/topics/pubs/Invisible%20 No%20More.pdf. Accessed October 11, 2009.

Flores-González, Nilda, Amalia Pallares, Cedric Herring, and Maria Krysan. 2006. *UIC Immigrant Mobilization Project: General Survey Findings*. July 17. http://www.wilsoncenter .org/news/docs/uicstudy.pdf. Accessed October 11, 2009.

Gutiérrez, David. 1995. *Walls and Mirrors: Mexican Americans, Mexican Immigrants, and the Politics of Ethnicity*. Berkeley: University of California Press.

Haney-López, Ian F. 2003. *Racism on Trial: The Chicano Fight for Justice*. Cambridge: Belknap Press of Harvard University Press.

Immigration Policy Center. 2008. *The New American Electorate: The Growing Political Power of Immigrants and Their Children*. October. http://www.immigrationpolicy .org/images/File/specialreport/NewCitizenVotersWEBversion.pdf. Accessed August 8, 2009.

López, Mark Hugo, and Susan Minushkin. 2008. *2008 National Survey of Latinos: Hispanics See Their Situation in U.S. Deteriorating; Oppose Key Immigration Enforcement Measures*. September 18. http://pewhispanic.org/reports/report.php?ReportID=93. Accessed August 8, 2009.

Marquez, Benjamin. 1993. *LULAC: The Evolution of a Mexican American Political Organization*. Austin: University of Texas Press.

Mexico Institute. 2009. *Latino Migrant Civic and Political Participation*. www.wilsoncenter .org/migrantparticipation. Accessed August 17, 2009.

Monforti, Jessica Lavariega. 2008. "The Awakening of the Sleeping Giant? Latino Political Participation and the 2006 Immigrant Rights Protests." Paper presented at the annual meeting of the Western Political Science Association, San Diego, Calif.

Muñoz, Carlos, Jr. 2007. *Youth, Identity, Power: The Chicano Movement*. Rev. and exp. ed. New York: Verso.

Oropeza, Lorena. 2005. *¡Raza Sí! ¡Guerra No! Chicano Protest and Patriotism during the Viet Nam War Era*. Berkeley: University of California Press.

PART 1

Political and Historical Context

1

Taking the Public Square
The National Struggle for Immigrant Rights

NILDA FLORES-GONZÁLEZ
AND ELENA R. GUTIÉRREZ

Temporada de Caza (Hunting Season), a *corrido* by Waukegan, Illinois, brothers and musicians Ignacio and Santiago Echevarria, vividly describes current policies and practices that penalize immigrants who lack legal status in the United States. The song, which was played at several immigrant rights mobilizations in Chicago, reflects the current rapid escalation in work-site raids and deportation of undocumented immigrants:

Es temporada de caza,	It's hunting season
comentan los ilegales	The illegals are saying
Anda aguitada la raza	The people are agitated
por lo que pude escucharles	From what I could hear
Porque dicen que la Migra	Because they say that Immigration
ya nos quiere echar para Juárez	Wants to throw us to Juárez
Comenzaron las redadas	The raids have started
hay que andar con más cuidado	You have to be more careful
Porque algunos andan presos,	Because some are in prison
a otros ya los deportaron	Others are already deported
Que por no traer licencia,	For not having a license
por eso los castigaron.	That is why they were punished
Ya nos han relacionado	We have been associated
con los grandes terroristas	With the big terrorists
De todo nos han culpado	We have been blamed for everything
las gentes que son racistas	By racist people
Que saquen a los mojados	Pull out the wetbacks
es lo que algunos suplican.	Is what some are begging for.

—Ignacio Echevarria and Santiago
Echevarria, "Hunting Season"

Immigrants and their advocates across the nation have responded to these re-pressive actions by demanding legalization and humane treatment of immi-grants and their communities. Although the immigrant rights megamarches that began in the spring of 2006 are popularly characterized as spontaneous reactions to restrictive laws, they actually follow many years of concerted grass-roots, organizational, and legislative immigrant rights efforts. This chapter pro-vides a comprehensive history of national immigrant rights activism and mo-bilizations in light of immigration-related legislation since the mid-1980s. We counter depictions of Latinos as a "sleeping giant" by tracing the immigrant rights movement's development as an organic progression of concerted local and national efforts (Monforti 2008). While organized immigrants and their advocates attempt to shape immigration policy at the federal level, their activism is also shaped by the constraints and opportunities created by federal policy. A discussion of developments in national immigration policy and the resistance they have generated shows that the immigrant rights movement, although not always monolithic, has consistently orchestrated efforts to bring visibility and justice to immigrant communities.

The 2006 Immigrant Rights Marches

The spring of 2006 will forever be marked as the Primavera de los Inmigrantes (the Spring of the Immigrants). Between late February and May 1, an estimated 3.5 to 5 million people participated in immigrant rights marches and public demonstrations across the United States. Several factors in addition to the sheer numbers of participants make these mobilizations extraordinary. First, marches and rallies in support of immigrant rights occurred in many cities and towns. Fox, Selee, and Bada (2007) have counted 268 mobilizations between Febru-ary 22 and May 1 in forty-three states and the District of Columbia.[1] While the largest rallies took place in traditional immigrant gateway cities such as Los Angeles, New York, and Chicago, Charleston, South Carolina; Goshen, Indiana; and Smithville, South Carolina, also hosted significant marches. These efforts constituted not only the largest immigrant rights activities in U.S. history but also the largest mobilizations ever in such locales as Chicago, Dallas, Denver, Fresno, Los Angeles, and San Jose (Fox, Selee, and Bada 2007).

Second, despite police preparation for disruptive and violent behavior, all mobilizations were peaceful. Even when crowds were larger than anticipated or efforts at mobilization took place at the last minute, crowds displayed an extraordinary level of what Fox and Bada (forthcoming) term "collective self-discipline." Marchers wore white shirts as a symbol of peace, waved Mexican flags to express ethnic pride, and carried U.S. flags as a symbol of patriotism and loyalty to this country (Chávez 2008, 152).

Third, the mobilizations brought to the stage actors who had previously been uninvolved in U.S. civic and political life. Perhaps most significant was the overwhelming presence of families (see chap. 12). Parents often pushed strollers, carried toddlers, or marched alongside school-aged children. Teenagers marched with their parents and grandparents. Thus, Latin American immigrants and their institutions, such as Mexican hometown associations, debuted as new collective actors (see chap. 8). The marches also led to the forming of new coalitions and networks, essentially consolidating the immigrant rights efforts that emerged after the 1986 reform. These connections helped unite different Latino national-origin groups through their shared status as immigrants (Lazos-Vargas 2007).

When the U.S. House of Representatives ratified the Sensenbrenner Bill in December 2005, immigrant rights supporters knew that such a draconian proposal called for a drastic response. Far from offering a path to legalization, the Border Protection, Anti-Terrorism, and Illegal Immigration Control Act (H.R. 4437) sought to increase security and immigration enforcement at the border and to turn undocumented immigrants and anyone who assisted them into felons.

The idea of a nationwide mobilization, in which marches would occur simultaneously in different cities and towns, was born at a February 11, 2006, meeting in Riverside, California. Immigrant rights supporters representing unions, churches, community-based organizations, and advocacy groups converged and planned a National Day of Action on March 10. However, putting together a significant mobilization on such short notice proved nearly impossible. While some marches and rallies occurred—most notably in Washington, D.C., where twenty thousand people marched—before that date, only Chicago delivered big, with a march that drew more than one hundred thousand people to the city center. Although the turnout for the event surprised the nation and even the organizers, the march went largely unreported by the national media (Chávez 2008, 155). Yet the significance of this massive mobilization was not lost on immigrant rights activists around the nation, for whom Chicago confirmed that massive mobilizations were possible. Mobilizations in other cities soon followed, with the largest turnouts taking place in Los Angeles and Denver on March 25; Detroit on March 27; and Dallas, San Diego, and St. Paul, Minnesota, on April 9. Labor unions—particularly the Service Employees International Union—called for another National Day of Action on April 10, and this time at least eighty-five mobilizations occurred across the country, with the largest in Washington, D.C.; New York City; Phoenix; and Fort Myers, Florida (see Bada et al. 2007). The overwhelming response led activists to a call for a nationwide mobilization on May 1.

On April 19, U.S. Immigration and Customs Enforcement (ICE) conducted a nationwide raid at IFCO Systems work sites in several states, leading to the arrest of 1,187 workers (including 60 in Chicago) and 7 managers because of "faulty" or "no-match" social security numbers (that is, discrepancies between names or social security numbers provided by employers and those in Social Security Administration records). Immigrant rights advocates perceived ICE's action as a backlash against the marches and as a scare tactic intended to discourage people from marching on May 1. Instead of deterring the marches, however, the raids gave organizers further momentum.

Organizers learned important lessons from the March and April demonstrations. First, marchers had been heavily criticized for displaying Mexican flags and those of other countries (Chávez 2008, 156). Some critics contended that waving flags other than the U.S. flag called into question marchers' loyalty to this country. While some organizers disagreed, concern arose about the appearance of disloyalty or nonpatriotism (Chávez 2008, 158). Thus, many organizers called on people to wave only U.S. flags and to wear white shirts as a symbol of peace.

Second, with important exceptions, the earlier marches had comprised primarily Mexicans, with little participation from members of other groups (Fox and Bada forthcoming). For May 1, organizers sought to mobilize other groups; although the mobilizations remained largely Mexican, other nationalities participated. In Chicago, for example, the march included significant representation from the Polish, Filipino, Korean, and many other communities.

Third, initial calls for a national boycott day, during which people were asked not to go to work or school or spend money, encountered much resistance, particularly from labor unions and advocacy groups (Narro, Wong, and Shadduck-Hernández 2007). These organizations grounded their opposition on concerns about alienating voters, employers, unions, and Congress. For example, calls for a boycott created such strife among Los Angeles activists that two separate factions sponsored marches on April 25. The March 25 Coalition called for a boycott and held a march at noon in downtown Los Angeles that drew 250,000 people. A second march, headed by immigrant rights organizations, Cardinal Roger Mahoney, labor unions, and Mayor Antonio Villaraigosa, took place in the afternoon along Wilshire Boulevard and counted 400,000 participants.

The boycott ultimately did not materialize on a large scale (although some individuals observed it), but masses of workers and students attended the mobilizations, severely decreasing school attendance and leading businesses to close for the day (Narro, Wong, and Shadduck-Hernández 2007). High school students organized walkouts in Arizona, California, Nevada, New Mexico, Illinois, and Texas (Mora 2007; see also chap. 9). Many schools reported low attendance: Chicago's Benito Juárez High School, for example, had only 17 percent of the student body present on May 1 (Archibold 2006; see also chap. 9). A variety of businesses, including restaurants as well as large meatpacking plants in Nebraska, closed because workers did not show up, customers were scant, or owners sought to display solidarity with their mostly immigrant workforce (Narro, Wong, and Shadduck-Hernández 2007). The most dramatic display of employer-employee solidarity occurred in Las Vegas, where the Culinary Union worked with the casinos on a "no-pain" approach to the boycott: the march was held after work hours and a joint petition was sent to Congress (Lazos-Vargas 2007).

On May 1, seventy-three mobilizations took place across the United States (Bada et al. 2007). In Los Angeles and Chicago, home to the biggest demonstrations, crowds were estimated as high as 650,000 (Bada et al. 2007). Large marches in Denver, Seattle, San Antonio, Houston, and Milwaukee were joined by smaller ones in more than one hundred other cities and towns. This national mobilization sealed the fate of the Sensenbrenner Bill and made doubtful the passage of any measure that offered less than a path to legalization. Furthermore, the marches made immigrants visible on the national stage. They had come out in large numbers and shown a political potential that both legislators and immigrant advocates had underestimated. The marches' success can be attributed to years of organizing for immigrant rights in conjunction with strong opposition to a draconian law that affected, directly or indirectly, most Latinos in this country.

One Step Forward, Two Steps Back: Immigrant Rights in an Increasingly Restrictive Era

Although the Sensenbrenner Bill served as the catalyst for the spring 2006 mobilizations, discontent had been brewing among immigrants and their advocates since passage of the 1986 Immigration Reform and Control Act (IRCA).[2] IRCA constituted a victory for immigrant rights because it granted amnesty to three million undocumented persons who had entered the United States prior to January 1, 1982, and had subsequently resided here continuously. The victory was bittersweet, however, because hundreds of thousands of immigrants remained ineligible for amnesty because they did not meet the requirements or could not provide the necessary documentation (such as pay stubs, lease agreements, and electric or phone bills). In addition, in response to pressure from labor unions, which sought to minimize competition from undocumented immigrants, IRCA criminalized the hiring of undocumented immigrants and required employers to document employees' legal status (see chap. 6). Hiring undocumented immigrants could bring fines of up to ten thousand dollars and criminal prosecution for repeat offenders. IRCA also provided funds for the Border Patrol to bolster anti-illegal-immigration enforcement along the U.S.-Mexico border. According to Chicago activist Jorge Mujica, IRCA's mixed benefits for immigrants immediately set in motion the current immigrant rights movement (see chap. 7).

IRCA also bolstered the immigrant rights movement by leading to the development of a variety of community-based organizations that provided immigrants with services, outreach, information, and advocacy (Hondagneu-Sotelo and Salas 2008). The Illinois Coalition for Immigrant and Refugee Rights and various other local and national groups began to assist immigrants in gathering and completing the paperwork required for the adjustment from temporary to permanent legal status under IRCA.[3] By the 1990s, many of these organizations had shifted from amnesty assistance to other kinds of support and integration services for the immigrant population, such as classes in English as a second language and in citizenship. These organizations later became central in mobilizing against national and local restrictive immigration bill proposals.

While IRCA temporarily reduced undocumented immigration, the numbers had begun to rise again by 1990. IRCA led to the proliferation of fake documentation and human smuggling and to an increase in both legal and undocumented migration (Durand, Malone, and Massey 2002). While family reunification policies now made spouses and dependents eligible for visas, relatives of those legalized were also more likely to migrate without documents (Durand, Malone, and Massey 2002). In addition, civil war in Central America—particularly in Guatemala, Nicaragua, and El Salvador—led hundreds of thousands of people to flee to the United States and push for temporary protected status. To deal with these issues, the Immigration and Nationality Act (INA) was revised in 1990 to increase the limits on legal immigration to the United States, allow for the legal entry of family members of people covered under the 1986 reform, and grant temporary protected status to immigrants who would experience hardship as a result of civil war or natural disaster if they returned to their countries of origin. The INA thus represented another small but significant victory for immigrant rights.

A major setback soon followed, however, as restrictionist and nativist sentiments grew at the state and national levels during the early 1990s.[4] Immigrants were blamed for problems that actually resulted from an economic recession (Calavita 1996). Several states along the U.S.-Mexico border began demanding that the federal government foot the bill for costs related to the undocumented, such as educating and providing health care and other social services (Office of the Inspector General 1998). Restrictionist groups such as the Federation of American Immigration Reform (FAIR) expressed concerns about the breakdown of the "rule of law" at the border, contending that "illegality breeds illegality"—that is, that unauthorized entry leads both immigrants and employers to break other laws (see chap. 10). Vigilantism along the border increased as restrictionist groups dissatisfied with the Border Patrol took it upon themselves to protect the southern border. Hence, the attempt to restrict immigration and immigrant rights rested on a two-pronged strategy of increasing border enforcement and enacting restrictive measures at the state and local government levels.

The Border Patrol instituted three programs aimed to deter and prevent immigrants from entering without authorization. In 1993's Operation Hold the Line, Border Patrol agents in El Paso, Texas, assumed strategically visible positions along the border to provide twenty-four-hour surveillance of the area. Leading to a significant decline in apprehensions of undocumented immigrants, the program was lauded as a success. A year later, Operation Gatekeeper allowed the expansion of a fence along the Tijuana/San Diego border starting in the waters of the Pacific Ocean. This area had long been the preferred place of entry for undocumented immigrants and accounted for 40 percent of the apprehensions made by the Border Patrol (Office of Inspector General 1998). Operation Gatekeeper also established an immigration court to handle expedited (or on-the-spot) hearings and deportations of those caught entering without authorization and allocated funds for state-of-the-art surveillance equipment and increased personnel. A similar program, Operation Safeguard, was implemented in the Tucson, Arizona, border area. These initiatives brought down the number of undocumented arrivals apprehended but did not deter unauthorized entry; rather, immigrants were pushed into more isolated, less guarded, and more dangerous terrain (Nevins 2002). As a consequence, the death toll among undocumented immigrants has soared, particularly in the Arizona desert, even when there have been no increases in unauthorized entries (U.S. Government Accountability Office 2006). In the Arizona desert, the number of recorded deaths between 2004 and 2007 ranged from 214 to 241 a year ("Death on the Border" 2009). Because of the increased danger of crossing and the steep fees charged by smugglers, undocumented immigrants from Mexico have opted to stay longer in the United States rather than engaging in a circular migration pattern that took them back to Mexico in the off-season (Nevins 2002).

As Operation Gatekeeper unraveled, California started a new wave of state legislation that sought to curtail undocumented residents' rights and limit further immigration. Besieged by a recession, the 1992 Los Angeles riots, and natural disasters, the public turned toward immigration control (Chávez 1997; Perea 1997; Montejano 1999). A 1994 ballot initiative, Proposition 187, sought to deny undocumented immigrants social, health, and educational services (with the exception of emergency medical services). It also required local law enforcement, social service, health, and school personnel to report people with undocumented status to immigration officials. Despite the fact that Mexican migration to California had slowed considerably in the mid-1990s and that more Mexicans were leaving the state than were arriving, many supporters of increased immigration controls claimed that undocumented Mexican immigrants were flooding to the state and disproportionately using social, health, and educational services to which they contributed little (Hayes-Bautista 2004,

127). These public debates echoed long-standing nativist sentiments that characterized Mexican immigrants as a social burden and often legitimated coercive public policies and practices (Elena Gutiérrez 2003, 2008).

Although some Latinos voted in favor of Proposition 187 (Connell 1994; Newton 1998), the majority of Latino opposition to Proposition 187 was not based solely on support for the undocumented but constituted a response to what was perceived as an initiative that targeted all Latinos, not just the undocumented (Hayes-Bautista 2004, 135). On October 16, 1994, more than one hundred thousand people marched downtown from East Los Angeles to protest Proposition 187 (Mora 2007). Proposition 187 nevertheless passed, and Governor Pete Wilson pushed for its implementation even after the Mexican American Legal Defense Fund obtained an injunction against it. U.S. District Court judge Mariana Pfaelzer ultimately ruled Proposition 187 an unconstitutional attempt by the state to regulate immigration, which is the responsibility of the federal government.

Mobilizations against Proposition 187—the nation's first massive demonstrations focusing broadly on immigrant rights—provided a preview of the rallies of 2006 (Mora 2007).[5] Moreover, these mobilizations were marked by the building of coalitions and collaboration among labor, community organizations, and different ethnic/racial groups, setting the stage for such cooperation in the spring of 2006 (for more on coalitions in Chicago in 2006, see chaps. 4, 6, 7, 13). In addition, Proposition 187 mobilized many U.S.-born Latinos who felt attacked by the measure, related to the immigrant experience, and/or had immigrant relatives (see chaps. 9, 11).

While Proposition 187 was never implemented, the restrictionist momentum was paralleled at the federal level by a series of 1996 laws and legislative proposals that more directly limited immigrant rights. These measures restricted social benefits for undocumented immigrants and permanent legal residents, expanded the categories of criminal behavior that are grounds for deportation of noncitizens, and limited the recourses for appealing deportation decisions. Most importantly, a welfare reform bill, the Personal Responsibility and Work Opportunity Reconciliation Act (PRWORA) of 1996, effectively restricted legal immigrants' eligibility for federally funded assistance such as social security, food stamps, and Medicaid.[6] While PRWORA offered eligibility for federal assistance to certain categories of immigrants, such as refugees and victims of domestic violence, the elderly were excluded.[7]

The Illegal Immigration Reform and Immigrant Responsibility Act (IIRIRA) of 1996 extended PRWORA's restrictions on public assistance and social benefits for undocumented immigrants to the state and local levels.[8] It also opened the door for the extension of immigration enforcement functions to state and local police. Section 287(g) allowed federal authorities to train local enforcement officers to perform immigration law enforcement functions. Furthermore, the Anti-Terrorism and Effective Death Penalty Act of 1996, passed in response to the bombings of the World Trade Center and in Oklahoma City, cemented these relationships by allowing state and local police to arrest and detain undocumented immigrants convicted of felonies and therefore deportable for criminal behavior.

IIRIRA eased the process of deportation of undocumented immigrants by implementing a new expedited removal—an immediate or on-the-spot deportation without the right to a hearing or appeal process or legal assistance. Expedited removal can be carried out by an enforcement agent and does not require the approval of an immigration judge. It applies to undocumented immigrants who are detained while attempting to enter the United States, overstay their visas, or engage in unauthorized employment. Hence, people caught entering the United States without visas or who could not prove that they had resided here continuously for at least two years were to be immediately deported unless they could credibly claim political asylum and seek refugee status. IIRIRA also barred undocumented immigrants who were first-time offenders and had voluntarily agreed to leave the country within 120 days and/or prior to their scheduled deportation hearing from legally entering the United States for six to ten years, based on the length of their "unlawful presence." Those caught a second time were banned from entering for twenty years.

IIRIRA also expanded the categories of criminal behavior under which noncitizens could be deported. Previously, noncitizens who had committed aggravated felonies (mainly murder, assault, and drug dealing) and received sentences of five or more years in prison were deported after completing their sentences. IIRIRA modified the definition of aggravated felony to include twenty-eight offenses with minimum sentences of a year, even if the sentence was suspended or the offender was placed on probation. IIRIRA was also retroactive, turning offenses committed before 1996 and not considered felonies at the time into aggravated felonies that met the criteria for deportation. And deported felons were permanently banned from entering into the United States. At the same time, IIRIRA eliminated the right to a hearing with an immigration judge to appeal a deportation, substituting cancellation of removal.[9]

IIRIRA immediately increased the number of deportations of legal immigrants, particularly after the passage of the Anti-Terrorism and Effective Death Penalty Act. Whereas 67,000 immigrants were deported in 1996, that number rose to 210,000 a year later. Most of the deportees were not terrorists or threats to public safely but had committed misdemeanors that previously would not have resulted in deportation (Vila 1998). Many were longtime U.S. residents with jobs and families. Most were caught when they applied to adjust their status or when they reentered the country after traveling abroad. However, enforcement of many IIRIRA provisions lagged, and not until six years later were IIRIRA's most restrictive and punitive measures more widely implemented.

Immigrant rights advocates strongly opposed the restrictive and punitive measures imposed by PRWORA, IIRIRA, and the Anti-Terrorism and Effective Death Penalty Act, winning small victories in restoring some rights and benefits for undocumented immigrants. However, these advocacy groups had a variety of goals, resources, and relationships to the state and did not necessarily present a unified front. Most organizations were grassroots efforts, often staffed by immigrants or their children and serving an immigrant clientele. Some, such as the Farm Labor Organizing Committee, had ties to unions, while others, such as the Tepeyac Association of New York or Casa Aztlán in Chicago, were oriented toward social services. Usually possessing significantly more resources were national Latino civil rights and policy advocacy organizations, including the League of United Latin American Citizens, the Mexican American Legal Defense and Educational Fund, the National Council of La Raza, and the National Network for Immigrant and Refugee Rights, which worked with many of the state-level immigrant rights coalitions created after 1986. In the middle were some coalitions that formed between the mid-1990s and the early 2000s and strove to work with both types of organizations. Local unions also became involved at times. Despite some collaboration, however, differences in strategy often led various organizations to pursue parallel battles rather than working in concert.

In some cases, however, efforts at different levels dovetailed to bring about significant victories for immigrant communities. As a result of advocacy by national lobbying and community-based organizations, the U.S. Congress passed four bills that offered ways for some undocumented immigrants to adjust their status. One of these victories was the passage in 1994 and temporary extension in 2000 of Section 245(i) of the INA, which extended the status-adjustment deadline to January 14, 1998, for certain people illegally in the United States who paid a one-thousand-dollar penalty. In 2000, the Legal Immigration Family Equity Act extended the deadline for status adjustment petitions to April 30, 2001. Another extension of Section 245(i) was scheduled for a vote in the House of Representatives on September 11, 2001, but was tabled in the wake of the terrorist attacks that occurred on that day (Tsao 2008).

Other notable immigrant rights victories included an extension of asylum for Central Americans and Haitians. Advocates for the legalization of Central American refugees included the sanctuary movement, a network of more than two hundred churches supported by community-based organizations, universities, and the State of New Mexico that had been working on this issue since the 1980s (Mize 2005). The Nicaraguan Adjustment and Central American Relief Act of 1997 and the Haitian Refugee Immigration Fairness Act of 1998 enabled Nicaraguans, Salvadorans, Guatemalans, and Haitians who had entered the

United States before December 31, 1995, to ask for a suspension of their deportation proceedings and apply for legal status. However, qualification for a status adjustment required applicants to make a credible case for asylum. Finally, the Victims of Trafficking and Violence Protection Act of 2000 granted vulnerable undocumented populations, such as victims of human trafficking and domestic violence, temporary residence permits and made them eligible for federal and state assistance.

National Grassroots Coalitions, 1996–2005

The first national demonstration for immigrant rights occurred in Washington, D.C., on October 12, 1996, when Coordinadora '96, a national coalition of civil and immigrant rights organizations, organized the Latino and Immigrants' Rights March to protest restrictive laws and to demand amnesty and constitutional rights for undocumented immigrants.[10] Twenty-six Latino immigrant rights community-based organizations from thirteen states met in Tucson in 1994 to found Coordinadora '96 (Hernández 2005). According to Juan José Gutiérrez of Latino USA, Coordinadora '96 sought to create a nationwide coalition that would pressure President Bill Clinton to commit to immigration reform before the 1996 presidential elections (Juan José Gutiérrez 2008). One of the group's first actions was a boycott of Walt Disney and RJR Nabisco "because of major donations by corporate officers to the reelection of Gov. Pete Wilson and other pro-187 Republican candidates" (Arango 2008; Feldman and McDonnell 1994). Coordinadora's agenda also included other issues that attracted support from different sectors (such as unions) and from non-Latinos, especially African Americans and Asian Americans (Juan José Gutiérrez 2008). This broader civil and human rights agenda included support for affirmative action, a fair minimum wage, increased access to public health and education, and protection of the constitutional rights of all persons in the United States (Hernández 2005).

The Washington march represented another of Coordinadora '96's efforts to put Latinos on the map as political actors (Arango 2008; Juan José Gutiérrez 2008; Jiménez 2008). The group spent two years organizing the demonstration, garnering support with small mobilizations in Houston, Chicago, New York, Philadelphia, and Detroit as well as securing the endorsement of twelve hundred groups (Hernández 2005). The first national organizations to endorse the Coordinadora were labor unions, including the AFL-CIO, the United Farm Workers, the United Auto Workers, and the Service Employees International Union (Hernández 2005). In fact, the International Union of Electrical, Salaried Machine, and Furniture Workers donated space and resources to put together the Latino and Immigrants' Rights March on October 12, 1996 (Goldberg 1996;

Juan José Gutiérrez 2008; Holmes 1996; Rodríguez 1996). No major Latino civil rights and/or advocacy organization endorsed the Coordinadora, but the American Friends Service Committee, the National Network for Immigrant and Refugee Rights, and the League of United Latin American Citizens joined the effort at the last minute (Hernández 2005).

The rally represented "the first mass protest by Hispanic people in the nation's capital" (Holmes 1996). The historic three-mile march drew approximately twenty-five thousand participants of all races, ethnicities, and ages (Hernández 2005; Koppel and Stone 1996). Maria Jiménez of the American Friends Service Committee of Houston described it as a "marcha con otro sabor y con mucho color y alegría" (a march with another flavor and with lots of color and happiness) (2008). Dancers appeared in colorful traditional dress, and marchers waved U.S. colonial flags to assert their rights as people who had also helped build this country. Carlos Arango of Chicago's Casa Aztlán recalled that during the rally, marchers sang a literal Spanish translation of the U.S. national anthem (2008). The Congressional Hispanic Caucus endorsed the march, and four members attended: Democratic representatives Ed Pastor of Arizona, Nydia Velazquez and José Serrano of New York, and Luis Gutiérrez of Illinois. Journalist and talk show host Geraldo Rivera also supported the rally (Holmes 1996). The next day, more than one thousand college students gathered for the East Coast Chicano/a Student Forum at Georgetown University, a two-day event at which participants discussed solutions to problems affecting Latino communities (Rodríguez 1996).

The following year, Coordinadora '96 called for a March of Immigrants, Indigenous, and the Poor to be held on October 12 in New York City, with satellite marches to take place in Los Angeles, Chicago, and Austin (Catalinotto 1997). About fifteen hundred people marched to New York's United Nations Building to demand human rights for immigrants, including amnesty and a permanent extension for Section 245(i). Although predominantly Mexican and Salvadoran, marchers included people from Haiti, Bangladesh, Poland, Albania, Korea, and various African nations (Obrero Revolucionario 1997). On October 12, 1998, Coordinadora '96 gathered for its last march in Chicago, which was attended by about one hundred people.

Coordinadora '96 disbanded soon thereafter, partly because its main objective of organizing for the 1996 elections had been fulfilled but also because of disagreement among its leaders. Even though Coordinadora '96 did not obtain amnesty for the undocumented or prevent IIRIRA's passage, the group mobilized Latinos nationwide and demonstrated their political potential. Coordinadora '96 activists Juan José Gutiérrez (2008), Arango (2008), and Jiménez (2008) concur that despite the group's short life, it showed Latinos the road to Washington, D.C., paving the way to subsequent national efforts.

In April 1999, the National Coalition for Dignity and Amnesty for Undocumented Immigrants (Dignity and Amnesty) was formed to push for amnesty for undocumented immigrants in the United States. This assemblage of more than two hundred organizations, churches, and unions included some groups that had been involved in Coordinadora '96 as well as newcomers such as the Farm Labor Organizing Committee in Toledo, Ohio, the Centro de Trabajadores Latinos and the Asociación Tepeyac in New York City, and the Comité de Immigrantes en Acción in Providence, Rhode Island (Jiménez 2008; Maya 2008). According to two of its founders, Jiménez and the Farm Labor Organizing Committee's Beatriz Maya, Dignity and Amnesty sought to push for amnesty based on the realization that lack of legal status provided a major obstacle to organizing immigrant workers as well as the main source for labor problems faced by undocumented immigrants.

Dignity and Amnesty initially sought to recruit national policy advocacy organizations such as the National Network for Immigrant and Refugee Rights, the League of United Latin American Citizens, and the National Council of La Raza, but leaders of these groups believed that the time was not ripe for moving for amnesty, seeing a discussion of legalization as political suicide (Jiménez 2008). Despite this lack of funds and support, Dignity and Amnesty held an October 16, 1999, proamnesty march in Washington, D.C., that drew approximately fifteen thousand participants. This mobilization sparked attention, and in February 2000, the AFL-CIO endorsed the call for a general amnesty for undocumented workers.

With the AFL-CIO on board, other national advocacy organizations, the Catholic Church, the Methodist Church, and labor unions joined the movement for a general amnesty, and some helped fund the campaign (Maya 2008). On May 1, 2000, Dignity and Amnesty held rallies in eighteen states, mobilizing nearly thirty thousand people. The group then moved forward with a three-pronged strategy: it continued to hold mobilizations in Washington, D.C., as well as regionally and locally; it developed a highly participatory organizing program that included training immigrants to lobby in Congress; and it drafted the Freedom Act, an immigration proposal that contained Dignity and Amnesty's vision for immigration reform. The act had two components: an unconditional general amnesty that would grant permanent residency to the eight million undocumented immigrants in the country at the time; and status adjustments for future undocumented immigrants via the creation of a temporary resident status that would lead to permanent residency after three years (Maya 2002). This concept was incorporated into several bills later introduced in Congress by Republican senator John McCain of Arizona; Republican representatives Jim Kolbe and Jeff Flake, also of Arizona; Democratic senator Edward Kennedy of Massachusetts; and others (Maya 2008).

At least twice a year, Dignity and Amnesty held mobilizations timed to coincide with the symbolic dates of May 1 (International Workers' Day) and October 12 (Día de la Raza). These events began with congressional lobbying and ended with rallies. In 2000, Emma Lozano of Chicago's Centro sin Fronteras asked Representative Gutiérrez to introduce the Freedom Act in the House of Representatives (Jiménez 2008; Maya 2008). Although Gutiérrez did not endorse the measure, he supported the group's initiatives, and the following July he was a main speaker at a Washington, D.C., press conference and demonstration at which Dignity and Amnesty presented the act (National Coalition for Dignity and Amnesty 2000a). Other participants included members of Congress; top executives of the Laborers' International Union of North America, the National Council of La Raza, the Labor Council For Latin American Advancement, and the Farm Labor Organizing Committee; representatives of various religious denominations; and former district directors of the Immigration and Naturalization Service (INS, a forerunner to ICE) (National Coalition for Dignity and Amnesty 2000a).

By 2001, the immigrant rights struggle had become more diversified. Ironically, grassroots organizations' ability to call attention to the issue inspired other types of groups directly to assume the cause, drawing away some of the constituency and funds on which the grassroots efforts had relied. National civil rights organizations that had been reluctant to work on amnesty began campaigns, securing support from foundations that had previously funded Dignity and Amnesty (Maya 2008). The Catholic Church, which had provided crucial funds, also redirected those monies toward internal efforts at immigration reform (Maya 2008). In addition, newly created national organizations such as the National Alliance of Latin American and Caribbean Communities and older networks such as the National Network for Immigrant and Refugee Rights attracted some Dignity and Amnesty members (Jiménez 2008).

In 2001, Representative Gutiérrez drafted and introduced the U.S. Employee, Family Unity, and Legalization Act (H.R. 500) (Maya 2008). Although this bill did not include amnesty, it sought to reverse some of IIRIRA's retroactive provisions, particularly the clause that made noncitizens deportable for earlier offenses. Although Gutiérrez's bill fell short of the Freedom Act, Dignity and Amnesty activists and immigrant rights advocates supported it, collecting fifty thousand signatures, holding a March 2001 press conference on behalf of the measure, and planning a national mobilization for September 23, 2001, in Washington, D.C., to push the bill (Maya 2008). The September 11 terrorist attacks derailed the rally, however, and H.R. 500 died in committee.

Despite the increasingly restrictive environment that followed the September 11 terrorist attacks and other groups' sense that the moment for reform was not at hand, Dignity and Amnesty continued to advocate on behalf of immigrant rights. Although the group never regained the massive support it had previously enjoyed, Dignity and Amnesty continued to hold action days in the nation's capital and to participate in national and international forums on immigration until 2005.[11] Due to lack of funding, Dignity and Amnesty ceased coordinating national actions in 2005, but the coalition still functions as an immigrant rights network, and its members remain active, primarily at the local level. Dignity and Amnesty again came together as an organization to participate in the National Immigrant Rights Strategy Convention, held on August 11–13, 2006, in Chicago and sponsored by Chicago's March 10 Coalition (see chaps. 2, 7). Despite their short existences and infrequent policy successes, these national coalitions had a lasting impact. Jiménez (2008) believes that Coordinadora '96 and Dignity and Amnesty were the first campaigns/coalitions to create a network of community organizations that could communicate and coordinate simultaneous marches.

Labor and Immigrant Rights Advocacy

Although local unions participated in these immigrant rights efforts, labor struggles that included immigrant workers were neither articulated nor brought under the immigrant rights banner by the national unions until 2000. Recognizing that immigrants constituted a large segment of their membership, unions adopted immigrant rights as one of their most important issues (see chap. 6). In 2000, the AFL-CIO changed its long-standing stance against undocumented immigrant labor rights that had led to its historical support for restrictive measures. According to Fred Tsao, policy director of the Illinois Coalition for Immigrant and Refugee Rights, the AFL-CIO's move represented a "defining moment" for the issue of immigrant legalization: "When the AFL-CIO executive committee issued its change of policy, it was like a lightning bolt; it motivated a lot of people to think, [legalization] might actually be possible if this longtime organized labor institution is changing its policies towards immigrants generally but towards the undocumented specifically" (2008). The AFL-CIO's first step toward integrating its growing immigrant base was to sponsor forums in New York, Atlanta, Chicago, and Los Angeles, providing immigrant workers with an opportunity to talk about labor issues. A year later, the union led a campaign that resulted in one million people sending postcards to Washington in favor of legalization (Hondagneu-Sotelo and Salas 2008). In 2002, the AFL-CIO officially launched a campaign for legalization and family reunification for immigrant workers (AFL-CIO 2002). From September 20 to October 4, 2003, the union sponsored the Immigrant Workers Freedom Ride, in which about one thousand immigrant workers spent twelve days traveling to more than one hundred cities across the United States to call attention to issues faced by immigrant workers, converging on Washington, D.C., on October 1 to meet with 120 members of Congress.

In February 2001, U.S. president George W. Bush began negotiations with his Mexican counterpart, Vicente Fox, for the legalization of more than three million undocumented Mexican workers—what amounted to a guest worker program (Chen and Smith 2001). These negotiations and the increased involvement of labor as a key ally brought momentum to the immigrant rights movement's quest for more comprehensive immigrant reform than Bush proposed, but those hopes were dashed on September 11 (Maya 2002).

A Nation of Immigrants or a Nation of Suspects?

On September 11, 2001, America changed from a nation of immigrants to a nation of suspects (McKenzie 2004). Because the attacks were perpetrated by immigrants who held valid visas, immigration control became a matter of national security, and the quest to identify and apprehend immigrant terrorists led to the scrutiny, detention, and deportation of immigrants (Rudolph 2007; McKenzie 2004). U.S.-Mexican negotiations on immigration issues halted as President Bush and Congress scrambled to pass a set of bills to control entry and monitor immigrants. Within six weeks of the attacks, Bush had signed into law the Uniting and Strengthening America by Providing Appropriate Tools Required to Intercept and Obstruct Terrorism Act of 2001 (the Patriot Act), which expanded the search and surveillance powers of law enforcement agencies, especially immigration enforcement. The act restricted the entry of foreigners suspected of having links to terrorist organizations and allowed the deportation of immigrants who provided any kind of support, including donations, to suspected terrorist organizations.[12]

The Patriot Act was soon followed by the Enhanced Border Security and Visa Entry Reform Act of 2002, which required foreigners entering the United States to have machine-readable visas with biometric features such as fingerprinting and photos. It also mandated that airlines and ships submit lists of passengers before arrival in the United States rather than while the vessels were in transit, as had previously been the case; provided increased INS funding for personnel and surveillance technology; and allowed information sharing among governmental agencies.

The Homeland Security Act of 2002 followed shortly thereafter, creating the Department of Homeland Security (DHS) to consolidate efforts to prevent and respond to terrorist attacks within the United States. The DHS monitors domestic intelligence activities and develops new security technology, border security, and emergency readiness, including in the aftermath of natural disasters. Sweeping changes in immigration processing and enforcement resulted. Duties previously handled by the INS, including the processing of immigration documents, the prevention of undocumented migration, and the enforcement of immigration laws, were split into three separate agencies within DHS. The U.S. Citizenship and Immigration Services bears responsibility for processing of immigration documents such as visas, passports, and status adjustments. The U.S. Customs and Border Protection Agency deters the arrival of undocumented immigrants by conducting screening at points of entry and by patrolling the border. Finally, ICE enforces immigration laws, including capturing, detaining, and processing undocumented immigrants. Placing immigration under the purview of the Homeland Security Act makes it a national security issue. By extension, immigrants, both legal and undocumented, become threats to national security, thereby justifying restrictive and punitive measures against them.

Although IRCA and IIRIRA had contained restrictive and exclusionary anti-immigrant measures, not until the passage of the Patriot Act and the Homeland Security Act were these provisions widely implemented, rolling back immigrant rights advocates' gains against a system of "broken laws" that violate or can violate the immigrants' and citizens' civil rights (McKenzie 2004). All undocumented and many legal immigrants were directly affected by these policies. Expansions in the definition of *terrorist* to include "persons of interest" and "material witnesses" have led to the registration, detention, and deportation of thousands of immigrants, mostly those of Middle Eastern descent and/or Muslims, because of their suspected connections with organizations on the terrorist list.[13] Immigrant rights advocates contend that the problem has not been lack of restrictive immigration laws but rather a weak intelligence program that has failed to identify terrorists or to provide immigration officials with the names of those identified. Focusing on immigration enforcement has led to the "spending of millions of dollars rounding up and deporting undocumented Mexican workers at restaurants and factories around the United States" but has had no effect on national security (Stock and Johnson 2003).

These laws also broadened the definition of those who qualified for expedited removal, which from 1997 to 2002 had been applied only to people caught entering without documentation at ports of entry. The category was expanded in 2002 to undocumented persons arriving illegally by sea; in 2004 to undocumented persons caught within one hundred air miles of the U.S.-Mexico border who could not establish that they had been present in the United States for the past fourteen days; and in 2005 to the entire U.S.-Mexico border area (Siskin and Wasem 2005). In recent years, authorities have contemplated applying the category to anyone caught anywhere in the United States.

Federal officials led by attorney general John Ashcroft recruited both state and local governments and their police forces to help implement these laws (McKenzie 2004). Section 287(g) of the IIRIRA already allowed local and state police to partner with the INS to enforce immigration laws, but the provision was not implemented until 2002, when Florida put it into practice. By 2008, state and local governments in nineteen states had concluded sixty-three active agreements under Section 287(g) (U.S. Immigration and Customs Enforcement 2008a).[14]

Immigrant advocates argued that increased state and local police participation in immigration enforcement could lead to the violation of civil rights if officers were not properly or uniformly trained (McKenzie 2004). Yolanda Torrez, an attorney in Waukegan, Illinois, where the city council voted in favor of 287(g), explained, "The error that some people make is they think that 287(g) only affects the undocumented . . . but 287(g) gives the police probable cause to stop you based on the fact that they believe you're in violation of the immigration laws. So anyone can be stopped" (Ali 2007). Community organizer Alejandro Domínguez concurred: "We look at the history and what they're doing and we are worried [police] will abuse the law" (Ali 2007). Police departments also opposed the measure for fear that immigration enforcement would jeopardize the trust they had built with immigrant communities and deter immigrants from reporting crime (Jonas 2006). Moreover, localities, many of which are having financial difficulties, must bear the costs of Section 287(g) since the DHS does not provide funding (McKenzie 2004).

While immigration rights activists refer to immigration policy as a "broken system" because of inhumane laws that restrict regularization and increase deportations and family separations, restrictionists claim that the system is broken for other reasons. FAIR, the Americans for Legal Immigration Political Action Committee, Numbers USA, and the Minutemen believe that the system has not adequately restricted immigration or punished violators. Members of both groups call for comprehensive immigration reform, but supporters of immigrant rights seek to legalize all undocumented immigrants, while restrictionists argue for further limits and their strict enforcement both internally and at the border. In this battle, legalization and enforcement were positioned as polar opposites.[15]

Fixing Broken Laws

Congress saw a flurry of efforts at comprehensive immigration reform between 2003 and 2006. Many of these bills were compromise measures that attempted to include some of each side's demands.[16] In January 2004, President Bush joined congressional efforts to introduce new immigration legislation, announcing a plan that included a guest worker program, an increase in the number of immigrants allowed to enter the United States, and improvements in immigration enforcement.[17] While Bush's proposal departed from the trend in restrictive and punitive measures that had existed since 1996 and particularly since 2001, it generated mixed reactions among friends and foes of immigrant rights. Some immigrant advocates saw the proposal as a small step in the right direction; much more vocal were those who opposed the plan as reminiscent of the earlier and much-abused Bracero program for Mexican guest workers. Restrictionists denounced Bush's plan as "amnesty" and as a ploy to win over Latino voters. Both Democrats and Republicans developed alternative proposals, some of which focused on legalizing undocumented immigrants, others of which were compromise bills that offered more limited legalization along with punitive provisions, and still others of which sought expanded enforcement with no path to legalization.

The Development, Relief, and Education for Alien Minors (DREAM) Act sought a path to legalization for undocumented students. Initially introduced by Illinois senator Richard Durbin under a different name in 2001, the DREAM Act has been introduced in the Senate and House of Representatives multiple times since 2005 both as a standalone measure and as part of other immigration-related bills. The bill would allow states to charge in-state college tuition and provide a six-year conditional permanent resident status for undocumented students who graduate from U.S. public high schools and enroll in two- or four-year universities or serve in the armed forces. Those who complete at least two years of higher education or serve in the military for at least two years would receive permanent residence, placing them on the path to citizenship. No version of the DREAM Act has ever garnered enough support from Republican senators to come to a vote.[18]

More comprehensive immigration reform bills have met the same fate, dying in congressional committees.[19] The Safe, Orderly, Legal Visas and Enforcement Act (SOLVE) of 2004 (S. 2381/H.R. 4262) was introduced by Senator Kennedy and Representative Gutiérrez and would have led to legalization, labor protections, and reforms of the employment-based visa system. Despite its endorsement by organized labor and immigrant rights advocates, SOLVE languished in committee. Another bipartisan proposal, the Secure American and Orderly Immigration Act of 2005 (S. 1033/H.R. 2330, known as the McCain-Kennedy Bill), which provided a path to permanent residency for undocumented workers but required them to pay fines and back taxes, study English, and maintain employment, was introduced on the Senate floor but was filibustered when Republican senators overused their speaking time to prevent the bill from being discussed.

At the end of 2005, Republican representative James Sensenbrenner of Wisconsin introduced the Border Protection, Antiterrorism, and Illegal Immigration Control Act (H.R. 4437), which proposed making undocumented status a felony and criminalizing any person who provided assistance to undocumented immigrants, including family members and educational, health, and social services personnel. Most immigrant advocates expected that the Sensenbrenner Bill, like most other attempts at comprehensive immigration reform, would not reach the floor, but the measure passed the House of Representatives in a surprise vote held on December 5, 2005, during a session attended by few opponents. Opposition to the bill by immigrant advocates led to the massive spring 2006 mobilizations. Congress subsequently took no further action on H.R. 4437, but some of its provisions were reintroduced as three separate bills that offered no leniency for immigrants and sought further restrictions on immigration options and avenues for appeal.

Only two of these immigration-related bills became law. Sensenbrenner introduced the Real ID Act of 2005 (H.R. 418, now P.L. 109-13), which made it more difficult for immigrants to seek asylum, expedited construction of a fence along the Mexican-U.S. border, limited access to federal courts for appeals of immigration rulings, banned states from issuing driver's licenses to undocumented immigrants, and called on states to create separate identification cards for U.S. citizens and noncitizens. The Secure Fence Act of 2006 (H.R. 6061, P.L. 109-367) added seven hundred miles of fence along the Mexican-U.S. border.

A few other immigration-related bills have been discussed and put to a vote on the House or Senate floor but have not been enacted. One explanation lies in the disagreements between the more centrist approach of the Senate and the restrictionist orientation of the House of Representatives, which was controlled by Republicans through the November 2006 elections. The House's Immigration Reform Caucus (HIRC) has opposed any form of legalization, even bills introduced by Senate Republicans such as McCain (Building Democracy Initiative 2007).[20] HIRC has ties to FAIR and other restrictionist groups such as the Minutemen; its current chair, California Republican Brian Bilbray, formerly worked as a lobbyist for FAIR (Building Democracy Initiative 2007). As long as Republicans controlled the House, the caucus ensured that any proposal involving some sort of legalization had no chance of being brought for discussion in the House.

Congressional inaction during 2006 also resulted from pressure from the U.S. public in an election year. Restrictionists and immigrant rights advocates combined to create a climate in which officials seeking reelection saw coming down strongly on either side as too politically risky. After the Democrats regained the majority in both chambers, however, immigrant rights advocates had new reasons for optimism.

After 2006

In the wake of the massive marches and with the Democrats in control of Congress, immigrant rights advocates hoped that bipartisan, comprehensive immigration reform would be possible, so far to no avail. Compromise bills proposed in 2007 sought to pair legalization with stiffer border control and enforcement. In March 2007, Representatives Gutiérrez and Flake introduced the Security through Regularized Immigration and a Vibrant Economy (STRIVE) Act (H.R. 1645), which offered the undocumented a chance to "earn" legalization by paying set penalties. It also called for tighter border security, immigration enforcement, an employment verification system, and a new guest worker program. The STRIVE Act would have led to the legalization of approximately nine million of the country's estimated twelve million undocumented immigrants.

Two months later, the Secure Borders, Economic Opportunity, and Immigration Reform Act of 2007 (S. 1348), known as the Comprehensive Immigration Reform Act, was introduced. Devised by a group of Republicans later joined by Kennedy, the bill represented yet another attempt to strike a bipartisan compromise between legalization and increased border enforcement. The bill provided for mandatory verification of legal status by employers but also proposed a new temporary worker program, the elimination of family immigration backlogs, and a point system and would have allowed most undocumented immigrants currently in the country to earn legal status but not eventual citizenship. Some Democrats responded cautiously, worried about ruffling feathers so close to the 2008 presidential election and about maintaining their slight congressional majority. Other newly elected moderate Democrats as well as Democratic Party leaders concerned about keeping the party's slight numerical advantage in Congress were worried that supporting the bill would hurt the new Democrats' chances of reelection. For their part, HIRC and restrictionist groups expressed strong opposition, viewing the bill as offering amnesty. Restrictionists flooded Congress with three hundred thousand calls in one day to express their opposition, playing a large part in stopping the legislation's progress. Neither immigrant rights supporters nor restrictionist activists were satisfied with the bill, contending that it was either too soft or too hard on curbing immigration and enforcing the law.

Immigrant rights advocates were divided on the bill's merits, but most of the grassroots sector came down against it, concerned about the human rights aspects of a bill that would not lead to citizenship for those included, would not include everyone, and had too many punitive measures. Idealists took an all-or-nothing position, holding out for universal, unconditional legalization with no punitive provisions. Grassroots organizations also were concerned about the point system, which would award more visas to people with professional qualifications and fewer visas to people seeking family reunification. Finally, many Democrats, labor unions, and Latino organizations with close ties to labor feared that the temporary worker component would introduce a permanent vulnerable workforce that would compete with newly legalized immigrants and others. Even those who were open to supporting some type of guest worker program worried that the bill lacked sufficient protections, reproducing some of the problems of the Bracero program. In contrast, state- and national-level immigrant advocacy groups were more willing to accept a measure that they perceived as imperfect because of the benefits it offered. When the measure failed to reach cloture, some supporters of immigrant rights regretted their failure to accept the compromise.[21]

Other bills were introduced in 2008, but the realities of election-year politics ensured that they would go nowhere. All of these measures were restrictive; one, the Secure America through Verification and Enforcement Act (H.R. 4088), was deemed "baby Sensenbrenner" because of its punitive provisions. The immigrant rights movement continued to stage large mobilizations in 2007 and 2008, although none of these efforts has reproduced the megamarches of 2006. In August 2008, many grassroots and policy-oriented sectors of the immigrant rights movement, along with several elected officials, most notably Gutiérrez, launched the ¡Ya Basta! campaign, which urges a moratorium on raids and deportations until new immigration legislation is passed.

Barack Obama's election to the presidency lent new hope to the immigrant rights movement, since one of his campaign promises was the enactment of immigration reform during his first year in office (Sachetti 2008). On January 21, 2009, the day after Obama's inauguration, immigrant rights rallies took place in Washington, D.C., and several other cities. Despite record cold temperatures in the nation's capital, a diverse group of several hundred activists marched to ICE's headquarters, chanting "Sí Se Puede" (Yes We Can), a phrase created during the 1960s farmworkers' struggle, used extensively in the immigrant rights marches, and adopted by Obama during his presidential campaign (Aizenman 2009; Barbassa 2009). Gutiérrez told the crowd that the Congressional Hispanic Caucus had already sent a letter to President Obama requesting a meeting to discuss immigration (Barbassa 2009). In addition, a campaign organized by immigrant rights groups has yielded thousands of letters urging Obama to stop ICE raids and deportations. The Familias Unidas (United Families) Campaign, spearheaded by Congressman Gutiérrez and supported by the Congressional Hispanic Caucus, hosted a number of massive events in churches throughout the country in the spring of 2009, culminating in a Mother's Day event in the campaign's city of birth, Chicago. During these events, citizen and legal resident family members affected by deportation publicly testified about how their lives had been affected by the current policy. These events were attended not only by thousands of people affected by this issue and immigrant rights and religious leaders but also by local and national politicians, including House speaker Nancy Pelosi, who stated on March 2, that "taking parents from their children [is] un-American" (Zito 2009). While the campaign elicited thousands of petitions from citizens and legal residents asking that their family members not be deported, it also kept the immigration issue on the agenda. According to the ICIRR's Tsao, "Certainly the fact that thousands of people and dozens of families came out to these events was probably a really encouraging sign.

. . . I am sure that the Obama administration was paying attention to that, seeing that there was real pain in the community and that something needs to be done" (Tsao 2009).

The strategy of marching on International Workers Day also continued. On May 1, 2009, immigrant rights activists marked the first one hundred days of Obama's presidency with marches throughout the country. Though these rallies were definitely smaller than the megamarches, they nevertheless attracted thousands in major cities and reminded Obama of his campaign promise to address legalization.

But the Obama administration did not respond as quickly as activists had hoped. While initial expectations had held that that a bill would be discussed in the fall of 2009, the extended health care policy debate played a role in delaying the possible introduction of a bill by Senator Charles Schumer, a New York Democrat and the new chair of the Senate Immigration Subcommittee, until the spring of 2010. Moreover, Schumer's principles for the bill, announced in June 2009, emphasize both family unification and increased enforcement, leading activists to be concerned about the specter of harsher enforcement. At a national immigration rally in Washington, D.C., on October 13, Gutiérrez proposed the principles for a bill that is more supportive of immigrant rights.

As the difficulties encountered by recent immigration policy reform efforts have shown, however, this new push for comprehensive immigration reform does not guarantee the passing of legislation. Some activists suggest depending less on the idea of a comprehensive reform and more on separate efforts to ensure passage of some policy. The DREAM Act, for example, was reintroduced in March 2009. Activists also express concerns about increased enforcement, especially in light of the continuation, creation, strengthening, and extension of enforcement policies in the first year of the Obama administration, including the expansion of electronic verification systems and extensive auditing of employment records, leading many employers preemptively to fire employees; the expansion of 287(g) plans to eleven new locations; and the expansion of secure communities, which allows ICE agents into jails to identify and deport undocumented prisoners (Tsao 2009; "Obama Administration" 2009). National activist Robert Lovato expressed frustration that the Obama administration had not done away with some of the enforcement measures that only require an administrative order but instead had expanded them: "A lot of people were just expecting [that 287(g) enforcement] was going to be closed down . . . thought that with Obama, there was a new day in race and racial profiling. . . . In fact, they're expanding that program [which] has been proven to profile, prosecute, persecute, and jail and terrorize a lot of people" ("Obama Administration" 2009).

In sum, while activists remain hopeful that immigration reform may be passed in 2010, they are more concerned than ever about the trade-off between legalization and increased enforcement and view the Obama administration's current continuation and expansion of enforcement as a predictor of harsher enforcement in the future.

Temporada de Caza Intensifies

Legislative inaction has led to a rapid increase in the application of the most repressive immigration law provisions, particularly after 2004. While a majority of the American public seems to favor measures that would allow undocumented immigrants to stay in the United States (either as permanent residents or as temporary workers), Congress has failed to move on legislation or to enact a moratorium on deportations until the law is reviewed (Pew Hispanic Center 2006). Enforcement has been stepped up at both the national (ICE) and local levels. From January 2004 to June 2007, ICE deported more than 675,000 people, 74 percent of them in 2006–7. A 13 percent increase in removals occurred between 2005, when 170,000 people were deported, and 2006, when 195,999 were deported. That number jumped another 30 percent in 2007, when 276,912 people were deported (U.S. Immigration and Customs Enforcement 2009b).

Raids at work sites and arrests of undocumented workers have also burgeoned. In fact, the largest work site raids in U.S. history have taken place since 2006 (U.S. Immigration and Customs Enforcement 2009b). In addition to the arrests at IFCO Systems on April 19, 2006, 320 people were arrested at Michael Bianco in New Bedford, Massachusetts, on March 6 of that year (Nossiter 2008). The following December 12, 1,297 people were arrested at six Swift meat-processing facilities in several states (Nossiter 2008). On May 12, 2008, 389 undocumented workers were arrested at a single Agriprocessors plant in Postville, Iowa (Nossiter 2008). And on August 25, 2008, 595 undocumented workers were arrested at Howard Industries in Laurel, Mississippi (Nossiter 2008).

The rates of arrest during work site raids far exceed the increases in the rates of deportation for the same time period. From January 2004 to June 2007, ICE made 11,460 arrests at work sites, with 9,323 of these arrests (81 percent) in 2006–7. Arrests increased 71 percent from 2005 (1,292) to 2006 (4,383), and as of the end of August, work site arrests for 2008 had topped 5,527.

These actions would not have been possible without increases in ICE's budget that have considerably expanded the agency's enforcement capacity. At the same time, these raids are a result of ICE's need to justify those large budgetary increases (Camayd-Freixas 2008). From 2005 to 2009, ICE's budget increased from $3.5 billion to $5.9 billion (U.S. Immigration and Customs Enforcement 2005, 2006, 2007, 2008b, 2009a). Single raids that yield large numbers of arrests are cost-effective and expedient. ICE defends this tactic's efficiency in catching people guilty of the possession or sale of fraudulent documents, identity theft, social security fraud, and reentry after deportation. Immigrant rights advocates have raised concerns that ICE has failed to follow due process during raids and in detention and about arrestees' conditions during detention, isolation from family members, and lack of access to adequate information about legal representation (Camayd-Freixas 2008; Human Rights Watch 2007; National Council of La Raza 2007; National Network for Immigrant and Refugee Rights 2008).

In September 2008, in response to the sweeping raids, Kennedy and another Democratic senator, Robert Menendez of New Jersey, introduced the Protect Citizens and Residents from Unlawful Raids and Detention Act (S. 3594), which would have established due process standards for immigration detention, raids, and deportation. The bill would have required DHS to offer arrestees such due process protections as access to counsel and telephones, to provide for the humane treatment of all deportees, and to promote "alternatives to detention" programs that are more humane and cost-effective than traditional penal-style detention. The bill also would have required DHS to establish an ICE ombudsman to investigate complaints and to ensure that work site raids do not undermine labor or employment law investigations. The bill was referred to the Senate Judiciary Committee, and no further action was taken. In the first year of the Obama administration, most workplace raids have ceased as a consequence of a restriction by Department of Homeland Security secretary Janet Napolitano, who announced the need to delay and scrutinize workplace raids while placing a new emphasis on employer practices and employment verification (Hsu 2009). However, this emphasis on employment verification has led to procedures that some activists call "silent raids," such as the firing of twelve hundred workers for Minneapolis's ABM company in October 2009. Moreover, home raids, neighborhood raids, and other forms of detention (for traffic violations, for example) and subsequent deportations have continued.

Another consequence of Congress's failure to pass comprehensive immigration reform is that policies have gone local. Since 2005, the number of state bills related to immigration and immigrants—legal and undocumented arrivals, seasonal workers, and refugees—has increased by a staggering amount (National Conference of State Legislatures 2008, 2009). All fifty state legislatures have contemplated some sort of legislation, and as many as forty-three have enacted measures. The number of bills proposed in state legislatures mushroomed from 300 in 2005 to 574 in 2006 to 1,562 in 2007 to 1,305 in 2008, while the number enacted more than doubled each year between 2005 and 2007: 38 in 2005, 84 in 2006, and 240 in 2007. Most of these bills are restrictive and focus on licensing (driver's, professional, firearms, and fishing and hunting), employment (employer sanctions, employment eligibility verification), education (in-state tuition eligibility, programs that teach English as a second language), and law enforcement (immigrant detention processes, officer responsibilities). Perhaps the most restrictive state law, the 2007 Oklahoma Taxpayer and Citizen Protection Act (H.B. 1804), requires public employers to verify employees' immigration status, limits government identification to U.S. citizens and legal immigrants, and turns harboring, transporting, concealing, or sheltering undocumented immigrants into a felony (Catholic Legal Immigration Network 2007; Witt 2008). H.B. 1804 has resulted in an immigrant exodus that has left the state's businesses catering to the Latino community with too few workers and clients (Witt 2008).

The number of local ordinances has also grown, with most seeking to limit immigrants' access to housing options, city contracts, and business licenses as well as mandating enforcement of immigration restrictions and the adoption of English as the official language. Between roughly 2005 and 2007, at least fifty-five localities contemplated restrictive ordinances (Fair Immigration Reform Movement 2007), with Hazleton, Pennsylvania, passing the first such measure in 2006, when it prohibited the employment and the renting of housing to undocumented immigrants. A year later, courts declared the ordinance unconstitutional.

Restrictive and nativist sentiment has also led to an increase in hate crimes against Latinos, regardless of their legal or immigration status. From 2003 to 2006, the number of anti-Latino hate crimes increased by almost 35 percent nationwide and by 54 percent in California alone (Mock 2007). Especially after the spring 2006 marches, the Ku Klux Klan and other hate organizations have experienced a resurgence (Anti-Defamation League 2006). These groups have explicitly called not only for vigilantism at the border but also for violence against Latinos (Anti-Defamation League 2006). Such violence is not limited to organized groups: on July 12, 2008, three white teenagers unaffiliated with any nativist group beat to death an undocumented Mexican immigrant in Shenandoah, Pennsylvania. The increases in raids, deportations, restrictive local laws, and hate crimes support many immigrants' belief that *temporada de caza* has indeed arrived.

However, the picture is not uniformly bleak. Various states, cities, and towns have recently passed measures that support immigrant rights, such as charging in-state tuition to undocumented students and declaring sanctuaries where local police will not turn in immigrants who lack criminal records to the ICE.[22]

Immigrant rights activists and advocates have long worked to promote the fair and just treatment of immigrant communities, not only establishing immigration as an issue of national concern but playing a crucial role in the development of legislative immigration policy. This process has been particularly acute in Chicago, which has a rich history of pro-immigrant policies, stood at the vanguard of the sanctuary movement, and was hailed as leading the spring 2006 mobilizations.

Notes

1. Mobilizations did not take place in Hawaii, Montana, New Hampshire, North Dakota, Vermont, West Virginia, and Wyoming.

2. Immigrant rights activism predates IRCA, but we focus here on activism following this measure, the most recent comprehensive immigration reform.

3. Other immigrant rights coalitions created in this period include the New York Immigrant Coalition, the Northern California Coalition for Immigrant Rights, the Coalition for Humane Immigrant Rights of Los Angeles, and the Western Massachusetts Coalition for Immigrants and Refugee Rights, all of which fall under the umbrella of the National Network for Immigrant and Refugee Rights. Several other coalitions were established during the 1990s.

4. While restrictionists favor increasing limits on immigration and more restrictive immigration laws, nativists oppose immigration—in particular, by members of ethnic groups assumed to be unassimilable. Thus, all nativists are restrictionists, but not all restrictionists are nativists. Here, we use the more general term *restrictionists* to refer to both groups and use *nativists* when their views and/or actions set them apart from restrictionists.

5. Labor organizing had previously taken place in California, including the 1989 Janitors for Justice campaign, the 1992–93 drywall workers unionization, and the 1993 Latino American Truckers Association strike.

6. Legal immigrants who had entered the country before August 22, 1996, were eligible for these benefits after five years of residence in the United States, while immigrants who arrived after that date were eligible only after they became citizens. Undocumented immigrants were ineligible for any federally funded assistance except in the case of medical emergency.

7. Advocacy groups subsequently lobbied to mitigate the restrictions, and the Balanced Budget Act of 1997 rolled back a few of the more devastating provisions.

8. IIRIRA also required that immigrant sponsors be at least eighteen years old, reside in the United States, and show an income 125 percent higher than the federal poverty level.

9. Before 1996, noncitizen offenders had legal recourse: they appeared before immigration judges who established whether grounds for deportation existed and then determined if offenders should be deported (Morawetz 2000).

10. Other demands included a streamlined naturalization process, the enforcement of labor laws and the minimum wage, the establishment of civilian police review boards, and the provision of health care and quality education and equal opportunity for all (Hernández 2005; La Riva 1996; Rodríguez 1996).

11. On October 1, 2001, Dignity and Amnesty held a tribute in New York City for the immigrant workers who died in the attacks but whose families did not receive compensation because of their undocumented status. On May 1, 2002, the group carried out another mobilization in Washington, D.C., during which members met with members of Congress and White House officials in charge of immigration and held a rally, receiving a relatively warm reception. Dignity and Amnesty also participated in the Freedom

Rides in 2003. In September 2004, Dignity and Amnesty went back to Washington to protest President George W. Bush's principles for immigration reform and to present a Manifesto for Immigration Reform. In April 2005, Dignity and Amnesty held a National Day of Action in Washington, D.C., with visits to Congress and a rally and press conference. Fifty-four organizations endorsed what became Dignity and Amnesty's last national action.

12. It also called for the mandatory detention of suspected terrorists, and although charges must be filed within seven days of detention, detention may be extended indefinitely if the person is deemed a threat to national security.

13. Thousands of Muslim immigrants (including U.S. citizens) were subjected to investigation for possible connections to terrorist organizations. Bank accounts were frozen; people were detained without charges, often indefinitely, as "persons of interest"; and others were charged as "material witnesses" for their monetary donations to organizations, many of them legitimate but now on the government's terrorist watch list (Parker and Fellner 2004). Furthermore, the National Security Entry-Exit Registration System of 2002 required all male immigrants from Middle Eastern and Muslim countries who were sixteen years or older to report and register with the INS (Stock and Johnson 2003; Rudolph 2007).

14. Those states were Alabama, Arizona, Arkansas, California, Colorado, Florida, Georgia, Maryland, Massachusetts, Missouri, New Hampshire, North Carolina, New Mexico, Ohio, Oklahoma, South Carolina, Tennessee, Texas, and Virginia.

15. While the movement to support immigrant rights has paralleled the very effective restrictionist movement, this volume, with the important exception of Bleeden, Gottschalk-Druschke, and Cintrón, does not focus on the restrictionist movement or the relationship between the two camps, although the two movements clearly shape and inform each other as well as the state. An analysis of restrictionist activism merits a book unto itself. For more on restrictionism and nativism, see Perea 1997; Nevins 2002; Reimers 1999.

16. Because so many bills were introduced during this period, this section focuses on measures that were voted on, passed, or generated significant debate or controversy. For more detailed information on all the immigration-related bills introduced during this period, see the National Immigration Forum's Web site at www.immigrationforum.org.

17. The guest worker program would have allowed undocumented immigrants as well as foreigners to obtain three-year renewable work permits.

18. The Senate debated a version of the DREAM Act in October 2007, but the bill fell eight votes short of cloture. It has not been debated in the House.

19. Among these bills are the Immigration Reform Act of 2004 (S. 2010), also known as the Hagel-Daschle; the Comprehensive Enforcement and Immigration Reform Act of 2005 (S. 1438); and the Comprehensive Immigration Reform Act of 2006, also known as the Hagel-Martínez Compromise.

20. In 2007, the HIRC included 110 members of Congress, all of them white, including fourteen women (Building Democracy Initiative 2007). Its founder and first chair was Colorado Republican Tom Tancredo. Its members have introduced the most punitive immigration-related bills, including proposals to stop all legal migration and to

deny (and revoke) citizenship to the U.S.-born children of undocumented immigrants (Building Democracy Initiative 2007).

21. Cloture is "the only procedure by which the Senate can vote to place a time limit on consideration of a bill or other matter, and thereby overcome a filibuster. Under the cloture rule (Rule XXII), the Senate may limit consideration of a pending matter to 30 additional hours, but only by vote of three-fifths of the full Senate, normally 60 votes" (http://www.senate.gov/reference/glossary_term/cloture.htm).

22. Approximately eighty cities, four states, and five counties nationwide have declared themselves sanctuaries.

References

AFL-CIO. 2002. *The Immigrant Workers Freedom Ride: "On The Road to Citizenship."* August 7. www.aflcio.org/aboutus/thisistheaflcio/ecouncil/eco807d2002.cfm. Accessed May 13, 2009.

Aizenman, N. C. 2009. "Immigrant Activists Call for End to Raids." *Washington Post,* January 22.

Ali, A. 2007. "Battle Lines Being Drawn in Waukegan Immigration Debate." *Medill Reports: Chicago.* August 9. http://news.medill.northwestern.edu/chicago/news .aspx?id=46703. Accessed May 13, 2009.

Anti-Defamation League. 2006. "Extremists Declare 'Open Season' on Immigrants: Hispanics Target of Incitement and Violence." http://www.adl.org/main_Extremism/ immigration_extremists.htm?Multi_page_sections=sHeading_1. Accessed May 13, 2009.

———. 2007. *Ku Klux Klan Rebounds.* http://www.adl.org/learn/ext_us/kkk/klan_report .pdf. Accessed May 13, 2009.

Arango, Carlos. 2008. Interview by Nilda Flores-González. October 27, Chicago.

Archibold, Randal C. 2006. "Immigrants Take to U.S. Streets in Show of Strength." *New York Times,* May 2.

Bada, Xóchitl, Jonathan Fox, Elvia Zazueta, and Ingrid García. 2007. *Database: Immigrant Rights Marches, Spring 2006.* Woodrow Wilson International Center for Scholars. http://www.wilsoncenter.org/index.cfm?topic_id=5949&fuseaction=topics .item&news_id=150685#coverage_of_2006_marches. Accessed October 7, 2009.

Barbassa, Juliana. 2009. "Calls for Immigration Reform under Obama." *Orange County Register,* January 21.

Building Democracy Initiative. 2007. *Nativism in the House: A Report on the House Immigration Reform Caucus.* Center for New Community. http://www.buildingde-mocracy.org/reports/HIRC.pdf. Accessed May 13, 2009.

Calavita, Kitty. 1996. "The New Politics of Immigration: 'Balanced Budget Conservatism' and Prop 187." *Social Problems* 43 (3): 284–305.

Camayd-Freixas, Erik. 2008. "Interpreting after the Largest ICE Raid in U.S. History: A Personal Account." June 13. http://graphics8.nytimes.com/packages/pdf/ national/20080711IMMIG.pdf. Accessed October 7, 2009.

Catalinotto, John. 1997. "Immigrant Rights Marchers Head to UN." *Workers World,* October 16.

Catholic Legal Immigration Network. 2007. *Analysis of Recent Anti-Immigrant Legislation in Oklahoma.* November.

Chávez, L. 1997. "Immigration Reform and Nativism: The Nationalist Response to the Transnationalist Challenge." In *Immigrants Out: the New Nativism and the Anti-Immigrant Impulse in the United States,* ed. Juan Perea, 61–77. New York: New York University Press.

———. 2008. *The Latino Threat: Constructing Immigrants, Citizens, and the Nation.* Stanford, Calif.: Stanford University Press.

Chen, Edwin, and James F. Smith. 2001. "Bush and Fox Broach Issue of Migration." *Los Angeles Times,* February 17. http://articles.latimes.com/2001/feb/17/news/mn-26617. Accessed May 13, 2009.

Connell, R. 1994. "Prop 187's Support Shows No Bounds." *Los Angeles Times,* September 25.

"Death on the Border." 2009. *Arizona Daily Star,* June 30. http://regulus.azstarnet.com/borderdeaths/search.php. Accessed October 7, 2009.

Durand, Jorge, Nolan J. Malone, and Douglas S. Massey. 2002. *Beyond Smoke and Mirrors.* New York: Russell Sage Foundation.

Fair Immigration Reform Movement. 2007. *Database of Recent Local Ordinances on Immigration.* http://www.stateimmigrationlaws.com/NR/rdonlyres/edqegfctoziye73t dxebiaqdlvx3xos45xv36g3qwlojvgflxhllcdoxcqziubd6ftzcmhsshns5bedvvbiy2jtcmnf/ FAIRImmigrationLocalChart.pdf. Accessed November 14, 2009.

Feldman, Paul, and Patrick McDonnell. 1994. "Immigrant Activists Announce Boycott of Disney, Nabisco." *Houston Chronicle,* December 9.

Fox, Jonathan, and Xóchitl Bada. Forthcoming. "Migrant Civic Engagement." In *Rallying for Immigrant Rights,* ed. Irene Bloemraad and Kim Voss. Berkeley: University of California Press.

Fox, Jonathan, Andrew Selee, and Xóchitl Bada. 2007. "Conclusions." In *Invisible No More: Mexican Migrant Civic Participation in the United States,* ed. Xóchitl Bada, Jonathan Fox, and Andrew Selee, 35–40. Washington, D.C.: Woodrow Wilson International Center for Scholars.

Goldberg, Carey. 1996. "Hispanic Groups Prepare to March to Washington." New York Times, October 9.

Gutiérrez, Elena R. 2003. "Policing 'Pregnant Pilgrims': Welfare, Health Care, and the Control of Mexican-Origin Women's Fertility." In *Women, Health, and Nation: The U.S. and Canada since 1945,* ed. Molly Ladd-Taylor, Gina Feldberg, Kathryn McPherson, and Alison Li, 379–403. Toronto: McGill-Queens University Press.

———. 2008. *Fertile Matters: The Politics of Mexican-Origin Women's Reproduction.* Austin: University of Texas Press.

Gutiérrez, Juan José. 2008. Telephone interview by Nilda Flores-González. October 15.

Hayes-Bautista, David E. 2004. *La Nueva California: Latinos in the Golden State.* Berkeley: University of California Press.

Hernández, David Manuel. 2005. "Latino March on Washington." In *The Oxford Encyclopedia of Latinos and Latinas in the United States,* ed. Suzanne Oboler and Deena

J. González. http://www.oxford-latinos.com/entry?entry=t199.e494. Accessed May 13, 2009.

Holmes, Steven A. 1996. "Hispanic March Draws Crowd to Capital." *New York Times,* October 13.

Hondagneu-Sotelo, Pierrette, and Angelica Salas. 2008. "What Explains the Immigrant Rights Marches of 2006? Xenophobia and Organizing with Democracy Technology." In *Immigrant Rights in the Shadows of Citizenship,* ed. Rachel Ida Buff, 209–25. New York: New York University Press.

Hsu, Spencer S. 2009. "Delay in Immigration Raids May Signal Policy Change." *Washington Post,* March 29. http://www.washingtonpost.com/wp-dyn/content/article/2009/03/28/AR2009032801751.html?hpid=topnews. Accessed November 14, 2009.

Human Rights Watch. 2007. *Forced Apart: Families Separated and Immigrants Harmed by United States Deportation Policy.* July 16. http://www.hrw.org/en/node/10856/section/1. Accessed August 8, 2009.

Jiménez, María. 2008. Telephone interview by Nilda Flores-González. October 13.

Jonas, Susanne. 2006. "Reflections on the Great Immigration Battle of 2006 and the Future of the Americas." *Social Justice* 33 (1): 6–20.

Koppel, Martin, and Elizabeth Stone. 1996. "March on Washington: No Human Is Illegal!" *The Militant,* October 28. http://www.themilitant.com/1996/6038/6038_1.html. Accessed October 11, 2009.

La Riva, Gloria. 1996. "Conference Focuses on How to Defend Immigrants' Rights." *Workers World,* December 19. http://www.hartford.hwp.com/archives/45/124.html. Accessed November 18, 2009.

Lazos-Vargas, S. R. 2007. "The Immigrant Rights Marches (Las Marchas): Did the 'Gigante' (Giant) Wake Up or Does It Still Sleep Tonight?" *Nevada Law Journal* 7:780–825.

Lee, Taeku, Karthick Ramakrishnan, and Ricardo Ramirez. 2007. "Bridging Political Behavior and Social Movement Perspectives on the Immigration Protests of 2006." Paper presented at the Conference on Understanding the Immigration Protests of Spring 2006: Lessons Learned, Future Trajectories, Institute for Research on Labor and Employment, University of California, Berkeley, April 20.

Mailman, Stanley. 1995. "California's Proposition 187 and Its Lessons." *New York Law Journal,* January 3, 3.

Maya, Beatriz. 2002. "Mayday in D.C.: Immigrants Exercise Democracy." *Independent Progressive Politics Network.* Summer. http://www.ippn.org/legacy/legacy/ippn.org/articleb943.html?ID=sumnewso2e.html. Accessed May 13, 2009.

———. 2008. Telephone interview by Nilda Flores-González. September 25.

McKenzie, A. 2004. "A Nation of Immigrants or a Nation of Suspects—State and Local Enforcement of Federal Immigration Laws." *Alabama Law Review* 55 (4): 1149–65.

Mize, Ronald L. 2005. "Amnesty Movement." *Oxford Encyclopedia of Latinos and Latinas in the United States.* www.oxford-latinos.com. Accessed October 15, 2009.

Mock, Brentin. 2007. "Immigration Backlash: Violence Engulfs Latinos." *Intelligence Report.* http://www.splcenter.org/intel/news/item.jsp?site_area=1&aid=292. Accessed May 13, 2009.

Monforti, Jessica Lavariega. 2008. "The Awakening of the Sleeping Giant? Latino Political Participation and the 2006 Immigrant Rights Protests." Paper presented at the annual meeting of the Western Political Science Association, San Diego, Calif.

Montejano, David. 1999. "On the Future of Anglo-Mexican Relations in the United States." In *Chicano Politics and Society in the Late Twentieth Century,* ed. David Montejano, 234–57. Austin: University of Texas Press.

Mora, C. 2007. *Latinos in the West: The Student Movement and Academic Labor in Los Angeles.* Lanham, Md.: Rowman and Littlefield.

Morawetz, Nancy. 2000. "Understanding the Impact of the 1996 Deportation Laws and the Limited Scope of Proposed Reforms." *Harvard Law Review* 113 (8): 1936–62.

Narro, V., K. Wong, and J. Shadduck-Hernández. 2007. "The 2006 Immigrant Uprising: Origins and Future." *New Labor Forum* 16 (1): 49–56.

National Coalition for Dignity and Amnesty. 2000a. *Campaign for General Amnesty* (online petition). http://www.petitiononline.com/i1pacman/petition.html. Accessed September 9, 2008.

———. 2000b. *The National Coalition for Dignity and Amnesty Will Return to Washington, D.C. on July 20th.* July 17. http://www.nettime.org/Lists-Archives/nettime-l-0007/msg00079.html. Accessed September 9, 2008.

National Conference of State Legislatures. 2008. *2007 Enacted State Legislation Related to Immigrants and Immigration.* January 31. http://www.ncsl.org/default.aspx?tabid=13106. Accessed August 8, 2009.

———. 2009. *State Laws Related to Immigrants and Immigration in 2008.* January 27. http://lawprofessors.typepad.com/immigration/files/stateimmigreportfinal20081.pdf. Accessed August 8, 2009.

National Council of La Raza. 2007. *Paying the Price: The Impact of Immigration Raids on America's Children.* http://www.urban.org/UploadedPDF/411566_immigration_raids.pdf. Accessed August 8, 2009.

National Network for Immigrant and Refugee Rights. 2008. *Overraided, under Siege: U.S. Immigration Laws and Enforcement Destroy the Rights of Immigrants.* http://www.nnirr.org/resources/docs/UnderSiege_web.pdf. Accessed May 13, 2009.

Nevins, Joseph. 2002. *Operation Gatekeeper: The Rise of the "Illegal Alien" and the Making of the U.S.-Mexico Boundary.* New York: Routledge.

Newton, L. 1998. *Why Latinos Supported Proposition 187: Testing the Economic Threat and Cultural Identity Hypotheses.* Center for the Study of Democracy, University of California, Irvine. http://repositories.cdlib.org/csd/98–12. Accessed May 13, 2009.

Nossiter, Adam. 2008. "Hundreds of Workers Held in Immigration Raid." *New York Times,* August 26. http://www.nytimes.com/2008/08/26/us/26raid.html?_r=1&oref=slogin. Accessed May 13, 2009.

"Obama Administration Expands Law Enforcement Program 287(g), Criticized for Targeting Immigrants and Increasing Racial Profiling." 2009. *Democracy Now,* July 29. http://www.democracynow.org/2009/7/29/obama_admin_expands_law_enforcement_program. Accessed November 14, 2009.

Obrero Revolucionario. 1997. "Los Inmigrantes se Hacen Oír." *Revolutionary Worker Online,* October 26. http:rwor.org. Accessed May 13, 2009.

Office of the Inspector General. 1998. *Operation Gatekeeper: An Investigation into Allegations of Fraud and Misconduct.* July. http://www.usdoj.gov/oig/special/9807/index .htm. Accessed May 13, 2009.

Parker, Alison, and Jamie Fellner. 2004. "About the Law: Executive Power after September 11 in the United States." *Human Rights Watch World Report 2004.* http://www.hrw .org/legacy/wr2k4/8.htm. Accessed August 8, 2009.

Perea, Juan. 1997. Introduction to *Immigrants Out: The New Nativism and the Anti-Immigrant Impulse in the United States,* ed. Juan Perea, 1–10. New York: New York University Press.

Pew Hispanic Center. 2006. *The State of American Public Opinion in Spring 2006: A Review of Major Surveys.* May 17. http://pewhispanic.org/files/factsheets/18.pdf. Accessed August 8, 2009.

Reimers, David. 1999. *Unwelcome Strangers: American Identity and the Turn against Immigration.* New York: Columbia University Press.

Rodríguez, Roberto. 1996. "Students Play a Major Role at Historic Latino March on Washington." *Black Issues in Higher Education,* October 31.

Rudolph, Chris. 2007. *National Security and Immigration in the United States after 9/11.* http://www.ccis-ucsd.org/PUBLICATIONS/wrkg157.pdf. Accessed October 15, 2009.

Sachetti, Maria. 2008. "Obama Faces Pressure on Immigration Reform." *Boston Globe,* November 12. http://www.boston.com/news/nation/articles/2008/11/17/obama_ faces_pressure_on_immigration_reform. Accessed May 13, 2009.

Siskin, Alison, and Ruth Ellen Wasem. 2005. *Immigration Policy on Expedited Removal of Aliens.* http://www.au.af.mil/au/awc/awcgate/crs/rl33109.pdf. Accessed August 8, 2009.

Stock, Margaret D., and Benjamin Johnson. 2003. "The Lessons of 9/11: A Failure of intelligence, Not Immigration Law." *Immigration Policy Focus.* http://homeland.cq.com/ hs/flatfiles/temporaryItems/20031215_ailf.pdf. Accessed November 14, 2009.

Tsao, Fred. 2008. Interview by Amalia Pallares. February 22. Chicago.

———. 2009. Interview by Amalia Pallares. September 2. Chicago.

U.S. Government Accountability Office. 2006. *Illegal Immigration: Border Crossing Deaths Have Doubled since 1995.* http://www.gao.gov/new.items/d06770.pdf. Accessed May 13, 2009.

U.S. Immigration and Customs Enforcement. 2005. *Fact Sheet, Fiscal Year 2005.* http:// www.ice.gov/pi/news/factsheets/index.htm. Accessed May 13, 2009.

———. 2006. *Fact Sheet, Fiscal Year 2006.* http://www.ice.gov/pi/news/factsheets/index .htm. Accessed May 13, 2009.

———. 2007. *Fact Sheet, Fiscal Year 2007.* http://www.ice.gov/pi/news/factsheets/index .htm. Accessed May 13, 2009.

———. 2008a. *Delegation of Immigration Authority: Section 287(g) Immigration and Nationality Act.* http://www.ice.gov/partners/287g/Section287_g.htm. Accessed May 13, 2009.

———. 2008b. *Fact Sheet, Fiscal Year 2008.* http://www.ice.gov/pi/news/factsheets/index .htm. Accessed May 13, 2009.

———. 2009a. *Fact Sheet, Fiscal Year 2009.* http://www.ice.gov/pi/news/factsheets/index .htm. Accessed May 13, 2009.

———. 2009b. *Worksite Enforcement Overview.* April 30. http://www.ice.gov/pi/news/ factsheets/worksite.htm. Accessed May 13, 2009.

Vila, Daniel. 1998. "Record Number of Immigrants Deported." *People's Weekly World,* November 8.

Witt, Howard. 2008. "Where Have the Illegal Workers Gone? Oklahoma Law Targeting Illegal Workers Had Some Unforeseen Results." *Chicago Tribune,* February 10.

Zito, Kelly. 2009. "Pelosi: End Raids Splitting Families." *San Francisco Chronicle,* March 8. http://www.sfgate.com/cgi-bin/article.cgi?f=/c/a/2009/03/07/BAHJ16BE8V.DTL. Accessed November 14, 2009.

2

The Chicago Context

AMALIA PALLARES

Chicago's ability to stage the first megamarch of 2006 and the largest marches in 2007 and 2008 illustrates the existence of a vibrant scene of Latino/a activism that both precedes and postdates the marches. Moreover, many of Chicago's actors, institutions, and processes have parallels in other cities. Thus, an analysis of Chicago's historical and political conditions offers an indispensable starting point for examining immigrant activism.

This chapter first examines Chicago's demographic, institutional, and political development before turning to the politics of the marches and their immediate effect. The final section reflects on the marches' consequences for the movement, the social and political capital they have provided, and the ways in which they have shaped future political possibilities, completing a general narrative that will guide readers through the remainder of the book.

The Chicago Context

With a current population of 1.6 million, Latinos comprise approximately 20 percent of all Chicago residents, the largest ethnic minority in the nine-county metropolitan area. Whites constitute a majority of the population, at 55 percent, with blacks accounting for 19 percent and Asians for 6 percent (Ready and Brown-Gort 2005). Chicago has the nation's third-largest Latino population (trailing only Los Angeles and New York) and second-largest Mexican[1] community (after Los Angeles) (Ready and Brown-Gort 2005). Two-thirds of Chicago-area Latinos are citizens (Paral et al. 2004). The city's Latino population jumped from 5 percent in 1970 to 12 percent in 1990, 17 percent in 2000, and 20 percent in 2004. In the 1990s alone, the Latino population grew by 69 percent (Paral et al. 2004). By 2002, Latinos had surpassed African Americans to become the largest minority in the metropolitan area (Ready and Brown-Gort 2005).

Most Chicago Latinos are Mexican (74.9 percent), followed by Puerto Ricans (10.8 percent), Central Americans (2.6 percent), South Americans (2 percent), and Cubans (1.2 percent). While Chicago's Mexican presence dates back to the early twentieth century, Puerto Ricans arrived in the 1940s and other Latinos started migrating to the city in the late 1950s. U.S.-born Latinos constitute 53 percent of the total Latino population; however, the numbers are quite different for adults (just 35 percent of whom are U.S.-born) than for children (84 percent of whom are U.S.-born) (Ready and Brown-Gort 2005). Estimates show that about 26 percent of Chicago's 740,000 Latino immigrants are undocumented (Ready and Brown-Gort 2005). Finally, Latino arrivals to Chicago are joined by people from many other different parts of the world, including Filipinos, Chinese, other Asians, and Poles. Chicago is a city of immigrants, among whom Latinos account for just over half (Ready and Brown-Gort 2005). One in five Chicagoans is an immigrant, far higher than the 11 percent nationwide rate (Knight, Ready, and Barboza 2007).

Latino Activism

Chicago has been a site of Latino activism since the 1920s, when the newly arrived Mexican population organized mutual aid societies. During the 1950s, the growing Puerto Rican population added social organizations, and in the late 1960s and 1970s, a new generation of leaders and organizations arose to address both Mexican and Puerto Rican concerns. Like Chicano activists in the Southwest, Mexicans in the Midwest organized as farmworkers (the Farm Labor Organizing Committee) and as students (the Organization of Latin American Students and the Movimiento Estudiantil Chicano de Aztlán) and created community, civil rights, and political organizations (the Midwest Council of La Raza, La Raza Unida, and local chapters of the Mexican American Legal Defense Fund) (Parra 2004). The important political and community organizations created during the 1970s included the Centro de Acción Social Autónomo (CASA, formerly the Illinois Raza Unida Party), the Centro de la Causa, Casa Aztlán, Hogar de Niños, Mujeres Latinas en Acción, Latino Youth, and the Asociación Pro Derechos Obreros (Parra 2004). In addition, Mexican activism focused on immigrant rights, including the rights of the undocumented. According to Badillo, the Mexican American population saw "defense of undocumented workers and their political representation [as] the most important movement from 1975 to 1983" (2004, 41). Moreover, this activism developed in response to several aggressive raids in factories, parks, and theaters in the Pilsen area in the early to mid-1970s (41). (See figure 2.1 for a map of key sites of activism.)

Figure 2.1. Key Sites of Activism in Chicago.

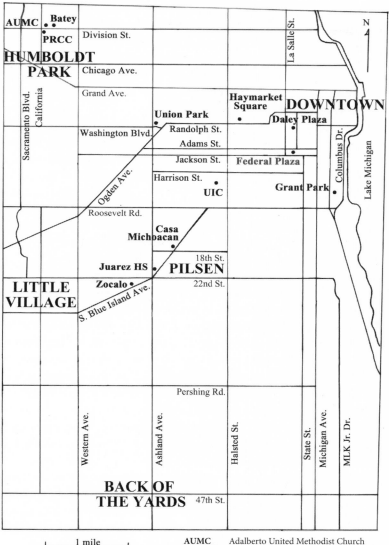

AUMC	Adalberto United Methodist Church
Juarez HS	Benito Juarez High School
PRCC	Puerto Rican Cultural Center
UIC	University of Illinois at Chicago

The work of activist Rudy Lozano encapsulates some of these struggles as well as the creation of panethnic and panracial coalitions and independent political organizing during the 1970s and 1980s. Lozano, a labor organizer, joined with Art Vásquez, Linda Coronado, Jesús "Chuy" García, Juan Soliz, and others in the Chicago Chapter of CASA, a California-based organization that focused on community issues, including labor rights and the rights of undocumented immigrants.[2] Lozano and other Mexican activists worked with Puerto Ricans for educational equality and other community issues. Puerto Ricans had mobilized around policy brutality and other urban issues in the late 1960s, creating the Young Lords Organization (Padilla 1985; Cruz 2007). In addition, the West Town Coalition of Concerned Citizens brought together Puerto Rican community organizers and progressives, among them the Reverend Jorge Morales, Peter Earle, and José "Cha-Cha" Jiménez. In 1973, while a student at the University of Illinois–Chicago Circle (now the University of Illinois at Chicago), Lozano joined a group of Mexican and Puerto Rican students who occupied the chancellor's office, demanding more resources and services as well as more Latino faculty and the creation of a Latin American studies curriculum. The university eventually created a Latin American studies program, the Latino Cultural Center, and the Latin American Recruitment and Educational Services Office. In 1979, Lozano became an organizer for the International Ladies' Garment Workers Union. In the early 1980s, Lozano and García founded an independent political organization that sought to challenge the Chicago machine by seeking more resources for Latino communities and political empowerment at all levels.[3]

During the 1980s, the lack of Latino electoral empowerment caused young activists to adopt other strategies for change, such as community organizing (Torres 1991). Mexicans and Puerto Ricans joined forces to promote access to jobs and create the Instituto del Progreso Latino (Padilla 1985, 120). In 1981, García and Lozano created the Independent Political Organization of Little Village in the Twenty-second Ward, and a year later, Lozano ran for the ward's seat on the Chicago City Council, falling seventeen votes short of a runoff. However, the Independent Political Organization helped to create a coalition that resulted in the election of African American Harold Washington as mayor in 1983. Grassroots black organizers attempting to challenge machine control selected Washington as an independent candidate and worked with lakefront white liberals and Latino independents to build a historic coalition for change. Washington carried 75.3 percent of the Latino vote, which gave him a narrow margin of victory (Torres 1991, 173). Lozano served briefly as part of Washington's transition team but was shot and killed in the summer of 1983.

Opponents on the city council at first thwarted Washington's efforts to govern. After special elections in 1986, however, the number of Latinos on the council doubled from two to four (a consequence of demographic growth and the Mexican American Legal Defense Fund's intervention in a lawsuit against gerrymandering), giving Washington supporters a governing majority.[4] Four of seven new Black and Latino districts were won by Washington supporters, while three were won by machine candidates. The mayor's new supporters on the council included García (Twenty-second Ward) and Puerto Rican social worker and former Washington adviser Luis Gutiérrez (Twenty-sixth Ward). A year later, Washington, Gutiérrez, and García were reelected and two other nonmachine candidates won in Latino wards (Córdova 1999), but the mayor died suddenly of a heart attack just as the progressive coalition was set to initiate an era of reform. By 1989, the independents no longer retained control of City Hall (Torres 2004, 93).

Some important advances in Latino empowerment occurred during Washington's term in office. He created the Commission on Latino Affairs to devise programs to address Latino issues both in the city and in immigrants' home countries. Commission members viewed themselves as advocates for the community rather than advisers to the mayor and pressed for public policies to address a number of key Latino issues. The commission also provided Latinos of all nationalities and neighborhoods a forum in which to discuss their shared concerns and develop an independent, progressive agenda (Torres 2004, 176). Washington also appointed at least one Latino to every city board and commission, although the low number of Latinos hired by the city disappointed commission members (Torres 1991, 179). In 1986, in response to commission pressure and economic conditions, Washington issued an executive order that prohibited city departments from collaborating with immigration officials and from making any reference to immigration status on city applications (Torres 1991, 179). In light of the Reagan era's federal disinvestment from local governments, the normally divided members of the city council unanimously agreed that the city could not enforce federal policy while the U.S. government was taking money away from the city (Torres 2008). Chicago was one of the first cities to enact such ordinances, which now distinguish sanctuary cities from nonsanctuary cities, and one of Mayor Washington's successors, Richard M. Daley, and the city council amended the municipal code in 2006 to prevent city workers from requesting information on legal status.

After Washington's death, Latino empowerment grew within the restrictive environment of the Chicago electoral machine, which sought to control Latino politicians and curtail independent candidates and public officials. In 1992, Gutiérrez was elected to the U.S. Congress from the Fourth District, which was created to maximize Latino representation.[5] His independent credentials and his allegiance to the Latino community, however, were questioned when he supported Daley over independent Timothy Evans in the 1989 special election to replace Washington. Gutiérrez initially received very little support from independent Latinos and relied mostly on white votes but later relied on the immigration issue to build a solid pan-Latino and panethnic constituency that has kept him in office, and he has become one of House's most vocal advocates for comprehensive immigration reform.

Between 1996 and 2007, the number of Latino elected officials in Illinois more than doubled from forty-one to ninety-seven (National Association of Latino Elected and Appointed Officials 2008). Many of these gains resulted from the significant increases in the city's Latino population, but Latinos remain underrepresented among the state's electorate, comprising 15 percent of Illinois residents but only 8 percent of eligible voters. (National Association of Latino Elected and Appointed Officials 2007). At the same time, however, independent political representation has declined as a consequence of the persistence of the Chicago political machine. While the machine's power waned in the 1960s and 1970s in response to a combination of reform movements, white flight from the city, and African American defection, it was reincarnated in the late 1980s. Richard M. Daley, the son of longtime Chicago political boss Richard J. Daley, has built a powerful political organization that has effectively turned many former independents into Daley supporters and permanent incumbents.

The machine's Latino arm, the Hispanic Democratic Organization (HDO), has worked consistently in the past decade to get independent Latino city and state public officials voted out, thwart the efforts of independent Latino candidates, and get machine candidates elected. The HDO, a political action committee made up mostly of Latino city employees (according to the Chicago Board of Election Commissioners, 482 of its 1,173 registrars were city employees in 2005 [Konkol et al. 2005]), was formally created in 1993 and has since helped elect Daley-endorsed candidates to the city council, the Illinois General Assembly, and the U.S. Congress. Until its demise in 2008, it recruited large numbers of campaign workers by promising them jobs and/or promotions.[6] According to Maria de los Angeles Torres, who served as executive director of the Commission on Latino Affairs from 1983 to 1987, "Latinos incorporated into machine politics often lose their independence and instead of advocating for the needs of their communities, end up being used to detain independent communities" (2004, 86). While a handful of independent public officials remain in office, holding onto their positions is frequently an uphill battle, and the possibility of a new independent reform era (and of an accompanying black-Latino coalition) is practically nonexistent.

Although the immigration issue cuts across machine politics (in Chicago, both machine and nonmachine officials have supported the marches and different sectors of the movement), the local context shapes activists' and community members' perception that formal politics offers an ineffective avenue for change and helps to explain the persistence of other types of political activism. However, the machine's persistence also raises doubts among local activists that civic participation through marches, even if followed by massive registration and unprecedented Latino voting, can lead to meaningful electoral and political change.

In addition to the effect that increased Latino empowerment has played in shaping immigration politics, other local factors must also be taken into account. Chicago and Illinois have generally provided a welcoming context for immigrants and immigrant activism. Chicago has a long history of receiving multiethnic migrations from both Western and Eastern Europe as well as Asia and Africa. Many public officials, including Daley and former Illinois governor Rod Blagojevich, are of immigrant descent and publicly and proudly identify themselves as such. The city traditionally hosts multiple large annual parades commemorating the ethnic holidays of Italians, Irish, Poles, Mexicans, and Puerto Ricans, among many others. White ethnics have a long history of political ascension in city politics, unions, and other public institutions that has been shaped by dense immigrant networks. Perhaps most important, despite the city's large Mexican presence, immigrants and immigration issues are equated not solely with Mexicans but with a wide variety of populations, including new arrivals from the Philippines, India, China, Sudan, Poland, Russia, Bulgaria, and most recently Myanmar (*Encyclopedia* 2004).

The fruits of Latino community activism and pro-immigrant politics include a wide array of organizations that work directly on immigrant issues. Some are policy and advocacy organizations (the Illinois Coalition for Immigrant and Refugee Rights [ICIRR] and Latino Policy Forum [formerly Latinos United]), while others, such as Casa Romero, the Erie Neighborhood House, and the Instituto del Progreso Latino, are social service organizations. Still others—Casa Aztlán, the Puerto Rican Cultural Center, the Albany Park Community Center, and the Centro sin Fronteras—combine advocacy and service and community activism for education, housing, health, and immigrant rights, addressing immigrants' needs.

More recently, the State of Illinois itself has implemented a number of policies designed to facilitate immigrant incorporation. In November 2005, Governor Blagojevich signed the New Americans Executive Order, which created an office to coordinate policies and programs to help new immigrants and study the impact of immigration policy. Further, he appointed José Luis Gutiérrez, a Mexican activist who was pivotal in the growth and consolidation of hometown associations, as director of the Office of New Americans Policy and Advocacy, which is charged with integrating immigrant-related efforts by state agencies, community organizations, private funding sources, and experts. In 2007 the office's first Immigrant Welcoming Center opened in Melrose Park, a Chicago suburb with a population that is 53.9 percent Latino. In addition, the state has enacted legislation to protect day laborers against employer cheating, provide health coverage for immigrant children, and allow undocumented immigrants to pay in-state tuition to attend public universities.

The Marches—Historical Precedents

Like many other U.S. cities, Chicago experienced a proamnesty momentum in the 1990s that was stopped cold by the September 11 attacks. The subsequent linkage of immigration to security issues placed the movement on hiatus at a time when both legislative measures and diplomatic initiatives between Mexican president Vicente Fox and U.S. president George W. Bush had made some type of reform seem likely.

The Chicago immigrant rights struggle gained new strength as part of Coordinadora '96, a coalition that organized the first national Latino mobilization to Washington, D.C., on October 12, 1996 (see chap. 1). Headed by Carlos Arango, executive director of Casa Aztlán, the Chicago chapter of Coordinadora '96 took more than five thousand people to this mobilization, the largest delegation from any city. The Centro sin Fronteras, the St. Pius Catholic Church, the Comité Patriótico Mexicano (Mexican Patriotic Committee), and some union locals and college student groups were among the organizations that mobilized people. Chicago also had a strong presence in other Coordinadora '96 events, including an October 12, 1997, march to the United Nations. On October 12, 1998, Chicago hosted Coordinadora's national mobilization, with one thousand people marching from the Providencia de Dios Church in the Mexican neighborhood of Pilsen to the Tribune Plaza. Lázaro Cárdenas Batel, son of Mexican politician Cuauhtémoc Cárdenas, attended, as did delegations from Arizona, New York, Texas, and California.

In 1998, Coordinadora '96 ceased to exist, but the struggle for amnesty and for other legislative changes continued through the newly formed Coalition for Dignity and Amnesty for Undocumented Immigrants (Dignity and Amnesty; see chap. 1). The Centro sin Fronteras and Casa Aztlán participated in Dignity and Amnesty's first national march, held in Washington, D.C., on October 12, 1999. The following September 25, the ICIRR and various grassroots organizations and unions, including the Association of Community Organizations for Reform Now, Centro sin Fronteras, the Service Employees International Union (SEIU), and the Union of Needletrades, Industrial, and Textile Employees and the Hotel Employees and Restaurant Employees International Union (UNITE HERE), mobilized ten thousand people to march from Daley Plaza to Federal

Plaza (Tsao 2008). Also in 2000, the ICIRR held several town hall meetings on the issue, collected thousands of signatures on a petition for amnesty, and worked intensively though unsuccessfully to extend Section 245(i) of the Immigration and Nationality Act beyond its April 2001 deadline (see chap. 1).

On October 14, 2000, Dignity and Amnesty held marches in Atlanta, Chicago, Los Angeles, Seattle, Austin, and New York. In Chicago, Centro sin Fronteras was one of the main organizers, and the march theme was dual: amnesty for undocumented immigrants and the U.S. Navy's ouster from the Puerto Rican town of Vieques. At the rally, Representative Gutiérrez called on President Bill Clinton to restore Section 245(i) and extend amnesty to Haitians, Salvadorans, Guatemalans, and Hondurans as well as to undocumented immigrants left out of the 1986 Immigration and Reform Control Act amnesty. On May 1, 2001, immigrant rights activists joined Puerto Rican activists to create the Amnesty-Vieques Human Chain (see chap. 13).

The period from the aftermath of the September 11 attacks to 2005 saw both retrenchment and growth for Chicago's immigrant rights movement, as changes in local organizing helped to prepare the terrain for the creation of networks that facilitated later marches. In the wake of the AFL-CIO's decision to support the rights of undocumented immigrants (see chap. 1), immigrant rights organizations as well as local unions revisited their assessment of what was politically possible. Local unions became increasingly active in immigrant rights issues, in the process recruiting more Latino leaders (see chap. 6). In 1998, twenty organizations that provided services to immigrants had created the Coalition of African, Arab, Asian, American, European, and Latino Immigrants of Illinois, pooling resources and ideas for citizenship work and immigrant advocacy. The coalition subsequently provided training and public education to many immigrants and immigrant activists. Moreover, ICIRR made the transition from a primary focus on policy research and advocacy to more direct involvement in immigrant political incorporation and community organizing, working closely with grassroots organizations.

Mexican hometown associations also began developing more leadership capacity and creating extensive networks (see chap. 8). The Mexican consulate as well as the Enlaces de América program run by the Heartland Alliance for Human Needs and Human Rights played important roles in this process.[7] Hometown associations also expanded their focus beyond local development issues in Mexico to include broader policy concerns, lobbying both the Mexican and U.S. governments for policies that would benefit immigrants, such as dual citizenship and the ability to use a consular identification in the United States (see chap. 8). Immigrants who had political experience in Mexico began to organize political parties in Chicago, joining with representatives of hometown associations to participate in the newly created Instituto de Mexicanos en el Exterior, which, in turn, solidified and expanded existing Mexican immigrant networks (see chaps. 7, 8).

Multiple immigrant-led organizations, many of them local to Chicago, formed the National Alliance of Latin American and Caribbean Communities (NALACC), which sought to develop an agenda by and for immigrants. Immigrant and second-generation youth in Humboldt Park and Pilsen also organized cultural groups in which people could share their views on the social and political conditions facing their communities. Many of the founding youth leaders of Batey Urbano, Zócalo Urbano, and the May 1 Youth Network were also community activists with deeply intertwined political and cultural agendas (see Flores-González, Rodríguez, and Rodríguez Muñiz 2006; see also chap. 11). Church activism for immigrant rights intensified through the work of individual parishes and congregations, interfaith coalitions, and more formal campaigns initiated by the Catholic Church hierarchy (see chap. 4). Finally, local Spanish-language media began to take a more proactive role in the immigrant issue (see chap. 3). All of these developments would prove crucial in the formation of the actors and networks that would play a central role in the immigrant marches.

By 2003, the immigrant rights movement was gaining new momentum. In May, the ICIRR achieved one of its first major successes at the state level, the enactment of H.B. 60, which allowed undocumented students who had graduated from Illinois high schools to pay in-state tuition at public colleges and universities. According to the ICIRR's policy director, Fred Tsao, the state legislature's newly enlarged Latino Caucus showed some muscle and made this issue a priority, persuading overwhelming numbers of General Assembly members to vote for the bill (2008).

Tsao also saw 2004 as an important year for the revival of activism in Chicago: "It wasn't really until Bush made his announcement of principles back in January 2004 that the energy started picking up again. . . . Basically, it was a guest worker proposal. . . . We even bought TV spots to protest what we thought was wrong with the proposal. [The announcement] set up the dynamic that this was going to be an issue that was going to be alive again. . . . Luis Gutiérrez and Senator [Edward] Kennedy were working on their own immigration proposals. . . . I think the bills got introduced after Bush made the announcement, but all the same, it's one step further that helped energize the process" (2008). The ICIRR launched New Americans Vote, its first major immigrant voter mobilization program, the same year, following up in 2005 with the state-funded New Americans program to promote naturalization. The issue of family separation had become more central beginning in 2002, as the Centro sin Fronteras, NALACC, and ICIRR organizers underscored the ways in which the full implementation of the 1996 law had affected even legal immigrants (see chap. 12). Their efforts primarily involved lobbying in Chicago, Springfield, and Washington as well as mobilizing communities to lobby in an effort to keep families together. While all these efforts were bearing fruit, the massive outpouring of street activism would not become a reality until 2005.

The Spring of the Immigrant

While 2006 will be remembered as the year of the immigrant megamarches, the first massive march in Chicago was held in 2005 in response to declarations by the Minutemen published in the newspaper *Hoy*. A Chicago Minuteman chapter was being created, and its president, Rosanna Pulido, a Mexican American, was openly recruiting members. The public reaction to this article was intense, leading various community leaders and personalities to weigh in on the issue. Father Marco Cárdenas of Our Lady of Guadalupe Roman Catholic Church and Rafael "El Pistolero" Pulido, a DJ on a Univision radio affiliate, called for a mass response. The Centro sin Fronteras, Casa Aztlán, and the ICIRR helped organize a July march in the mostly Mexican Back of the Yards neighborhood. The rally surprised even organizers by drawing about fifty thousand people even though the press devoted little attention to the plans in part because of its location and low expectations for its success. Thousands of West and South Side residents appeared, dressed in white shirts symbolizing amnesty, bearing Mexican and U.S. flags, and carrying signs that read "I am illegal, not a criminal"; "We come to work, not to steal from anybody"; and "We demand our place" (Martínez and Piña 2005). Most hometown associations did not participate on the grounds that the South Side location would have little impact. Congressman Gutiérrez joined in, however, and Senator Kennedy later expressed his support (Martínez and Piña 2005, 9). The event's success showed many activists the issue's potential to produce massive mobilizations.

As the Sensenbrenner Bill made its way to passage in the House of Representatives (see chap. 1), activists agreed that a more visible mobilization was necessary to stop the measure from reaching a Senate vote. In December 2005, several SEIU representatives met in San Juan, Puerto Rico, and decided that they all must work locally to mobilize supporters of immigrant rights. One of those representatives, Artemio Arreola, a member of Casa Michoacán (a union of hometown clubs from that Mexican state), undertook those efforts when he returned to Chicago, recruiting help from members of other hometown associations, churches, unions, and grassroots organizations. In addition, Emma Lozano, president of Centro sin Fronteras, as well as Marcia Soto from the Confederación de Mexicanos en el Exterior (a regional coalition of hometown associations) traveled to Riverside, California, in early February 2006 and attended a meeting at which immigrant rights activists decided to stage marches across the country on March 10 (see chap. 1).

Although organizers in most cities could not pull events together so quickly, Chicago activists began mobilizing immediately through the March 10 Coalition, whose founding members included Lozano, Soto, Salome Amezcua, Omar López, Artemio Arreola, Jorge Mujica, and Maria D'Amezcua, among many others. Regular meetings were held in Casa Michoacán to plan the event. Organizers began to suspect that the rally would attract a tremendous number of participants after learning that all the buses in the Chicago metro area had been reserved and that groups from the suburbs were having difficulty securing transportation (Arreola 2008). Numerous calls from church and community groups, each of which committed to sending several dozen people, also indicated that the march would be a success. Disagreements about which elected officials would be allowed to speak to the crowds led Sin Fronteras organizers to withdraw from the coalition on the eve of the march, but representatives of all the founding groups were among the estimated one hundred thousand to three hundred thousand marchers at Union Park the following day.[8]

Although the march had some union financial support, it relied heavily on indigenous resources, Spanish-language media, and word of mouth (see chap. 4). Most signs had handwritten, improvised messages. While the march was intensively and meticulously planned, it had an element of surprise and spontaneity that distinguishes it from later marches. Many employers gave their workers time off, in some instances providing transportation so that employees could attend: "Commercial sectors such as 26th Street [in Little Village] were deserted" (Espinosa 2006, 11).

Politicians who spoke at the rally included Senators Durbin and Barack Obama, Governor Blagojevich, Mayor Daley, and Congressmen Gutiérrez and Bobby Rush. According to Daley, "The United States was built by immigrants and we are not going to turn them into criminals" (Espinosa 2006, 11). Blagojevich told those assembled, "You are not criminals, you are workers," while Gutiérrez urged them to raise American flags because "this is our country, and it is where we will remain" (Banda Sifuentes 2006, 13).

A few days later, several activists from the March 10 Coalition decided to continue the pressure, using the experience and energy they had gained to mobilize even more people on May 1. Chicago leaders traveled to California to gather support for their idea of a national march to be held simultaneously in multiple cities. Though some California activists pondered the idea of a national labor and consumer boycott (see chap. 1), that suggestion gained little traction in Chicago. The proposal for the May 1 march was also complicated by the fact that SEIU organizers in other parts of the country had promoted April 9 as the date for a national demonstration.

After a series of marches across the country in April, between four hundred thousand and six hundred thousand people marched in Chicago on May 1. The event attracted broad participation among progressive forces, including labor, religious, educational, and community organizations; socialists; anarchists; and antiwar activists. Polish, Korean, and Filipino immigrants also participated. Signs and T-shirts were more professional than had been the case at the earlier rally. It was a sunny day, and the mood was festive, as families with children in strollers and wagons marched alongside youth activists with drums, community organizers, clerics, union members, and socialists.

What Next?

Observers generally believe that the immediate result of the marches was the defeat of the Sensenbrenner Bill. However, there has been very little consensus about what else the marches accomplished. Some immigrant rights advocates argued for continuing the pressure by marching again in 2007, whereas others contended that lobbying represented a better option. This dichotomy was less central in Chicago than in other cities, and intense activism for immigration reform continued, as organizers sought to keep the momentum going to push for what appeared to be a very possible immigration reform. The May 1, 2006, march was followed by an intense wave of activism. Supporters of immigrant rights staged a July 2006 march against deportations and a walk to Batavia over four days in September to pressure U.S. House speaker and anti-immigrant politician Dennis Hastert. Chicago's attention was also drawn to the movement by the trials of the IFCO workers arrested in the spring of 2006 (see chap. 1), the March 10 Coalition's hosting of a national meeting of immigrant rights activists in August, Elvira Arellano's bid for sanctuary in the Adalberto Unido Church in August (see chap. 12), and commissioner Roberto Maldonado's successful effort to have Cook County declared a sanctuary county.

For immigration activists in Chicago, 2007 was a year of hope and determination as well as profound disappointment. In the November 2006 elections, Democrats retook control of Congress, defeating Hastert, among others. While most political analysts view opposition to the Iraq War as the main explanation for this shift and give a very marginal role—if any—to the pro-immigrant vote, it was at the very minimum clear that defeated Republicans did not benefit electorally from their pursuit of an anti-immigrant agenda. Whatever the reason for the decline in Republican power, immigrant activists saw this change as a sign of hope for policy reform in the immediate future. However, many of the new congressional Democrats were quite moderate and were as unwilling to vote in favor of comprehensive immigration reform as the Republicans had been. Chicago's immigration activists pondered their next move.

Some local officials and Latino community leaders in Los Angeles proposed a switch to a primary focus on lobbying rather than marching. Localities passed a series of anti-immigrant ordinances, raising the possibility that the marches had led to a backlash and that more demonstrations would only increase restrictionist ire and decrease public support. Most important, no galvanizing issue such as the Sensenbrenner Bill existed around which to mobilize.

Chicago's leaders generally remained supportive of the idea of marching but feared that people would become exhausted, especially because policy changes were not forthcoming. Nevertheless, efforts to move away from marching that prevailed in other cities did not take hold in Chicago. In the early spring of 2007, rumors that both the March 10 Coalition and the Centro sin Fronteras were planning marches led DJ El Pistolero to launch a successful mediation effort to combine the marches.[9] On May 1, more than 150,000 people marched from Union Park to Grant Park, again surprising organizers, who had expected a much smaller crowd. Many activists believed that an April 24 raid by U.S. Immigration and Customs Enforcement officials at the Little Village Discount Mall triggered public outrage and increased the number of participants.[10] At a march held the same day in Los Angeles, police officers fired rubber bullets at the crowd, but the tenor in Chicago remained peaceful although somewhat more somber than in 2006. In contrast to the numerous Illinois political luminaries who spoke in 2006, the main political speaker at 2007 rally was Mayor Daley.

The 2007 march helped to maintain visibility for the issue of immigration reform, but two years of massive marches, combined with a lack of concrete policy changes at the federal level and the consideration of local anti-immigrant ordinances, including some in Carpentersville, Waukegan, and Elgin in the Chicago area, sobered Chicago's immigration activists. According to Jorge Mujica of the March 10 Coalition, when the Secure Borders, Economic Opportunity, and Immigration Reform Act of 2007 failed, "on the one hand, we say that's good, because it was a Frankensteinish legislation, but on the other hand, it's bad. It's bad because then you have two years of marches . . . marches in 2006, marches in 2007, public pressure, and nothing happens, that causes disappointment, disenchantment. People start saying we don't achieve anything by marching" (2008).

Fear that the struggle would die led Arellano to leave the Adalberto Unido Church in August 2002 to make surprise appearances at sanctuary churches throughout the country (see chap. 12). Arellano's subsequent arrest and deportation created a climate of hesitation and even fear among members of her organization, La Familia Latina Unida, linked to Centro sin Fronteras. In addition, later in 2007, when the city of Waukegan sought to train local police officers as immigration enforcement agents under Section 287(g) of the Illegal Immigration Reform and Immigrant Responsibility Act, Chicago activists worked with members of the Waukegan community to organize a boycott to protest the city council's decision and to register Latino voters.

Keeping the Cause Alive

By the spring of 2008, activists understood that inaction on immigration reform remained likely until after the fall presidential election and consequently approached May Day with two different plans. One group, consisting of Sin Fronteras, Latino members of Operation PUSH (People United to Serve Humanity), some founding members of the March 10 Coalition, and various grassroots, union, and religious activists, sought to highlight brown-black unity. Proponents of this approach sought to merge the immigrant rights agenda into a common human, civil, and economic rights agenda with African Americans, emphasizing solidarity among people of color and deemphasizing the declining numbers of march participants. Group members took "We are the new majority" as their motto and listed among their demands legalization for all, an end to the war in Iraq, increased access to housing, the preservation of families, and an end to violence.

The reconstituted March 10 Coalition took a different approach. First, in March, it hosted a conference of activists from Illinois, Indiana, Minnesota, Wisconsin, Iowa, and Ohio that was designed to create a regional coalition as well as to plan the participation of activists from other states in the Chicago May Day march. Although the conference generated important dialogue, most activists ultimately decided to march in their home states. The March 10 Coalition also opposed the idea of pursuing black-brown unity, arguing that the legalization issue should not be diluted. The two factions continued to meet separately throughout the spring, holding sessions at the same time and thereby impeding the efforts of people and organizations who were interested in both strategies. However, the two groups never considered the possibility of staging separate marches, given declining participation levels and the intensification of immigrant detentions and deportations. In both groups, youth played an unprecedented role as organizers and secured the presence of several young speakers on the stage.

After intense negotiations, the two groups ultimately worked out a combined program for the May 1 march. The "We are the new majority" slogan proved particularly controversial, since some March 10 Coalition activists feared that it could be interpreted as antagonistic toward whites. Other organizers stressed the ideological element—that is, the idea of the new majority as part of a new ideological vision attached to new presidential options in the run-up to the election—whereas others maintained that it did in fact have a racial component and reflected U.S. demographic realities. Organizers finally hung a banner across the stage that read, "Together we are America's majority" and signed an agreement stating that speakers at the rally would alternate between union, March 10 Coalition, and Sin Fronteras representatives.

The May 1, 2008, rally opened with a prayer session in Union Park and ended with a celebration involving several groups of *danzantes aztecas* who joined together to make one *capulí,* an unprecedented occurrence.[11] While the turnout of between fifteen and twenty thousand was much lower than in past years, it was higher than many activists had expected. Organizers from the various groups involved reported that people's interest in march participation had declined, perhaps because of fear but also because of a growing sense of futility. One activist called it the "¿Marchar para qué?" (March for what?) syndrome. The somber tone of 2007 persisted, police attended in riot gear, and the English-language press offered only scant coverage of the event. Nevertheless, the march provided an important source of hope, confirming to those who participated that the struggle remained imperative and that the lives and hopes of immigrants are meaningful, even when their claims are not heard. Mayor Daley again attended, joined by antiwar activists, representatives of gay and lesbian groups, and youth activists. Rage Against the Machine guitarist Tom Morello led the crowd in an emotional rendition of Woody Guthrie's "This Land Is Your Land."

Agency, Representativity, and Mobilization

According to Artemio Arreola, "This is a phase in U.S. history in which it is difficult to explain and even more difficult to understand what the [immigrant rights] movement is. Nobody can speak for the movement, but you can't claim that someone does not speak for the movement" (2008). These words capture the complexity and diversity of this book's goals. Has immigrant rights activism in Chicago become primarily a series of coordinated marches or a social movement? And if it is a movement, is it one or many? Differences in goals, strategies, and visions plague almost all movements, and Chicago immigrant activism is no exception. Moreover, most of the differences visible in Chicago are faced by immigrant activists throughout the country.

According to social movement theory, social movements are groups of people and networks with common goals who sustain contentious collective action for an extended period of time (Tarrow 1998, 3). This definition excludes many events and actors. A single march or protest is not a movement; while there are social movement organizations, an organization is not a movement, as movements rely on a set of set of networks, coalitions, and interactions. While organizations may overlap with movements, movements need not be tied to organizations. Chicago has a dense set of social service, community, grassroots, and policy organizations as well as informal groups that facilitate networking for the immigrant movement. In addition, immigrant activism tapped into networks such as informal youth groups and hometown associations that had not previously been as active in local politics (see chap. 8). And many immigrant activist leaders have overlapping relationships. For example, Arreola has been active in the SEIU, Casa Michoacán, and the Confederación de Mexicanos en el Exterior and more recently has served as ICIRR's political director (see chaps. 7, 8); Maria D'Amezcua has occupied important positions in the local chapter of the League of United Latin American Citizens and the RainbowPUSH Coalition's Latino chapter and been active in the Institutional Revolutionary Party's Chicago chapter and her hometown association; Emma Lozano has served as president of Sin Fronteras and as a board member of the Coalition of African, Arab, Asian, European, and Latino Immigrants of Illinois; and Rosie Carrasco is a founding member of the March 10 Coalition and a member of the ICIRR board. The 2006 planning meetings for the March 10 Coalition provided several activists with their first real opportunity to network with a wide array of social and political actors.

The process of mobilizing has resulted in a clear articulation of the shared goal of comprehensive immigration reform that would provide a path for legalization and eventual citizenship for most undocumented immigrants. Beyond this initial point of agreement, activists' opinions differ regarding a number of important positions, including the extent to which legalization needs to be accompanied by enforcement measures; the level of openness toward alternatives to legalization that would not ultimately lead to citizenship (an option that some activists consider throwing the baby out with the bathwater); and the inclusion of a guest worker program. Pragmatists believe in supporting the best available option in an imperfect political context, while idealists insist on working to create a political environment that is more conducive to the needed reforms in their entirety. These differences become most apparent when activists must decide whether to support particular legislation. As Tsao stated,

> Everyone who favors legalization wants to legalize as many immigrants as we can and reunite as many families as we can. But immigration policy is a matter of federal legislation, so any changes need federal and in particular congressional action. So we need to not only take principled stances about what we want but also to understand how Congress works, what we can achieve with the Congress we have, and what capacity we have to influence what Congress does. We need to make fully informed decisions about not just what we want but also what we would agree to or not agree to and how willing we would be to compromise. Would legalizing only some but not all undocumented immigrants be accept-

able? Would certain conditions and restrictions be okay? Maybe most important, is accepting a bill that doesn't have everything we want or even includes things we don't want better or worse than no bill at all? Different people and groups will answer these questions in different ways, but everyone must understand that these decisions have real-life consequences and that those who are directly affected should have an important voice in the process." (2008)

Hence, the movement has no single voice but rather a plethora of voices, all seeking a common goal but with very different ideas about how to get there (see chap. 7).

Virtually all activists have supported the use of marches as the movement's main muscle. In fact, the marches have reinvigorated and redefined the immigration reform movement after the interruption caused by September 11. The rallies have both demonstrated marchers' capacity to mobilize and pressure and symbolized a promise for future political potential, as embodied in the slogan, "Today we march, tomorrow we vote." The success of the July 2005 and March 10, 2006, mobilizations motivated activists to organize more marches. Such persistence, particularly in the wake of immigration's post-9/11 association with terrorism, is practically unequaled by any other contemporary U.S. movement.

While all of these points show that these marches are not brief and isolated events but are in fact the most dramatic expressions of a broader social movement, it is important to keep in mind that this movement is very heterogeneous. It is characterized by tensions that make it difficult sometimes to discern the position of "the movement" or where the movement may be going. While the specific variations these debates take may be unique to the Chicago scene, many of them are present in immigrant activism throughout the country. Hence, a brief overview of some of the main issues in Chicago provides a basis for comparisons with other cities.

MOBILIZATION VERSUS ORGANIZATION

Some observers argue that although Chicago activists have staged tremendous marches, their energy has not adequately been harnessed into organization; others, in contrast, have praised the spontaneity and vibrancy of the marches as evidence of their grassroots nature. Many members of organizations that rely on more formal modes of advocacy feel that the marches have not reached their full potential—people have been mobilized not for consistent engagement but for a sort of "vacation activism," once a year. Anti-immigrant forces have demonstrated their ability to flood Congress with calls and emails to express opposition to immigration reforms perceived as too lenient, but according to NALAAC's executive director, Oscar Chacón,

If half of the population that participated in the marches [in 2006] had sent an email, a fax—one email, one fax per week—we would have a different reality. . . . Inadvertently what is promoted is the idea that if we go out to march, that is how we will make a difference, and I am telling you that marching alone is not how you ultimately make a difference. I think we need to learn to make more rigorous use of all the tools that technology offers us, that we learn how to lobby, not only in Washington but here, in Chicago, in Illinois. . . . Of the people who come to a march, very few get involved in other tasks, and of course, at the end of the day, this indicates the difference between mobilizing and organizing. Because if you don't have a way of organizing the population, it's going to be very hard for you to transform the will of participating in a march into the discipline of sending one email per week, one fax per week, or making one phone call a week to advance the cause you are interested in. (2007)

Such a campaign would require a more systematic and extensive organizational effort designed to pursue concrete goals. However, other activists are less concerned about creating an organizational model and more concerned about highly visible acts of protest and opposition as well as alternative forms of mobilizing (see chap. 7). But even these activists seek to use the capital provided by the marches to organize other events and acts of civil disobedience—that is, to keep the contentious action going—and increasingly have come to agree that mobilization requires a certain degree of organization. The different paths pursued by organizations and activists reveal where they see the movement headed. Some options may not involve naturalization, registration, and legislative advocacy work, but most activists are working to channel the momentum of the marches into activities that will promote some form of empowerment.

QUESTIONING REPRESENTATIVITY

Representativity deals with who should represent undocumented immigrants. This issue is heavily contested, given the heterogeneity of activists involved. Since most marchers were Latinos and immigrants, many observers consider members of those groups to be the base of the movement. However, the question of who can speak for them is quite complex.

On one level is the issue of immigrants versus nonimmigrants. Organizations servicing and defending the rights of immigrants have always been heterogeneous, including immigrants as well as members of the second generation and others who have no recent immigrant origin. NALACC and many of its constituent organizations argue, however, that immigrants should represent immigrants. In Chacón's words, "The immigrant rights movement must, in first place, recognize the primacy of empowering the immigrant. We cannot continue to promote the idea of a strong pro-immigrant-rights movement in which immigrants are not at the front. This is like talking about a civil rights movement forty years ago in which blacks are not at the front or like speaking about a woman's suffrage movement in which women are not at the front. So the full recognition of this is a premise that we must accept" (2007). But this premise becomes somewhat more complicated as youth involvement in the movement increases. Many leaders of the youth movements are the children of immigrants rather than immigrants themselves (see chap. 11). Moreover, second-generation Latinos as well as Puerto Ricans often explain their role as speaking for or representing those who lack U.S. citizenship (see chaps. 11, 13).

This scenario is intimately tied to existing racial structures in which nonimmigrant Latinos see the movement as belonging to them, too, not only because of their personal or familial associations with immigrants but also because of a racial solidarity with immigrants as well as lived experiences such as racial profiling (see chap. 11). Hence, it is limiting to consider immigrant rights as a single-issue movement in the narrowest sense of the term. The movement involves the rights of both undocumented and legal immigrants as well as the rights, status, and dignity of Latinos as a racialized group. Further complicating matters is the question of the political agency of the undocumented as distinct from that of legal immigrants. If status has become an important determinant of people's well-being, the question arises of whether the undocumented should represent themselves. Moreover, who speaks for undocumented immigrants? Do they have only one voice? When Elvira Arellano claimed to speak for undocumented immigrants, some activists responded that was she just one voice among many.

Finally, grassroots organizations have fewer resources than more policy-oriented or lobbying organizations but played a pivotal role in mobilizing marchers, whereas policy groups may be in a better position to use the political capital gained from the marches in their lobbying efforts. But national lobbying organizations focused on Washington, D.C., can also lose touch with the pulse of the grassroots movement. According to Mujica,

> What the march generates is a lot of political power, a precious political capital, enormous, massive, gigantic. . . . But we start to suffer from our political success, because it's one thing to be the voice of the mobilization and quite another to be able to use that enormous political capital. We can't, because we don't have the structures, the contacts, and the mechanisms to be the ones who sit down in Congress to discuss anything. So it's the institutions that sit down in Congress and start discussing a reform. . . . They are the ones who get the Senate to refuse [the Sensenbrenner Bill] and produce something very different and well to defeat Sensenbrenner. But we had given them the possibility to do it, no? (2008)

Chacón however, pointed out the downside of this arrangement: "When you are talking about Washington groups, these groups are permeated with a logic in which they think they will achieve change if they only lobby in the right way, without really taking the pulse of the national factors—not in D.C. but at the national level—that are really and profoundly influencing the debate over public policy, in this case immigration policy. So it's very easy to create castles in the air in terms of what is achievable, and it's also easy to summarize the success or failure of an effort as the result of good or bad lobbying" (2007). Grassroots' organizations lesser resources and access to national-level policymakers have led some activists to express concern about such groups' ability to get their perspectives included in high-level legislative policy negotiations. Some grassroots activists even perceive a disconnect between themselves and Latino advocacy organizations and express a desire to play a more active role in policy creation. One long-term effect of the marches may be the redefinition of the relationship between grassroots and community associations and national advocacy organizations such as the National Council of La Raza, the National Immigration Forum, and the American Immigration Lawyers Association. According to Tsao, many local and regional organizations are already working with national organizations such as the Center for Community Change to affect the immigration debate in Congress: "D.C. groups and local and regional groups increasingly understand that effective advocacy requires both inside and outside games working in coordination to put pressure on legislators and to educate and inform them on the right thing to do. In particular, lobbying groups in D.C. must be informed by and accountable to the organizations in the field who have a stake in the debate and ultimately to the people who would be directly affected by policy choices" (2008).

Choosing Strategies

Another important recurring theme involves differing views on the direction of political action. While some activists have supported local and national politicians who are working toward some type of reform, others believe that this option is at best a limited strategy and at worst is simply wrong. When Congressman Gutiérrez, a longtime supporter of immigration reform, proposed the STRIVE Act, Chicago activists disagreed about the measure's wisdom (see chap. 1). Many members of the March 10 Coalition believe that the proposal split the grassroots immigrant community, broadening the institutional/grassroots divide, while the Centro sin Fronteras has worked quite closely with Gutiérrez despite his proposal's acknowledged imperfections.

Such issues are manifestations of the more profound divide regarding the potential of an electoral strategy in the current political system. Some members of the March 10 Coalition have pointed to the limitations of the Democratic Party, arguing that it has not done enough in a context of local machine politics and national restrictionist and nativist activism. As a consequence, the original

March 10 Coalition and Sin Fronteras split in 2006, with March 10 activists taking the position that a clear separation from elected officials was necessary to keep the movement more independent and Sin Fronteras members considering Gutiérrez as well as other local officials (whether machine politicians or independents) to be key allies. Running as a member of the Green Party, coalition member Omar Lopez ran for Gutiérrez's congressional seat in 2008. This dispute is not unique to Chicago but mirrors splits at the national level.

Conclusion

Immigrant rights activism in Chicago seems to be transitioning away from the era of megamarches toward a new phase that involves a plethora of initiatives and campaigns. While the marches have been a key muscle of the movement (and most activists continue to consider them crucial in the effort to pressure for reform) they are not, in and of themselves, the movement.

While policy changes are the most tangible and immediate way of measuring a movement's success, they are not the only way. Social movement scholars have explained that movements can have a number of consequences—both intended and unintended—that transform the world from which they came. In Chicago, the legacy of the immigrant rights movement lies in the articulation and recognition of the political agency of immigrant activists and the empowerment of their communities. Such effects not only are the product of consistent work by many social and political actors but also are in many ways the children of the marches, providing a stimulus as well as a certain level of political capital that would not have been available otherwise.

These developments include the growing role of youth in the movement (see chap. 9); individual as well as collective gains by hometown associations (see chap. 8); state legislators' ability to allocate funds for immigrant integration and education; the creation of the New Sanctuary Movement; the creation of a variety of coalitions; the Chicago City Council's unanimous October 8, 2008, call for a moratorium on all raids and deportations until comprehensive immigration reform is passed; and the registration of fifty thousand immigrant voters in Illinois prior to the 2008 presidential election and the creation of Immigration PAC to campaign on behalf of candidates who support immigrant rights. The marches have also facilitated other changes whose full impact cannot yet be measured.

The marches have unquestionably ushered in a new political period in which immigrant empowerment—and, more specifically, Latino immigrant empowerment—is no longer an oxymoron. The movement's goals *después de las marchas* (after the marches) include not only legalization but a broader preoccupation with the human, social, and civil rights of a population that is collectively claiming its right to have rights.

Notes

1. I use *Mexican* to refer to Mexican immigrants and those of Mexican descent because that term is used by a majority of Chicago's population of Mexican origin. *Chicano* and *Mexican American* are not generally used.

2. The Chicago chapter of CASA remained active long after the national organization had disbanded (Torres 1991).

3. Machine politics refers to the tight (but officially invisible) organizational structure designed to maintain strict allegiance to a groups of local public officials in exchange for patronage that rewards supporters. In Chicago, machine politics dominated from the 1930s through the 1970s, reaching its peak with former Mayor Richard J. Daley. For more on Chicago machine politics, see Gosnell 1977; Guterbock 1980; Grimshaw 1995; Simpson 2001. Other members of what became the Near West Independent Political Organization included Carlos Arango, Linda Coronado, and Lidia Bracamonte (Córdova 1999).

4. For a detailed description of this lengthy and complicated redistricting process and its impact on Washington's term as mayor, see Córdova 1999.

5. Redistricting occurred as a consequence of pressure to create a majority-Latino district exerted by the Mexican American Legal Defense Fund. The Fourth District has an irregular shape that includes several Puerto Rican and Mexican neighborhoods on the city's East and West Sides.

6. HDO recently came under federal scrutiny because of the city hiring system's favoritism toward HDO members and other pro-Daley political workers. In July 2008, HDO closed its campaign committee, basically becoming extinct.

7. The Heartland Alliance is a Chicago-based organization that provides social services to immigrants and refugees. It serves the broader Midwest region, primarily in the areas of housing, legal protection, health care, and economic security.

8. The numbers of marchers counted by police, reporters, and activists vary greatly. In this chapter, I note the range of estimates, although most of the chapters in this volume rely on Bada, Fox, and Selee 2006.

9. These rumors have been disputed by some activists and confirmed by others. Flyers definitely circulated announcing two different start times.

10. Eighty-four customs officers conducted the raid, which targeted producers of counterfeit identification, and arrested twelve people. The operation sparked spontaneous protest among members of the Little Village community who were outraged that heavily armed officers initially rounded up more than one hundred people and prevented them from exiting the mall, scaring shoppers and their children.

11. There are ten groups of *danzantes* in Illinois. While some *danzantes* view themselves as activists and/or have been participating in immigrant movement events for several years (hunger strikes, vigils, small protests, sit-ins, conferences, and marches), other groups remained separate, claiming that *danza* was about culture rather than politics. Shortly before the 2008 march, all the *danzante* groups met and concluded that their involvement in the movement was appropriate since this particular political struggle was also cultural, and indigenous displacement and migrant displacement had important parallels. Nine of the ten *danzante* groups ultimately participated.

References

Arreola, Artemio. 2008. Interview by Amalia Pallares. April 10, Chicago.

Bada, Xótchil, Jonathan Fox, and Andrew Selee, eds. 2006. *Invisible No More: Mexican Migrant Civic Participation in the United States.* Washington, D.C.: Woodrow Wilson International Center for Scholars. www.wilsoncenter.org/topics/pubs/Invisible%20 No%20More.pdf. Accessed October 11, 2009.

Badillo, David. 2004. "From La Lucha to Latino: Ethnic Change, Political Identity and Civil Rights in Chicago." In *La Causa: Civil Rights, Social Justice, and the Struggle for Equality in the Midwest,* ed. Gilberto Cárdenas, 37–54. Houston: Arte Público.

Banda Sifuentes, Exequiel. 2006. "Sensenbrenner fue el Principal Promotor de la Movilización." *MX Sin Fronteras,* April, 13–14.

Chacón, Oscar. 2007. Interview by Amalia Pallares. July 5, Chicago.

Córdova, Teresa. 1999. "Harold Washington and the Rise of Latino Electoral Politics in Chicago, 1982–1987." In *Chicano Politics and Society in the Late Twentieth Century,* ed. David Montejano, 31–57. Austin: University of Texas Press.

Cruz, Wilfredo. 2007. *City of Dreams: Latino Immigration to Chicago.* Lanham, Md.: University Press of America.

The Encyclopedia of Chicago. 2004. Chicago: University of Chicago Press. http://www .encyclopedia.chicagohistory.org. Accessed November 13, 2009.

Espinosa, Leticia. 2006. "Cuando un Mar de Emigrantes Inundó el Centro de Chicago." *MX Sin Fronteras,* April, 10–11.

Flores-González, Nilda, Matthew Rodríguez, and Michael Rodríguez Muñiz. 2006. "From Hip-Hop to Humanization: Batey Urbano as a Space for Latino Youth Culture and Community Action." In *Beyond Resistance! Youth Activism and Community Change: New Democratic Possibilities for Practice and Policy for America's Youth,* ed. S. Ginwright, P. Noguera, and J. Cammarota, 175–96. New York: Routledge.

Gosnell, Harold. 1977. *Machine Politics: Chicago Model.* Chicago: University of Chicago Press.

Grimshaw, William. 1995. *Bitter Fruit: Black Politics and the Chicago Machine.* Chicago: University of Chicago Press.

Guterbock, Thomas M. 1980. *Machine Politics in Transition.* Chicago: University of Chicago Press.

Knight, Roger, Timothy Ready, and Gia Barboza. 2007. "Attitudes towards Immigration: Findings from the Chicago Area Survey." *Latino Research* 4 (5): 1–8.

Konkol, Mark J., Scott Fornek, Fran Spielman, and Art Golab. 2005. "HDO Grows into Political Powerhouse." *Illinois Police and Sheriff's News,* June 12. http://www .ipsn.org/hired_truck_scandal/hdo_grows_into_political_powerho.htm. Accessed November 13, 2009.

Lozano, Emma. 2008. Interview by Amalia Pallares. January 10, Chicago.

Martínez, Cindy, and Francisco Piña. 2005. "Chicago en Marcha por Reforma Migratoria." *MX Sin Fronteras,* August 20, 6–9.

Mujica, Jorge. 2008. Interview by Amalia Pallares. May 19, Chicago.

National Association of Latino Elected and Appointed Officials Educational Fund. 2007. *A Profile of Latino Elected Officials in the United States and Their Progress since 1996.* http://www.naleo.org/downloads/NALEOFactSheet07.pdf. Accessed May 13, 2009.

———. 2008. *2008 General Election Profile: Latino Candidates in Federal and State Races.* http://www.naleo.org/downloads/2008GenElecProf_fin.pdf. Accessed May 13, 2009.

Padilla, Felix. 1985. *Latino Ethnic Consciousness: The Case of Mexican Americans and Puerto Ricans in Chicago.* South Bend, Ind.: University of Notre Dame Press.

Pallares, Amalia. 2009. *Family Matters: Strategizing Immigrant Activism in Chicago.* http://www.wilsoncenter.org/news/docs/Chicago%20Pallares.pdf. Accessed August 19, 2009.

Paral, Rob, Timothy Ready, Sung Chun, and Wei Sun. 2004. *Latino Demographic Growth in Metropolitan Chicago.* December. http://latinostudies.nd.edu/pubs/pubs/paral.pdf. Accessed August 19, 2009.

Parra, Ricardo, 2004. "Latinos in the Midwest: Civil Rights and Community Organization." In *La Causa: Civil Rights, Social Justice, and the Struggle for Equality in the Midwest,* edited by Gilberto Cárdenas, 1–18. Houston: Arte Público.

Ready, Timothy, and Allert Brown-Gort. 2005. *State of Latino Chicago: This Is Home Now.* South Bend, Ind.: University of Notre Dame Institute of Latino Studies.

Simpson, Dick W. 2001. *Rogues, Rebels, and Rubber Stamps: The Story of the Chicago City Council from 1863 to the Present.* Boulder, Colo.: Westview.

Tarrow, Sidney. 1998. *Power in Movement: Social Movements and Contentious Politics.* Cambridge: Cambridge University Press.

Torres, Maria de los Angeles. 1991. "The Commission on Latino Affairs." In *Harold Washington and the Neighborhoods: Progressive City Government in Chicago, 1983–1987,* ed. Pierre Clavel and Wim Wievel, 167–87. New Brunswick, N.J.: Rutgers University Press.

———. 2004. "In Search of Meaningful Voice and Place: The IPO and Latino Community Empowerment in Chicago." In *La Causa: Civil Rights, Social Justice, and the Struggle for Equality in the Midwest,* ed. Gilberto Cárdenas, 81–106. Houston: Arte Público.

———. 2008. Interview by Amalia Pallares. October 29, Chicago.

Tsao, Fred. 2008. Interview by Amalia Pallares. February 22, Chicago.

Elvira Arellano marching next to her son, Saul, religious leaders, and Guerrero and Michoacán home-town association members, March 10, 2006.
Credit: Artemio Arreola

Representatives of community organizations in a planning meeting for the March 10, 2006, mobilization in Casa Michoacán.
Credit: Artemio Arreola

By 2007, the family unity theme was prevalent in the march. This banner, created by Waukegan marchers, was also displayed in the 2008 and 2009 marches.
Credit: Hector González

Youth marching in 2007.
Credit: Jhonathan F. Gómez

Youth from Batey Urbano marching in 2007.
Credit: Jhonathan F. Gómez

Marchers in 2007.
Credit: Victor Espinosa

A group of marchers created a rendition of the Statue of Liberty, 2007.
Credit: Victor Espinosa

Members of the Confederation of Mexican Federations in Chicago (CONFEMEX) onstage in 2008.
Credit: Nilda Flores-González

One marcher's expression, 2008.
Credit: Sandro Corona

One of the Azteca dancers who came together for the 2008 march.
Credit: Victor Espinosa

PART 2

Institutions

3

Competing Narratives on the March

The Challenges of News Media Representations in Chicago

FRANCES R. APARICIO

In *Brown Tide Rising,* Otto Santa Ana (2002) extensively documents the major metaphors for immigration—movements of water, invasion, animals, and diseases or burdens—that have dehumanized immigrants. For example, in 2007, Trent Lott, Republican senator from Mississippi, referred publicly to his way of dealing with "illegal" immigrants: "People are at least as smart as goats. Now one of the ways I keep those goats in the fence is I electrified them. Once they got popped a couple of times, they quit trying to jump it." Such metaphors enable the U.S. public to see immigrants as Others, to consider them not as fellow human beings but as enemies, parasites, and "foreign bodies" that have come to destroy this country (Inda 2000). Such discourse echoes the strategies previously used against African slaves. While academics, particularly Latino/as, and think tanks such as the Pew Hispanic Center have publicized statistics that reflect the complex human aspects of immigration, the larger U.S. public relies on mainstream media—television, print, radio, and the Internet—to gather information on the issue of immigration. Outlets such as Lou Dobbs's CNN television show, Web sites, and conservative radio talk shows continue to nurture fears about immigrants. In a particularly egregious recent example, former speaker of the U.S. House of Representatives Newt Gingrich announced that "young Americans are being massacred by people who should not be here" (Neikirk 2007). Contesting such discourse, ethnic alternative media and independent productions disseminate constructs of Latino/a immigrants as human beings strongly motivated to better themselves in this country, as members of families facing complex and painful issues of separation across borders, and as individuals who came to the United States to work hard, live the American Dream, and in the process contribute to the larger U.S. economy.

Spanish-language radio and television played a major role in exhorting people to participate in Chicago's May 1, 2006, immigrant rights march: half of the marchers heard about the march in the media, particularly via television (56 percent), the radio (49 percent), and newspapers (28 percent) (Flores-González et al. 2006). Moreover, media coverage promotes public discussion and eventually leads to the creation of public opinion (Park 1999). This chapter focuses on print media, which have historically underrepresented Latinos. My analysis is based on the reading of 367 immigration-related articles published in three Chicago newspapers—the *Tribune,* the *Sun-Times,* and *Hoy*—between December 2005 and June 2006 as well as on interviews with six of the city's journalists.[1] Specifically, I examine the ways in which these newspapers have represented (or failed to represent) the marches and the debates over immigration as a human and social issue and Latinos as agents of history in the making. I began the research with the assumption that in light of the enormous publicity the Sensenbrenner Bill was receiving at the time, mainstream publications would focus primarily on the legislative actors in Washington, D.C.—the elite white sector—and less on mobilization as a local and national social movement.

Mainstream Media and Latino Media

Scholars generally agree that despite the significant demographic growth of U.S. Latino/as, mainstream media and news programming in particular have devoted very little attention to these communities (Rodríguez 1999; Molina Guzmán 2006; Vargas 2000; Santa Ana 2002). Despite Latino/as' recent visibility in U.S. film and television—with programs such as *Ugly Betty* winning Golden Globe Awards—Latino/as remain underrepresented. In 2005, less than 1 percent of news features on ABC, CBS, and NBC involved Latino stories (National Association of Hispanic Journalists 2006). Thus, Latino broadcast media such as Univision Television and Radio and Telemundo and Spanish-language newspapers such as *Hoy* and *La Raza* represent an alternative discourse that highlights Latino/as as agents of history, role models, and sources of authority. Yet the Latino media continue to struggle for mainstream respectability: as Isabel Molina Guzmán argues, "The history of Spanish-language news media in the United States illustrates the complex tensions between the ethnic media and the nation-state with regards to the formation of imagined community" (2006, 283). Analyzing mainstream newspapers such as the *Miami Herald* and its Spanish-language counterpart, the *Nuevo Herald,* Molina Guzmán concludes that Cuban Americans remain outside of the U.S. body politic: "Miami Cubans were positioned within the local general-market media as racialized ethnics who refused to assimilate into dominant definitions of U.S. citizenship" (292). For its part, the *Nuevo Herald* exemplified "the role and function of the ethnic media" as it has "the potential to influence dialogue in the public sphere by engaging in an oppositional relation-ship with general-market media reports on issues of immigration and providing alternative narratives for the public in their local communities" (292).

However, Latino media institutions are "increasingly influenced by the com-mercial imperative of news conglomeration." In other words, changes in own-ership, U.S.-based investments in Latino newspapers and television stations, and corporate mergers affect these outlets' public service values and ideologies (Molina Guzmán 2006, 284). As Arlene Dávila (2001) also suggests, most Latino media have been informed and structured by the transnational flow of programs and productions coming from Latin America, giving them a globalized nature and a transnational audience appeal. It thus makes sense to categorize Latino news media as advocating immigrant rights and including the Latino perspec-tive on immigration politics.

The Latino media have generally justified their existence precisely on the basis of cultural and linguistic difference—that is, the idea that United States has a Latino, Spanish-speaking audience that specifically needs to be addressed as a group. If Latinos watched only mainstream news and entertainment, there would be no need for Spanish-language media. Thus, the Latino media have constantly reiterated their value as advocates for the rights of U.S. Spanish-speakers, most of whom are immigrants. The Latino media thus locate themselves outside of the mainstream media, resisting any sort of recognition of hybrid Latinos who engage both mainstream and Spanish-language outlets.[2]

Chicago's Latino news media therefore advocate for the rights of Latino immi-grants and define themselves as a source of information and community service for the Latino community, their ideal audience and market niche. According to *Hoy* reporter Leticia Espinosa (2006), they want to provide Chicago's Latino/as with all the knowledge they need to make informed decisions. Indeed, La-tinos often call the newspaper for legal advice and recommendations on their immigration status, and despite their lack of formal legal training, *Hoy* staff-ers feel a sense of responsibility toward the Spanish-speaking community. In this sense, they identify themselves as public servants. Even if they provide the same information available in the *Chicago Tribune* and the *Chicago Sun-Times,* it serves very different purposes for *Hoy's* audience.

In contrast, the two Latino *Chicago Tribune* reporters I interviewed saw them-selves as part of a larger national agenda of presenting all of the perspectives for and against undocumented immigration in a coherent and comprehensive fashion. They talked about serving as a "bridge" between the non-Latino and Latino communities, suggesting that the presence of Latino reporters can have a larger impact in the newspaper's politics of representation. This perspective also offers a reminder that the construction of particular audiences is a major factor in deciding "what" as well as "how" to understand events (Hall et al. 1999, 253).

Another central tenet in news journalism is objectivity. Although already contested by scholars, it remains part of the professionalization of journalists. To bolster claims about objective reporting, journalists are told to use quotation marks, to find "accredited sources," to present both the pros and cons of any issue, and to refrain from including their personal opinions. However, mainstream media cannot claim to be "objective" in their news when they systematically exclude Latino/a perspectives. This question has serious ramifications with regard to news about immigration, a topic of great importance to U.S. Latino/as.

Molina Guzmán concludes that "the routine journalistic practices of objectivity . . . with [their] focus on event-centered coverage, conflict over analysis and 'pro and con' sourcing practices (Schudson 2003) contribute to an ideological narrative grounded in dominant 'White' definitions of law, order and citizenship. Such a narrative embeds U.S. Cubans within anti-immigration discourses prevalent in general-market news through two strategies: the construction of U.S. Cuban actions as outside the law and the construction of U.S. Cubans as ethnic outsiders" (2006, 290). América Rodríguez (1999) also critiques the standard of objectivity as a professional construction that has been juxtaposed to "ethnicity." In other words, the debate about whether media can be truly objective if they serve particular ethnic or racial markets has been deployed to subordinate the validity and quality of ethnic media productions. In this context, Latino journalists in the United States have been defined as "advocates" because of their focus on Hispanic issues. Discussing the impact of big corporations' purchases of Latino news media, Marcelo Ballvé argues that "many reporters at Spanish-language newspapers controlled by mainstream media corporations say there is an ongoing culture clash between an activist vision of Latino journalism and the strict standards of 'objectivity' still preferred by media corporations" (2004, 22). Reporters from *Hoy* had begun covering immigration issues well before the immigration mobilization took place and thus believed that the marches reinforced their roles as ethnic reporters and the value of cultural and linguistic specificity.

Chicago's English-language newspapers claim to offer high-quality, objective, and in-depth journalism. Spanish-language newspapers, in contrast, are seen as purveyors of "local news"—what one *Chicago Tribune* reporter called the "small wrinkles of the day to day." In his view, *Hoy,* which is also owned by the Tribune Company, has a different mission from the *Tribune* "when it comes to covering the Latino community. [*Hoy*] must cover the community on a daily basis because that is their core audience. [The *Tribune*'s] role is to step back and provide more context to the rhythms within the community and how they may affect the city and country at large." For him, the difference was not ideological but was based on varying yet overlapping audiences.

Hoy foregrounds Latinos in Chicago and across the country as sources of knowledge about the situation at hand, as "authoritative subjects with valuable perspectives" rather than as "objects of the news" (Vargas 2000, 285). According to Stuart Hall and his coauthors, "the hierarchy of credibility" (1999, 254) ensues precisely from the tenets of journalistic objectivity. Reporters seek sources accredited as experts, usually finding people who are aligned with dominant institutions and giving them the power to establish and define the issues at stake, the "primary interpretation" (254). By constantly quoting these sources, the media "reproduce symbolically the existing structure of power in society's institutional order" (254). Latino media turn to alternative "experts," creating major epistemological, ideological, racial, and gender differences in which perspectives are perceived as having value.

My readings demonstrated that English-language newspapers emphasized the debates in Washington over the Sensenbrenner Bill, and *Hoy* focused much more significantly on local activism, families, deportations, and the larger national events and issues that would affect Latinos as an immigrant community. This is revealing, then, of important differences in epistemology; that is, the construction of knowledge about Latinos in *Hoy* is informed by Latinos themselves as sources of authority and as agents of history, not by white experts or legislators in Washington D.C.

This discussion about objectivity is closely linked to the issue of visibility and invisibility for U.S. Latinos, as it also informs my analysis of the news media narratives about the march. As one sign carried by a marcher read: "El pueblo habla, tiene rostro, debemos de ser escuchados" (The people speak and have a face, we must be heard) (*La Primavera* 2006). The visual narrative about the marchers as agents who have a voice and who were speaking against the Sensenbrenner Bill through the movement of their bodies in the public space of downtown Chicago is itself an important symbolic moment of opposition in the history of U.S. Latinos. As Vargas (2000) indicated for mainstream news media, and as Isabel Molina Guzmán has also analyzed in the case of the *Miami Herald* (2006), both the *Chicago Tribune* and the *Chicago Sun-Times* have undermined Latinos first as historical agents of a social movement for the legalization of undocumented immigrants and second as experts on issues of immigration. A basic count on the number of times that each of the three newspapers quoted a Latino/a or referred to a Latino/a as a source of authority reveals the clear binary between the mainstream media and the Spanish-language newspaper.

These numbers do not take into account the ideologies of the persons who served as sources, however. For example, the Latino sources included not only the Pew Hispanic Center, elected officials, workers, advocates, undocumented immigrants, and students but also Rosanna Pulido, the conservative Mexican American spokesperson for the Illinois Minutemen, and other Latinos who oppose legalization for undocumented immigrants. The white and non-Latino authorities cited included African Americans, elected officials, representatives

Table 3.1. Sources for Quotes and References, Chicago
Newspapers, December 2005–June 2006

	Latino	White and Non-Latino
Chicago Tribune	140	213
Chicago Sun-Times	128	302
Hoy	256	130

Source: Author's analysis of 367 immigration-related articles.

of think tanks, and Joshua Hoyt, the director of the Illinois Coalition for Immigrant and Refugee Rights. Nevertheless, Latinos clearly remain underrepresented in discussions of immigration. Emma Lozano's name rarely appeared in either the *Chicago Tribune* or the *Chicago Sun-Times* despite her prominent role as an advocate of immigrant rights, an omission that is also indicative of gender bias (see Vargas 2000). When those newspapers did refer to Lozano, they generally described her as a "friend" or "supporter" of Elvira Arellano.[3] *Hoy*, in contrast, cited Lozano as president of the Centro sin Fronteras. Moreover, mainstream news media never reported on the fact that Jorge Mujica, a member of the March 10 Coalition, received the state's Altgelt Award for Freedom of Expression, although the event at the Newberry library received coverage in *Hoy*. Mainstream readers thus continue to receive the message that the only voices worthy of national coverage are those of elected officials in Washington, including President George W. Bush, who was cited repeatedly in both English-language newspapers.

My reading of the three Chicago newspapers suggests that there are clear ideological differences between the English-language, mainstream newspapers and their Spanish-language counterpart in terms of the inclusion of Latino/as as agents of history and as experts on issues of immigration. However, in terms of content, there were also many overlapping themes and contradictory views that seemed to be present across these news venues. A brief content analysis for each newspaper and a close reading of the coverage of the May 1st march yields some significant knowledge about the competing narratives on the march.

Content Analysis

The *Chicago Tribune* extensively covered the congressional debates on the Sensenbrenner Bill and published articles on border control, fake identification, and the number of undocumented immigrants. The paper also published a significant number of articles that focused on the Chicago-based activists, among them Oscar Avila's (2006) profile of Rafael "El Pistolero" Pulido, a Spanish-language radio personality who exhorted Latinos to attend the March 10 mobilization, and the story of one man deported to Mexico without his family (Dellios 2006). Also featured in the *Tribune* were articles on the drive for naturalization and on the Mexican government's position on the immigration debate. The newspaper humanized immigration to the extent that it printed stories about the impact of raids on workers and families, rally participants who lost their jobs after failing to report for work, and child advocates of immigrant rights. Pieces about student march participation, undocumented workers' contributions to the U.S. economy, and Elvira Arellano and Flor Crisóstomo's hunger strikes acknowledged local activists' role in the immigration mobilization. Yet the *Tribune* also quoted Minutemen and reported on national disagreements about undocumented immigrants. On April 16, 2006, Timothy J. McNulty, a *Tribune* public editor, summarized readers' arguments that the newspaper had portrayed immigrants and the March 10 rally in an overly good light. McNulty responded that the immigration story was "one of the two or three top stories in the city today" and that the *Tribune* would cover "any group of 100,000 demonstrating in the Loop, whatever the cause." However, he also acknowledged that the newspaper had less systematically covered the negative impact of undocumented immigrants on U.S. workers and that the paper should also document the growing intolerance toward the undocumented.

The *Chicago Sun-Times,* in contrast, published very few articles that focused on the human face of immigrants. The exceptions included a story on the death of a sixteen-year-old immigrant girl while waiting for a liver transplant and a short piece on a young undocumented cook living in the shadows of Chicago society. Most of the *Sun-Times* articles addressed larger national issues involving legalization, congressional debates, President Bush's public comments, and border control. The paper did provide some coverage of March 10 and May 1 marches. Perhaps the most oppositional article in the *Sun-Times* focused on a Chicago Mexican family's negative reaction to Bush's May 15 speech (O'Donnell 2006).

Hoy published the most articles focusing on Latino activism at both the local and national levels, including such topics as a boycott of Miller beer, a group of Chicago activists who traveled to Mexico City to meet with elected officials, march preparations, and voter mobilization. In the pages of *Hoy,* staff offered the most systematic coverage of Latinos as agents of history, and the immigration debate appeared less a Washington affair and more a grassroots social movement. The paper's reporters brought attention to Arellano well before either the *Tribune* or the *Sun-Times* did so and informed readers about immigration raids both in Chicago and elsewhere. Though *Hoy*'s coverage, particularly of Chicago deportation cases, long predated the immigration marches, the "bomb exploded," in Espinosa's words (2005), with the Sensenbrenner Bill, and staffers decided to focus intensely on these debates. Indeed, the paper covered the unpublicized July 1, 2005, march in the Back of the Yards neighborhood that was organized as a response to Rosanna Pulido's anti-immigrant comments published in *Hoy*. This is significant as it foregrounds the major role that Latino news media played in triggering the wave of marches, a fact that has escaped journalists in the English-language newspapers and the larger reading public. This content analysis, then, reaffirms the ideological differences between English and Spanish-language media, yet recognizes that the *Chicago Tribune* made significant efforts to provide a much more humane and Latino-centered coverage.

Competing Narratives of May 1, 2006

On May 1, 2006, the *Chicago Tribune* published an article recognizing local activists' impact on immigrant advocacy as a national social movement (Avila and Martínez 2006). The article quoted many of the city's Latino activists, discussed potential conflicts in the organizing of the march, noted that various community organizations rather than one individual had led the mobilization, and foregrounded the potential marchers' racial and cultural diversity. The article also recognized the role of the immigrant hometown associations and of Spanish-language radio stations in exhorting Latinos and other immigrant groups to participate (see also Avila 2006). However, the same edition of the paper also included a piece that summarized the Illinois Minuteman Project's views regarding the criminality of all undocumented immigrants (Masterson 2006). Focusing on a white couple active with the Minutemen, the article humanized the group and argued that its members were not racists but rather were interested in doing away with the criminal aspects of undocumented immigration.

The following day, the *Tribune* offered extensive coverage of the May 1 marches nationwide. The paper's main article (Martínez 2006) summarized worker shortages, labor boycotts, turnouts, and the marchers' cultural and racial diversity. The focus on diversity was empowering in that it reaffirmed that immigration touched many other groups in addition to Mexicans and Latinos; however, it also could be deployed to undermine some Mexicans' claims that the anti-immigration debate represents an articulation of racism against Mexicans in particular. In this case, then, the focus on diversity could censor antiracist voices. The *Tribune* also noted the predominance of Spanish-speakers among the marchers and the existence of groups opposing the marches and supporting tougher border enforcement.

The paper also printed short interviews with two young white mothers at the Los Angeles rally who explained that they had participated to teach their young children about U.S. history and expressed disappointment at the presence of "few white people" (Martínez 2006). This section exemplifies the marches' transcultural potential to educate, inform, and perhaps transform white people's attitudes toward immigrants. The white women's participation may have exoticized Latino/a immigrants by making them objects of curiosity, but it also made an important point about whites' need to move into the public space of cultural and racial heterogeneity in which whites are the numerical minority and may feel a decreased sense of power. The inclusion of these interviews suggests that the *Chicago Tribune*'s coverage of the marches was addressed primarily toward a mainstream white readership.

The *Tribune*'s coverage of the Chicago march focused on racial and cultural diversity, estimates of the size of the crowd, and arguments for and against legalization (Martínez 2006). The paper noted the coalition of labor, religious leaders, employers, and community organizations that had made possible the march and briefly touched on the traffic problems caused by the throngs.

On May 3, the *Tribune* included a commentary (Schmich 2006) in which the author argued that the people at the march "weren't alien faces, this is what Chicago looks like in 2006." This article constituted an attempt to include immigrants as part of the city, to remind readers that very real, Latino physical bodies populate Chicagoland despite their invisibility. Although "a lot of us preferred not to see," wrote the author, "now that we've seen, we have to choose." This statement is central to the representation of Latino immigrants in the news media. It jolted white readers into the recognition of the growing Latino presence in Chicago as well as in the suburbs. It forced readers to come to terms with the past erasures of Latinos as the silent workers, the invisible labor force—in many ways, a true summation of the march's transcultural impact on Chicago. Latino/a bodies became visible in the public space of downtown Chicago, which has been racialized as a white space for tourists, businesses, and members of the upper class.

The May 1 and 2 editions of the *Chicago Sun-Times* offered less extensive and much more negative coverage of the march. The main article on the day of the rally (Flaccus 2006) highlighted the economic effects of workplace absences rather than the agency of the Latino activists and community organizations. By using *illegal immigrants* in the piece's title, the *Sun-Times* explicitly demonstrated its editorial policy regarding the appropriateness of the term. Although the *Tribune*'s policy also permits the use of *illegal immigrant* (but not *illegal alien,* the official term used by the federal government), I have not seen that phrase in the titles of any *Tribune* articles. The May 1 *Sun-Times* coverage also omitted any accounts of immigrants' personal, human, or family stories.

In another piece (Konkol et al. 2006), however, the *Sun-Times* included anecdotes that reflected participants' diversity. The article also discussed the estimates of the size of the crowd and quoted many Latino marchers, allowing them to reaffirm the need for rights, respect, and social justice for immigrant laborers and for Latinos to be seen as productive individuals rather than as criminals or terrorists.

Hoy's coverage centered on the national unity evidenced by the marches and boycotts. Articles used phrases that reaffirmed Latino political power, such as "la marcha más grande en la historia de Chicago" (the biggest march in the history of Chicago) and "triunfo histórico" (a historical triumph), indicating the awareness that these marches made history locally as well as nationwide. While the articles also quoted the Minutemen, the institutional perspective clearly favored the marchers' collective history-making power. A May 2 editorial ("Orgullo Inmigrante" 2006) argued that Latino immigration must be seen as part of the continuum of larger U.S. immigration history. *Hoy* also published an article (Agencias 2006) that described Mexico's positions regarding the boycott of U.S. companies.

One *Hoy* article used *inundaron* (to flood) to refer to the massive size of the crowds in Chicago and other U.S. cities (Espinosa and Reyes 2006).[4] The strategic deployment of this term clearly had an oppositional value, evincing the way that these loaded terms engage a discursive struggle over power. *Inundaron* recollects the reactionary, fear-producing use of the term *flooding* in mainstream, conservative media, suggesting that anti-immigrants' fear of invasion became real as more than a million bodies came out to be seen and to be heard. Specific words' meaning and social power shift based on who uses those words. In this case, *flooding* could have opposing ideological values, embodying the power wars behind the immigration debate.

Conclusions

In the recent film *Bordertown* (2006), Jennifer Lopez plays a Mexican American journalist who writes for a mainstream Chicago newspaper and is investigating the killings of working-class women in Ciudad Juárez, Mexico. Her supervisor, played by Martin Sheen, reminds her that newspapers no longer engage in investigative reporting, since journalists now work for major corporations that reject oppositional writing. Although fictional, this scene illustrates the ideological challenges that socially committed reporters face in these times of globalized, corporate-driven news media (Ballvé 2004).

Although my analysis clearly supports the existence of a binary opposition between mainstream and ethnic news media, the *Chicago Tribune*'s immigration coverage offers some challenges to this thesis. Although the paper's march coverage was addressed primarily at white readers, the two Latino *Tribune* journalists I interviewed had significant freedom to choose their topics, leading to the growing prominence of Latino issues in the mainstream newspaper. Progressive Latino reporters closely connected to local communities can still make a meaningful difference. In addition, one reporter noted that in the wake of the 2006 marches, Latino issues have become part of the *Tribune*'s daily discussions about coverage, and the paper has significantly increased its coverage of Mexico, where Oscar Avila served as a foreign correspondent. These developments suggest that *Tribune* editors have a clear understanding of the transnational nature of Chicago's Mexican community and have begun to address its informational needs.

However, the *Chicago Tribune*'s coverage of the May 1 march also addressed white readers, exhorting them to reflect on the historical and economic contributions of undocumented immigrants to the region and to recognize the potential for transculturation that this sector can effect on American society. The *Tribune* is thus attempting to expand its audience to a multiethnic readership, pursuing a strategy that allows for a negotiation of multiple audiences. Nevertheless, audience differences continue to play a strong role in editorial decision making and the practices of objectivity. Indeed, there are real limits to the extent to which mainstream news venues can truly represent the social, cultural, and political agency of U.S. Latino/as, for such coverage still largely exemplifies the dominant white gaze on minority communities.

The *Chicago Sun-Times* also exemplifies the idea that reporters' ideologies can significantly affect the way readers perceive newspapers but does so in the opposite way. *Sun-Times* columnist Esther Cepeda alienated Latino/a supporters of immigrant rights with her vehement writings against the undocumented and against the public mobilizations. Cepeda, a Mexican-Ecuadorian journalist, was a columnist for the *Chicago Sun-Times* until January 2008, and she exemplifies the ideological heterogeneity of the Latino/a population in the United States. The issue, then, is not whether a newspaper has Latino/a journalists but whether they are committed to covering stories of interest to Latinos/as and to foregrounding their social activism and political agency, even at the local level.

The fact that human interest stories catch the audience's attention has had great benefits for immigrant mobilization. The focus on individuals, on families, and on U.S.-citizen children of undocumented parents attests to the real human experiences, conflicts, and challenges posed by the lack of productive immigration laws and the need for cheap labor. Although mainstream newspapers have not foregrounded Latino/a and immigrant agency, human interest stories may—unintentionally, perhaps—have reminded the rest of the country of the complex human situations that immigrants face. Nonetheless, Spanish-language media continue to play a critical role in asserting the legal, political, social, cultural, family, and economic factors that affect Latino/a immigrants' future in the United States and their ability to come out of the shadows.

Both before and after the May 1, 2008, Chicago march, the city's media discussed the usefulness of public demonstrations on behalf of undocumented immigrants. Despite its smaller size, the 2008 march provided a strong reminder that Chicago has an established public ritual for bringing undocumented immigrants' rights and needs to local, state, and national attention. The marches' symbolic visibility as public, political performances has helped to transform the collective thinking about immigration. News outlets stood ready to cover the 2008 march with helicopters and reporters, a stark contrast from the conditions of March 2006. These changes suggest that at least in Chicago's news media, Latino/as are increasingly considered to be historical and political actors worthy of representation and inclusion but do not necessarily mean the transcendence of the traditional ideologies that have rendered U.S. Latino/as invisible. Although the marches opened up a new space for this population, the shift does not yet represent a new chapter in the coverage of Latino/a issues. It remains to be seen whether, as one reporter commented, the marches have been "a good experience for the media" and will lead to "long-term changes, . . . to more in-depth coverage of the community, not just when the events happen."

Notes

I thank research assistants Jillian Báez, Joanna Maravilla, Emma Olivera, and Daniela Ruiz for their help and express my appreciation to Professors Isabel Molina Guzmán and Otto Santa Ana for their productive suggestions.

1. The *Chicago Sun-Times* refused to allow me to interview its reporters, citing their need to remain publicly objective and their lack of time. I omitted the Spanish-language *La Raza* from my analysis because it is a weekly rather than daily newspaper. However, I included *La Raza* as part of the quantitative analysis of references to Latino/as as sources of authority and reference.

2. According to Rodríguez, "born-again Hispanics" constitute a marketing and audience category of Latino/as who have longer residence in the United States, more formal education, have disposable income, and thus have more hybrid viewing interests (1999, 66–68).

3. I thank Amalia Pallares for this observation.

4. The article also mentioned that no arrests were reported during the Chicago march. Depictions of events as peaceful and nonviolent may be seen as evidence of the media's gendering of the march as feminine but may also undermine the criminalization of immigrants as a whole and foreground the law-abiding nature of U.S. Latinos.

References

Agencias. 2006. "México le dice sí al boicot." *Hoy,* May 2.

Avila, Oscar. 2006. "Shooting for a Big Turnout." *Chicago Tribune,* March 10.

Avila, Oscar, and Michael Martínez. 2006. "Immigrants at Crossroads." *Chicago Tribune,* May 1.

Ballvé, Marcelo. 2004. "The Battle for Latino Media." *NACLA Report on the Americas* 37 (4): 20–25.

Dávila, Arlene. 2001. *Latinos Inc.: The Marketing and Making of a People.* Berkeley: University of California Press.

Dellios, Hugh. 2006. "Migrant Laws Breaking Hearts, Homes." *Chicago Tribune,* March 13.

Espinosa, Leticia. 2005. "Llega a Chicago el Proyecto Minuteman." *Hoy,* June 1.

———. 2006. Interview by Frances R. Aparicio. July 13, Chicago.

Espinosa, Leticia, and Jaime J. Reyes. 2006. "Miles Piden Legalización para Todos." *Hoy,* May 2.

Flaccus, Gillian. 2006. "Illegal Immigrants and Their Allies Boycott." *Chicago Sun-Times,* May 1.

Flores-González, Nilda, Amalia Pallares, Cedric Herring, and Maria Krysan. 2006. *UIC Immigrant Mobilization Project: General Survey Findings.* July 17. http://www .wilsoncenter.org/news/docs/uicstudy.pdf. Accessed January 11, 2007.

Hall, Stuart, Chas Critcher, Tony Jefferson, John Clarke, and Brian Roberts. 1999. "Policing the Crisis" (excerpt). In *News: A Reader,* ed. Howard Tumber, 249–56. New York: Oxford University Press.

Inda, Jonathan Xavier. 2000. "Foreign Bodies: Migrants, Parasites, and the Pathological Nation." *Discourse* 22 (3): 46–62.

Konkol, Mark J., Annie Sweeney, Lucio Guerrero, and Eric Herman. 2006. "More Than 400,000 Rally for Immigrant Rights." *Chicago Sun Times,* May 1.

Latino reporter for the *Chicago Sun Times.* 2006. Email to Frances R. Aparicio, July 19.

Latino reporter for the *Chicago Tribune.* 2006. Interview by Frances R. Aparicio. June 13, Chicago.

Latino reporter for the *Chicago Tribune.* 2006. Interview by Frances R. Aparicio. June 19, Chicago.

Latino reporter for the *Chicago Tribune.* 2008. Email to Frances R. Aparicio, January 9.

Lott, Trent. 2007. "Verbatim." *Time Magazine,* July 9, 10.

Martínez, Michael. 2006. "Rallies Draw over 1 Million." *Chicago Tribune,* May 2.

Masterson, Kathryn. 2006. "Illegal Is Illegal—It Has Nothing to Do with Race or Color." *Chicago Tribune,* Red Eye edition, May 1.

McNulty, Timothy J. 2006. "Covering Immigration Fairly." *Chicago Tribune,* April 16.

Molina Guzmán, Isabel. 2006. "Competing Discourses of Community: Ideological Tensions between Local General-Market and Latino News Media." *Journalism* 7 (3): 281–98.

Nanez, Dianna M. 2007. "Student May Still Face Being Deported." *Arizona Republic,* August 12.

National Association of Hispanic Journalists. 2006. *Network Brownout Report: The Portrayal of Latinos and Latino Issues on Network Television News, 2005.* Washington, D.C.: National Association of Hispanic Journalists.

Neikirk, William. 2007. "Gingrich Rips Bush on Immigration." *Chicago Tribune,* August 15.

O'Donnell, Maureen. 2006. "President Disappoints Mexican-American Family." *Chicago Sun-Times,* May 16.

"Orgullo Inmigrante." 2006. *Hoy,* May 2.

Park, Robert E. 1999. "News as a Form of Knowledge: A Chapter in the Sociology of Knowledge." In *News: A Reader,* ed. Howard Tumber, 11–15. New York: Oxford University Press.

La Primavera del Inmigrante (DVD). 2006. Directed by Alexy Lanza. Chicago: En el Ojo.

Rodríguez, América. 1999. *Making Latino News: Race, Language, Class.* London: Sage.

Santa Ana, Otto. 2002. *Brown Tide Rising: Metaphors of Latinos in Contemporary American Public Discourse.* Austin: University of Texas Press.

Schmich, Mary. 2006. "Faces of March Are Image of a New Chicago." *Chicago Tribune,* May 3.

Schudson, Michael. 2003. *The Sociology of News.* New York: Norton.

Vargas, Lucila. 2000. "Genderizing Latino News: An Analysis of a Local Newspaper's Coverage of Latino Current Affairs." *Critical Studies in Media Communications* 17 (3): 261–93.

4

The Role of the Catholic Church in the Chicago Immigrant Mobilization

STEPHEN P. DAVIS,

JUAN R. MARTINEZ, AND

R. STEPHEN WARNER

Chicago's March 10, 2006, demonstration to support undocumented immigrants in the face of the Sensenbrenner Bill was remarkable in its size, in that it led to a series of huge marches nationwide, and in that most of the marchers and their leaders were Latinos. Its significance and scope surprised many observers, among them social scientists at the University of Illinois at Chicago (UIC), a racially, ethnically, and culturally diverse university situated less than a mile from where the march began.

Steve Warner, a teacher and researcher in the sociology of religion with a particular interest in the connections between religion and immigration, received his only inkling that anything unusual was happening on March 10 when he saw a brief item in the *Chicago Tribune* warning commuters that a demonstration might cause some afternoon traffic problems in the West Loop. Warner was away from the university that day, and only when he opened the March 11 paper did he learn that he and his colleagues had missed a historic event. However, on the morning of the demonstration, Juan Martinez, who is one of Warner's graduate students and has conducted research in a suburban parish for his master's thesis on ethnic succession in Catholic parishes, was told by one of his Latina students that she would be absent from class that day because she was attending a demonstration, and he subsequently was told by other students that they would be leaving for the rally immediately after class. One Catholic student reported that her pastor had told her and her friends to go. When Martinez headed downtown for a meeting, he saw that Harrison Street was jammed with traffic, and he was forced to get off his bus at Canal Street.

Steve Davis, who has lived in and near Pilsen, a port-of-entry neighborhood for Chicago Mexicans, and has volunteered with the youth program at the area's St. Pius V Church, had learned about the march a day earlier. Father Brendan Curran had invited participants at a teen support-group meeting to join the march and to travel to the site on one of the three buses the church had rented. When Davis said that he had to teach a class and could not get to St. Pius in time, Father Brendan said that there would be "a sea of people" at the march and that Davis would be unlikely to find the St. Pius contingent. The next morning, Davis participated in the march on his own before attending the annual conference of the Association of American Geographers at a downtown Chicago hotel. He was disappointed at how little attention conference participants paid to the march, although one geographer lamented that they were missing out because people were taking to the streets right outside.

Having learned about the church's role in the March 10 mobilization not from our colleagues or from the media but from our churchgoing Mexican American students and contacts in Chicago Catholic parishes, we felt our most advantageous contribution to the Immigrant Mobilization Project was to focus on the role of religion in the subsequent May 1 rally. For this purpose, we used the results of the surveys we and other UIC researchers conducted at the march as well as information gleaned from interviews with Catholic clergy and lay leaders and observations and written materials collected from Chicago's parishes.[1]

The students and church contacts knew something that most social scientists had thus far missed: the Catholic Church played a key role in mobilizing hundreds of thousands of Chicago's Mexican Americans in support of immigrant rights. At the May 1 march, 68 percent of survey respondents described themselves as Catholic (figure 4.1), and 67 percent of the Catholics reported that they attended church at least two or three times a month (what we call "frequent" attendance) (figure 4.2). Cross-tabulations indicate that 64 percent of all marchers were both Latino and Catholic and that 46 percent of all marchers were Latino Catholics who frequently attended church.

This is not to say that the march was a religious event. The second-largest group of marchers (14.5 percent) described themselves as having "no religious preference" (figure 4.1), a rate that jumped to 44 percent for non-Latino participants. Moreover, 15.3 percent of the Latino Catholics who attended the march "rarely" went to church. As observing participants in the May 1 march, we can say that the two predominant groups among the marchers were secular white leftists and religious Mexican Catholics.[2]

Nine percent of the Latino Catholics who frequently attended church said that they had been convinced to participate by someone at church, and fewer than 3 percent came to the march with someone from church.[3] But only 57 percent of respondents said that anyone at all had convinced them to participate, and

Figure 4.1. Marchers' Religious Preferences, 2006

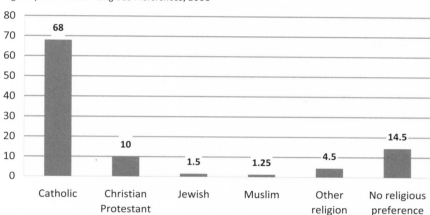

Figures in this chapter are from the 2006 report by Nilda Flores-González, Amalia Pallares, Cedric Herring, and Maria Krysan, *UIC Immigrant Mobilization Project: General Survey Findings,* available at http://www.wilsoncenter.org/news/docs/uicstudy.pdf.

Figure 4.2. Church Attendance among Latino Catholic Marchers, 2006

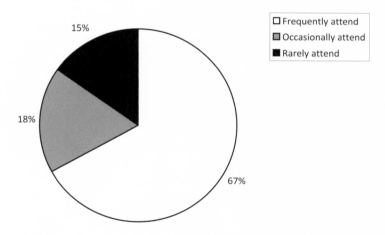

most respondents reported that they came with family members. Father Michael Boehm of St. Maurice's Parish, on Chicago's Far Southwest Side, suggested the possibility of arranging transportation from the church, but his parishioners told him not to bother because they would be going directly from work or school. He told us that "nearly all the Latino parishioners" subsequently reported that they had joined in the march.

Seventy-nine percent of those who frequently attended church received encouragement from church leaders to attend the march, with 62 percent receiving strong encouragement; only 48 percent of those with less frequent attendance received such encouragement. Small numbers of participants in the march reported that teachers, classmates, neighbors, coworkers, family members, or friends had discouraged participation; however, no one received such a negative message from someone at church (figure 4.3).

Figure 4.3. Catholic Church Leaders' Encouragement by Parishioner Attendance Frequency, 2006

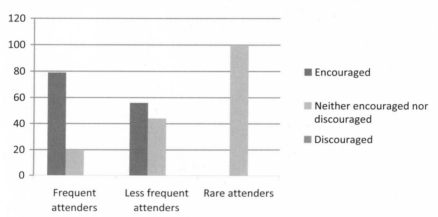

Findings from the Qualitative Research

The Catholic churches we studied promoted parishioner involvement in the May 1 march in a variety of ways:

* direct encouragement from Catholic pastors;
* indirect encouragement through such means as priests' making known their opposition to anti-immigrant legislation and support for immigrant rights and urging employers to allow workers to take the afternoon off;
* earning respect from parishioners through culturally sensitive responses to material and spiritual needs;
* regular integration of immigration-related concerns into parish activities;
* empowerment via a long-term, multifaceted, only partly articulated program that promotes the substantive citizenship of Latino constituents, even those who are not yet eligible for legal citizenship.

DIRECT ENCOURAGEMENT

On May 4, Davis asked participants at a youth group meeting at St. Pius how they had heard about the march. Said one young woman, "There was flyers everywhere." When Davis asked if the flyers had been posted in the church, the woman responded, "No, [but] Father Brendan was talking about it [at] Sunday mass." A young man at the meeting recalled that Brendan had come to an April planning session for the rally and suggested that marchers wear white shirts and bring American rather than Mexican flags. Similarly, the pastor at a parish in the mostly Mexican suburb of Cicero, just west of Chicago's Little Village neighborhood, reported that he had promoted the march in his homilies and bulletins, as did a priest in Melrose Park, farther west. In addition, this cleric had helped arrange funding for thirty-two buses to transport parishioners to the march and had organized youth and young adult leaders to provide participants with guidance about logistics and the peaceful nature of the protest. In some parishes, lay leaders offered even more direct encouragement, nearly always with priests' blessings. A pastor in Little Village, for example, described one of the lay leaders from his congregation as "far more knowledgeable" and more directly involved than the priest himself.

INDIRECT ENCOURAGEMENT

Several of our clergy informants participated in public events designed to influence policy and/or public opinion, and these efforts indirectly encouraged parishioners to participate. Three of the priests we interviewed said that they had joined other priests in fasting and periodic pilgrimages to the office of former House speaker Dennis Hastert to protest the Sensenbrenner Bill and other repressive measures. Such actions generated publicity from such sources as the *Chicago Tribune* (Ramírez 2006):

> As hundreds of activists held small rallies in Cicero and the South Chicago neighborhood Monday to support immigration reform, others picketed. . . .
>
> Hours later, Latino Catholics held a prayer vigil to support a small group of priests who are fasting, not just to grow spiritually during Lent, but to show solidarity with immigrants who come to this country for work and food.
>
> Rev. Mark Bartosic said . . . "I'm also fasting for the people in my parish. This is the reason why they come here. They come because they're hungry." . . .
>
> Catholic leaders in Illinois and nationwide are rallying for reforms that help their immigrant parishioners. Several bishops support legislation that would offer illegal immigrants a chance to legalize their status and establish a temporary worker program. . . .
>
> The six bishops of Illinois' Catholic dioceses, including Chicago's Cardinal Francis George, issued a joint statement denouncing the current immigration system and outlining elements they said should be included in a new law. . . .
>
> Rev. Gary Graf of Holy Family Church in Waukegan, who conceived the idea [of fasting], is fasting 15 days, until Good Friday. Monday night, Latino Catholics held a prayer vigil at Our Lady of Tepeyac Church in Chicago's Little Village neighborhood to support the priests.

One well-known marketing principle holds that redundancy of messages is necessary to stimulate a decision; thus, such news reports, combined with direct encouragement from pastors and celebrities, contributed to the mobilization. Indirect encouragement was also vital in the workplace, where priests were sometimes uniquely able to gain an audience with management. Parish leaders in Melrose Park and elsewhere asked business owners to give employees the day off or to contribute financial support for church contingents.

EARNED RESPECT

Religious leaders' direct and indirect encouragement would not have figured into the Chicago mobilization had priests not enjoyed legitimacy and respect among their congregants. Many Latinos and their spokespersons regard the Catholic Church with suspicion because it sided with the wealthy in their countries of origin or because they believe it has neglected or discriminated against Hispanics in the United States. To address such suspicions, the National Conference of Catholic Bishops conducted the National Hispanic Encuentro in 1972 to promote Hispanic leadership and decision making in the church. Progress has been uneven, but the archdioceses of Chicago and Los Angeles in particular have worked to meet the needs of their Mexican American charges. These projects rely heavily on the observations of bishops and priests but are also informed by lay groups such as individual parish councils and archdiocese-wide pastoral councils. Many progressive priests and parishes also have taken independent action.

In Pilsen and other such neighborhoods where new, often undocumented, arrivals land, they immediately need food, clothing, shelter, and jobs. Father Charles Dahm, the longtime pastor of St. Pius V Church in Pilsen, begins his recent book *Parish Ministry in a Hispanic Community* with a story that he says "was repeated hundreds of times" during his more than twenty years there: "Maria" and "José" arrive on his doorstep after a three-month journey from Guatemala. They have forded the Rio Grande, walked 150 miles across the Texas desert, and ridden freight trains to Chicago, where someone in the emergency room at Cook County Hospital directs them to St. Pius. The priest offers them clothing from the secondhand store, and lay volunteers prepare a table for them in the church basement and serve *menudo* from the soup kitchen. The new arrivals are offered a shower and bed in the rectory and bus fare to a relative's home in Rock Island and leave promising never to forget the parish's generosity (2004, vii–viii).[4] In another parish, several families have formed an organization that provides refugee groups with temporary home stays, local transportation, and a "welcome to America pack" with "all the necessary things." More than mere charity, such offers meet urgent human needs.

Yet it is not enough for a church to provide necessities, especially if such offers are made in a condescending or culturally insensitive manner (for example, if the soup were borscht instead of *menudo*). Many heavily Latino parishes only recently began to offer masses in Spanish and to display Mexican iconography, especially statues, murals, and banners featuring the image of La Virgen, Our Lady of Guadalupe (Dahm 2004, 161–67; Elizondo 2000a, 2000b). Other features that are becoming more common include Christmastime *posadas* (Dahm 2004, 191–96); the open-air Good Friday pageant known as Via Crucis Viviente (Dahm 2004, 172–76; Hurtig 2000); and commemorations of Día de los Muertos (Day of the Dead, coinciding with the European All Souls' Day) (Dahm 2004, 177–80). The events have been incorporated not only in city parishes such as Pilsen, Little Village, and Back of the Yards and on the Southeast Side but also in the suburbs of Cicero, Berwyn, and Melrose Park (Badillo 2006, 134–53). The accommodation of Mexican customs has generated friction in some cases (Dahm 2004, 14–17): in one Southeast Side parish, Polish and Mexican parishioners jockey to obtain favored positions for their effigies of Our Lady of Czestochowa and Our Lady of Guadalupe, and in one west suburban parish, Italians resent hearing Spanish spoken during the annual procession for Our Lady of Mount Carmel. Many parishes provide separate masses in Spanish, English, Polish, and other languages, but one pastor we interviewed insists on a unified approach to major holidays in which "multicultural but not bilingual masses" juxtapose hymns and other elements in different languages without repeating with translations.

Cultural accommodation goes well beyond matters of formal religion. Many parishes host *quinceañeras* (coming-of-age ceremonies for Mexican girls) (Badillo 2006, 144; Dahm 2004, 196–99), although some priests worry about the extravagance of the celebrations and the risk that families may sink into debt. Dahm learned a tradition of presentation of infants (not a formal baptism) from his parishioners (2004, 128) and believes that some Mexican families prefer St. Pius over their neighborhood parishes because he honors that practice. A three-story mural of Dahm presenting a baby adorns a building across the street from his church.

REGULAR ATTENTION TO IMMIGRATION-RELATED CONCERNS

Exhortations for parishioners to get involved in protest marches do not occur in a vacuum, and church leaders work hard to make them consistent with the rest of the church's teachings. Week after week, parishioners communally pray the Our Father, commemorate Jesus' sacrifice for their salvation, and hear their pastor relate these familiar religious rituals to the often new and strange threats they face in their adopted country. At mass on October 29, 2006, St. Pius observed Todos los Santos (All Saints' Day) and Día de los Muertos. Father Dahm told the congregation of a petition in which more than one hundred members of Priests for Justice for Immigrants requested a halt to deportations until there is a comprehensive reform to the immigration laws. Unfortunately, the government is doing the opposite. They made two worrisome raids of almost 30 people last week. . . . Last Sunday, at 6:00 A.M., immigration agents entered the house of —— and arrested her in front of her husband and three daughters and took her into custody for not having appropriate documents. —— is a catechist at St. Pius for disabled children. She has lived in the U.S. for 15 years, has paid her taxes, and serves her community. Her youngest daughter is a citizen; she is disabled and it would be nearly impossible for her to survive without her mother. . . . At least 13 laborers who work with —— were detained in their homes early on Sunday. Each one needs $2,000 bond to be free. Why were these workers detained? It seems that the company was getting revenge, because the union had won a court case on October 16 against it.[5]

Dahm then invited the parishioner to the pulpit to tell her story. The church had posted bond for her that morning, and the congregation greeted her with thunderous applause as she approached the altar.

At St. Pius and other churches, those who attend regularly expect messages that comfort the soul and challenge the imagination. One pastor referred to these messages as "raising issues" and consciousness. Between March and May, he explained, "what we were doing was educating the people as to their rights, . . . and so we raised the issue of justice, we raised the issue about employment, education, health care . . . a blanket of different threads that tie into this immigration issue." Another priest marveled, "We had a program [about being] an immigrant, about the history of immigration, about social justice. . . . We had about a total of twenty to twenty-five people taking this [class]. We asked them to bring themselves into community organizing." Such efforts generated overwhelming results: "Five years ago, to have thirty-two buses [bringing parishioners to a march] was unthinkable. Five years ago, to have *one* bus was unthinkable."

Not all Mexican parishes in Chicago have pastors as outspoken as these men. Indeed, Father Dahm believes that some St. Pius parishioners found him "too political" and gravitated toward another parish with a less challenging pastor. But even priests less activist than Dahm and his successor at St. Pius, Curran, do not espouse the kind of conservatism that would have discouraged immigrant mobilization (Robledo 2006).

Research reported by Kraig Beyerlein, Edwin Hernández, and David Sikkink (2007) strongly supports our findings about how Chicago Catholic churches encouraged participation. In Beyerlein, Hernández, and Sikkink's analysis of an August–October 2006 Pew Hispanic Center survey of 4,016 Latino adults nationwide, the dependent variable was whether the respondent had participated in protest activities in the past year. The independent variables were aspects of respondents' religion: denomination, salience, frequency of prayer and attendance, attitude toward the Bible, ethnic makeup of their churches, and whether their churches organized immigrant rights protests and had sermons on the topic.[6] Beyerlein, Hernández, and Sikkink controlled for more than a dozen demographic and contextual variables and then entered the independent variables sequentially into nine different models. Being Catholic remained a significant predictor of protest participation through the first eight models but became insignificant when the last two variables (whether the church organized immigrant rights protests and had sermons on the topic) were considered. The authors' interpretation of their results is consistent with our finding that some but not all Catholic parishes and pastors encouraged the mobilization. Mobilization efforts are predominantly found in the Catholic Church, yet many clergy, even in majority-Latino parishes, did not encourage the mobilization. Just which Catholics participated is explained by characteristics of their parishes, especially whether their priests spoke out for immigrant rights.

EMPOWERMENT VIA SUBSTANTIVE CITIZENSHIP

Although large segments of the Latino immigrant population enjoy rights of formal citizenship, millions cling to the precarious legal handholds offered by temporary visas and green cards, and millions more cope with even less secure standing as undocumented immigrants. For members of the latter two groups, formal citizenship (and its concomitant rights and responsibilities, such as voting) might be seen either as far in the future or as a prize beyond their reach. But in many immigrants' and Catholic leaders' eyes, formal citizenship remains somewhat insufficient in that it does little or nothing to build better neighborhoods, parishes, and countries. While parishes may offer citizenship classes, far more meaningful or substantive are efforts to promote homeownership, neighborhood initiatives (taking back streets, parks, and schools), and larger political actions (including immigrant rights marches). These actions build the foundations of substantive citizenship—that is, civic engagement, activism, and an accompanying sense of being a stakeholder in the larger system.[7] The ideal is for Latino immigrants to possess both formal and substantive citizenship, but when both are not possible, immigrants who remain undocumented and unrecognized by the central government may still negotiate and achieve substantive citizenship through social and civic involvement.

The Catholic Church historically has promoted societal participation through ties to the local community, particularly in the form of homeownership (McGreevy 1996). When immigration researcher Cecilia Menjívar (1999) first began to study how churches met the needs of Salvadorans in the United States, she expected that the Catholic Church, as an enormous international organization, would facilitate transnational ties binding people to their country of origin. She found instead that Protestant churches were more likely to stress home-country ties, whereas the Catholic Church worked to integrate people into local parishes. One priest we interviewed agreed, saying that he wants the church to help "integrate people into the country." Another said that although some parishioners aspire eventually to return to Mexico, he wants them "to become invested in being a citizen in the community." These goals apply particularly to young people. One priest perceives that children are more interested in staying in the United States than are their parents, and another wants to help secure the funding young people will need to go to college. These and the other priests we spoke with are strongly motivated by the claims of social justice. As one said, "Where people are suffering, the church is there. We need to be." But the long-term way to address this suffering is to help immigrants get a stake in this society.

Dahm invites his parishioners to share responsibility for the church's efforts to meet their needs—for example, by presenting the congregation with detailed budgets that show where St. Pius's funds come from and where they go. As Menjivar (2003) observes, despite its hierarchical structure, the Catholic church involves parishioners as local citizens.

Peter Skerry offers a similar interpretation of the role of the Resurrection Project, a community development corporation founded in 1990 by a coalition of Pilsen churches, in promoting "civic integration" of immigrants (2003–4, 26–29). Inspired by Saul Alinsky's militant, self-help approach to organizing, the Resurrection Project uses material self-interest to teach broader lessons about community involvement, helping residents become homeowners but also requiring them to participate in "intensive counseling sessions and months-long courses on personal finance and credit, home-ownership, refinancing and home improvement . . . with guidance in 'how to be responsible tenants and home owners'" (31).

Dahm emphasizes that the Resurrection Project had to supplement Alinsky's approach with a culturally explicit religious component: "Because of the importance of faith in the lives of Mexican people, the courses included a deeper reflection on the teachings of Jesus and the role of the church[, and] they were taught in Spanish to predominantly monolingual Hispanics" (2004, 264; for Dahm's understanding of church-based community organizing, see 252–80).

The churches that participate in the Resurrection Project have greater credibility when they urge people to increase their civic and political involvement. The program registers voters and trains community leaders who act on a range of social justice issues. Yet despite the success of recent voter-registration drives in Pilsen and Little Village,[8] civic and economic integration cannot be limited to U.S. citizens. An alternative, informal citizenship may be desired for many undocumented adults, particularly when their contributions go unrecognized by politicians and the public at large. One Pilsen priest explained that "citizenship classes" in his parish took many forms, including educating people about their

rights when confronted by police officers and promoting voting and neighborhood responsibilities:

> In a sense, . . . we're working to . . . raise consciousness [through classes on] reg-
> istrations, legal residency, getting voters signed up, education about what your
> rights are. . . . [But it is not] only about a matter of rights. Two of the classes
> were for responsibility, too. Even though you're not a voter, even though you're
> undocumented, you are still responsible to support actions. You can still show
> up to marches, you can still be part of educational programs. . . . Of course, their
> big fear is if they put their name down on anything they get picked up by the
> Migra, by the Immigration, but . . . they can still participate, they can still pray,
> they can still donate, they can still volunteer . . . raise the consciousness of being
> a good citizen, working in your neighborhood, keeping your house clean, mak-
> ing sure that your garbage can is closed—little things or bigger things, working
> with your neighbors to get a block club. [Because] being a good Christian means
> being a good citizen.

In this vision, the church calls parishioners to duty and service as citizens even
when formal paths to citizenship are barred. "Being a good Christian" means
being engaged civically, just as for many law-abiding yet progressive priests and
bishops, it may mean placing social justice and human rights above the letter
of immigration law.

Father Boehm echoed his colleagues' notion of "flawed immigration policies":
"There's eleven to twelve million undocumented immigrants . . . all paying taxes
but not getting the money back. They all work very hard." Politicians recognize
only the U.S.-born children of these immigrants, but as those children reach
the age of eighteen, their visibility will increase, according to Boehm. Another
priest tells the U.S. citizens in his flock, "Take a look at your brother and sister.
All of you . . . know someone who's come over the border illegally, and the only
way to make sure that they're treated with dignity [and] respect . . . is to make
sure you exercise your power. . . . You've got their lives in your hands. . . . You
can't just sit back and let [this door] close. If you [can] vote, you should vote."

Local church governance may serve as a pathway toward substantive citizenship, where both documented and undocumented parishioners gain leadership
experience, social confidence, and networking skills while sharing in day-to-
day parish activities. The immigrant rights movement may also be producing
church and civic leaders. According to Father Claudio Holzer of Melrose Park,
this type of movement places parishioners in conversation with local politicians,
calls forth new leaders, and is clearly relevant to peoples' lives.

Some of our informants used the secular language of integration to explain
the cooperation necessary between priests and parishioners, but others we interviewed spoke in more intimate terms of union and familial bonds. In the

words of one Pilsen pastor, "Life in a parish is like a marriage. Sometimes the priest steps [to the front], and other times the people lead. It happens all the time. And church history is full of that, where the people have taken the lead on things and all of the sudden the . . . authorities will come around, or vice versa. [In] most parishes . . . the priest usually gets a start—at least, I think he gets a start because he goes . . . to a lot more meetings and he hears some of the stuff. . . . If there's a labor problem at a factory or something like that, they come to the priest and say, 'This is what's happening,' and he'll say, 'Well, let's mobilize. Let's go.'" This pastor clarified that volunteerism has been particularly evident in his parish council, whose members talk about immigrant rights and mobilizations "even though it's not technically parish stuff. But it is something the Christian community at large would be interested in." As in a successful marriage, healthy communication—dialogue—is key to the coordinated efforts of a church. Though some dialogue takes place in formal parish councils and lay committees, often with the priest in attendance, much of what constitutes church-centered communication occurs informally—in conversations at the back of church, at the Mothers' Club, and on the sidewalks out front where a group of women talk for "an hour after mass" every Sunday. The strength of a union depends on effective information-sharing and support networks.

The Church as a Catholic Institution

Of course, the Catholic Church does not represent or minister solely to Latinos or immigrants. It claims to be universal, and its U.S. constituency is multiracial, multiethnic, and both rich and poor. Church members disagree about immigration policy, and our interviews and observations record these disputes between supporters and opponents of the rights of undocumented immigrants. One pastor of an ethnically mixed parish lamented that some "priests . . . have never been out of the country [and consequently] are 'American First' and then [they're] Catholic. And I know a lot of [lay] Catholics that are that way, too." The archdiocese of Chicago officially but rather quietly takes the position that the church does not support "total amnesty" for undocumented immigrants (Archdiocese 2007, 3a). Yet over the past thirty years, the National Conference of Catholic Bishops has communicated support for the cultural and social interests of Latinos generally and Mexican Americans specifically. The priests we interviewed have received ecclesiastical support for their pro-immigrant activities, which one informant described as a change from policies of the not-too-distant past. Cardinal George has publicly supported immigrant mobilizations, blessing the March 10 rally before its start in Union Park and participating in an interfaith prayer service in Grant Park at the conclusion of the May 1 march.

From the late 1800s through World War I, the American Catholic Church had a dominant working-class constituency of immigrants from Europe and their offspring.[9] The church often accommodated new immigrants by authorizing national or ethnic local parishes. Not without struggle, first Irish and Germans and then Poles and Italians were allowed to venerate their saints, worship in their accustomed style, and hear homilies in their native language. In Chicago beginning in 1874, European groups in Pilsen founded St. Pius V (Irish), St. Adalbert (Poles), St. Procopius (Bohemians), St. Stephen (Slovenians), and St. Michael (Italians). During the tenure of Archbishop James Quigley (1903–15), Chicago saw the founding of 113 ethnic parishes, and by the 1930s, Pilsen had fourteen parishes, only two of them based on parishioners' place of residence rather than ethnic or national origins.

But nativist sentiment increased as the country went to war. National legislation curtailing immigration as well as efforts by Chicago Catholic leaders, led by the powerful Cardinal George Mundelein (1916–39), to Americanize their constituents slowed the growth of ethnic parishes. But as the tide of immigrants from Poland, Italy, and other Eastern and Southern European countries ebbed and the archdiocese began to favor the creation of territorial parishes, American industry rebounded from the postwar slump and the demand for labor soared, resulting in a south-to-north migration bringing African Americans and Mexicans to midwestern cities. Mundelein allowed the creation of only two Mexican parishes, Our Lady of Guadalupe on the Far South Side and St. Francis of Assisi on the Near West Side. After World War II, a Hispanic mission was set up at Immaculate Heart of Mary in Back of the Yards. With only three widely spaced parishes, Mexicans faced rejection, often racially motivated, from the parishes serving most neighborhoods.

The development of the UIC campus in the 1960s forced the West Side Mexican community farther south, into Pilsen, which started to become the overwhelmingly Mexican neighborhood that it is now, but the national parishes there did not welcome Latinos: "For years, on Sundays, Euro-American ushers had stood in the front door [of St. Pius] to head off Hispanics coming to church, directing them to 'their parish,' St. Francis, about a mile away" (Dahm 2004, 17). Only under Cardinals Joseph Bernardin (1982–96) and Francis George (since 1997) has the church truly made room for its growing Mexican constituency so that there are now de facto Mexican parishes in Pilsen, Little Village, and other neighborhoods, and many other parishes offer Spanish-language masses. Though Chicago's longtime Latino activists well remember the decades of exclusion, the newer practices of a few visionary priests and the increasingly accommodating policy of the archdiocese have made the church far more inviting to the masses of Mexican immigrants who have arrived in the past twenty years.

Many priests who support immigrant rights worry more about neutralizing opposition within their non-Latino parishes than about what their ecclesiastical superiors may say. One priest in a parish that is 60–70 percent Latino (mainly Mexican), with the remainder mostly working-class Anglos, knows priests in non-heavily-Latino parishes who fear speaking out on immigration/solidarity, dreading parishioner disapproval: "It's a very sensitive issue to communities, very sensitive, and if you offend your parishioners, you affect your collection." Nonetheless, this man found inspiration from other pastors: "I've been very impressed with the Polish priests in the Priests for Justice [group,] cause the Poles come out too, and people notice that." That Poles and Latinos share a concern for immigrant rights is evident in official Chicago archdiocesan periodicals, including the Spanish-language *Católico,* published since 1985, and the Polish-language *Katolik,* which began appearing in September 2006. Many Polish priests are immigrants or guest workers, and a significant number of Chicago Poles were undocumented prior to the 1996 amnesty.

Other priests mobilize support from parishes that do not contain large numbers of immigrants. The African-immigrant priest in a progressive, affluent, white suburban parish related his experiences with racial profiling by U.S. immigration authorities. That experience, as well as his commitment to social justice ("Christ wiped out the divisions among people"), causes him to identify with the struggles of undocumented immigrants and to preach on their behalf. Although his parishioners do not for the most part join pro-immigrant demonstrations, three thousand of them signed a petition in favor of "humane immigration reform."[10]

During the summer of 1965, social scientist Jeffrey Hadden was studying a liberal Protestant workshop on inner-city ministry for Chicago-area clergy. Some of the workshop participants took part in a civil rights sit-in and were arrested. Hadden's analysis (1969) found that all four of the ministers who served inner-city integrated congregations were arrested but that only one of the ten pastors who served suburban congregations was arrested. In part, these men were doing what they thought their congregations expected. But those workshop participants who had jobs with social-justice-oriented denominational agencies and seminaries also had high rates of arrest. Hadden conceptualized their position as one of "structural freedom." Unlike the pastors of predominantly conservative white suburban congregations, these ministers did not perceive their livelihoods as threatened by civil rights activism. Hadden concluded that hierarchical institutions are not necessarily inimical to popular, democratic mobilization when they provide structural freedom to those whose livelihoods depend on those institutions.

Thus, Chicago's Catholic Church provides resources and leadership that encourage immigrants and their supporters to mobilize in favor of their rights and encourages leaders of nonimmigrant communities to act in solidarity with immigrants.

Conclusion

The marches of 2006 demonstrate the fruits of the U.S. Catholic Church's thirty-year-effort to accommodate its growing Hispanic constituency after more than a century of neglect. Like a battleship, the world's oldest formal organization has powerful momentum but is very slow to turn and has a large formal hierarchy. Unlike a battleship, however, more complex patterns of leadership also exist, and the church has turned and set a new course. As a whole, the Chicago church has come around to a commitment to justice for immigrants and their progeny, especially to helping them become fuller participants in society.

Nonetheless, the U.S. Catholic Church is not a revolutionary agent. It has a stake in the society, and it wants its constituents to receive the benefits of that stake. Its deep culture leads it to be critical of militarism and unrestrained capitalism as much as of sexual freedom and public profanity, but it accommodates itself to its worldly environment and recognizes that some of its members do not share compassion for immigrants' plight. Progressive Catholic laity must maintain support for like-minded priests and prevent the church from yielding to the proponents of fear. Among U.S. religious institutions, the Catholic Church stands out for connecting its laity to public life. Partly because of those connections, the Catholic Church is a major presence in American life. But partly because of the large size of many parishes, partly because of stresses caused by a shortage of priests, and partly because of the heterogeneity of parishes, the Catholic Church in general is less effective than Protestant churches in making its members citizens of the church itself. Catholics are less accustomed to choosing and demanding accountability from their religious leaders. This reticence is exacerbated in the case of recent immigrants from historically Catholic cultures. The most progressive of the priests we interviewed are aware of this problem and work to involve their faithful as active participants in parish life. These efforts must continue. The Catholic Church is an important—perhaps *the* most important—institutional vehicle for the mass mobilization of Chicago's Mexican Americans. If the church is to continue in that role, however, Mexican Americans, other Hispanics, and progressive laypersons in general must make sure that their voices continue to be heard.

Notes

Earlier versions of this essay were presented at the March 1, 2007, IMP conference; at the March 30, 2007, conference on the Good Samaritan in the Global Age: Migration, Religion, and the World Economy at Princeton University; and at the Chicago Area Group for the Study of Religious Communities on November 24, 2007. For their comments, we are grateful to those attending these sessions, especially Merída Rúa and Mary Ellen Konieczny. We are also grateful to Natalia Serna for research assistance.

1. We formulated interview questions that would explore Catholic churches' roles in the immigrant rights movement and then identified churches and parish leaders who were involved with immigrant rights. Six of the eight congregations we studied have a significant number of Mexican-immigrant parishioners and their children. Most members of the other two churches are native-born, non-Hispanic whites, although one parish includes numerous Irish and Polish immigrants. We conducted tape-recorded interviews with eight priests and two lay leaders and then transcribed the interviews, checked them for accuracy, and coded them.

2. Activists on all sides took pride in the coalition building that led to the event. Moreover, many leftists were commemorating International Labor Day. As one West Side priest put it, "I think they must have chosen May 1st because of . . . Labor Day . . . the communists' May Day. . . . I don't know if that was a part of it or not, but we also, for that day, wanted to reach out to other people like unions, other races, other nationalities, other creeds."

3. Many participants opted not to join church groups for the May 1 march because buses chartered for the March 10 mobilization had gotten stalled in traffic long before reaching the assembly point.

4. Dahm, who holds a doctorate in political science, continues to serve St. Pius as an associate pastor.

5. Quoted from a document in possession of the authors and translated by Davis.

6. The Pew survey asked a retrospective recall question and in that sense has less face validity than the Immigrant Mobilization Project's survey. But Beyerlein, Hernández, and Sikkink have variation in the dependent variable, whereas we do not.

7. The term *substantive citizenship* overlaps somewhat with the concept of Latino cultural citizenship articulated by Rosaldo (1994) and others. Cultural citizenship is said to involve group claims to community formation, shared spaces, and social rights, encompassing "a broad range of everyday activities as well as the more visible political and social movements" (Flores 2003, 88–89); it may also help to elucidate "the racialized subjugation of both citizen and non-citizen Latinos" and "political agency . . . not confined to the state's formal constructions of juridical citizenship and rights" (De Genova and Ramos-Zayas 2003, 222). The U.S. Conference of Catholic Bishops (1999) uses a term that we may link with substantive citizenship; its "faithful citizenship" initiative encouraged lay activism in the 2000 elections, sending out "Faithful Citizen" kits, including a video on civic responsibility, to almost twenty thousand parishes.

8. One Pilsen priest estimated that sixteen thousand voters had recently been registered in Pilsen and Little Village.

9. This section is based primarily on Dahm 2004; Dolan 1985; see also Orsi 1996; Warner 2005.

10. During the 1980s, this parish was home to an outspoken group of supporters of sanctuary for refugees from Central America's civil wars (Lorentzen 1991). For further discussion of sanctuary, social justice, and the preferential "option for the poor," see Campese 2007.

References

Archdiocese of Chicago. 2007. "Annual Financial Report, 2006." *Catholic New World*, January 6.

Badillo, David A. 2006. *Latinos and the New Immigrant Church.* Baltimore: Johns Hopkins University Press.

Beyerlein, Kraig, Edwin Hernández, and David Sikkink. 2007. "Latino Religion and Immigrant Rights Protest Participation." Paper presented at the annual meeting of the Society for the Scientific Study of Religion, Tampa, Florida, November 2–4.

Campese, Gioacchino. 2007. "Beyond Ethnic and National Imagination: Toward a Catholic Theology of U.S. Immigration." In *Religion and Social Justice for Immigrants,* ed. P. Hondagneu-Sotelo, 175–90. New Brunswick, N.J.: Rutgers University Press.

Dahm, Charles W. 2004. *Parish Ministry in a Hispanic Community.* Mahwah, N.J.: Paulist.

De Genova, Nicholas, and Ana Y. Ramos-Zayas. 2003. "Latino Racial Formations in the United States: An Introduction." *Journal of Latin American Anthropology* 8 (2): 2–17.

Dolan, Jay P. 1985. *The American Catholic Experience: A History from Colonial Times to the Present.* Garden City, N.J.: Doubleday.

Elizondo, Virgilio. 2000a [1977]. "Our Lady of Guadalupe as a Cultural Symbol." In *Beyond Borders: Writings of Virgilio Elizondo and Friends,* ed. T. Matovina, 118–25. Maryknoll, N.Y.: Orbis.

———. 2000b [1977]. "Popular Religion as Support of Identity." In *Beyond Borders: Writings of Virgilio Elizondo and Friends,* ed. T. Matovina, 126–32. Maryknoll, N.Y.: Orbis.

Flores, William V. 2003. "New Citizens, New Rights: Undocumented Immigrants and Latino Cultural Citizenship." *Latin American Perspectives* 30 (2): 87–100.

Hadden, Jeffrey K. 1969. *The Gathering Storm in the Churches.* Garden City, N.Y.: Doubleday.

Hurtig, Janise D. 2000. "Hispanic Immigrant Churches and the Construction of Ethnicity." In *Public Religion and Urban Transformation: Faith in the City,* ed. L. W. Livezey, 29–55. New York: New York University Press.

Lorentzen, Robin. 1991. *Women in the Sanctuary Movement.* Philadelphia: Temple University Press.

McGreevy, John T. 1996. *Parish Boundaries: The Catholic Encounter with Race in the Twentieth Century Urban North.* Chicago: University of Chicago Press.

Menjivar, Cecilia. 1999. "Religious Institutions and Transnationalism: A Case Study of Catholic and Evangelical Salvadoran Immigrants." *International Journal of Politics, Culture and Society* 12 (4): 589–612.

———. 2003. "Religion and Immigration in Comparative Perspective: Catholic and Evangelical Salvadorans in San Francisco, Washington, D.C., and Phoenix." *Sociology of Religion* 64 (1): 21–45.

Orsi, Robert A. 1996. *Thank You, St. Jude: Women's Devotion to the Patron Saint of Hopeless Causes.* New Haven: Yale University Press.

Ramírez, Margaret. 2006. "As Activists Rally, Priests Show Support by Fasting." *Chicago Tribune,* April 11.

Robledo, Vanessa. 2006. "How Latinos Are Changing the U.S. Catholic Church." Term paper, Department of Sociology, University of Illinois at Chicago.

Rosaldo, Renato. 1994. "Cultural Citizenship in San Jose, California." *PoLAR: Political and Legal Anthropological Review* 17 (2): 57–64.

Skerry, Peter. 2003–4. "Citizenship Begins at Home: A New Approach to the Civic Integration of Immigrants." *Responsive Community* 14 (1):26–37.

U.S. Conference of Catholic Bishops. 1999. *U.S. Bishops' Conference Preparing Unprecedented Program Calling for "Faithful Citizenship."* November 16. http://www.usccb .org/comm/archives/1999/99-269.shtml. Accessed April 28, 2008.

Warner, R. Stephen. 2005. *A Church of Our Own: Disestablishment and Diversity in American Religion.* New Brunswick, N.J.: Rutgers University Press.

5

Hoy Marchamos, Mañana Votamos

It's All Part of the Curriculum

IRMA M. OLMEDO

This chapter examines educational dimensions of the recent immigrant rights mobilizations in Chicago, including the classroom-based activities of teachers designed to engage students in inquiry on the issues and the participation and perspectives of children as a result of these activities. Many young people attended the March 10 and May 1, 2006, rallies, including children with their families and/or their teachers. Given that both marches took place during school time, it is important to explore what these children were learning about the reasons for marching, the controversies being addressed, the educational meaning of protest, and other related issues. Although many students may acquire this knowledge from families and or the media, schools and teachers also have played a role in helping students think about these issues.

Immigration, Teacher Education, and Curriculum

An extensive body of literature addresses immigration to the United States. Much of this literature is taught in classrooms as part of the history curriculum and traditionally focuses on nineteenth-century waves of immigration, changes in immigrants' places of origin since the mid-1800s, the types of persecution that immigrants were fleeing, and the meaning of the Statue of Liberty (Takaki 1993).

Changes in immigration patterns from the mid-1960s through the beginning of the twenty-first century have stimulated new interdisciplinary research, much of which examines the differences between the old immigration (involving primarily white Europeans) and this new one, highlighting the racialization of immigrants, their diversity, and new patterns of acculturation by the second and subsequent generations (Brettell and Hollifield 2000; De Genova and Ramos-Zayas 2003; Portes and Zhou 1993; Suarez-Orozco, Suarez-Orozco, and Baolian 2005). More recent studies address the educational dimensions of immigration into the United States, which is generally not covered in school curricula (Ream 2005; Suarez-Orozco and Suarez-Orozco 1995, 2001; Trueba and Bartolome 2000). This literature, which can provide guidance to policy-makers and scholars, examines the challenges immigrant families, children, and schools face in light of the growth of immigration and the need for educational policies and curricula that address the special requirements of these populations of students.

As immigrants have continued to cross the southern U.S. border, frequently settling in communities with sizable numbers of fellow countrymen, schools and communities have responded with varying degrees of urgency and com-mitment. The growth of immigration and the continued presence of diverse groups of students in American classrooms have motivated some educators to explore the curriculum's value for social justice. In Chicago, progressive urban educators who seek to improve their expertise in educating children of immi-grants have formed organizations such as Teachers for Social Justice in which participants collaborate to question traditional curricula, addressing issues of racism and economic injustice and challenging the power structures that limit opportunities for the most disadvantaged students.

Current trends encourage teachers to examine how to address controversial issues and make the curriculum relevant to students. For teacher educators, these directions are informed by research on teacher education and critical pedagogy, especially recent studies focusing on urban schools characterized by significant cultural, linguistic, racial, and ethnic diversity. One important body of literature addresses the value of curriculum orientations that seek to connect children's home and community lives with the academic content of the school as explored through the "funds of knowledge" of families (González, Moll, and Amanti 2005; Moll et al. 1992). The concept of funds of knowledge comes from anthropologically based research that seeks to identify the accumulated knowl-edge base of families resulting from their experiences in everyday survival, a kind of cultural capital of which educators may be unaware (Velez-Ibanez and Greenberg 1992). This anthropological orientation toward families encourages teachers to learn about the knowledge that children bring to the classroom from their homes and communities and then to use this knowledge as a building block for curriculum development. Children thus are not seen as blank slates or empty vessels to be filled with new knowledge; rather, teaching requires a recognition that children know many things and that connections must be built from that existing knowledge to new knowledge.

The social studies curriculum can be an important area for engaging in criti-cal pedagogy because that content area covers the study of history and issues of contemporary society, including considerations of race, ethnicity, social class, and relationships among nations and groups. New approaches to teaching social studies highlight the sociocultural goals of history teaching: its focus on enduring human dilemmas and human agency; the interpretive nature of history, with concerns about which voices are heard and which are ignored or omitted from the historical record; the value of connecting the micro and macro levels; and the recognition that history is dynamic and deals with controversy (Banks and Banks 1999; Levstik and Barton 2005; Parker 2005). Unfortunately, social studies content teaching recently has been deemphasized in schools given the focus on reading and math as a result of the No Child Left Behind Act and its orientation toward high-stakes testing. Promising directions nevertheless remain open through new orientations to teaching social studies content to address multiple perspectives, controversial issues, student engagement in inquiry-based learning, and constructivist orientations toward classroom teaching (Bigelow 2006; Lanman and Wendling 2006; Levstik and Barton 2005; Seixas 1993). New teachers often receive exposure to these ideas as part of their educational programs and social studies methods courses.

Research and writing in the curriculum field confirm the value of inquiring into teachers' classroom approaches as a way of understanding the educational processes of schools. Schubert (1996) has written extensively about curriculum theory and a variety of positions that have characterized writing in the field. He identifies four recurrent conceptions on curriculum thought: "intellectual traditionalist, social behaviorist, experientialist, and critical reconstructionist." In theorizing about curriculum and pedagogy, it is important to explore how educators explain what they do in their classrooms and their motivation for teaching particular topics in specific ways. This research also affirms the value of examining teaching philosophy through the rationales that teachers articulate and the ways they organize their classrooms and their instruction. Curriculum is therefore not a static document but rather a resource that can be enhanced by thinking professionals who plan, make decisions, reflect on goals, and consider the needs of their students and the broader community. These teacher interviews illustrate the richness of what may be accomplished when thoughtful educators work collaboratively and creatively to deliver a dynamic curriculum.

Interviewing Teachers about Their Lessons on Immigration

This project involved interviews with teachers, mostly from Chicago Public Schools, to explore what classroom projects, lessons, and activities they undertook in light of the controversies over immigration and the immigrant rights mobilizations. Initially, letters were sent out to school administrators, teachers, and college students to identify teachers willing to be interviewed about classroom-based activities in which they engaged in relation to the immigrant rights mobilizations and immigration controversies. From among those teachers who responded positively, we selected and interviewed twenty-seven, representing five Chicago elementary schools, one high school, one Catholic school, and one suburban school. All except the suburban school had large percentages of students who were still learning the English language; most were of Mexican background, although some were Puerto Rican or Central American. These schools had extensive bilingual education programs and were located in neighborhoods with large Latino populations, including many undocumented immigrants. Since these teachers identified themselves as educators who taught about this topic and were willing to be interviewed, the sample is not necessarily representative of what Chicago's teachers taught about immigration. Nevertheless, the interviews provide a snapshot of how some educators responded to the "teachable moment" created by these mobilizations.

The interview guide included an open-ended six-question protocol that asked about the teachers' immigration-related classroom-based projects, their objectives, what teachers thought students actually learned, and how the teachers would revise the lessons or activities in light of their experiences. I sought to explore not only the kinds of projects developed but also how the teachers legitimated these activities into the curriculum and integrated them into the school's overall educational mission. The teachers' philosophy of their role as critical urban educators is revealed through the ways that these class projects addressed the topic of immigration and the mobilizations.

In addition to the interviews, samples of student work were analyzed to examine the nature of student learning from the projects. Qualitative analysis of the teacher interviews forms the basis of the results reported here.

Teachers' Rationales for Teaching about Immigration

Several themes emerged from the interviews with the teachers. Some of the lessons focused on traditional learning about immigration to the United States, while others focused on issues of citizenship and voting rights and still others involved more activist projects such as writing to members of Congress to express views and organizing to participate in the marches. Most of the interviewees argued that teaching about immigration controversies was important because the children and their families would be affected by whatever decisions the government made. The themes that emerged from the interviews show several different conceptions of teacher identity or role:

* teacher as curriculum developer;
* teacher as anthropologist/ethnographer;

* teacher as citizenship educator;
* teacher as psychologist;
* teacher as sociopolitical activist.

TEACHER AS CURRICULUM DEVELOPER

Teachers occasionally used curricular rationales for their lessons, reasoning that discussing the mobilizations provided an opportunity to integrate language arts and other content areas such as social studies, mathematics, and art content in a thematic approach to teaching. Teachers showed concern with covering the content areas of the curriculum and with meeting the state and district teaching standards. As Emilia[1] argued, "I integrate it to the class. . . . I met the goals they want us to meet. They want us to meet writing goals, they want us to meet reading goals, they want us to meet basic expression, research and so forth. It's all part of the curriculum." Carmen taught a lesson in which she asked children to develop math problems using the march as a theme: for example, "Carlitos went to the immigrant march on Friday. He walked two miles during the four hours. How many miles did Carlitos walk in one hour?"

Some of the teachers who focused on the curriculum developer role conceptualized the study of these mobilizations as a part of the social studies content area, which has recently been downsized as a result of the pressure to prepare students for No Child Left Behind testing, which thus far has been limited to reading and mathematics. Given the emphasis on testing, teachers have been encouraged to focus their classroom time on reading, writing, and mathematics. Teachers who organized lessons on immigration as part of the social studies content area, although adhering to a somewhat traditional rationale for discussing immigration as part of curriculum, nevertheless defined the content area in a rather progressive departure from the "heroes and holidays" approach that too often characterizes elementary school social studies (Banks 1997). Such teachers argued that children need to learn about the "pull/push" factors in immigration, make comparisons between previous immigrant groups and contemporary immigrants, and understand multiple perspectives, such as why some people support and others oppose immigration. Joseph, a fifth-grade special education teacher, taught an ambitious unit on the U.S.-Mexican border: "We started with the Mexican revolution and the battle of Texas, then the Mexican-American War, the creation of the border patrol, [and] the Braceros program, where a lot of immigrants came."

Teachers in this group also included the development of "media literacy" as a component of the curriculum, arguing that students need to understand what they read in local newspapers and newsmagazines, see on television news programs, and learn from Internet news sources. According to Norma, her students learned "how to gather information, how to research, how to question, not just to assume just because it is written down, printed out in a newspaper or [on] the Internet, to just assume that it is right, to critically look at the media in general."

TEACHER AS ANTHROPOLOGIST/ETHNOGRAPHER

All teachers expressed the desire to give priority to the topic of immigration and the mobilizations because the issues affected the students and their families. In addition, some teachers saw themselves as learners in the community and the children and their families as potential teachers. This "funds of knowledge" approach recognizes that families have a great deal of knowledge that comes from their lived experiences and that can serve as a base for curriculum development and classroom instruction (Moll et al. 1992). Many students and their families know what it is like to be undocumented in the United States, to cross the border with all its dangers, and to continue to live in the shadows of urban communities. As Joseph argued, "Many of them have crossed the border, illegally and legally, so that they really understand that and why people would want to cross." These teachers engaged their students in conducting oral histories with family members to learn their experiences firsthand (Olmedo 2006). As Angela explained, "We asked them to go home and ask their parents about it, and they brought a lot of rich material from home." Students were then encouraged to write letters and poems based on their families' experiences.

TEACHER AS CITIZENSHIP EDUCATOR

Some of the teachers connected standard curricular learning with an understanding of the importance of being active citizens in a democratic society—that is, with encouraging and practicing political behavior. Such teachers had children learn how laws are made and how individual citizens can affect government policy. They wanted students to be well informed about current events, to see varying perspectives, and to take and defend stances. According to Mindy, an eighth-grade teacher, "As the issue of the march came up, we were in the middle of talking about the Constitution. I put a lot of emphasis on First Amendment rights and the Bill of Rights in general." She continued, "We also emphasized the right of assembly, which is one of the five freedoms, such as freedom of speech, the right to petition, the right of free press, and so on." Diana offered a similar rationale: "They learned a lot about government stuff through doing this, because we had to talk about how does a bill become a law."

Some teachers also found ways to engage children at a higher level. As Barbara, a sixth-grade teacher, explained, "They wrote a letter to the president, talking about the law and how they felt about it, and then what I had them do was exchange with someone else, and that someone else had to be the president responding to them." Such role-playing helped students not only articulate their positions but also understand other perspectives. Carmen and other teachers had children draft "persuasive" letters to the various members of Congress, including James Sensenbrenner, expressing their opinions of the law and the reasons for their stance. Some of the letters were quite moving, with children explaining that they did not want to be separated from their undocumented parents or siblings. One child questioned the use of the term *illegal* to refer to the undocumented, arguing that they had not robbed or killed anyone but were only here to work and that "immigrants produce many supplies we need, like food, clothes and other important stuff." Barbara and other teachers also organized classroom debates in which students considered varying perspectives, such as those of Minutemen and immigrant rights activists.

TEACHER AS PSYCHOLOGIST

In 2006, a California eighth-grader, Anthony Soltero, committed suicide after the principal of his school threatened to suspend him for attending an immigrant mobilization march. Some educators may underestimate the fear and emotional turmoil that children experience when they perceive themselves or members of their family as threatened. Teachers who embraced the psychologist role were concerned that classrooms be a safe environment where students could express themselves freely, learn, and feel good about themselves. As George, an eighth-grade teacher, explained, "Children should be made to feel safe discussing this topic in school." Another eighth-grade teacher, Juan, had similar concerns and started his lessons with class meetings at which "students share stories [and] fears and explored what they understood. . . . A lot of times it was having them talk and having them verbalize a lot of this anxiety of what was going on at that time." Andrés, a social studies teacher, was sensitive to how the controversy was affecting the families and used that as a principal rationale: "Every student was affected by it in one way or another by their own family and by relatives. . . . As an educator, [I] couldn't run away from it." Said George, "The students get to explore themselves, and ask those questions: Who am I? Why am I me?" Emilia wanted students "to basically come out of their shell and not be shy, speak for what they believe in." Geraldo offered a similar rationale: "It validated their culture. They learned that they have a voice, that they are not alone in the city."

In this conception, teachers focused on students' emotional well-being, seeking to use academic learning as a tool for personal affirmation and to constitute the school as a kind of sanctuary where children would be protected.

Antrop-González explores the idea of school as haven, arguing that one small alternative high school in Chicago has "sanctuary-like attributes" that include "multiple definitions of caring relationships between students and their teachers, the importance of a familial-like school environment, the necessity of psychologically and physically safe school spaces, and allowing students a forum in which they are encouraged to affirm their racial/ethnic pride" (2006, 273). Valenzuela (1999) has also theorized about this important role of schooling in relation to U.S.-Mexican youth, characterizing its absence as a form of "subtractive schooling."

TEACHER AS SOCIOPOLITICAL ACTIVIST

Teachers who embraced this role considered themselves advocates for their students and wanted to model social activism. Mindy "grew up as a social activist because of a church that was socially active, and I boycotted grapes and lettuce. . . . That is the Chicano civil rights movement or the parallel." Her personal experiences thus influenced her approach to the topic of immigration. She wanted the children "to start to really realize at this age—eleven and twelve and thirteen years old—they are starting to understand the political implications of what these things mean . . . how that plays out and how discrimination and racism . . . have inhibited immigration." Graciela, a third-grade teacher, sought to teach her students that "protest might change the government, the politicians' point of view." Likewise, Carrie, a seventh-grade teacher, wanted her students to learn that "they have a voice and their voice matters, and if they get together and unite, that they can actually be heard."

Many of these teachers participated in the march in solidarity with the community. Emilia estimated that 70 percent of her students participated, and she joined in "because I felt that I love everything it stands for. It stands for social justice, and the kids really know how, I make them aware of that, and we are really into government, politics, ancient history, and how it's affected us in the modern world as well. . . . I am teaching you guys to be vocal, be active in your community and standing up for yourself." Andrés, one of the older teachers interviewed, was reminded of the African American civil rights movement: "As being at my age—close to fifty—it is probably the closest event as I have seen since the civil rights movement. So it is real big to me. I lived through the civil rights, and my neighborhood was affected by civil rights, . . . and my neighborhood changed. . . . You can't teach people this. It's not in the books. They have to be a part of that."

Teachers had to take personal days to participate in the march, but George believed that doing so was worthwhile: "Because I am politically active and an advocate for my students and their families, I wanted to be out with them." Other teachers, in contrast, wanted to participate in the march but also wanted to be at the school to help students who were not marching be involved. Alicia, a special education teacher, was torn by that dilemma: "What about my kids who come to school?" She did not march but used the occasion to have students read a book about a janitors' strike in Los Angeles, ¡Sí Se Puede!, and connect that issue to the march. She also showed a video of the March 10 mobilization and had students make posters about the march.

The teachers who identified as sociopolitical activists often benefited from supportive administrators. Reinaldo, a sixth-grade teacher, appreciated the backing from his principal: "He said what he could do is rent us two or three buses and we could choose students from the middle school, bring parents, make banners, bring the custodial staff, and go and march." Similarly, Lillian, an eighth-grade teacher, reported that "our principal allowed our student council and upper grades to participate." Such principals considered the event a kind of field trip and therefore a legitimate activity for their students, an extension of the curriculum. Marta, a teacher from a Catholic school, acknowledged the rhetorical support of her school's administration as a result of its religious mission: "As Catholics, part of our deal is to be on the side of people who are marginalized. Immigrants are being marginalized by this law, and our motto is to be men and women for others." However, Marta also argued that her school's administration offered a manipulative response in arguing against student attendance at the march: "Well, you have an education, and so you should exercise your right to obtain that education." Marta challenged that position, telling students, "No one is asking you to give up your education. To give up one day of school is a very different thing than to be giving up an entire education." She thus taught her students to critique the principal's flowery rhetoric and to recognize the gap between that language and genuine support for the cause.

Activist teachers who lacked supportive administrators used a variety of strategies to circumvent this lack of support. Juanita and her colleague "pretty much did our own thing." They believed that they could defend what they were teaching in spite of administrators' advice not to get "too political."

An Integrated Approach

All of the teachers blended aspects of these five orientations, which are not contradictory but rather represent meaningful teaching that helps students investigate, understand, sympathize, and take action—in short, critical pedagogy in action. The richest interviews came from teachers who integrated all of these perspectives at a school whose mission valued such integration. This school caters to native English speakers as well as native Spanish speakers. Immigration is an ongoing theme in both the fifth and eighth grades and is incorporated into many areas of the curriculum. These teachers spoke about the importance of having children make connections—from literature, historical issues they studied, conversations with parents, and television programs. Samuel explained, "We set up three components of immigration: the history of immigration, immigration to Chicago, and immigration today. . . . We looked at four immigrations to Chicago: Swedish, Polish, Chinese, and Mexican. The students investigated some of the reasons [these groups] immigrated to Chicago as well as the areas that they settled in Chicago. . . . We also visited some of the museums. . . . The kids had initially created a biography of an immigrant." The goal was for children "to realize that the U.S. was a nation of immigrants." According to another teacher at the same school, Margarita, "In eighth grade my focus is for them to understand the economic basis of the United States. When we did the Civil War, we saw how slaves helped boost the economy. In doing this unit, I asked them to evaluate how immigrants helped boost the economy, . . . how without the labor of immigrants, the economy of the country would change." Another activity had students explore the stances of the president and elected representatives, watching George W. Bush's address on the immigration issue and looking online at congressional voting records: students then "created a timeline of immigrant policies and they added to this timeline the recent policies that are going on."

The teachers in this school argued that academic study should be supplemented with opportunities for children to take real-world action. According to Clara, "Last year, the kids really wanted to do something that helped immigrants. We did some fund-raising stuff to donate money to an immigration association or an organization that helps immigrants." The class regularly goes to a community center "where they help people fill out their immigration documents." Children thus gain firsthand experience with the citizenship application process.

One important theme in teacher education is the effective preparation of educators who offer instruction on controversial issues with courage and conviction, especially when these controversies involve issues of race, ethnicity, social class, and the law. Undocumented immigration and the immigrant rights mobilizations offered a "teachable moment" that propelled these teachers beyond the formal curriculum found in textbooks and district documents to a critical pedagogy that legitimated controversy as curriculum. The teachers we interviewed framed their rationales in the rhetoric of "curricular goals and standards," "media literacy," and "citizenship education," interpreting those phrases to maximize opportunities for students to engage in the creation and exploration of a dynamic curriculum.

Our interviewees demonstrated the value of curriculum orientations that seek to connect children's home and community lives with the school's academic content. In this way, these teachers gave voice to the children and their families, thereby challenging media portrayals of "illegal aliens." Acknowledging the immigration experiences of the children's families as legitimate curriculum content takes issue with the deficit conceptions of minority students that too often characterize educational policy development.

Educators in urban schools characterized by cultural, linguistic, racial, and ethnic diversity have opportunities to create a critical pedagogy that affirms the value of such diversity. In personifying their roles not only as curriculum developers but also as anthropologist/ethnographers, citizenship educators, psychologists, and sociopolitical activists, these teachers demonstrate that education can be a tool for liberation.

Educators and schools must find ways to help students understand the nature of national and local sociopolitical events and how they affect students' lives, particularly when those students come from families that are generally underserved by societal institutions because they are poor, non-English-speaking, or lack documentation or citizenship rights. Education that helps students formulate and answer questions and take the next steps toward action can help prepare students for effective citizenship in a democratic society.

Students need to be able to understand media rhetoric, sort out facts from opinions and truth from propaganda, and make appropriate, informed judgments. Schools are the best place for this education to take place in a safe environment that recognizes students' rights to know, to make decisions, and to act based on their best judgments. Teachers who value student inquiry will not avoid addressing controversial issues in their classrooms but will seek ways to engage students, in the process helping to create future citizens who can challenge oppressive and unjust sociopolitical policies and practices.

Note

1. All teachers' names used in this chapter are pseudonyms.

References

Antrop-González, R. 2006. "Toward the School as Sanctuary Concept in Multicultural Urban Education: Implications for Small High School Reform." *Curriculum Inquiry* 36 (3): 273–301.

Banks, J. A. 1997. *Teaching Strategies for Ethnic Studies.* 6th ed. Boston: Allyn and Bacon.

Banks, J. A., and C. A. McGee Banks. 1999. *Teaching Strategies for the Social Studies: Decision Making and Citizen-Action.* New York: Longman.

Bigelow, Bill. 2006. *The Line between Us: Teaching about the Border and Mexican Immigration.* Milwaukee: Rethinking Schools.

Brettell, C., and J. Hollifield. 2000. *Migration Theory: Talking across Disciplines.* New York: Routledge.

De Genova, N., and A. Ramos-Zayas. 2003. *Latino Crossings: Mexicans, Puerto Ricans, and the Politics of Citizenship.* New York: Routledge.

González, N., L. C. Moll, and C. Amanti. 2005. *Funds of Knowledge: Theorizing Practices in Households, Communities, and Classrooms.* Mahwah, N.J.: Erlbaum.

Lanman, B. A., and L. M. Wendling. 2006. *Preparing the Next Generation of Oral Historians: An Anthology of Oral History Education.* Lanham, Md.: Rowman and Littlefield.

Levstik, L., and K. C. Barton. 2005. *Doing History: Investigating with Children in Elementary and Middle Schools.* 3rd. ed. Mahwah, N.J.: Erlbaum.

Moll, L., C. Amanti, D. Neff, and N. González. 1992. "Funds of Knowledge for Teaching: Using a Qualitative Approach to Connect Homes and Classrooms." *Theory into Practice* 31 (2): 132–41.

Olmedo, I. M. 2006. "Creating Contexts for Studying History with Students Learning English." In *Preparing the Next Generation of Oral Historians: An Anthology of Oral History Education,* ed. B. A. Lanman and L. M. Wendling, 163–70. Lanham, Md.: Rowman and Littlefield.

Parker, W. C. 2005. *Social Studies in Elementary Education.* Boston: Pearson.

Portes, A., and M. Zhou. 1993. "The New Second Generation: Segmented Assimilation and Its Variants." *Annals of the American Academy of Political and Social Science* 530 (1): 74–96.

Ream, R. K. 2005. *Uprooting Children: Mobility, Social Capital, and Mexican American Underachievement.* New York: LFB.

Schubert, W. H. 1996. "Perspectives on Four Curriculum Traditions." *Educational Horizons* 74 (4): 169–76.

Seixas, P. 1993. "Parallel Crises: History and the Social Studies Curriculum in the USA." *Journal of Curriculum Studies* 25 (3): 235–50.

Suarez-Orozco, C., and M. Suarez-Orozco. 1995. *Transformations: Migration, Family Life and Achievement Motivation among Latino Adolescents.* Stanford: Stanford University Press.

———. 2001. *Children of Immigration.* Cambridge: Harvard University Press.

Suarez-Orozco, M., C. Suarez-Orozco, and Desiree Baolian. 2005. *New Immigration: An Interdisciplinary Reader.* New York: Routledge.

Takaki, R. 1993. *A Different Mirror: A History of Multicultural America.* Boston: Little, Brown.

Trueba, E., and L. Bartolome. 2000. *Immigrant Voices: In Search of Educational Equity.* Lanham, Md.: Rowman and Littlefield.

Valenzuela, A. 1999. *Subtractive Schooling: U.S.-Mexican Youth and the Politics of Caring.* Albany: State University of New York Press.

Velez-Ibanez, C., and J. B. Greenberg. 1992. Formation and Transformation of Funds of Knowledge among U.S.-Mexican Households." *Anthropology and Education Quarterly* 23 (4): 313–35.

6

Labor Joins la Marcha

How New Immigrant Activists Restored the Meaning of May Day

LEON FINK

Two contradictory impressions first beckon for understanding organized labor's reaction to Chicago's March 10 movement. By one frame, the unions were latecomers, out of touch with the depth of frustrations welling up in the Latino community and unaware of the scale of a mobilizing process centered in Mexican hometown associations, Spanish-language radio stations, and church pews and basements. As someone "who doesn't move off WBBM [a local radio station], I'd never heard of Pistola, Pistolero, or whatever his name is," admitted Tom Balanoff, president of Local 1, Service Employees International Union (SEIU), who was, in fact, the first of the city's major union leaders to support the marches. The Chicago Federation of Labor (CFL), which loosely coordinated citywide labor strategies, was slower yet to comprehend the new phenomenon. When Jorge Mujica contacted the CFL about supporting the 2006 May Day march, a staff director suggested that he get in touch with the Illinois Labor History Society, which had organized a modest program the preceding two years at the newly installed "free speech" monument at the original Haymarket corner of Randolph and Desplaines. According to Mujica, the director asked, "Who are you? Why don't you join our event?" He responded that she did not understand: "You're talking about a hundred-person event; we're talking about a half million people. We'd like the CFL to be with us! . . . They never quite got it."

But another frame must also be considered. In the months leading up to the May 1 megamarch, Chicago's labor movement forged a strong and enduring connection with the new tide of immigrant rights mobilization. A select group of labor unions embraced the new movement with gusto, effectively providing the infrastructural funding for subsequent May Day rallies and generally lifting their voices to demand legalization alongside more sweeping immigration and labor law reforms. Even more important, the protests brought to the fore a cadre of organizers—both inside and outside the unions—who by their energy and creative tactics gave a new, expanded meaning to the term *labor movement*. Ten years earlier, such an alliance between organized labor and those—including undocumented workers—demanding a liberalization of immigration laws would have been unimaginable. In short, how labor came to belong to the immigration rights movement is significant.

By the time of the Chicago mobilizations, a sea change had transformed organized labor's outlook on immigration policy. "Next to the abundant economic opportunities available to wage earners in this country, immigration has been the factor most guilty of the incohesiveness of American labor," declared Selig Perlman in his classic formulation of the aims and strategy of the American labor movement (1928, 168). According to this conventional wisdom, embraced at least from World War I through the 1960s by the American Federation of Labor and later the AFL-CIO, new immigrants—and especially uncontrollable waves of new immigrants—constituted a "cheap labor" threat to the maintenance of an American standard of living, as vouchsafed by collective bargaining and strong labor unions. Operating in this light, the labor movement had supported a crackdown on Chinese immigration as early as 1880, backed the tight quotas of the 1924 restrictive legislation, and applauded the termination of the Bracero program in the early 1960s. By 1965, during a period of economic growth and liberal reform, the labor federation endorsed the Immigration and Nationality Act, including the abolition of racist and ethnic quotas, but twenty years later, in a more hostile political and economic climate and again worried by an influx of strangers, the AFL-CIO strongly supported the Immigration Reform and Control Act (IRCA) of 1986, combining amnesty for several million undocumented workers with promised "employer sanctions" on further hiring of the undocumented. Yet neither IRCA nor the subsequent restrictionist legislation of the early 1990s stemmed the tide of new arrivals (Milkman 2006, 114–24).

Circumstances on the ground (more specifically, in workplaces, where unions were increasingly losing their grip) ultimately forced a change in attitude as well as policy. Harbingers had already foretold a more robust approach to immigrant organizing in specific unions and locales. In Southern California, for example, the International Ladies Garment Workers Union (ILGWU) embraced new immigrant workers as early as the 1970s, and the United Farm Workers had given the nation its first great Hispanic labor icon in Cesar Chavez (Milkman 2006, 116–17). But in the 1990s, especially within the reform regime of newly elected AFL-CIO president John Sweeney (former head of the SEIU), signs of a strategic change were visible, first suggested by Sweeney's 1998 visit to Mexico. Eager to organize the masses of nonunion workers, labor's new leaders quickly discovered that the nation's immigration policy stood directly in their way. Time and again, campaigns foundered when U.S. Immigration and Naturalization Service (INS) tactics, such as do-not-hire letters dispatched to Nebraska and Iowa meatpacking plants in 1998, ran potential workers out of town. In 1999, the Holiday Inn Express in Minneapolis responded to a Hotel and Restaurant Workers (HERE) organizing drive by turning over nine undocumented workers to the INS; that same year, San Francisco's SEIU janitor campaign was similarly devastated by a massive INS deportation. In this climate, the AFL-CIO Executive Council formally declared in February 2000 that the employer sanctions it had backed in the 1986 legislation had failed and that the only viable solution was to offer amnesty so that undocumented immigrants could assume full rights, including union membership, as American citizens (Murolo and Chitty 2001, 315). Hard numbers have accompanied the unions' change of heart: immigrant membership in unions has risen about 30 percent from 1996 to 2006, when the nearly two million unionized immigrant workers represented 12 percent of the union totals (McGee 2007).

If the national labor mood had moved steadily in the direction of greater sympathy toward the new immigrants' cause, the positive feelings in Chicago were likely ahead of the curve. For multiple reasons, not merely tolerance but an active alliance, however uneven and slightly delayed, emerged between the unions and the new immigrant activism. The immigrant rights marches of early 2006 caught local labor organizations at a particularly propitious moment. With a strong self-image as residents of both a blue-collar and an immigrant city, Chicagoans, though often riled by ethnic as well as racial divisions, had long celebrated the hardworking immigrant arrival eager to support a family. More-over, in the midst of a general flattening (even outright decline) of population in many of its urban Midwest neighbors, a steady influx of new immigrants—especially Mexicans but also Poles, Central Americans, and South Asians—had contributed to continuing growth in the metropolitan Chicago region. Although the "new immigration" brought some social tensions—especially manifest in youth gang and drug rivalry between Latinos and African Americans and strains on public resources such as schools and hospitals—it did not generate the same shock waves in Chicago as in Southern California, Arizona, and other centers of anti-immigrant mobilization. Perhaps more important, several key Chicago unions—particularly SEIU, UNITE-HERE (formed by HERE's 2004 merger with the garment and textile worker union, the Union of Needletrades, Industrial, and Textile Employees [UNITE]), and Local 881 of the United Food and Commercial Workers (UFCW)—had already formed positive connections with the new immigrant and especially Latino communities at both the national and local levels. To the extent that these unions had incorporated a community approach to organizing, they were quick both to sympathize with and to align their collective strength with the defense of immigrant workers, documented or undocumented. Finally, in addition to the dynamics within individual unions, Chicago labor as a whole was more politically attuned than usual to signals emerging from the city's sizable Latino constituency. In the months leading up to the May Day 2006 march, the CFL had taken as its top political priority passage of a "big box ordinance"—a minimum-wage measure specifically aimed at retail giant Wal-Mart, which was targeting African American and Latino neighborhoods. In a rare confrontation with Mayor Richard M. Daley, who had announced his opposition to the proposal, labor, desperate to stem the further loss of high-wage, union jobs, eagerly reached out to minority communities. (Indeed, Daley vetoed the measure two months after it passed the city council with substantial Hispanic aldermanic support in July 2006.)

The SEIU's Balanoff first learned of the budding Chicago movement from Artemio Arreola in the weeks leading up to March 10. A school janitor in a western suburb, Arreola embodied the intersection of labor and immigrant community activism. At once active in his local union (he had participated in several campaigns for Locals 1 and 73) and in his hometown Michoacán association, the forty-one-year-old Arreola had already served an extended political apprenticeship. Gravitating to the regional capital of Morelia following high school and working as a computer teacher, he early on witnessed the power of well-disciplined teachers' union strikes. He also quickly absorbed himself in political issues, even running at age twenty-three as a candidate for state representative. In 1989, drawing on family connections, Arreola moved to Chicago, where he soon found himself working in a factory where management was colluding with a corrupt SEIU local boss at the expense of workers who "didn't even know they had a union." A reform campaign that ultimately aligned his shop with Local 1 served as Arreola's baptism in American union politics. In the same period, he was attracted to the hometown associations as a practical resource for resolving everyday immigrant social problems. He soon became president of Club Oaxaca, even though it was not his hometown state but that of his aunt. He helped charter the first Chicago Michoacán club in 1996 and traveled to California to inaugurate a nationwide Michoacán Federation. In 2003, Arreola and the federation joined HERE and other unions in the Immigrant Workers Freedom Ride (see chap. 1), demanding federal legislation to offer legalization and a path to citizenship for the undocumented. Continually working on multiple fronts, Arreola also nurtured an acquaintance with Omar López, a longtime Chicago Mexican American activist, head of the Confederation of Mexican Clubs, and founder of the Instituto de los Mexicanos en el Exterior, an elected council of Mexican diaspora representatives. Though Arreola lost his first bid for election to the council in 2004, he worked with López to find ways that the Instituto might work with the Mexican government to aid Mexican workers in the United States.

When the House of Representatives passed the Sensenbrenner Bill in December 2005, Arreola's extended networks and previous experience left him as well positioned as anyone in Chicago to respond. A rising sense of urgency had already led SEIU staffers and rank-and-file leaders to push for a nationwide Latino Caucus within the union, a move catalyzed by a late 2005 meeting in Puerto Rico that Arreola attended alongside SEIU vice president Eliseo Medina, a former United Farm Worker activist who had emerged as one of the union's leading voices on new immigrant issues. Such meetings led to growing national networks and new calls for action. Recognizing Arreola's uncommon connections to the Mexican working-class community, Balanoff released Arreola from other obligations to organize full-time on the immigration rights front. January and February 2006 found him meeting regularly with community groups at Casa Michoacán, sessions that led to the creation of the March 10 Coalition, a leadership committee uniting the city's major Mexican American organizations and many longtime activists in anticipation of a march from Union Park to Federal Plaza.

Balanoff arrived at the March 10 rally immediately after returning from Europe and found a jubilant but somewhat disorganized atmosphere: "There was some struggling on stage, and I realized no one really had control of the mike." A few days later, Arreola was invited to address the SEIU State Council, where he found everyone wondering how organizers had staged such a successful march.

People would undoubtedly have been further surprised to learn that not only Arreola but several other members of the March 10 Coalition self-consciously identified with the labor movement. Among the most experienced was Jorge Mujica. By the time he arrived in the United States in the late 1980s, Mujica had passed through several cycles of radical labor politics in Mexico. The Mexico City native had come of age amid the student movement of the 1960s, and he and his comrades at the National Autonomous University of Mexico had reached out to peasants losing their land to try to "unionize the countryside." Mujica also joined the city's left-wing independent union movement before settling into a career as a journalist and writer. After arriving in Chicago at the tail end of the first amnesty wave in the late 1980s, Mujica had his first experience with a U.S. union; unfortunately, its practices reminded him of the corrupt Mexican unions he had hoped to leave behind. In the wake of the 1986 amnesty, when workers in SEIU's Building Service Local 25, run by Eugene Moats, sought to drop the false names and social security numbers they had acquired to gain employment, the union administration refused to recognize their seniority rights (Gruelle 1996, 8–9). Mujica subsequently took a job with the original production team at Chicago's Spanish-language Univision outlet and helped organize technicians there into a union in 1995.

As a self-identified "radical labor activist," Mujica watched the city's immigration rights mobilization begin from an unexpected social base. In early 2005, the local Latino community was shocked when Aurora resident Rosanna Pulido emerged as the public face of the Illinois Minutemen, which confronted would-be immigrants at the Mexican border and called for repatriation of illegals. When local Spanish-radio DJ Rafael "El Pistolero" Pulido started talking about the threat of the Minutemen, community activist Emma Lozano challenged him on the air to do something. The first demonstration quickly materialized entirely from within the Mexican community, as some thirty thousand people assembled in Back of the Yards—"a private party for our own consumption," in Mujica's words. With the added threat of the Sensenbrenner legislation, Mujica, Arreola, and López became determined to tap the energy evident in Back of the Yards for greater political impact.

A third early participant in the March 10 movement was Martin Unzueta, a salaried organizer with the Chicago Workers' Collaborative in Little Village. This group brought four busloads of people to the march, indirectly closing down hundreds of workplaces by organizing workers' petitions demanding the right to participate. Unzueta saw "no fear" in the faces of those who boarded the buses: the typical reaction was, "Okay, I left my job. I don't care if they fire me." Unzueta was well able to gauge the fear of joblessness among the undocumented. Born in Mexico City and drawn into radical politics as a high school student in 1968, he transferred his activism to the printing trade before moving to Chicago and taking a job at a printing firm in 1996. In March 2002, the U.S. Supreme Court issued a controversial decision in *Hoffman Plastic Compounds, Inc. v. National Labor Relations Board*, finding that an undocumented immigrant worker illegally fired from his job for union organizing was not entitled to compensation for lost wages (National Immigration Law Center 2004). Soon thereafter, a friend of Unzueta's who was working to organize a nonunion print shop was fired—a victim of the *Hoffman* decision. Unzueta worked with labor, church, and immigrant organizations to "understand what had happened." After educating himself on the issues, he began conducting workshops on worker rights at Pilsen's Rudy Lozano Library: "Some people asked me, 'Why you gonna do worker rights? That's the work of the unions.' I said, 'No, it's the work of the community.'" In 2004, such sentiments carried him into the Chicago Workers' Collaborative, an organization started in 1999 that offers multipronged programs in the Mexican American community and works to secure rights for "temporary workers." In Unzueta's words, "The labor movement is not only the people who sit in the unions; I think the labor movement is everybody who is a worker."

Reclaiming May Day

As immigrant rights activists sought to turn the growing backlash against the Sensenbrenner Bill into a nationwide mobilization, Chicago's March 10 Coalition leaders adopted an explicit labor strategy, reaching out to the city's unions and selecting May 1, International Workers' Day, for the next immigrant megamarch. The date was an obvious choice for the Mexican-born activists, who had turned out for years in the *zócalos* (central squares) of Mexico City and other towns for May Day celebrations that increasingly served as sites of protest during the 1970s and 1980s. Recalled Mujica, "We won the right to express May Day as a day for workers to fight, not [a day for] a mere parade: nobody works on May Day, everybody marches on May Day. And that's what we were proposing here."

Arreola became Chicago's May Day ambassador abroad. He first met with both the Instituto de los Mexicanos en el Exterior in Mexico City (where some sixty U.S. cities were represented by two hundred delegates) and the Michoacán club federation in Morelia. He moved on to Los Angeles, where, in the days leading up to the city's huge March 25 mobilization, he continued his pitch in a complicated political setting. Nativo López-Vigil and other Los Angeles community leaders were loathe to cede momentum to a "labor day" focus, targeting other dates for what they were calling a Great American Boycott, and Los Angeles County Labor Federation leader María Elena Durazo was initially "too busy" to see Arreola. Ultimately, however, the idea of the May Day march won out.

Rallying Labor's Rank and File

Margarita Klein, Chilean-born staff director of UNITE-HERE and a Chicago immigration activist since the mid-1980s, received a phone call from Jorge Mujica and his wife, Maria Teresa, on March 12, 2006. "Excited" about the May Day idea, they urged her to summon a Labor Committee of the March 10 Coalition to plan for the new actions. Klein, the daughter of a victim of General Augusto Pinochet's violence against left-labor advocates, was eager to jump on the bandwagon, and she soon pulled together a core of about a dozen Latino organizers, including Laura Garza and others from the SEIU as well as representatives from UFCW Local 881; the United Electrical, Radio, and Machine Workers of America; and the Jobs with Justice coalition. The group eventually drew in others, including representatives of the steelworkers, the laborers, the operating engineers, and the Labor Council for Latin American Advancement (the official Latino constituency group within the AFL-CIO), who would rally the troops for May Day marches over the next three years.

A select but powerful group of representatives of Chicago's larger labor community thus partnered with the immigrant rights activists. In SEIU and UNITE-HERE, the coalition drew on the city's two most dynamic unions, although many of the conservative building trades that had traditionally buttressed the CFL were missing from the front ranks of immigration mobilization. Still, changing realities within the labor movement were apparent. According to Balanoff, Bill

Dugan, president of Operating Engineers Local 150, "is as conservative as they come but got very much into this issue because of workers they're dealing with." Perhaps the most conspicuous union absence from the May Day organizing was the American Federation of State, County, and Municipal Employees, which coalition organizers explained as motivated by the union's constituency of prison guards (who might be especially sensitive to helping "illegal" immigrant workers) and by running tensions between new immigrants and African Americans (who comprise a large segment of the union's base). SEIU Local 1, which faced similar tensions given that Latinos accounted for just under a third of the forty thousand members, was very conscious of involving its own black leadership within the immigrant rights protests: said Balanoff, "We tried to connect African American and Latino workers, we purposefully put African Americans in our press conferences and speaking roles. One of the basic principles of trade unionism is unity, right?"

One of the core members of the Labor Committee was Moises Zavala, an organizer for UFCW Local 881. Raised in Back of the Yards by his Michoacán parents, Zavala first worked as community organizer on the South Side, targeting housing-related issues. He initially connected with the UFCW in the mid-1990s as a community worker and then moved on to UNITE before returning to Local 881 in 1998 as a grocery store organizer. He now serves as both an executive board member and director of the local's organizing department. For a diverse union roughly equally divided between white and minority workers, involvement in immigrant rights issues was a matter of necessity. Just as national food processors such as Smithfield Foods have threatened to call federal immigration officials as a means of disrupting union campaigns, Chicago has seen fears regarding new immigrants figure in the decline of a once-solid unionized grocery workforce (Geary 2005). In Chicago, the big unionized chains (Jewel, Dominick's, Cub Foods) have declined or at best remained stagnant, while non-union "ethnic supermarkets" or *supermercados* (with an estimated 90 percent Latino workforce) have expanded rapidly. Immigration, the union discovered, was a key issue. In "probing" (sending organizers into the *supermercados* as workers), what Zavala calls the "fear factor" among new immigrants proved a major obstacle. Rather than complain and risk losing their jobs, many workers put up with abuse. According to Zavala, "If we're going to organize those workplaces, then we need to understand those workers and what affects them." At the national level, the UFCW sued Immigration and Customs Enforcement in 2007 to delay raids on immigrant workplaces. Such police actions, argues Zavala, "spill over from attacks on individuals to affect their community and institutions. We took it on as a human rights issue."

Zavala thus sees the May Day marches as part and parcel of Local 881's attempt to form an organic bond with the workers' community: "Unions need to become part of the workers' vision, especially that [the unions] are the best option for immigrant workers." Union involvement helped extend the marchers' demands beyond green cards to worker health care, a living wage, union rights, and job security: "It's about more than 'I need my papers.'"

Indeed, its connections to the March 10 Coalition and the May Day marches have led Local 881 to undertake an imaginative—perhaps unprecedented—initiative with the Mexican consulate in Chicago. Because the consulate already reaches deep into the immigrant community (receiving some six hundred visits per day from displaced Mexican nationals, most of them workers), officials there could help overcome the fear factor. The consulate recently has begun providing information to employees on such issues as job safety and basic worker rights and even, according to Zavala, "literature on our union." To further such connections, Zavala joined a Latino labor delegation that traveled to Mexico City in May 2008 courtesy of Mexico's secretary of foreign relations. He and other group members, including a representative from the Chicago Workers' Collaborative and organizations from other parts of the United States, met with government and union leaders from both "official" and "independent" federations.

* * *

Chicago's May 1, 2006, immigrant rights rally had a decidedly more confident tone than its March 10 predecessor: in Unzueta's words, "It was more like we know who we are and what we are." This and subsequent May Day marches took on more of a Mexican style, with chanting and shouting—"something that we were exporting" to the United States.

The reemergence of mass May Day celebrations in the United States likely could only have come about via an outside stimulus. May Day marches began in this country on May 1, 1886, when the forerunner of the American Federation of Labor inaugurated a nationwide wave of strikes to win the eight-hour workday. The Haymarket bombing and riot in Chicago on May 4 of that year inextricably linked the May Day marches to the left wing of the workers' movement, however, and the September Labor Day became the official U.S. workers' holiday in 1894. The Mexican celebration of May Day, conversely, fits with the worldwide tradition of an International Workers' Day, loosely connecting the martyrdom of the original eight-hour marchers to continuing demands for social justice. Thus, when immigrant rights supporters prepared for the May Day marches in Chicago, they did so within an interpretive frame of their own choosing, a spirit of innocent suffering.

In many respects, participation in the March 10 Coalition may be considered one of the Chicago labor movement's brightest, most creative recent moves. Union support not only helped to bring the needs and aspirations of the area's Latino community broad public notice but also strengthened labor's ties to a vital sector of the Chicago labor force. In this light, it is all the more curious that Arreola remembers some resistance when he first raised the May Day march idea in a meeting with Chicago labor union leaders. "You don't know the history," they said. Many people think of May Day as a "bad day for Chicago," when there was "killing the police and all that." He responded, "It's time to write our own history. . . . In the rest of the world, people from the laboring class take to the streets and talk about the martyrs of Chicago." He also told the naysayers that the March 10, 2006, march had taken place without their assistance, "and we'll do it again." After Artemio's moment of defiance, Tom Balanoff cut him off, saying, "I'm convinced" and officially moving to embrace the proposal. In deference to the CFL's "official" celebration, march organizers rearranged their route to pass by the Haymarket monument at Randolph and Desplaines. "Most of the immigrant community had no idea there was a monument there," explained Jorge Mujica.

Local education worked both ways, however. In April 2008, Richard Berg, the newly elected reform-minded president of Chicago Teamsters Local 743, spoke at an organizational meeting of the Labor Council for Latin American Advancement for that year's May Day march. According to Berg, members of his local had marched with Martin Luther King in Washington, D.C., in 1963, and they were determined to march again in the struggle for "full equality." It was important to the labor movement, Berg continued, to make May Day "big and strong." The "immigrant community, mostly Germans," he reminded his audience, had "started" May Day in 1886. In commemoration of those who fought for the eight-hour day, it had ultimately become "international workers' day" everywhere but in the United States. Berg thanked the members of his overwhelmingly Mexican American audience "for bringing May Day back to us." Balanoff similarly cited the immigrant-worker coalition as uniting the SEIU's Eastern Europeans (especially Poles) and Latinos: "I had had this fantasy that some day I'd march on May Day with masses of workers. I just never realized it would happen this way."

References

Arreola, Artemio. 2008. Interview by Leon Fink. May 30, Chicago.

Balanoff, Thomas. 2008. Interview by Leon Fink. May 30, Chicago.

Becerra, Ramon. 2008. Interview by Amalia Pallares. May 14, Chicago.

Geary, Bob. 2005. "Tar Heel Pinkertons: Smithfield Foods Is Anti-Union in the Worst Way." July 20. http://www.indyweek.com/gyrobase/Content?oid=oid%3A24777. Accessed July 1, 2008.

Gruelle, Martha. 1996. "What Happens When Union Officials Are Paid Like Management?" *Labor Notes*, October, 8–9. http://www.cpcs.umb.edu/labor_notes/files/21108.pdf. Accessed June 27, 2008.

Kelland, Lara. 2005. "Putting Haymarket to Rest?" *Labor: Studies in Working Class History of the Americas* 2 (2): 31–38.

Klein, Margarita. 2008. Interview by Leon Fink. June 3, Chicago.

Labor Council for Latin American Advancement. 2008. Meeting attended by author. April 23. Teamsters Local 743 Hall, Chicago.

McGee, Patrick. 2007. "More Immigrants Joining Unions." *Fort Worth Star-Telegram,* September 3.

Milkman, Ruth. 2006. *L.A. Story: Immigrant Workers and the Future of the U.S. Labor Movement.* New York: Sage.

Mujica, Jorge. 2008. Interview by Leon Fink. May 22, Chicago.

Murolo, Priscilla, and A. B. Chitty. 2001. *From the Folks Who Brought You the Weekend.* New York: New Press.

National Immigration Law Center. 2004. "Statement on 'Evaluating a Temporary Guest Worker Proposal.'" February 12. http://www.nilc.org/immlawpolicy/cdev/NILC_statement_Guest-Worker_Prog.pdf. Accessed May 13, 2009.

Perlman, Selig. 1928. *A Theory of the Labor Movement.* New York: Macmillan.

Thindwa, James. 2008. Interview by Leon Fink. May 20, Chicago.

Unzueta, Martin. 2008. Interview by Leon Fink. May 22, Chicago.

Zavala, Moises. 2008. Interview by Leon Fink. June 2, Chicago.

PART 3

Agency

7

Marchando al Futuro

Latino Immigrant Rights Leadership in Chicago

LEONARD G. RAMÍREZ,

JOSÉ PERALES-RAMOS,

JOSÉ ANTONIO ARELLANO

According to an editorial in the Latino newspaper *La Raza,* the July 1, 2005, immigrant rights march in the Back of the Yards, a predominantly Mexican neighborhood, occurred because the Latino immigrant community was "fed up with so much abuse of [its] rights" ("Leadership Vacuum" 2005). Community discontent, not the encouragement of leaders or organizations, was responsible for the marches' success.

Two years later, Esther Cepeda, a conservative columnist for the *Chicago Sun-Times,* also addressed the issue of a leadership vacuum: "Today's burning question," asked Cepeda after a Los Angeles protest march during which police brutalized participants, is "Why isn't our community outraged over this? Where is 'our' Jesse Jackson or our Al Sharpton? Why is there no great Hispanic leader to take these people to task?" (2007). Cepeda concluded that such leaders did not "and never will" exist because the Latino community has never needed a Martin Luther King Jr. Because immigrants are here by choice, Cepeda implies, whatever injustices they face are self-imposed, and they thus lack the standing to protest.

The historic importance of immigrants to the U.S. labor movement and the 2006 outpouring of millions of people on city streets across the country would seem to argue otherwise (see, e.g., Higham 1969; Preston 1963). Despite Cepeda's questioning of the legitimacy of Latino protest, her assertion indirectly underscores the concerns voiced in the *La Raza* editorial.[1] Yet social movement theorists do not agree about the role and value of leadership.[2]

Certain researchers argue that organization, an important task of leadership, facilitates the coordination of available resources into a strategic and concerted effort to wrest concessions from the ruling class (McCarthy and Zald 1977; McAdam 1982; Tilly 1978). Furthermore, the success of such efforts sustains a social movement over time. Stated simply, organization is understood as a vehicle of power. Yet in a landmark study of poor people's movements, Frances Fox Piven and Richard Cloward describe the drive to organize during times of heightened resistance—that is, when a community is willing to protest—as effectively stifling the disruptive force of collective action: "The presumption of most reformers and revolutionaries who have tried to organize the lower classes is that once the economic and political resources of at least modest numbers of people are combined in disciplined action, public or private elites will be forced to yield the concessions necessary to sustain and enlarge mass affiliation" (1977, xx–xxi).

According to Piven and Cloward, this reasoning has a flaw: "It is not possible to compel concessions from elites that can be used as resources to sustain oppositional organizations over time" (1977, xxi). Disruption, not organization, largely bears responsibility for whatever concessions are possible. Leaders of mass-based organizations, however, tend to reorient their efforts toward negotiation with elites, often discouraging disruption and protest in an effort to establish their legitimacy and to solidify relationships with economic and political power holders. The effort to create mass-based organizations of the disenfranchised, then, often leads to co-optation and the decline of social movements (xx–xxii). In light of these debates, it is important to examine leadership and organization in the context of the development of Chicago's immigrant rights campaign.

We sought to understand how the city's activists built a movement aimed at securing comprehensive immigration reform despite a perceived lack of organizational and charismatic leaders.[3] We also sought to identify areas of leadership activity that might open the way for co-optation or that might disrupt or otherwise dissipate the movement's momentum, with a focus on community needs that are unlikely to become media concerns.[4]

This study draws from interviews with fourteen organizers as well as informal conversations with many others who participated in the marches.[5] We examined what individuals saw as the primary goals of the movement and how they defined their tasks. The people with whom we spoke included those acting independently as well as those participating in grassroots and membership-based organizations. Political officials, while important to the process of securing immigrant rights, did not fall within the scope of this project.

Between the late spring of 2006 and the late summer of 2007, we asked leaders about their background, affiliations, and roles in the megamarches as well as the nature of the current leadership, goals for the immigrant rights movement, and the vision that guided mobilization efforts. We conducted the interviews at activists' places of work, at union offices, at community agencies, and on the campus of the University of Illinois at Chicago. Interviews typically lasted between an hour and a half and two hours; we held informal follow-up discussions with a few activists. Participants have been encouraged to review our work and to approve statements personally credited to them. Names and organizational affiliations are used when interviewees have permitted us to do so.

We recruited the interviewees based on their role as mobilizers and/or their affiliations with various organizing initiatives. We sought to include voices from across a broad range of movement perspectives as well as representatives from specific sectors of the community. All interviewees were U.S. citizens or permanent residents with strong ties to the Latino community. Nine were immigrants, while five were U.S.-born. Twelve were of Mexican descent, while the others were Chilean natives. Participants involved in the coordination of the marches not only saw themselves as personally affected by the issue but also understood the importance of immigration reform to the Mexican and entire Latino community. We used newspaper articles and Internet and other sources to track the activities of the various organizations and community activists.

Indigenous Resources

Similar to the black civil rights struggles in the second half of the twentieth century, the immigrant rights movement has been seen as a spontaneous response to oppressive conditions.[6] The deteriorating situation of immigrants and the immediate threat of criminalization embedded in the Sensenbrenner Bill ignited the massive 2006 rallies; however, community resources were nonetheless important in facilitating the protests. As in the case of black civil rights, the "material resources, and the less tangible ones provided through informal communication networks and communal solidarity, predated the boycotts and protests" (Kling 2003, 730). Moreover, the transformation of discontent into a social movement aimed at obtaining comprehensive immigrant reform relies in part on the quality and effectiveness of leadership. Leadership is itself an aspect of the development of local resources, and the emergence of the immigration movement is a consequence of the maturity of the Mexican community.

Community Development

The Chicago metropolitan area's economic diversity has made it home to the largest U.S. concentration of Mexicans outside of the Southwest (Paral et al. 2004). However, the development of the Mexican community at the beginning of the twentieth century was initially limited by several factors and totaled less than twenty thousand at the end of the 1920s (Kerr 2000). That number dropped further as a consequence of deportations during the following decade (Kerr 1976; Valdes 2000). In the early years of settlement, Mexicans did not constitute a numerical majority in any of the three initial ports of entry—South Chicago, Back of the Yards, and the Near West Side. The number of Mexican professionals was minimal, and most immigrants were laborers. Furthermore, Mexicans were at times recruited as strikebreakers, which increased racial and ethnic animosities and reinforced union antagonism toward Spanish-speaking immigrants (Arredondo 2004, 2008; A. E. Jones 1928; Kerr 1976).

Although opportunities for organization were initially limited, immigrants formed mutual aid societies that provided assistance for basic needs such as the costs of burial. In addition, Mexicans established grocery stores and pool halls, and a few religious centers developed to serve the specific needs of the population (Kerr 1976, 2000). In 1943, the Mexican Civic Committee was formed, with the Mexican American Council following in 1950. However, the limited number of Mexican organizations that could serve as advocates may account for the lack of an organized response to deportations during the 1950s and 1960s (Padilla 1985).

The emergence of Pilsen, just south of the Near West Side, as a majority-Mexican community occurred in tandem with the rise of political activism during the 1960s and 1970s.[7] The establishment of a number of new social service and grassroots organizations resulted largely from the efforts of the Chicano activist generation. The Centro de la Causa (Center for the Cause) housed service and educational programs including the Organization of Latin American Students, the community office of a network of college activists. Casa Aztlán (Aztlán House), another major neighborhood center, offered meeting, workshop, and organizational space for artists and advocacy groups such as Chicago's Brown Berets (Fernández 2005). Mujeres Latinas en Acción (Latina Women in Action) and the Latino Youth Alternative High School were two other local initiatives that were by-products of the era's youth activism.[8]

Between 1970 and 1990, Chicago's Latino community grew from 836,905 persons (7 percent of the area's population) to 1,405,116 (almost 20 percent) (Chicago Fact Book 1992). By 2030, Latinos are expected to account for 33 percent of the area's population (Ready and Brown-Gort 2005). In 2000, Mexicans comprised almost 76 percent of Chicago's Latino population (Paral 2006). The growing Mexican presence in the Chicago area is reflected in the most of the city's residential neighborhoods and increasingly in nearby suburbs (Paral 2006). This demographic explosion has brought an increase in neighborhood resources. Immigrant neighborhoods have witnessed the growth of businesses and religious centers as well as civic organizations and social service agencies. Little Village ranks as one of the city's most successful business districts, second only to the Magnificent Mile (Sampson 2008). The many initiatives that specifically serve immigrants include the Instituto del Progreso Latino (Institute for

Latino Progress), established at the end of the 1970s, and Latinos Progresando (Latinos Progressing), founded in 1998. The 1990s saw the establishment of the Resurrection Project, an alliance of six Catholic parishes serving the Pilsen neighborhood that focuses on the creation of "local leadership . . . so that area residents become catalysts for social change at the local, regional, and national levels. This initiative provides leadership development formation, building community leaders that tackle issues facing the community such as: health, safety, housing, immigration, and education" (*Resurrection Project* n.d.).

Unions also offer opportunities to build leadership skills. Illinois ranks among the strongest states in unionization rates, and although Mexicans have relatively low rates of union membership, immigrants from that country are often favorably disposed toward unions. The success of such organizing efforts as the Justice for Janitors campaign in Los Angeles has encouraged unions to recruit Mexicans and other Latino workers who had previously been seen as difficult to organize (Zavala 2006). Over the past decade or so, the AFL-CIO has followed this trend, taking a more positive stance toward immigrants (AFL-CIO n.d.). Unions organizing workers in service industries, such as the Service Employees International Union (SEIU) and the Union of Needletrades, Industrial, and Textile Employees and the Hotel Employees and Restaurant Employees International Union (UNITE HERE), have made special efforts to target the many Mexicans who work in this sector (Milkman 2005; see chap. 6).

In the decade preceding the megamarches, activists noted a change in the mix of Mexican immigrants that increased the capacity for mobilization. The devaluation of the Mexican peso and the economic crisis of the 1990s moved increased numbers of Mexican professionals to enter the United States, and teachers, artists, and journalists could be found working in Chicago's restaurants and factories. These better-educated and largely urban immigrants, including those from the Mexico City area, may have added another dimension of experience and skills that contributed to the organization of the marches.[9]

Jorge Mujica, an organizer who has been active on both sides of the border, stated, "I believe that we have a generation of Mexican immigrants here that has also been politicized in the last twenty years. People living here are people that went through the 1988 election process in Mexico, as well as the dismemberment of the [Institutional Revolutionary Party] and the failed election of [progressive candidate] Cuauhtémoc Cardenas. People are living here that participated in the student movement in the late 1980s." New organizers with a history of activism in Mexico or from other areas of Latin America brought with them valuable political insights.[10] This group of individuals joined Chicago's already vibrant local scene, creating a diverse community of activists.

Convergence

Despite the U.S. Mexican community's awakening as a force, racial, class, political, generational, and other differences have created division and diminished Mexican influence. Suspicions and rivalries historically have existed across Mexican community networks, organizations, and agencies, and the growth of Mexico-focused initiatives added an additional layer of complexity. During the 1990s, newly arrived immigrants helped to establish or further develop existing home town associations (HTAs), which sought primarily to raise funds for improvements in Mexico (Heredia 2007; see also chap. 8). Associations commonly included members of opposing Mexican political parties, leading to contentious relationships within groups. However, the campaign to secure immigrants the right to vote in Mexican elections (which Mexico's Chamber of Deputies approved in 2005) and the increasingly difficult situation that immigrants faced in the United States (see Martínez 1998) encouraged collaboration. HTA members began to interact with activists representing the spectrum of Mexican political parties based in the United States. According to Claudio Gaete, "A lot of new people who are used to fighting the fights in Mexico"— individuals whose "sights are in Mexico—began to put aside their political differences and work together." According to Maria D'Amezcua, group members then established working relationships with one another and with other groups despite their ideological differences.

Omar López, a service provider on Chicago's North Side whose experience in the city dates back to the 1960s, experienced this network-building process firsthand. He found the campaign for dual citizenship "a very unifying issue for the Mexican community; it created a kind of energy that brought people together [from] different political positions to work on one issue, and I think that was a primer to the march." The process invigorated networks: "I ran for *consejero* [counselor] of the [Instituto de Mexicanos en el Exterior (Institute of Mexicans Living Abroad)], so it was then that I reestablished communication with a lot of the Mexican activists." Accordingly, "Even if the only objective of the hometown associations was to send money for the church in their hometown, they were nevertheless organizing. For the last ten years we have been pushing and fighting for establishing a very clear political link between Mexico and Mexicans living abroad."

According to Luis Gutiérrez, an organizer from the Pilsen community, this effort has also involved an important reorientation of the HTAs' political interests:

> They started to realize that a lot of their power doesn't just lie in Mexico. For the
> last couple of years, a lot of their work was sending money back home, building

roads, building schools, things of that nature. But over the last couple of years, they've really made a push to try to get involved in policy that's happening in the U.S. and how policy both in the U.S. and Mexico work[s] together and affect[s] everyone on both sides of the border. To get them out of the mentality that they should not only work on issues going on in Mexico but on issues that are going on here was a really big step.

The second thing that happened was that they formed [the Confederation of Mexican Federations in the Midwest]. Basically, all the heads of the federations got together and created one organization where each federation is represented. They were all sitting down together to figure out how all the federations could start working together.

The confederation was in part promoted by the Instituto de Mexicanos en el Exterior, an initiative designed to develop a network of émigré leaders, activists, and organizations (Alarcón 2006; González Gutiérrez 2006; see also chap. 8).[11]

Continued immigration in the 1990s coincided with a downturn in the economy that fueled a nativist backlash, characterized by "English only" referenda in states with large Latino populations and the growing presence of outspoken anti-immigration politicians (Castro 1999). Anti-immigrant sentiment reached its peak with the Sensenbrenner Bill; in response, the HTAs and various Mexican political parties in the United States came together with advocacy groups that had been involved in international solidarity but were primarily focused on community issues such as education and housing (Gaete 2007). Leaders of community agencies proved critical in this developing collaborative environment. Left-of-center groups, including socialists distrustful of mainstream politicians, worked alongside individuals involved in gubernatorial and aldermanic political campaigns. Grassroots organizations normally skeptical of grant-oriented entities' ability to make independent decisions came together with leaders who had previously focused more exclusively on one side of the border or the other. Union organizer Moises Zavala described the unity among so many diverse groups as "magical."

The March 10 Coalition

On a national level, Armando Navarro, professor of ethnic studies at the University of California at Riverside and a member of the National Alliance for Human Rights, responded to the Sensenbrenner vote in the House by organizing the Latino Mobilization Summit Conference. More than 550 individuals from across the country, including Chicago leaders Emma Lozano and Marcia Soto, arrived at the Riverside Convention Center on February 11, 2005, to discuss what form the resistance would take. Participants decided to conduct a nationwide protest on March 10. Lozano and Soto returned to Chicago and worked with representatives of other groups to plan the rally. Recalled López, "The very first meeting we had like sixteen people. . . . We said, 'Okay, this is February 16. We got less than a month, but let's do it.' We formed a series of committees, and we started working on logistics, press and propaganda, the outreach committee, and we moved from there. We decided that we needed to bring in other groups, and then other organizations really began to come in to the meetings."

After the success of the March 10 megamarch, the activists adopted the name March 10 Coalition and continued to meet to plan further actions. The group initially attracted a broad range of individuals and organizations interested in fighting for comprehensive immigration reform—representatives of unions, various religious denominations and churches, civic associations, community agencies, student groups, and social justice networks. Participants agreed on what were termed the Seven Points of Unity (later expanded to ten) (Arreola 2007).[12] Salome Amezcua remembered a comment made at one of the organizing meetings: "We can't just leave this. Look at all these people. Look around [at] who's next to you. How many places have you gone where all these different ethnic groups [were present], and they are all fighting for the same thing? There's so many things we still have to fight for. We have to stick together."

The coalition met at Casa Michoacán, the center for the HTAs of that Mexican state, a renovated two-story building near the corner of Blue Island and Eighteenth Street in Pilsen. It was, in Amezcua's words, a "house for everyone." The coalition generally met on Mondays. Folding chairs were arranged auditorium style and along the sides of a room on the building's first floor. Board members sat at the front table. Interest remained high, and later arrivals often had to stand because all the chairs were filled.

According to union representative Cynthia Rodríguez and other participants, these early meetings were highly democratic. Amezcua saw no differentiation among leaders, activists, and community members; all received an equal say because "that one person that's quiet all the way in the back that you might not have ever heard, [that person] might be a future leader of the organization." Anyone in attendance, regardless of affiliation, could vote on proposals, and representatives of large organizations wielded no greater clout than persons who were there as individuals, not representing any group (Rodríguez 2007). In Amezcua's words, "This was something beautiful. Sitting at the table were everyday people, people that weren't members of any group or organization. They were there simply because of their desire to participate." Another coalition member, José Artemio Arreola, concurred: "All opinions were heard, [and] we tried to reach a consensus."

Problems arose from the outset, however. One of the coalition's "drawbacks," stated Carlos Heredia, was "that there is so much to discuss." Meetings lasted hours, and participants grew frustrated. It was difficult to plan and to address all the issues raised. Discussions at times veered off on tangents or rehashed matters debated earlier. Moreover, some participants began to suspect that the confusion in the general meetings was being used to control the discussion.

Caught in the vise between democracy and efficiency, the organization attempted to move to a more effective organizational structure by using existing subcommittees to address specific concerns and narrow the focus of the general sessions. The coalition would continue to function as an umbrella group but would redirect issues and activities to smaller working groups that would focus on specific functions or aspects of mobilization. This structural adaptation met with only limited success, however.

Despite its internal tensions and pressures, the March 10 Coalition soon demonstrated its potential as an important leadership vehicle. According to longtime activist Juan Salgado, López "was the voice of experience," while Arreola "was an important glue. [Businessman] Fabian Morales handled all the logistics. Salome [Amezcua] brought her own talents." The meetings also brought Salgado into contact with other activists he had not previously met. Coming together for the mobilizations provided an opportunity for leaders to collaborate and build trust not just in Chicago but across the country (Arreola 2007).

The March 10 Coalition brought together resources as well. Over time, individuals, organizations, unions, local merchants, and major businesses provided funding. After some initial controversy, Miller Brewing Company helped fund an immigrant rights conference. Groups provided volunteers, and a network of churches and organizations served as sites of information (Arreola 2007; Salgado 2007). Between 2006 and 2007, the coalition became a center for planning, networking, resource identification, and collaboration among leaders.

Cross-group collaboration has numerous benefits, particularly in light of the barriers that have historically divided the Mexican community and diminished its potential impact. However, Salgado and other participants did not see the need for the coalition to continue as a permanent and broadening organization: "I think there is enough leadership that's worked together on something that at a moment's notice we can get back together. I would go back to that table. I'm not going to stay at the table because I don't think that's how we're going to get the most work done." Although the Centro sin Fronteras, headed by Lozano, left the coalition in March 2006, the group has continued to collaborate on specific activities, including the May 1, 2008, march.

The historic divisions within the Mexican community probably mean that activists could not have coalesced under one organization or behind one leader. The 2006–7 protests did not result in a single mass-based organization that sought to defend immigrant rights but rather an organizing center around which groups, activists, and networks could work cooperatively for the purposes of mobilization.[13] The March 10 Coalition has functioned as a mobilizing and organizational magnet, occasionally drawing other important initiatives outside the coalition into dialogue when necessary.

Creating Democratic Leadership

The absence of civic leaders standing at the helm of a single organization caused some observers to perceive Chicago as suffering from a leadership vacuum. Immigrant rights organizations tended to emphasize more democratic leadership structures that sought to subsume individual identities behind organizational affiliations. Centro sin Fronteras and the March 10 Coalition, for example, received more attention than did specific activists, although the identities of spokespersons became familiar both locally and nationally.

In 2006 and 2007, activists generally supported the idea of transcending traditional leadership models: said one, "We're trying to demystify the whole one leader type of mentality." Some organizers believed that these models create a false dichotomy between those who direct and those who follow, and most of those we interviewed voiced the necessity to move away from specific organizing perspectives such as those associated with Saul Alinsky and the Industrial Areas Foundation because of the elevated role of leadership (Gaete 2007). According to Mujica,

> We frankly refused to have leadership. We believe in collective leadership more than in the personal leadership of anybody. Of course, there are people that you might see more on TV or hear on the radio, but that doesn't mean that person is the leader. We consciously refused to have a Cesar Chavez here. We don't want a Cesar Chavez. We don't need a Cesar Chavez. What we need is one hundred people working nationwide, coordinating over the phone, over the Internet, coordinating actions and coordinating statements and setting up dates for the whole movement to keep moving forward. Because this was originally a grassroots movement, and we don't want to deny people in the grassroots their movement.

Organizers cited specific theorists as inspirations, including Brazilian educator Paulo Freire, known for his literacy work among the rural poor, and Myles Horton and his Highlander Folk School. This approach focuses on creating spaces for reflection and interaction and provides an environment for the sharing of stories that support leadership development (Gaete 2007). Regardless of whether they embedded their ideas in a specific theoretical model, organizers generally advanced perspectives rooted in notions of participatory democracy and shunned traditional models that value the presence of charismatic or organizational leaders. These evolving models of participatory leadership, however, have not solidified into a clearly articulated alternative. (For an exploration of the tension between participatory democracy and authoritarianism, see Breines 1980.)

Immigrant rights activists have not necessarily superseded traditional leadership practices despite consciously rejecting them. For example, some March 10 Coalition spokespersons have been seen as defaulting into traditional roles. The repeated presence of the "same old faces" has been viewed as an attempt by certain individuals to monopolize the spotlight and define the movement according to their perspectives. Forces both within and outside of the coalition have been faulted for adopting "street populism" while promoting strategies that depend on politicians' agendas.

In addition, activists' efforts to incorporate newly mobilized constituents and blur the line between leaders and followers have not resolved issues related to the incorporation of youth. Veteran activists occupy most positions of responsibility, and Rudy Aguilar, a student organizer, was among several activists who wanted to see more youth in leadership positions. Those most integrated into the March 10 Coalition structure seem to be those affiliated with unions, civic and political organizations, and HTAs, although the coalition's constituent base includes youth. The minimal leadership presence of those under thirty is a concern. The ascendance of youth to leadership is not necessarily a linear or natural process. Young activists may need guidance in taking on greater responsibility, and no organized process for doing so appears to exist.

Charting a Course for Change

Theoretical debates regarding the value and function of leadership became especially relevant in the aftermath of the 2006 and 2007 mobilizations. If building mass-based organizations is not critical to the process of social change, where should leaders direct their energy? What role do leaders play in helping move "from the old to the new" (Hobsbawm 1978)? Piven and Cloward (1977) identify two central responsibilities of leadership: assessing what can be gained at every step in a movement's trajectory, and helping to create the conditions for future mobilizations.[14]

The megamarches highlighted immigrants' predicament and hinted at the potential role that they and their allies can play in the country's future political realignment. Mass mobilization also provided an opportunity to create a collective consciousness, enrich constituent perspectives, stimulate organization, create networks, integrate the newly activated, and establish a process to encourage mobilization. The outpouring of millions of people across the nation also disrupted the status quo and served as an initial impetus for reform.

However, the same dynamic and democratic process that led to the coming together of vastly different and heterogeneous groups and the creation of these multiple mobilizational leaders rendered the coalition vulnerable and collaboration among leaders tentative. Leaders who unite despite their differences but with a common goal of coordinating a massive event may find reaching agreement on other issues difficult. After a march ends, differences arise among leaders with very different ideas about what is or should be the movement's agenda. Since, at least in theory, no one's views are particularly privileged, reaching a consensus is often difficult. Different leaders' visions imply different strategies for change and different organizing approaches. Organizers weighed specific legislative initiatives and favored certain alliances over others. Tactics were then chosen based on how the movement was seen to be progressing. Such tensions affected the dynamic of collaboration and enthusiasm that characterized the movement's first two years. Indeed, according to Gaete, "Right now, it's a Mexican-led movement, and it's split."

The Pace and Possibilities for Change

Veteran activists have long understood that U.S. immigration policies have evolved over time, attracting immigrants when labor is necessary and expelling workers or making their existence difficult when the need for labor declines— for example, during the Great Depression and during Operation Wetback in the 1950s (Balderrama and Rodríguez 1995; García 1996; Hoffman 1974). Many of these activists believe, however, that the sporadic and piecemeal approaches that have previously characterized immigration reform have not addressed the underlying structural issues. Said Mujica, "I think that what we are living now is just the mobilization phase of a movement that has always been there. I would say that the movement for the undocumented started the day some people were left out of the amnesty program in 1986. I mean, three and a half million people were legalized; half a million people were not. So that day, this movement started. And of course, it has ups and downs and variations in the number of people working on the issue, but there's always been people working on the issues of undocumented workers."

Although the Immigration Reform and Control Act of 1986 granted amnesty to millions of immigrants, it did not provided the necessary systemic reform, and Mujica believes that by 2015, "we're going to have another five million undocumented workers, so the movement is going to be here indefinitely." Activists argue for a more sober immigration policy that recognizes immigrants' right to provide for their families and be united with loved ones. The system must address the inevitable immigration flows that result from globalization and the economic dislocation and disequilibrium that are a consequence of the relationship between the United States and Latin America, particularly Mexico.

But mobilizers have disagreed about specific legislation. Conflict surfaced when some community leaders appeared ready to back a proposal supported by Illinois Democratic representative Luis Gutiérrez that would have provided a route toward citizenship only for some of the undocumented. Many of those involved thought that the marches had opened the way to secure the possibility of citizenship for all immigrants and that accepting less left too many people's needs unaddressed; others, in contrast, were willing to accept the incremental logic of the legislative process, arguing in favor of taking what can be gained now and continuing the fight to obtain more. Subsequent legislative initiatives also generated criticism: some activists believed that the STRIVE Act, for example, continued to criminalize immigrants by including in reform measures features such as the building of detention centers (Lydersen 2008).

Less controversial is the idea of using the impact of the mobilizations to address immigrants' immediate needs.[15] Illinois' mass mobilizations initially provided a favorable context for the acquisition of funds and services, awakening political officials to Latinos' power. Officials eager to be seen as supportive opened up lines of communication with community representatives, and in 2005, under Governor Rod Blagojevich, the state established the Office of New Americans Policy and Advocacy, requiring "every state agency to come up with a plan for how it will better welcome immigrants" (Salgado 2007). Local organizations also received funding for provision of services related to citizenship preparation. Salgado, executive director of the Instituto del Progreso Latino, a community organization that addresses the needs of immigrants, applauded the state's efforts to provide ten million dollars for English-language programs and three million dollars for citizenship preparation. López and other veteran leaders see pragmatic gains in services and resources as important steps along the path to comprehensive reform.

Electoral Strategies for Change

After the first two megamarches, leaders began to speculate about future organizing approaches and strategies, given the inevitable decline in turnout. The March 10 Coalition's perceived single focus on large public events prompted one organizer to refer to it as a "parade committee." Salgado agreed about the need to think beyond marches and consider other strategies to effect change (2007). Although the issue of political alliances remains a source of debate, activists have advanced at least three electoral strategies: general support for the Democratic Party; a focus on building a vocal Mexican constituency within the Democratic Party; and the encouragement of independent electoral alternatives that address immigrant issues.

Many of those involved in the mobilizations hope that the movement can help tilt the country's political balance. Activists have generally seen the Reagan Revolution and the 1994 Republican Contract with America as signaling a policy shift away from addressing the needs of the middle classes and the poor.

Adherents of the Democratic Party and supporters of specific public officials have emphasized the general need to partner with these forces. A Democratic congressional majority, many believe, offers a better political context for immigration reform and thus should be a priority in the developing movement agenda. Cultivating legislative allies in the fight to obtain immigration reform, then, remains a major goal.

Within and outside the March 10 Coalition, activists have debated the proper place of political officials. Lozano and some other leaders outside of the coalition welcome all public officials who support immigrant rights, even when those officials have a mixed record on other issues that affect Latinos. The presence of politicians at pro-immigrant events, including the major marches, is seen by others as lending added legitimacy to this position and was the main reason for Sin Fronteras' departure from the coalition.

A somewhat different perspective accepts Democrats as potential allies but feels that the movement should seek to create independent community bases of power that can bring a much-needed and long-awaited Mexican presence to local and national politics. These leaders see the need to develop a policy agenda with the Mexican community firmly at the center. As community activist Luis Gutiérrez said, "I just want to see leadership. I want to see leadership from our community. I want our community to represent itself, which I don't think happens enough." This is not a nationalist strategy per se but an acknowledgment that Mexicans have for some time been divided by agendas imposed from outside the community. As such, Mexican interests have often been marginalized or discounted completely.

Salgado also sees the development of local political representation as important. He enthusiastically supported the formation of a Mexican political action committee "with the stated purpose of moving a Mexican agenda forward in the United States." He argued for the need to focus on gaining the congressional votes that would support comprehensive immigration reform while focusing less on marches, in accordance with his "personal belief . . . that we need a legislative strategy right now." Salgado recognized that politicians are necessary to advance a legislative agenda and believed that their presence served the movement's aims (2007).[16]

Still, within the coalition is a great deal of resistance to making Democratic Party politics central to the movement. In Mujica's words, "One big, huge, deep discussion in this movement is that we are going to sell out to the Democratic Party. They have not won our esteem, our confidence. I mean, so many Democrats voted [for] HR 4437. Then Democrats approved 2611, the bill that doesn't legalize everybody—it only legalizes from maybe 25 to 30 percent of the undocumented immigrants. So how can you push forward for votes for the Democratic Party? We just don't agree with it."

Where some view electoral politics as the answer to immigrant grievances, others see the present political configuration as part of the problem, wondering if electoral politics functioned as a "graveyard for social movements." Orlando Sepulveda, a student activist, believed that electoral politics as practiced by the Democratic Party were detrimental to social movements, although such does not always have to be the case: "The movement has radicalized people, and that's where the role of the Democratic Party enters. I think the Democratic Party has a role in American politics, which is the co-optation of the movement."

Independent politics is one response to the disillusionment and distrust of the Democratic Party. In 2008, López, representing the Green Party, challenged incumbent Luis Gutiérrez for the Illinois's Fourth Congressional District seat. López's bid was controversial not only because Gutiérrez is known as an immigrant rights supporter but because major environmentalist leaders at the national level have been unsupportive and even hostile to immigrants. López nevertheless believes that the Greens' environmental and social justice agenda can accommodate immigrant rights issues. The party officially supports permanent border passes for Mexican and Canadian citizens and seeks an end to immigration-related racial profiling and English-only laws while promoting policies based on fairness, nondiscrimination, and family unification. It also believes that "any free trade pact should have free passage over borders," as in the European Union (Lydersen 2008).

Partnering Labor and Immigrant Rights

The presence of a large number of working-class immigrants in the 2006 mobilizations provides hope that Latino workers will reinvigorate a labor movement weakened over the past fifty years by economic changes and a hostile policy environment. As Mujica noted, the May 2006 march clearly promoted workers' rights: "I think the most important repercussion [these protest marches are] going to have is the labor movement. Immigrant populations are working populations, and the fact that you obtain your immigrant papers is not going to increase your wages. It is not going to give you health care in the workplace; it's not going to give you seniority and respect in the workplace. So this movement is going to provoke, I think, a whole revival of the labor movement in the United States. That's why we wanted and we needed and we still need, and we will continue wanting the labor unions."

According to those with a labor perspective, immigration rights and workers' rights are complimentary and reinforcing. A labor focus may also provide a bridge across racial and ethnic divides. Some observers see the presence of enthusiastic African American union members at the May 1, 2006, protest as suggesting the potential to find common ground and extend alliances. The working-class character of most Mexican immigrants and the continuing support of unions are seen as having the potential to stimulate a comprehensive labor agenda. From this perspective, immigration reform represents only the first step toward developing a labor politics in the United States.

As publicity and support for the May 1 march increased, organizations with electoral and labor agendas began to contribute increased resources, including money and personnel, giving rise to questions about the extent of collaboration with unions and others that mirrored the issues that arose with regard to politicians and political parties. Lozano pointed out that many groups involved in the mobilization, including SEIU and Operation PUSH, have agendas. For certain leaders, the growing influence of unions and other organizations within the movement raised concerns about maintaining the independence of the immigrant rights struggle.

Union members initially participated largely as individuals but subsequently became official representatives to the March 10 Coalition. Financial resources soon followed (Rodríguez 2007). Labor's growing organizational influence motivated even those affiliated with unions to wonder whether their participation might have a muting effect on grassroots enthusiasm or change the spontaneous and community character of the first march.

Developing Leadership for Mobilization

Grassroots organizers see immigration reform as an important step in a broader social justice agenda. They see the marches' most important consequence as the increased capacity for future mobilization, including the development of social-justice-oriented leaders who can address the comprehensive needs of the primarily working-class Latino community. Activists are enthused by community mobilization and progressive movement within the labor's ranks. Some participants support electoral strategies that offer an alternative to the domination of conservative Republicanism or the probusiness centrist politics of the Democratic Party. However, activists focused on social justice are generally more likely to see immigrant rights as a critical element in a broader agenda that includes "issues that are important to the development of the Mexican community" (Heredia 2007).

In addition to mobilization, social-justice-oriented activists tend to emphasize leadership development and community education as an arena of intervention and as a means of fighting for reform. For these mobilizers, the key is not the alliance with politicians but the development of community understanding and networks that build capacity, including the cultivation of a committed leadership. Activists bear responsibility for facilitating engagement and integrating participants in a process of reflection that can foster their role as mobilizers (Gaete 2007).

All Mexican/Latino leaders see community development and an informed citizenry as important ingredients for long-term success. All of the interviewees acknowledged the important role played by the Spanish-speaking media. However, some saw a need for the Latino media to move beyond the simple entertainment aspect of their programming to focus on creating a more aware and sophisticated Latino public that can make informed decisions. Community forums and popular education initiatives were suggested as playing important roles in this process (Heredia 2007; Gaete 2007; Gutiérrez 2006).

Those with a solitary focus on comprehensive immigrant rights, however, caution that broader visions and strategies should not interfere with the core agenda. These activists, who include Amezcua, see immigration reform as the beginning and end of the movement. With years of experience in such organizations as the League of United Latin American Citizens and more currently with the Latino Chapter of the RainbowPUSH Coalition, Amezcua participated in the March 10 Coalition with one main goal: "This is not an organization as in membership. There are no fees. This organization is only structured for after [comprehensive immigration reform is attained]. If you don't have a location, go to RainbowPUSH, SEIU, or a community organization." In short, comprehensive immigration reform is the sole unifying goal.

Moving Forward

Despite its success, the March 10, 2006, protest was seen in some quarters as rudderless and lacking leadership, largely as a consequence of the prominence of organizations and coalitions rather than individuals. Many immigrant rights organizers reinforced this view by challenging the traditional leader-follower relationship. These organizers obtained permits, coordinated transportation, recruited hundreds of volunteers, arranged for publicity, raised funds, and converted sympathizers into protesters. A smaller but important sector of these individuals undertook the complex responsibilities of leadership in an effort to transform a groundswell response into an organized and sustainable constituency, a movement capable of advancing an immigrant rights agenda.

The growth of Chicago's Mexican population over the past hundred years has provided fertile ground for the development of the financial, social, and human resources that facilitated the twenty-first-century mobilizations. The city has witnessed the development of community-based organizations, civic and political groups, HTAs, and service agencies as well as loosely organized cultural and political networks that offer a rich variety of venues for association and platforms for leadership. The March 10 Coalition provided a central location for the resources needed for large-scale mobilization without undermining existing organizations and leadership structures. Even groups not part of the coalition could work with it when needed circumstances warranted such collaboration.[17]

The March 10 Coalition facilitated the development of information networks, encouraged mobilization, and at various times showed itself capable of responding quickly to issues. However, the same leadership style that helped the group mobilize hundreds of thousands of demonstrators has faced postmarch challenges, with differences arising over the assessment of possibilities, alternative pathways to achieve social change, and the selection of allies.

Today, the March 10 Coalition appears to be adopting a more streamlined and limited skeletal structure. Part of the reason for the shift is that the process became cumbersome even for those who initially lauded the group's participatory character. At its peak in 2006, more than 200 organizations were affiliated with the coalition; that number dropped to 197 in 2007 and to just over 100 in 2008 (Amezcua 2006).

The high energy and intensity of purpose that characterized the March 10 Coalition during its first two years have waned to some extent. For a time, it appeared that the group would develop into an intermediate organization that would unite local leaders. Such groups characterized the civil rights movement in its early stages, prior to the creation of the Southern Christian Leadership Conference. It is now unclear precisely where the coalition is heading and whether it will continue to serve as an umbrella organization for organizations and individual activists. The executive committee currently comes together only when a joint effort is needed.[18] Committee members often communicate via conference calls instead of face to face. While this approach reflects the goals of efficiency and allowing local leaders to operate primarily in their respective spheres, it also appears to be a mechanism for moderating the differences among activists.

The process of globalization will continue to produce transnational migratory flows and generate new challenges. The movement's unifying goal is comprehensive immigration reform. This central objective may advance all agendas if activists continue to keep their eyes on the prize. The appreciation that more can be accomplished through coordinated action perhaps provides the best chance for the continuation and success of the immigrant rights movement.

Mexicans' rare 2006 display of unity represented an important step, as anti-immigrant sentiment encouraged a fractured community to at least temporarily circumvent "the multicultural, multiracial, regional, generational, and class character of the Mexican American people" that has historically divided Mexicans and impeded their formation into a strong, cohesive political constituency (Muñoz 1989, 10). We hope that the community and its leaders remain firm in the belief that social change is possible and that they continue to march together toward a better future.

Notes

1. Following the classic work of Weber (1968), two general forms of leadership are typically assumed: bureaucratic leaders, who stand at the forefront of organizations; and charismatic leaders, who rely on the force of their personality to inspire others. *La Raza* seems to be referring to the former, while Cepeda refers to the latter.

2. Debate regarding the function and importance of leadership erupted shortly after the publication of Piven and Cloward 1977 and resumed in *Perspectives on Politics* in 2003 (see Block 2003; Kling 2003; Piven 2003; Schram 2003; Tarrow 2003).

3. For the purposes of this study, the terms *leader, activist,* and *mobilizer* are synonymous and refers to anyone directly involved in mobilization efforts that aided in the success of the 2006–7 megamarches.

4. Qualitative researchers have often identified alternative ways to measure the validity of their work, including the impact or contributions they can make with respect to participants' goals (Lather 2004).

5. We originally intended to interview additional activists, but some were reluctant to speak publicly, and logistical issues prevented others from participating.

6. Morris 1984 discusses how the black civil rights struggle was initially viewed as a spontaneous movement, dependent on external leaders and resources. His emphasis on the importance of community infrastructure highlights the centrality of indigenous organization and leadership in the mobilization process.

7. Gentrification of the Near West Side and the consequent displacement of Mexicans was one factor that led to Pilsen's transformation into a largely Mexican community.

8. Mujeres Latinas grew out of the June 1973 Latina Women's Education Awareness Conference, La Mujer Despierta (Women Awake) at Centro de la Causa. Subsequent meetings were held throughout the community to decide on a course of action. Some of these discussions were held at the Librería Nuestro Continente (Our Continent Bookstore), the Chicago's first and only Chicano bookstore (Vital 2008).

9. Chicago activists' perceptions regarding the changes in the nature of immigrants' previous occupations are supported by data from California (Cornelius and Marcelli 2000).

10. For the involvement of people with political experience, especially from Mexico City, in political organizations, see de la Garza and Hazan 2003.

11. The Instituto de Mexicanos en el Exterior served some of the "movement halfway house" functions Morris (1984) describes with respect to such organizations as the Highlander Folk School and American Friends Service Committee. The institute sponsored leadership seminars and other organizing projects and helped to identify and bring together leaders.

12. The Ten Points included (1) opposition to the Sensenbrenner Bill and other such restrictive measures; (2) the criminalization of immigrants; (3) the construction of walls and the militarization of the border; (4) guest worker programs and employer sanctions; (5) deportations; (6) the use of local law enforcement for immigration purposes; (7) support for expedited family reunification visas; (8) protection of labor civil rights; (9) civil liberties; and (10) unconditional legalization for all (Zavala 2006).

13. The March 10 Coalition initially seemed to be what Morris (1984) terms an intermediate organization. Formal nonbureaucratic organizations "facilitate mass participation, tactical innovations, and rapid decision making" (285). One of their attributes is that they unite leaders despite historic divisions, suspicions, and personal rivalries.

14. Block provides a more specific listing of these leadership tasks: leaders can "help the poor overcome their structured inequalities . . . not by organizing the poor but by participating in activities that can contribute to the mobilization of the poor" (2003, 733). This process can take such forms as challenging dominant and legitimating narratives; supporting claims made by the poor; developing strategies that link protest to specific political goals; identifying allies who can make mobilization more effective; framing arguments in defense of the poor; and drafting proposals and legislation that can at some point become concessions. He also underscores the need for mobilizers continuously to test the waters for environmental fissures, "probing for weaknesses in the arrangements that keep the poor in their place" and seeking reforms that can help establish "durable political forces" and "create political capacity" (734).

15. A grant secured by a person affiliated with a local HTA generated some controversy since it was said to be obtained with the help of Republican Dennis Hastert, who represented Illinois' Fourteenth Congressional District from 1987 to 2007 and served as speaker of the House from 1999 to 2007.

16. The degree of participation by elected officials at the rally at the end of the March 10 protest route constituted perhaps the main point of contention among the various wings of the immigrant rights movement.

17. The Centro sin Fronteras independently organized for the May 1, 2007, march. A year later, the New Majority Coalition paralleled the March 10 Coalition's organizational efforts. The New Majority Coalition included four founders of the March 10 Coalition, among them the Centro sin Fronteras, as well as several other organizations and unions that also participated in the concurrent March 10 Coalition's planning meetings.

18. In keeping with the coalition's commitment to democratic practices, persons not affiliated with any organization receive two votes on the executive committee, while each organization has one representative and an alternate (Amezcua 2008).

References

AFL-CIO. N.d. *Building Understanding, Creating Change: Defending the Rights of Immigrant Workers: What Union Members Should Know about . . . the AFL-CIO Policy on Immigration.* http://www.aflcio.org/issues/civilrights/immigration/upload/AFLCIOPO.pdf. Accessed July 1, 2007.

Aguilar, Rudy. 2006. Interview by Leonard G. Ramírez, José Perales-Ramos, and José Antonio Arellano. June 28, Chicago.

Alarcón, R. 2006. "Hacia la Construcción de una Política de Emigración en México." In *Relaciones Estado-Diáspora: Aproximaciones desde Cuatro Continentes,* ed. C. González Gutiérrez, 157–79. Mexico City: Secretaria de Relaciones Exteriores, Instituto de Mexicanos en el Exterior.

Amezcua Frieri, Salome. 2006. Interview by Leonard G. Ramírez, José Perales-Ramos, and José Antonio Arellano. July 28, Chicago.

———. 2008. Personal communication. June 24.

Arredondo, G. F. 2004. "Navigating Ethno-Racial Currents: Mexicans in Chicago, 1919–1939." *Journal of Urban History* 30 (3): 399–427.

———. 2008. *Mexican Chicago: Race, Identity, and Nation, 1916–1939.* Urbana: University of Illinois Press.

Arreola, José Artemio. 2007. Interview by Leonard G. Ramírez, José Perales-Ramos, and José Antonio Arellano, July 9, Chicago.

Bada, Xótchil, Jonathan Fox, and Andrew Selee, eds. 2006. *Invisible No More: Mexican Migrant Civic Participation in the United States.* Washington, D.C.: Woodrow Wilson International Center for Scholars. www.wilsoncenter.org/topics/pubs/Invisible%20 No%20More.pdf. Accessed July 16, 2007.

Balderrama, F. E., and R. Rodríguez. 1995. *Decade of Betrayal: Mexican Repatriation in the 1930s.* Albuquerque: University of New Mexico Press.

Barker, C., A. Johnson, and M. Lavalette. 2001. "Leadership Matters: An Introduction." In *Leadership and Social Movements,* ed. C. Barker, A. Johnson, and M. Lavalette, 1–23. Manchester: Manchester University Press.

Block, F. 2003. "Organizing versus Mobilizing: *Poor People's Movements* after 25 Years." *Perspectives on Politics* 1 (4): 733–35.

Breines, W. 1980. "Community and Organization: The New Left and Michels' 'Iron Law.'" *Social Problems* 4 (27): 419–29.

Castro, M. 1999. "Toward a New Nativism? The Immigration Debate in the United States and Its Implications for Latin America and the Caribbean." In *Free Markets, Open Societies, Closed Borders? Trends in International Migration and Immigration Policy in the Americas,* 33–52. Miami: North-South Center Press.

Cepeda, E. J. 2007. "A Horse Is a Horse." *Chicago Sun-Times,* May 10.

Chicago Fact Book. 1992. In "Promoting Hispanic Immigrant Entrepreneurship in Chicago," by Marta Tienda and Rebecca Raijman. *Journal of Developmental Entrepreneurship* 9 (1), April 2004.

Cornelius, W. A., and E. A. Marcelli. 2000. *The Changing Profile of Mexican Immigrants to the United States: New Evidence from California and Mexico.* Bonn, Germany: Institute for the Study of Labor.

D'Amezcua, Maria. 2006. Interview by Leonard G. Ramírez, José Perales-Ramos, and José Antonio Arellano. November 1, Chicago.

De la Garza, R. O., and M. Hazan. 2003. *Looking Backward, Moving Forward: Mexican Organizations in the U.S. as Agents of Incorporation and Disassociation.* http://www .trpi.org/PDFs/Looking_Backward.pdf. Accessed September 15, 2008.

Fernández, L. 2005. "From the Near West Side to 18th Street: Mexican Community Formation and Activism in Mid-Twentieth Century Chicago." *Journal of the Illinois State Historical Society.* http://findarticles.com/p/articles/mi_qa3945/is_200510/ai_ n15984337n. Accessed July 7, 2008.

Gaete, Claudio. 2007. Interview by Leonard G. Ramírez, José Perales-Ramos, and José Antonio Arellano. January 7, Chicago.

García, J. 1996. *Mexicans in the Midwest, 1900–1932.* Tucson: University of Arizona Press.

González Gutiérrez, C. 2006. "Del Acercamiento a la Inclusión Institucional: La Experiencia del Instituto de los Mexicanos en el Exterior." In *Relaciones Estado-Diáspora: Aproximaciones desde Cuatro Continentes,* ed. C. González Gutiérrez, 189–219.

Mexico City: Secretaria de Relaciones Exteriores, Instituto de Mexicanos en el Exterior.

Gutiérrez, Luis. 2006. Interview by Leonard G. Ramírez, José Perales-Ramos, and José Antonio Arellano. May 17, Chicago.

Heredia Ortiz, Carlos. 2007. Interview by Leonard G. Ramírez, José Perales-Ramos, and José Antonio Arellano. April 7, Chicago.

Higham, J. 1969. *Strangers in the Land: Patterns of American Nativism, 1860–1925.* New York: Athenaeum.

Hobsbawm, E. J. 1978. "Should the Poor Organize?" *New York Review of Books.* http://www .nybooks.com/articles/article-preview?article_id=8224. Accessed July 16, 2007.

Hoffman, A. 1974. *Unwanted Mexican Americans in the Great Depression: Repatriation Pressures, 1929–1939.* Tucson: University of Arizona Press.

Jones, A. E. 1928. "Conditions Surrounding Mexicans in Chicago." Ph.D. diss., University of Chicago.

Jones, C. E. 2003. "From Protest to Black Conservatism: The Demise of the Congress of Racial Equality." In *Black Political Organizations in the Post–Civil Rights Era,* ed. O. A. Johnson III and K. L. Stanford, 80–98. New Brunswick: Rutgers University Press.

Kerr, L. A. N. 1976. "The Chicano Experience in Chicago, 1929–1970." Ph.D. diss., University of Illinois at Chicago.

———. 2000. "Chicano Settlements in Chicago: A Brief History." In *En Aquel Entonces/ In Years Gone By: Readings in Mexican-American History,* ed. Manuel G. Gonzales and Cynthia M. Gonzales, 109–16. Bloomington: Indiana University Press.

Kling, J. 2003. "*Poor People's Movements* 25 Years Later: Historical Context, Contemporary Issues." *Perspectives on Politics* 1 (4): 727–32.

Lather, P. 2004. "Research as Praxis." In *Harvard Educational Review Reprint Series,* ed. R. A. Gastimbide-Fernández, H. A. Harding, and T. Sorde-Marti, 38:41–60. Cambridge: Harvard Educational Review.

"A Leadership Vacuum." 2005. *La Raza,* July 8. http://www.laraza.com/print .php?nid=24146&origen=1. Accessed February 1, 2007.

López, Omar. 2007. Interview by Leonard G. Ramírez, José Perales-Ramos, and José Antonio Arellano. January 10, Chicago.

Lozano, Emma. 2007. Interview by Leonard G. Ramírez, José Perales-Ramos, and José Antonio Arellano. January 8, Chicago.

Lydersen, K. 2008. "The Browning of the Greens." *Chicago Reader,* August 14, 17–19.

Mansbridge, J. J., and A. D. Morris. 2001. *Oppositional Consciousness: The Subjective Roots of Social Protest.* Chicago: University of Chicago Press.

Martínez, E. 1998. *De Colores Means All of Us: Latina Views for a Multi-Colored Century.* Cambridge, Mass.: South End.

McAdam, D. 1982. *Political Process and the Development of Black Insurgency, 1930–1970.* Chicago: University of Chicago Press.

McCarthy, J. D., and M. N. Zald. 1977. "Resource Mobilization and Social Movements: A Partial Theory." *American Journal of Sociology* 82 (6): 1212–41.

Milkman, R. 2005. *Labor Organizing among Mexican-Born Workers in the U.S.: Recent Trends and Future Prospects.* http://repositories.cdlib.org/ccpr/olwp/CCPR-029-06. Accessed September 15, 2008.

Morris, A. D. 1984. *The Origins of the Civil Rights Movement: Black Communities Organizing for Change.* New York: Free Press.

Mujica, Jorge. 2006. Interview by Leonard G. Ramírez, José Perales-Ramos, and José Antonio Arellano. August 31. Chicago, Illinois.

Muñoz, Carlos, Jr. 1989. *Youth, Identity, Power: The Chicano Movement.* London: Verso.

Padilla, F. M. 1985. *Latino Ethnic Consciousness: The Case of Mexican Americans and Puerto Ricans in Chicago.* Notre Dame, Ind.: University of Notre Dame Press.

Paral, R. 2006. "Latinos of the New Chicago." In *The New Chicago: A Social and Cultural Analysis,* ed. J. P Koval, L. Bennett, M. I. J. Bennett, F. Demissie, R. Garner, and K. Kim Kiljoong, 105–14. Philadelphia: Temple University Press.

Paral, R., T. Ready, S. Chun, and W. Sun. 2004. *Latino Demographic Growth in Metropolitan Chicago.* http://latinostudies.nd.edu/pubs/pubs/paral.pdf. Accessed August 28, 2008.

Piven, F. F. 2003. "Retrospective Comments." *Perspectives on Politics* 1 (4): 707–10.

Piven, F. F., and R. A. Cloward. 1977. *Poor People's Movements: Why They Succeed, How They Fail.* New York: Vintage.

Preston, W., Jr. 1963. *Aliens and Dissenters: Federal Suppression of Radicals, 1903–1933.* New York: Harper Torchbooks.

Ready, Timothy, and Alert Brown-Gort. 2005. *The State of Latino Chicago: This Is Home Now.* http://latinostudies.nd.edu/pubs/pubs/StateofLatino-final.pdf. Accessed August 18, 2008.

The Resurrection Project. N.d. http://www.resurrectionproject.org/display.aspx?pointer =4761. Accessed August 13, 2008.

Rodríguez, Cynthia. 2007. Interview by Leonard G. Ramírez, José Perales-Ramos, and José Antonio Arellano. January 10, Chicago.

Santa Ana, O. 2002. *Brown Tide Rising: Metaphors of Latinos in Contemporary American Public Discourse.* Austin: University of Texas Press.

Salgado, Juan. 2007. Interview by Leonard G. Ramírez, José Perales-Ramos, and José Antonio Arellano. January 19, Chicago.

Sampson, Robert J. 2008. "Rethinking Crime and Immigration." *Contexts* 7 (1): 28–33.

Schram, S. F. 2003. "The Praxis of *Poor People's Movements*: Strategy and Theory in Dissensus Politics." *Perspectives on Politics* 1 (4): 715–20.

Sepulveda, Orlando. 2006. Interview by Leonard G. Ramírez, José Perales-Ramos, and José Antonio Arellano. July 12, Chicago.

Tarrow, S. 2003. "Crossing the Ocean and Back Again with Piven and Cloward." *Perspectives on Politics* 1 (4): 711–14.

Tilly, C. 1978. *From Mobilization to Revolution.* Reading, Mass.: Addison-Wesley.

Unite Here! n.d. http://www.unitehere.org/about. Accessed September 19, 2008.

Valdes, D. 2000. *Barrios Norteños: St. Paul and Midwestern Mexican Communities in the Twentieth Century.* Austin: University of Texas Press.

Vital, Cristina. Conversation with Leonard G. Ramírez. August 13, 2008.

Weber, M. 1968. *Max Weber: The Theory of Economic and Social Organization.* Ed. A. M. Henderson and. T. Parsons. New York: Free Press.

Zavala, Moises. 2006. Interview by Leonard G. Ramírez, José Perales-Ramos, and José Antonio Arellano. July 18, Chicago.

8

Mexican Hometown Associations in Chicago

The Newest Agents of Civic Participation

XÓCHITL BADA

In the spring of 2006, Chicago-based hometown associations (HTAs) mobilized their social capital and organizational resources during the planning stages of the large-scale demonstrations to protest the Sensenbrenner Bill. The following fall, a very prominent HTA leader and organizer of the Chicago marches expressed his opinion of this bill while reflecting on the surprisingly overwhelming participation in the demonstrations: "Sensenbrenner suddenly became Saint Sensenbrenner. I feel that we should thank him for being the real catalyst of this movement [laughing]. He produced a spark, and we took care of transforming it into a real fire." From March to May of that year, HTA members participated in large marches, carrying the important message that civic participation is not only exercised through voting. One of the most popular slogans was, "Today we march, tomorrow we vote."

HTAs are immigrant membership organizations formed by people from the same community of origin. Though many began as informal groups, by the turn of the twenty-first century, hundreds had become formal organizations. HTAs function as social networks as well as transmitters of culture and values to the U.S.-born generation. At times, HTAs have responded to Mexican government encouragement by federating with other groups from their home states. These scaled-up forms of representation increase immigrant leverage with their home state governments. As their organizational capacity matures, HTAs become involved in social development projects on behalf of their communities of origin as well as in the defense of immigrant rights in their U.S. communities.

This chapter focuses on the evolution of HTAs in the United States, with a special emphasis on Chicago-based groups. It presents empirical evidence of new forms of binational engagement among Mexican immigrant communities in the United States, leading to the creation of a fledging Mexican immigrant civil society.[1]

A relative informality and political isolation characterized HTAs in the mid-1990s, but they have subsequently consolidated their structures. Their activities have also changed, growing from initial, haphazard, and infrequent infrastructure projects to current cross-border fund-raising and investment projects of a larger scale. Increased visibility has led to recognition in public and political spheres, encouraging dialogue with federal, state, and municipal governments both in Mexico and in the United States.

Between 1998 and 2006, the total number of HTAs registered nationwide almost doubled from 441 to 815. Although the data are incomplete, HTAs have clearly expanded into parts of the United States beyond traditional immigrant destinations, and there are now HTAs from twenty-eight Mexican states in thirty-five U.S. states (Secretaría 2006). Mexican HTAs are heavily concentrated in California, Texas, and Illinois: 69 percent of the U.S. total is concentrated in the metropolitan areas of Los Angeles, Chicago, Dallas, and Houston, a figure consistent with the current clustering of the Mexican immigrant population (Fox and Bada forthcoming).

HTAs initially worked only in the area of self-help, providing support and resources to newcomers experiencing unemployment, sickness, and funeral/burial expenses. In the past decade, however, they have expanded their activities to include the promotion and defense of human and labor rights in the United States, participating in immigrant rights coalitions, legalization campaigns, immigrant marches, and labor organizing. For example, Mexican HTAs' participation in the 1993 campaign against California's Proposition 187 is considered the first involvement of HTAs in domestic politics affecting immigrant rights (Escala Rabadán 2005).

This chapter examines the inner dynamics, organizational challenges, and expanding roles of HTAs, placing special emphasis on the evolution and expansion of the social networks that led to the participation of these groups in the 2006 immigrant rights marches. This new system of binational organizing needs to be examined as a potentially democratizing element involving the expansion of substantive citizenship practices in transnational contexts in both sending and receiving societies.

Methodology

This chapter builds on dissertation research conducted in Chicago and its metropolitan area; Morelia; and Mexico City between 2005 and 2007. Most of the evidence presented is based on participant observation analysis aided by a few in-depth face-to-face interviews and conversations with immigrant activists engaged in transnational practices, Mexican government officials, and practitioners in the field of binational activism. All face-to-face interviews were semistructured, conducted in Spanish, and translated by the author. Data for the chapter were collected in Chicago, Aurora, Carpentersville, and Hillside, Illinois, and in Morelia and Mexico City, with a focus on the fifth Binational Forum of Michoacano Migrants Living Abroad and the first Migrant Summit in Morelia; the first meeting of Mexican HTAs, held at Chicago's West Side Technical Institute; the eighth annual advisory board meeting and the forty-ninth informative presentation for appointed and elected officials of the Institute for Mexicans Abroad, held in Mexico City; the first national convention of the March 10 Coalition in Hillside, Illinois; and a unionization drive informational meeting held at a Lutheran church in Aurora, Illinois. I digitally recorded some of the events, and I always took detailed field notes, which I subsequently analyzed.

Toward Binational Collective Action

Formal Mexican HTAs appeared by the late 1960s, when the post-1965 wave of Mexican migrants started to settle in the Chicago metropolitan area. By organizing by village or town of origin, immigrants recast their local or regional identities along with their national allegiance. Some organizations had their origins in successful sports clubs or religious associations (Badillo 2001; Pescador 2004).

The amnesty granted by the 1986 Immigration and Reform Control Act enabled thousands of Mexican migrants living in the Chicago metropolitan area to legalize their status and travel more easily between Mexico and the United States. With each return trip, they became more aware of the economic disparities between their current U.S. communities and their rural hometowns, which lacked many of the comforts of modernity, such as running water and electricity. While playing soccer or sharing home-cooked meals at their weekly gatherings, club members talked about people and places back in Mexico. Improved telephone service, cheaper air transportation, the proliferation of fax machines and handheld video cameras, and the Internet increased the speed with which news spread and helped in the coordination and development of infrastructure projects (Bada 2003).

From their beginning, Mexican HTAs had the clear agenda of helping their communities of origin obtain basic services such as water, roads, electricity, and school renovations. In their negotiations with municipal and state governments regarding funds for community development, HTA leaders became increasingly interested in the issues affecting their hometowns. Some even decided to return and run for political positions. For example, Timoteo "Alex" Manjarrez, a Chicago-based HTA leader from Guerrero, won the mayoral position in his home municipality in 2004 with the moral support of his Chicago-based *paisanos* (Olivo and Ávila 2007). Others remained active both in Mexico and in the United States, which led to their increasing involvement in local U.S. issues such as improvements in schooling and neighborhood safety and in organizations such as unions, block clubs, and churches.

Since 2000, HTA members and leaders have increasingly become embedded in a developing binational civil society. Members of HTAs commonly have multiple affiliations—they are members of Mexican political parties, U.S. political parties, local school boards, faith-based organizations, neighborhood associations, and labor unions. These multiple memberships allow them to exercise a binational activism, working to protect immigrant rights in the United States and to counteract the effects of economic globalization and neoliberal strategies on their communities of origin. Thus, the view of immigrant organizations as politically disengaged from their host country is no longer accurate.

This increased binational civic engagement has gained visibility for Chicago's HTAs. For example, the groups helped to organize the election of Chicago's representatives to the first advisory board of the Instituto de los Mexicanos en el Exterior (Institute for Mexicans Abroad), a governmental organization created in 2002 to strengthen relations with the Mexican diaspora. The first advisory board had more than one hundred members, most of whom were appointed by the Mexican consulates; only Chicago's seven representatives were directly elected by the community. Interested in obtaining national recognition and increasing the strength of Mexican organizations in Chicago, the HTAs, along with many other Mexican organizations and the Mexican consulate, formed an ad hoc committee to organize the election at Pilsen's Benito Juárez High School, during which 814 votes were cast; elected representatives were to serve three-year terms. Subsequent Instituto de los Mexicanos en el Exterior elections in Chicago have become more organized, with higher turnouts, improved accountability mechanisms, and more diverse candidates.

In 1995, the Mexican consulate in Chicago recorded 35 Mexican HTAs in the metropolitan area. By June 2006, that number had grown to 285, and groups represented 16 Mexican states of origin as well as Mexico City. These associations are organized into seventeen federations and one confederation that includes representatives of nine of the seventeen federations. The vast majority of the leaders and board members of these associations are naturalized citizens or legal permanent residents and belong to either the middle class or the entrepreneurial sector.

While membership in U.S. voluntary associations such as the Red Cross, parent-teacher associations, and Lions and Kiwanis Clubs has declined overall since the 1970s (Putnam 2000, 48–64), immigrant-led associations have developed vigorously in the last decade. The Pew Hispanic Center surveyed 4,000 Mexican migrants and found that 14 percent were members of HTAs (Suro 2005). The Pew Hispanic Center's 2006 National Survey of Latinos also shows important differences in immigrant civic participation by national origin both at the individual and associational level (Waldinger 2007). The study of 1,429 foreign-born Latinos revealed that 9 percent belonged to civic organizations, social clubs, or sports teams of people from their native land. Participation in these activities decreased with years of residence, from roughly 12 percent of recent arrivals to only 5 percent of those who had lived in the United States for between twenty and twenty-nine years. This finding suggests that attachment to the country of origin fades over time. Only 6 percent of Mexican nationals declared themselves to be members of ethnic immigrant civic or social organizations, a striking difference from the results of the previous Pew Hispanic Center Survey.[2]

A 2006 survey of 1,512 foreign-born and native-born Latinos in the Chicago metropolitan area conducted by the University of Notre Dame found that 6 percent of foreign-born Latinos belonged to HTAs. In addition, the data suggest that membership in transnational community organizations "does not lower the probability of being involved in local community groups. In fact, 70 percent of members of hometown associations belong to at least four additional Chicago-based community organizations" (Ready, Knight, and Chun 2006, 3). The results also indicate a strong correlation between nativity and propensity to participate in civic life in Chicago metro area: "Foreign-born Latinos are much more likely to belong to a community or civic organization than are the U.S. born; 53 percent of the foreign born belong to one or more community or civic organizations compared to only 37 percent of the U.S. born" (3).

Furthermore, the proportion of Mexican immigrants involved in "individually oriented" transnational activities such as sending remittances home, traveling to their communities of origin, and calling home on a weekly basis rises with each decade of settlement in the United States and then falls sharply among those who have lived in the country for thirty years or longer, with a peak participation of 17 percent among the cohort who have lived in the United States for between twenty and twenty-nine years (Waldinger 2007, 10). A recent survey of Latinos in the Chicago metropolitan area suggests that civic engagement in the United States is positively correlated to remittance behavior for both first- and second-generation Latinos and is also related to engagement in binational social action (Chun 2005).

Such low rates of immigrant participation in civic organizations might seem to bode ill for the future consolidation of a vibrant binational immigrant civil society. However, compared to the general trend of declining civic participation in membership-based organizations, Mexicans' rate of participation in HTAs is an inspiring sign.

Some authors remain skeptical that participation in voluntary civic groups can be positively correlated with increased political participation or increased interest in altering the prevalent status quo. Elizabeth Theiss-Morse and John R. Hibbing (2005) argue, for example, that civic participation in voluntary associations in the United States should not be directly associated with an increase in political participation because many voluntary groups consider political democracy messy, inefficient, and conflict-ridden. Members of these groups are quite homogeneous and tend to display a distaste for formal politics. Therefore, the authors claim, these associations have not usually been credited as promoters of public policy changes because they confine their concerns to practical fundraising projects that support noncontroversial goals. The authors conclude that "voluntary groups perform wonderful services and have undeniable value to society, but their effect on democratic politics is tenuous and possibly negative" (2005, 244).

While this argument may hold for many voluntary associations concerned exclusively with national issues, it does not apply to binational organizations. The case of Mexican HTAs and their creation of public policy initiatives to address development in their communities of origin offers evidence of such groups' potential as agents of social change. In 2002, several HTAs won an extension to the Mexican federal level of the government's matching fund program for migrants, the Programa 3 × 1 para Migrantes. Very few Mexican state governments previously had formally implemented state-level programs involving federal, state, municipal, and collective remittance funds to address the development needs of rural towns in regions of high outmigration (Escala Rabadán, Bada, and Rivera-Salgado 2006).

Increasing quantitative and qualitative evidence also shows that involvement in HTAs has led to greater interest in U.S. politics. The new evidence contradicts Samuel Huntington's zero-sum hypothesis of transnational incorporation, which argues that participation in home country politics decreases the possibilities of civic and political involvement in U.S. politics (cited in McCann, Cornelius, and Leal 2007). McCann, Cornelius, and Leal (2007) find a positive and highly significant correlation between Mexican immigrants' engagement in Mexican and U.S. public affairs. Evidence also shows that organized group membership is correlated with practices of civic binationality. For example, the creation of Mexicans for Political Progress in Chicago resulted directly from HTAs' interest in U.S. domestic politics. In June 2006, as a consequence of HTAs' participation in the immigrant rights marches, a group of Chicago-based HTA leaders formed a political action committee (PAC) to support electoral candidates committed to the agenda and demands of Mexican immigrants. The group is registered as a nonpartisan organization, although most of the candidates it has backed are Democrats. Through its ad hoc group, Mexicans for Blagojevich, the PAC endorsed the reelection of the former Illinois governor and raised twenty-five thousand dollars for his campaign. Moreover, the group registered 150 volunteers to participate in voter registration, canvassing, and logistical support on Election Day (Federación 2007). During the 2007–8 presidential primaries, the PAC organized regular gatherings to watch the Democratic candidates' debates and determine support for immigrant rights before endorsing a candidate (Mexicanos 2007).

Within the past decade, the activities of Mexican HTAs and state federations in the Chicago area have diversified. While they continue to address development in Mexico, they are also participating in U.S. domestic issues. Their leaders increasingly play key roles in local institutions such as labor unions, block clubs, parent-teacher associations, neighborhood organizations, March of Dimes volunteering efforts, immigrant advocacy organizations (such as the Illinois Coalition of Immigrant and Refugee Rights [ICIRR]), and the Illinois Office of New Americans Policy and Advocacy. Probably the most significant factor in this change is a new leadership more attuned to interests in the United States that has promoted more active binational civic engagement.

Many Mexican immigrant leaders are proud that Governor Blagojevich appointed a former HTA leader from Michoacán as the first director of the Office of New Americans Policy and Advocacy. More recently, ICIRR appointed a Michoacán HTA leader who had been very active in labor organizing and the immigrant rights movement as its new political director. However, these highly visible positions mark new challenges for these leaders more familiar with the mechanics of the Mexican political system than U.S.-style politics. As a result, the HTAs have faced some difficulties in handling the national press and in securing trustworthy advisers. In their efforts to increase their visibility within formal political channels, immigrant leaders have slowly gained important decision-making positions, although they need to acquire more experience to master the difficult transition from the world of activism to public policy making.

The Chicago-Michoacán Connection

HTAs from the state of Michoacán are among the most prominent in the Chicago metropolitan area and offer a good snapshot of the road the city's HTAs have traveled over the past decade. Chicago's first Michoacano HTAs were established around the late 1960s, and the Federation of Michoacano Clubs in Illinois was formed in 1997. In Mexico, these organizations have fought corruption and demanded government attention and resources for their communities.

Financial, political, and civic influence have flowed continuously back and forth between the two countries. Michoacano migrants have utilized the mass media to criticize their state government, both for its authoritarian politics and for forcing them to become economic exiles. After 2001, when the opposition gained power, communication between Michoacano immigrant organizations and the new state government became much smoother. Michoacano migrants have forged a strong network of more than one hundred HTAs, most of them in California, Illinois, Nevada, Washington, and Texas (Reynoso Acosta 2005).

In 2004, during Michoacán's midterm congressional elections, several immigrant candidates ran for seats in the state legislature, and the 2005–7 Michoacán Congress included at least seven legislators who obtained their seats after returning from the United States. In addition to supporting immigrant candidates, the Michoacán government sought to extend its presence beyond its geographical borders in several domains, including health, education, and job training, especially in California and Illinois. Several government agencies now offer services such as job training, medical treatment, and distance-learning high school education for Michoacanos living in the United States. In Chicago, these programs are housed in Casa Michoacán, which is in Pilsen, historically a port-of-entry neighborhood for Mexican immigrants, and provides space for hometown clubs, grassroots organizations, and university events. Planning for the spring 2006 immigrant rights marches also took place at Casa Michoacán.

Michoacano HTAs have also become interested in labor organizing in Chicago. Several HTA members and leaders also serve as union representatives or labor organizers. For example, many members of the San Miguel Epejan HTA in Aurora, Illinois, work for Fox Valley Forge, a foundry. In late 2005, some former HTA leaders organized a unionization drive at the factory, and the union struck in March 2007 to protest work conditions and declining wages. The strikers had the backing of some town council members, several HTAs, and AFL-CIO Solidarity International in Mexico City, which offered strategic advice and gained media attention on both sides of the border. By July, management agreed to reopen negotiations after the strike's leaders announced that they were asking two Mexican companies to suspend all transactions with Fox Valley Forge. The National Labor Relations Board dismissed the union's unfair labor practices complaint against the company in September 2007, and an appeal is pending. The immigrant community's support has been vital to the union's efforts.

Michoacano immigrant participation in local issues in the United States remains limited in part because improving social conditions in their communities of origin has proved easier than navigating U.S. local and national politics. Circumstances may soon change, however, as HTAs mature and learn to become effective advocates for social change in both host and home communities. In fact, the HTAs' engagement in country-of-origin politics has recently advanced their civic and political integration and advocacy.

The Promise of a Binational Agenda

Most of Chicago's HTAs and federations have extended their networks both within and outside of their traditional webs of relations. In 2003, many of the Mexican hometown federations created the Confederation of Mexican Federations in the Midwest (CONFEMEX), an umbrella organization representing nine federations of Mexican migrants (see Vonderlack-Navarro 2007). CONFEMEX has a mission to work with the Mexican immigrant community to achieve a more dignified life for immigrants and their families both in Chicago and in Mexico. CONFEMEX's membership includes 179 metropolitan Chicago HTAs, who elect an executive committee every two years.

In 2004, CONFEMEX became one of the founding members of the National Alliance of Latin American and Caribbean Communities, a network of ninety immigrant-led organizations working to improve the quality of life in their communities in the United States and in countries of origin. Through this alliance, CONFEMEX has worked to support the immigrant rights marches, a petition demanding emergency protected status for immigrant victims of Hurricane Katrina, Illinois bills that would allow undocumented persons to obtain driver's licenses, a bill that would validate the consular identification card as an official form of identification in the state of Illinois, education reform, day laborers' rights, voter registration, naturalization drives, and economic development in Latin America.

In 2005 and 2006, some CONFEMEX members were invited speakers at the annual conference of the RainbowPUSH Coalition and Citizenship Education Fund in Chicago, where they discussed how immigration laws affect employment, citizenship, and human rights. CONFEMEX's participation in these events resulted from the relationships that some members have established with African American organizations. Since its establishment in the early 1980s, Chicago's Latino Chapter of the RainbowPUSH Coalition has worked to establish more permanent relations with the African American community. In the past decade, the Latino Chapter has worked to impress on African American parents the benefits of education in a second language for their children. The former president of the Latino Chapter explained, "I always tell black parents that I would love if their kids can do business in immigrant Latino barrios and vice versa. I always tell them that if they speak Spanish, they can do business with Latin America. It is a win-win situation. I want Latino kids to learn English, but I also think that black kids can benefit from learning Spanish through good-quality bilingual education." Other issues on which blacks and Latinos have found common ground include minority access to higher education, police brutality, and support for candidates for police commander positions in some districts.

From Mexican Elections to the Immigrant Rights Movement

During the campaign to register Mexican voters to exercise their newly acquired right to participate in Mexican elections through absentee ballots in 2006, CONFEMEX, the largest umbrella organization of HTAs, registered fourteen hundred people in three days with support from the Massachusetts-based Solidago Foundation. In spite of the various challenges of registering, 3,439 Mexicans registered in Cook, DuPage, Will, Lake, McHenry, and Kane Counties, 10 percent of the total Mexican electorate registered in the United States (Instituto Federal Electoral 2006).[3]

Mexican migrants of different political affiliations were united in their desire to obtain the right to submit absentee votes in the Mexican presidential elections. Many of Chicago's most active HTA leaders had undergone political training in Mexico and, because of the country's long history of one-party rule, were affiliated with the Institutional Revolutionary Party, although others were active in the opposition. These activists thus acquired their leadership abilities, organizational skills, and interest in political participation before they arrived in the United States, an observation that is consistent with the history of other immigrant organizations in the late nineteenth and early twentieth centuries (Bodnar 1985, 121). In fact, the trend of prior political engagement in communities of origin contradicts previous explanations of HTA dynamics. Some scholars have contended that Mexican HTAs encourage immigrants to integrate into their host society by providing them with U.S. democratic values, but this argument incorrectly assumes that Mexicans lack these attributes before immigrating (De la Garza and Hazan 2003; Leiken 2002).

In the past decade, migrants in Chicago have mobilized to demand legalization for undocumented immigrants. In September 2000, under the leadership of ICIRR and with the participation of the Association of Community Organizations for Reform Now, the Service Employees International Union, Centro sin Fronteras, and other Chicago-based immigrant rights organizations, approximately ten thousand people rallied in downtown Chicago to demand legalization for the undocumented. After the September 11 attacks, however, immigration became connected to the issue of national security, and proponents of legalization needed a new context for regaining public visibility.

In Chicago, that opportunity was provided by attacks by the Minutemen. In response to those attacks, migrants led by Marco Cárdenas, a priest at Our Lady of Fátima Church, and with the urging of Rafael "El Pistolero" Pulido, a Mexican-born radio DJ, mobilized in July 2005 in the Back of the Yards. The HTAs miscalculated, declining to participate because leaders believed that the media would not cover the demonstration (Martínez and Piña 2005).

The Sensenbrenner Bill was passed a few months later, while many HTAs and other Mexican political groups were preparing to register voters for the following year's Mexican presidential elections. Regardless of their legal status or country of origin, many immigrants living in the United States perceived the measure as a unifying force, demanding dignity, respect, and a reaffirmation of their rightful place as productive law-abiding members of U.S. society. Mexican migrant organizations understood the importance of orchestrating an immediate response to the Sensenbrenner Bill despite their busy workload with the Mexican election campaign. After some unsuccessful attempts to encourage the Mexican Federal Electoral Institute to move quickly with the distribution of absentee ballots, the HTAs soon realized that their efforts to increase voter registration for Mexican elections would bring scant success as a consequence of the highly restrictive voting rules. HTA leaders consequently decided to use the momentum created by the voter registration drive to fight the Sensenbrenner Bill. The simultaneous orchestration of mobilization campaigns in Mexico and Chicago offers supporting evidence to McCann, Cornelius, and Leal's (2007) finding of a positive and highly significant correlation between engagement in Mexican and U.S. public affairs.

HTAs' direct involvement in the organization of the immigrant rights marches was a new development in the scope of their local activities. HTAs had participated in the September 2000 march only as members of a large organizational network coordinated by ICIRR and had played no organizing role. During the spring 2006 protests, however, Mexican HTAs displayed their new ability to mobilize their constituents for domestic issues. HTA representatives were key members of the March 10 Coalition. Some HTA leaders spoke during the rally, rubbing elbows with local politicians, established Latino activists, and immigrant leaders of different nationalities.

The leaders of the March 10 Coalition quickly understood that the rally would require support from other minorities. In Cook County (where Chicago is located), Latinos represent 22.5 percent of the population, while African Americans account for 25.8 percent and Asians 5.4 percent (U.S. Census Bureau 2007). At first, the meetings to plan the march took place almost entirely in Spanish, but in a creative and sophisticated adjustment, instant translations were soon provided through special headsets (Ávila and Martínez 2006).

African American leaders also provided support. Jesse Jackson spoke at Casa Michoacán during one of the organizing meetings. Jackson had committed to speak at the May 1 rally in New York City but publicly endorsed the Chicago march in late April, announcing, "There is real fear among blacks about the loss of jobs. But it's not because of the undocumented workers that are the cause. It's cheaper wage jobs" (Konkol 2006, 48). Jackson also attributed the problems with obtaining decent pay to the exodus of manufacturing jobs overseas (Ayi

2006; Konkol 2006). Estimates show that 3 percent of Chicago's May 1, 2006, marchers were African American (Flores-González et al. 2006; see also chap. 2). The most visible organized groups with large African American constituents included the Association of Community Organizations for Reform Now and the Student/Tenant Organizing Project, a group of housing activists from the city's South Side (Ginsberg-Jaeckle 2006).

The 2005–8 wave of mobilizations gave Mexican immigrant organizations an opportunity to develop a campaign to encourage legal permanent residents to acquire U.S. citizenship and promote their formal electoral participation while making sure that legal status did not prevent people from volunteering with immigrant rights advocacy organizations.

The momentum created by the immigrant marches in Chicago reached the suburbs in the fall of 2006, when the town trustees of Carpentersville, forty miles to the northwest, unsuccessfully tried to pass an ordinance penalizing landlords for renting to undocumented migrants and businesses for hiring undocumented workers. Facing $372,000 in uncollected ambulance fees, some of which were owed by people with Latino surnames, members of the town council concluded that undocumented immigrants posed an excessive burden. Officials were surprised, however, at the organized immigrant community's strong reaction: more than two thousand protesters attended the next council meeting to denounce the ordinance (Kotlowitz 2007).

Some protesters were residents of Carpentersville, while others came from Elgin and Chicago. Many members of one Michoacano HTA, Club la Purísima, reside in Carpentersville and attended the demonstration. La Purísima leaders not only urged people to join the protest but organized a voter registration campaign prior to the next town council elections. Mexican parents encouraged their U.S.-born children to go out and register young voters. The effort generated mixed results, however, and the number of Latino voters remained low, in large part because many of Carpentersville's immigrant residents are recent arrivals who lack voting rights. During a public presentation at the First Latin American Migrant Community Summit held at Morelia, Michoacán, in 2007, city council member Linda Sánchez declared with tears in her eyes, "When I ran for this position, only 79 Mexicans voted for me in the election and this hurts me so much because my parents are Mexican."

In the fall of 2006, La Purísima Club members had been busy organizing the presentation of a book about their hometown written by historian James Cockcroft. They were very proud that the book presentation was going to take place at Casa Michoacán. Once again, they gathered to discuss issues pertaining to their community of origin. However, according to Cockcroft, the meeting quickly turned into a political planning session around the persecution taking place in Carpentersville (Cockcroft 2006). The HTAs' role in fighting the Carpentersville ordinance became highly visible when it became the subject of a cover article in the *New York Times Magazine* in August 2007 (Kotlowitz 2007).

CONFEMEX helped to organize the first Latin American Community Migrant Summit, held in Morelia, Mexico, in May 2007. The event brought together more than one thousand individuals and Canadian, European, and U.S. grassroots organizations to promote the development of healthy communities in both countries of origin and destination. The summit sought to develop innovative proposals to alleviate the south-north migratory flows in the Americas by providing a deeper understanding of the root causes of emigration. Participants also discussed the need to increase immigrants' civic and political participation by taking into account the political experiences and cultural frames in immigrants' countries of origin. Illinois Democratic congressman Luis Gutiérrez served as the meeting's keynote speaker, presenting the main components of the STRIVE Act, which he sponsored. During one session, organizers urged participants to contact their congressional representatives to demand support for immigration reform.

Conclusions

While Mexican HTAs' are still devising civic and political strategies to defend immigrants' human, social, and economic rights, their new avenues of participation indicate the emergence of a fledging immigrant civil society working simultaneously in Mexico and the United States. The most important challenge for these organizations will be the definition of a feasible binational agenda and a determination of priorities. Since many HTAs have not yet decided to register as 501 (c) 3 organizations, division of labor among members will need to be highly efficient if the conversion of the informal HTA model into formal nonprofit organizations is further delayed.

Despite many members' political disenfranchisement, Mexican HTAs have transformed traditional forms of civic participation. Nevertheless, there are still very few organizations with both transnational agendas and the resources needed to participate in the global arena.

Binational civic engagement is not a zero-sum game for many HTAs, which have slowly but steadily increased their social and political integration into both sending and receiving societies. Some critics of the binational civic engagement approach (e.g., Huntington 2004; Renshon 2005) are deeply concerned with the issue of divided loyalties, but they have not produced convincing evidence to demonstrate that existing and potential binational citizens pose a real threat to U.S. sovereignty and national identity. The Mexican side of the equation also has its share of scholars and journalists who oppose immigrant political participation in home country affairs, although they have been mostly concerned with the very high cost of implementing the Mexican electoral system abroad (Riva Palacio 2005).

In contrast to mostly ideologically driven claims, the empirical evidence shows that rather than producing a contradiction of divided loyalties, migrants' dual commitments tend to be mutually reinforcing. Specifically, many immigrant organizations' efforts to help their Mexican hometowns have led to engagement in U.S. society. In the 1980s and early 1990s, Mexican HTAs were more inward-looking, focusing almost exclusively on their home communities. However, since the turn of the century, they have increasingly engaged with a wide range of U.S. civil society actors and elected officials in Illinois and elsewhere. In the past decade, HTAs have pursued two-track strategies, sustaining their commitments to their communities of origin while working to improve their home communities in the United States. We do not claim that this is a widespread practice, but there are some positive signs that might lead in that direction.

This new visibility has brought several of Chicago's Mexican HTAs legitimacy and credibility among local elected officials. Immigrants are increasingly organizing along the model of HTAs and state and regional federations. Chicago-based federations are also recruiting HTAs throughout the Midwest, and HTAs in Ohio, Minnesota, Indiana, and Michigan have flourished. In the near future, Mexican HTAs hold great promise for increasing the quality and density of migrants' social capital while brightening the possibilities for the consolidation of a robust civil society in which immigrants have direct representation in the social fabric of Mexico and the United States.

Notes

1. The concept of an immigrant civil society refers to immigrant-led grassroots organizations and public institutions that sometimes engage with communities of origin. This category is useful for understanding the broader significance of civic binationality practices, where migrants simultaneously engage with U.S. civic life and their communities and countries of origin. For a more detailed analysis of these concepts, see Fox and Bada forthcoming.

2. The differing results with the previous Pew Survey of Mexican immigrants might have to do with the sample size. In a sample of 1,429, fewer Mexicans were captured in the analysis.

3. Registration required a valid voting card, which many Mexicans in the United States lacked. In addition, registrants had to travel to a consulate or have access to the Internet to obtain a registration form and pay the postage to submit the application via certified mail.

References

Ávila, Oscar, and Michael Martínez. 2006. "Immigrants at Crossroads: Stakes Are High for Legalization Campaign." *Chicago Tribune,* May 1.

Ayi, Mema. 2006. "Jackson: We're All in This Immigration Battle Together." *Chicago Defender,* April 26.

Bada, Xóchitl. 2003. *Mexican Hometown Associations.* Albuquerque: Inter-Hemispheric Resource Center.

Bada, Xóchitl, Jonathan Fox, and Andrew Selee, eds. 2006. *Invisible No More: Mexican Migrant Civic Participation in the United States.* Washington, D.C.: Woodrow Wilson International Center for Scholars.

Badillo, David A. 2001. "Religion and Transnational Migration in Chicago: The Case of the Potosinos." *Journal of the Illinois State Historical Society* 94 (4): 420–40.

Bodnar, John E. 1985. *The Transplanted: A History of Immigrants in Urban America.* Bloomington: Indiana University Press.

Chun, Sung. 2005. "Remittance Behavior, Assimilation, and Socio-Cultural-Economic Factors: A Case Study of Latinos in the Chicago Metropolitan Area." Paper presented at the Annual Meeting of the Population Association of America, Philadelphia.

Cockroft, James. 2006. E-mail to author, December 1.

De la Garza, Rodolfo O., and Myriam Hazan. 2003. *Looking Backward, Moving Forward: Mexican Organizations in the U.S. as Agents of Incorporation and Dissociation.* Los Angeles: Tomás Rivera Policy Institute.

Escala Rabadán, Luis. 2005. "Derechos Humanos y Asociaciones de Migrantes Mexicanos en California." *Migraciones Internacionales* 3 (2): 84–107.

Escala Rabadán, Luis, Xóchitl Bada, and Gaspar Rivera-Salgado. 2006. "Mexican Migrant Civic and Political Participation in the U.S.: The Case of Hometown Associations in Los Angeles and Chicago." *Norteamérica Academic Journal* 1 (2): 127–72.

Federación de Clubes Michoacanos en Illinois. 2007. "Mexicanos for Political Progress (MX-PP): Un Paso Más en la Participación Cívica de la Comunidad Mexicana." *Presencia Michoacana en el Medio Oeste,* 60.

Flores-González, Nilda, Amalia Pallares, Cedric Herring, and Maria Krysan. 2006. *UIC Immigrant Mobilization Project General Survey Findings.* http://www.wilsoncenter .org/news/docs/uicstudy.pdf. Accessed May 13, 2009.

Fox, Jonathan, and Xóchitl Bada. Forthcoming. "Migrant Civic Engagement." In *Rallying for Immigrant Rights,* ed. I. Bloemraad and K. Voss. Berkeley: University of California Press.

Ginsberg-Jaeckle, Matt. 2006. "Unity in the Community: Housing Activists March for Immigrants' Rights." *Fight Back!* July–August, 6.

Huntington, Samuel P. 2004. *Who Are We? The Challenges to America's National Identity.* New York: Simon and Schuster.

Instituto Federal Electoral. 2006. "Informe de los resultados de la votación emitida por los mexicanos residentes en el extranjero." Mexico City. http://www.ife.org.mx/portal/ site/ifev2/Internacional/. Accessed March 11, 2010.

Konkol, Mark J. 2006. "Chicago Immigration March Gets PUSH support: Jackson Pledges Participants, Says Blacks Need Not Fear." *Chicago Sun-Times,* April 26.

Kotlowitz, Alex. 2007. "Our Town." *New York Times Magazine,* August 5.

Leiken, Robert S. 2002. *The Melting Border: Mexico and the Mexican Communities in the United States.* Washington, D.C.: Center for Equal Opportunity.

Martínez, Cindy, and Francisco Piña. 2005. "Chicago en Marcha por Reforma Migratoria." *MX sin Fronteras,* August, 7–9.

McCann, James A., Wayne Cornelius, and David Leal. 2007. "Does Engagement in Campaigns and Elections South of the Border Pull Mexican Immigrants away from U.S. Politics? Evidence from the 2006 Mexican Expatriate Study." Paper presented at the International Congress of the Latin American Studies Association, Montreal.

Mexicanos for Political Progress. 2007. Líderes Mexicanos Invitan a Presenciar y Analizar el Debate Presidencial Demócrata. September 8. Binational Michoacano Front (FREBIMICH). Electronic discussion group. http://groups.google.com/group/frebimich. Accessed October 3, 2007.

Morawska, Ewa. 1999. *The New-Old Transmigrants, Their Transnational Lives, and Ethnicization: A Comparison of 19th/20th and 20th/21st C. Situations.* San Domenico di Fiesole, Italy: European University Institute.

Olivo, Antonio, and Oscar Ávila. 2007. "Influence on Both Sides of the Border: Activists' Political Power Is Rising in Chicago and Their Homeland, as They Seek Reforms through Marches and Money." *Chicago Tribune,* April 6.

Pescador, Juan J. 2004. "¡Vamos Taximaroa! Mexican/Chicano Soccer Associations and Transnational/Translocal Communities, 1967–2002." *Latino Studies* 2 (3): 352–76.

Putnam, Robert D. 2000. *Bowling Alone. The Collapse and Revival of American Community.* New York: Simon and Schuster.

Ready, Timothy, Roger Knight, and Sung-Chan Chun. 2006. *Latino Civic and Community Involvement: Findings from the Chicago-Area Survey.* Notre Dame, Ind.: Institute for Latino Studies, University of Notre Dame.

Renshon, Stanley A. 2005. *The 50% American: Immigration and National Identity in an Age of Terror.* Washington, D.C.: Georgetown University Press.

Reynoso Acosta, Eneida. 2005. *Relación de Clubes de Michoacanos en los E.U.A.* Morelia: Coordinación General de Atención al Migrante Michoacano.

Riva Palacio, Raymundo. 2005. *Tacto de Elefante.* February 25. http://www.eluniversal.com.mx/columnas/45939.html. Accessed February 2005.

Secretaría de Desarrollo Social de Mexico. 2006. *Programa 3 por 1 para Migrantes.* www.sedesol.gob.mex. Accessed September 2009.

Suro, Roberto. 2005. *Mexican Migrant Worker Survey.* Los Angeles: Pew Hispanic Center, University of Southern California, Instituto de los Mexicanos en el Exterior.

Suro, Roberto, and Gabriel Escobar. 2006. *2006 National Survey of Latinos: The Immigration Debate.* Washington, D.C.: Pew Hispanic Center.

Theiss-Morse, Elizabeth, and John R. Hibbing. 2005. "Citizenship and Civic Engagement." *Annual Review of Political Science* 8 (1): 227–49.

Thelen, David. 1999. "Rethinking History and the Nation-State: Mexico and the United States." *Journal of American History* 86 (2): 439–52.

Tuan, Yi-fu. 1974. *Topophilia: A Study of Environmental Perception, Attitudes, and Values.* Englewood Cliffs, N.J.: Prentice-Hall.

U.S. Census Bureau, 2006–8. *American Community Survey Demographic Estimates.* http://factfinder.census.gov. Accessed November 19, 2009.

Vonderlack-Navarro, Rebecca. 2007. *Chicago Mexican Hometown Associations and the Confederation of Mexican Federations: Experiences of Binational Civic Participation.* http://www.wilsoncenter.org/news/docs/Chicago%20Vonderlack.pdf. Accessed May 5, 2008.

Waldinger, Roger. 2007. *Between Here and There: How Attached Are Latino Immigrants to Their Native Country?* Washington, D.C.: Pew Hispanic Center.

Permission to March?

High School Youth Participation in the Immigrant Rights Movement

SONIA OLIVA

On April 28, 2006, the Chicago Public Schools (CPS) sent home a letter warning parents of the consequences students would face if they missed school to participate in the May 1, 2006, immigrant rights march. Students had to choose from among three options: they could attend school all day, attend the march and miss school, or attend school and walk out in protest. Students' decisions were further complicated by the fact that they received mixed and often contradictory messages about participation: some teachers, administrators, and staff supported student participation by looking the other way, openly encouraging students to attend, or even leading "field trips" to the march, but the CPS's official position, backed by other educators, was that students should be in school and that they would face severe disciplinary action if they missed school or walked out. In spite of these threats, many students marched.

In this chapter, I examine how and why so many high school students participated despite CPS policy. I first examine the contradictory attitudes of CPS officials, underscoring the specific ways in which principle, policy, and practice often conflicted and the practices educators and administrators used to encourage or discourage students from attending the march. I subsequently examine how students dealt with these contradictory policies and practices and worked within the system to find ways of attending the marches while avoiding major penalties. Finally, I reflect on the effects of this and subsequent marches on students' political development as well as on the school board's policy.

We conducted seventeen semistructured interviews with CPS high school students who participated in the March 10 and May 1, 2006, immigration marches. The majority of the interviews were conducted in June and July 2006. Interviewees attended ten different high schools, seven of them predominantly Latino.[1] During the last month of the 2006 academic year, I asked high school teachers in

Latino communities to refer me to students who had participated in the marches. I recruited other students through community organizations or through the Immigrant Mobilization Project. All the respondents were between the ages of fourteen and eighteen. Students were asked why they marched and in what ways their school supported or discouraged their participation. In addition to analyzing interviews, I examined the CPS's attendance policy and Student Code of Conduct and newspaper articles that specifically addressed youth (which I define as students in grades K–12) participation in the Chicago marches.

Defining Engagement

According to Spring (1985), public education in the United States was originally designed to produce civically and politically engaged students who could participate and sustain democracy. Broadly defined, civic engagement involves providing for the public good by volunteering, while political engagement involves making changes in governmental and political institutions through voting and other activities (Zukin et al. 2006). In this manner, schools are responsible for providing students with civic and political knowledge and skills needed to become engaged in the democratic process (Torney-Purta 2002). Schools are purportedly one of the central sites where youth become politicized (Andolina et al. 2003; Youniss et al. 2002). Schools often teach youth about government functions, current political issues, and the importance of voting. Several scholars have noted that schools indeed have the greatest potential for fostering civic and political engagement, but only when they meet certain criteria: providing students with a rigorous curriculum in civic education, securing a safe space for discussing and debating issues that matter to them, and encouraging students to become involved in student government and other community service projects (Andolina et al. 2003; Torney-Purta 2002).

In recent years, the practice of civics has been institutionalized in programs such as service learning (Billig 2000). CPS defines service learning as "a teaching and learning methodology that connects classroom curriculum with identified community issues and needs. Service Learning engages students in projects that serve the community and build their social and academic capacities. . . . Service Learning is designed to enhance social and academic learning while developing character and citizenship skills" (CPS, Office of High School Programs 2007). CPS students are now required to complete forty hours of service learning to graduate from high school.

Institutionalized political practices in schools include student governments that provide youth with the opportunity to run for elected office, campaign, make speeches, and convince their peers that they are the best potential representative. In addition, many schools run mock local or national elections and mock United Nations or debate teams. Most schools do not explore new ways of exposing students to forms of political engagement that fall outside of this narrowly defined scope, more so when this entails protesting. In Chicago, many high schools saw the marches as a potential problem, declaring the rallies unsafe and punishing students who missed school. However, some schools or individual teachers viewed the immigrant rights marches as a novel opportunity to expose students to another form of politics (see chap. 5).

Latino Student Protests: Then and Now

Despite public schools' role in the politicization of youth, school and police authorities historically have repressed youth who engage in protest (Barrera 2004; Escobar 1993; Mora 2007). Previous work has documented that Latino youth in the United States have a long history of participating in social movements, particularly in the areas of education and immigration. In the late 1960s and early 1970s, the struggle for educational equality was not limited to one geographic region but spread to many Latino communities across the United States. Parents, youth, and community members protested two related issues: segregated schools and unequal treatment within them (Alvarez 1986; Donato 1997; Munoz 1989; Valencia 2002). In Los Angeles, Houston, and Chicago, youth boycotted schools, staged sit-ins, and walked out of schools to voice their discontent with the educational system. During the 1968 East Los Angeles blowouts, school authorities locked the gates so that students could not walk out, squad cars were sent to schools to scare students, and the police used force on many of the demonstrators (Escobar 1993). In 1973, Puerto Rican students and activists in Chicago were arrested for minor incidents, and some were charged with mob action after a school protest where several police officers were injured and personal property was damaged (Aronson 1973; Soll and Herman 1973; Herman 1973).

Aside from isolated bouts of activism by college students in the 1980s, Latino youth activism on a large-scale basis was dormant from the early 1970s until 1994, with another resurgence in 2006. The reasons why Latino young people took to the streets in 1994 and 2006 differed substantially from earlier years. Latino students, citizens, and legal and undocumented residents were now protesting proposed legislation to restrict immigrant rights and terminate basic social services for and deport the undocumented. In 1994, Proposition 187, introduced as a ballot initiative in California, sought to deny undocumented immigrants access to most social services, including education and health, and some of the state's high school students walked out in protest. Police responded with tear gas, barricaded the streets, and locked protesters inside a football stadium (Mora 2007, 39). While police treatment of youth in 1994 paralleled the response to youth activism in the 1960s and 1970s, the more recent protests were very different in scope, as they targeted federal policy, not the public school system or school property. So while previous police repression could be explicated as a defense of the schools as well as a questioning of student behavior, the sole focus in 1994 was student behavior.

In general, protest by any student population is constructed as deviant. While schools in principle promote a civically engaged student body by inculcating in youth civic education and opportunities to become socially responsible citizens, certain types of student activities—protests, sit-ins, boycotts, and most forms of civil disobedience—are systematically excluded. In addition, Latino and African American youth are perceived as untrustworthy troublemakers and criminals (Giroux 2003a, 2003b). The crime-prone image of Latino youth fuels existing racial and ethnic stereotypes and justifies the creation of oppressive policies (Collins 2000; Glassner 1999; Males 1999). In many urban schools, when Latino and other students of color walk into school buildings, they are mandated to walk through metal detectors and are treated as criminals, with their bodies and personal belongings subject to inspection (Saltman and Gabbard 2003). This increased presence of metal detectors, armed police officers, and surveillance cameras has resulted in the militarization of schools, which now resemble prisons (Mukherjee 2007; Saltman and Gabbard 2003). In addition, it has also justified the creation of punitive zero-tolerance policies that call for suspension and expulsion of students for major and minor disciplinary problems (Noguera 1995). Schools and school leaders who view their role as repressing and controlling students do not necessarily view Latino youth as good citizens or even as potential good citizens but rather see such students as deviant individuals who need to be policed and punished for their activism.

In the case of the immigrant rights marches of 2006, this criminalization of youth resulted in the purported need to repress, contain, and punish students for their social activism. In the spring of 2006, protests against the Sensenbrenner Bill led to the massive mobilization of millions of people, including high school students. The unprecedented number of people participating in the marches necessitated extra police on the streets. School authorities and police in cities across the country tried to stop students from participating in the marches. In Los Angeles, students received truancy citations, and several were told that they could be suspended or expelled and could face two hundred dollars in fines and twenty days of community service if they walked out of school to attend the march (*Police* 2006). In Escondido, north of San Diego, police used pepper spray on students and arrested twenty-four (Maass 2006). In Houston, students were told they could be placed in detention or in-school suspension; those who repeatedly walked out could be suspended or removed (*Saavedra's Statement* 2006). Some efforts to deter students from participating were quite drastic and punitive. One case that gained national attention was that of Anthony Soltero, a California eighth-grader who committed suicide after his principal threatened to have him imprisoned, banned him from graduation activities, and fined his mother $250 after he led immigrant rights walkouts at his school (Johnson 2006; McNary 2006).

The Chicago Context

These rather harsh experiences were not replicated in Chicago, where most of the students I sampled faced only an unexcused absence (the CPS term for any occasion when a student lacks a justifiable reason for being absent from school). Moreover, while the Chicago high school students interviewed were warned about more severe consequences, those threats were empty. Two related factors explain Chicago's exceptionalism: the set of macropolitical conditions that distinguish Chicago from other settings and the set of micropolitical environments in schools. School conditions are influenced by macropolitical conditions and allow for a number of contradictions between policy and practice, creating a gray area in which what is permissible and what is possible do not necessarily coincide. Teachers' and students' ability to identify and utilize this gray area enabled students' massive participation in the May 1 march.

CITY POLITICS

Unlike many other mayors, Chicago's Richard M. Daley has openly supported and participated in immigrant rights marches. Following his lead, many Illinois politicians, including former governor Rod Blagojevich, Senator Dick Durbin, and Congressman Luis Gutiérrez, along with religious figures and Spanish-language radio disc jockeys, have also expressed their support. This "immigrant-friendly" approach led the city of Chicago and Cook County to adopt sanctuary policies for the undocumented (Avila 2006). Furthermore, unlike some cities in California and Texas, the Chicago police and school board have not cracked down on students, issued truancy tickets, or fined students. The actions taken by local authorities and elected officials during and after the marches are not surprising, given Chicago's history and current standing as a city of immigrants with a strong ethnic base. Chicago has one of the country's largest and most diverse populations and continues to welcome new immigrants (Ready and Brown-Gort 2005). This widespread support for newcomers and immigrant rights expressed by influential and powerful individuals in various institutions makes Chicago unique.

Chicago is also unique because the city's schools operate as one unified district headed by the mayor. In light of Daley's public support of the movement, CPS officials issued a letter to students and parents expressing support for immigrant rights but not for student participation in the marches. Schools and teachers, in turn, did not strictly enforce this official policy. Although students were told that missing school to participate would result in an unexcused absence, many students did not receive such absences, and officials did not work to track down those who attended the rally. Furthermore, these policies were either ignored and/or enforced selectively by individual schools and staff members.

School Policies and Practices: A Study in Contradictions

A contradiction between school policy and practice occurs when an official school policy exists but is not enforced by all schools, school administrators, teachers, or staff members. An in-depth examination of the messages that high school students received systemwide (CPS), from their schools (administrators), and from the classroom (teachers) concerning their participation in the immigrant rights movement reveals a fundamental contradiction between school policy and practice.

SCHOOL BOARD POLICY

The March 10, 2006, mobilization took the CPS officials by surprise: they had not expected large numbers of students to miss school to attend the march. For the May 1 march, therefore, the school district implemented a policy geared toward deterring students from participating. Nonetheless, several schools with large Mexican populations reported very low attendance rates that day. For example, only 15 percent of students at Farragut High School showed up, and only 14 percent were present at Juárez (Konkol et al. 2006). These data corroborate other information that confirms that the immigrant rights marches drew very large numbers of young people. The Immigrant Mobilization Project survey found that 51 percent of the marchers in May 2006 and 54 percent in May 2007 were youth between the ages of fourteen and twenty-eight. Moreover, in 2006, 25 percent of the marchers were aged eighteen or younger; a year later, that figure had risen to 38 percent (Flores-González et al. 2006).

On April 28, 2006, the CPS's chief executive officer, Arne Duncan, sent home a letter urging parents to send their children to school because "schools are the best and safest place for children to be during the school day," march attendance would disrupt the educational process, and students who missed school to participate would receive punishment (Duncan 2006). The letter thus painted the marches as dangerous and implied that attending had no educational value. Duncan nevertheless stated the school system's backing of the marches: "The Chicago Public Schools—following the lead of Mayor Richard M. Daley— staunchly supports the rights of all immigrants, especially the right to a quality education." Exactly what "support[ing] the rights of all immigrants" meant was left open to interpretation. Thus, a gray area emerged in which it was not necessarily permissible to march but was possible.

Perhaps influenced by their schools' view of the marches, their parents' warnings, or by the media hype, some students expressed fear about the marches. For example, Maritza, a sixteen-year-old sophomore, said, "I was afraid that riots were going to start and people were going to go wild." She and many other students nevertheless participated and found that their fears were unfounded. Carlos, another sixteen-year-old sophomore, discovered that "they were exaggerating when they would say that it was going to get crazy in the marches, that people were going to hit us." However, Carlos also "felt like I needed to get in trouble to make it official." Such statements, in conjunction with CPS's message about the safety of schools, attest to the ways in which school systems can associate protest marches with danger and trouble, even when they are generally perceived as legitimate ways of political expression.

In fact, CPS policies dictate that students will get in trouble for most forms of protesting. Understanding the origins of Duncan's letter requires a brief examination of CPS policies concerning student protests. Every year, each student receives a copy of the CPS Student Code of Conduct. The booklet groups various inappropriate behaviors and outlines the punishment for each category. For example, Group 2 includes as acts of misconduct "that disrupt the orderly educational process in the school or on the school grounds" and includes "posting or distributing unauthorized or other written materials on school grounds; leaving the school without permission and interfering with school authorities and programs through walkouts or sit-ins." The possible penalties listed for these actions are student-teacher conferences, detention, and in-school or out-of-school suspensions for up to five days (Chicago Public Schools 2009).

An unexcused absence also constitutes grounds for punishment. CPS has strict attendance policies and guidelines about what counts as a legitimate excuse for missing school. According to CPS policy, the valid excuses include "illness, death in the immediate family, a family emergency, observance of a religious holiday, circumstances causing reasonable concern to the parent for the student's health or safety and other situations beyond the control of the student as determined by the principal, or principal's designee, on a case-by-case basis, including, but not limited to, homelessness and its attendant difficulties" (Chicago Public Schools 2006). Any excuse that falls outside of these parameters is considered "unexcused": "an absence which the school has reviewed and has determined not to meet the legal requirements for an excused absence. This is considered to be a truant absence" (Chicago Public Schools 2006).

SCHOOL PRACTICES

School officials also tried to prevent students from participating in the march through more informal practices, such as spreading rumors. Students heard rumors that schools would be locked down if students attempted to walk out, that harsh punishments would be imposed, and that students who marched would not be permitted to make up missed work or tests. Some students also heard these threats directly from teachers. Gabriel, a seventeen-year-old junior, heard that the entire school would be on lockdown and that "no one could enter or leave school during school hours. . . . But that's just what they said. It really wasn't like that. . . . I just walked out and just left, and I just went to the march." However, according to Gabriel, even though there was no lockdown, the rumor deterred many other students from attending the march. In another school, students who had already walked out to participate were told to go back inside. Herman, an eighteen-year-old senior, stated, "The principal took us into the auditorium and told us that we shouldn't be doing this, that when it's marches from other places, we do have permission, but when we organize them ourselves, we don't. . . . Everybody [had] already [been] outside chanting and ready to go." The principal's actions brought many students' participation in the marches to an abrupt halt, although some students nonetheless left.

In other instances, teachers and administrators used vague threats that students would "get in trouble" to instill a fear of punishment. Lourdes, a seventeen-year-old junior, heard that "people could get detention or suspended." A sixteen-year-old sophomore, Ana, mentioned that "some of the teachers had started rumors that you would get suspended if you went because it wasn't an excused absence, but nobody got in trouble." Rumors also circulated about teachers who deliberately scheduled tests or other assignments for the day of the march. According to Laura, also a sixteen-year-old sophomore, "Some teachers [said,] 'Because we're gonna have a big test, you can't miss,' and stuff like that. But I don't think kids really listened. They still went." Ana stated that if the teacher was "not so in favor of [the march], then you couldn't take the test, but it wasn't a major test, it was just like little tests." When students returned to school, they did not know whether tests had been given. None of these rumors were ever substantiated. No one I interviewed had concrete knowledge of anyone who received a suspension or detention. Students chose to attend despite these rumors and were willing to risk the threatened punishments.

In addition to rumors, some teachers and staff trivialized the movement and/ or belittled students for participating in the march. Maritza, a fourteen-year-old freshman, stated, "I remember one of the teachers saying, 'You students are stupid for attending the march.'" Some teachers expressed negative views of immigrants in general and the movement in particular. In Ana's words, "The teachers . . . said that, [immigrants] don't pay taxes and . . . they should just go back to their original country. 'Why do they want to come to a country that [they say] is so inhumane? [If the United States is] so wrong, then why don't they just go to their natural-born country and figure out the stuff over there?'" The teachers overlooked the fact that their students were immigrants or were from immigrant families.

These practices illustrate that schools view students not as agents of change but primarily as potential troublemakers who must be restrained from planning and engaging in mass protest. However, even these attempts were not always perfectly implemented, and some did not have their intended effects. Students were not easily deterred, even in the most restrictive environments.

In addition, some teachers, administrators, and staff were not entirely unsympathetic to the cause, while others were supportive but caught between a written school policy and their desire to support the march. Some high schools ignored the district's policies and arranged to take students on a field trip to the marches. More complicated, however, were the instances when a particular school's teachers and administrators had conflicting views about the movement and student participation. In some cases, teachers openly shared their personal views about the marches. Some teachers supported the cause but told their students that education had to take priority. Marco, a seventeen-year-old junior, stated that his teachers "said that we're gonna miss too much school already and there's no reason for [it]. They said to put education first and then the march second. . . . They said to do what we have in our hearts, to do what we wanna do, and that if you wanna stay in school, then you stay in school." Such statements validate the students' cause as well as their political agency and the responsibility that comes with it, simultaneously and subtly indicating the teachers' preferences and positing student choice. While the message seems on the surface to be contradictory, it actually underscores the gray area in which no right or wrong choice exists but in which students must make their own decisions. This type of statement implies that as developing citizens, students need to look beyond whether they have explicit permission to march.

Student Agency

Both formal policies and school practices were not always strictly enforced, and students found few practical barriers to marching. Those who walked out, passed out fliers without permission, or broke other rules or policies found ways to do so without getting caught or punished. Students often collaborated with faculty and staff to organize and participate. Teachers often looked the other way and did not punish students who missed class to march. Students also found ways to use their schools as sites of engagement.

Students who missed school had to have their parents or legal guardians account for the absence. Some parents wrote notes after the fact; although various reasons were given, only a few students reported that their parents lied for them. Other parents simply told the truth. The mother of Horatio, a sixteen-year-old sophomore, "wrote that I went with her to the march and [that] she felt it was important for me to be there. My teachers commented on that letter and how my mom was a smart woman, I guess because she was honest and didn't write something generic like that I stayed home because I was sick or something like that." All of those we interviewed made sure that their guardians called the school on the day of the march or wrote a letter the following day.

To avoid the difficulties of walking out, many students simply did not go to school the morning of the march. According to Herman, "They got security guards at every door, and we don't have open lunch, so I think everyone who wanted to go to the march knew they were better off not coming to school at all that day. Walking out wouldn't have been easy."

Many students planned to meet at public places near their school. Jocelyn, a seventeen-year-old junior, and her friends "met at the train station. We all have cell phones, so we just called each other to see where we were." Joel, a sixteen-year-old sophomore, and his group "took the train 'cause parking downtown is super expensive, and we didn't fit in one car." Gabriel "invited a lot of my friends from different classes and not all from this school, even other schools, and they didn't even go to school, so they just met me on the corner."

Students carefully observed what their peers and teachers were doing a few days before the march to get a sense of what would be permitted. Some students focused on mobilizing students by distributing flyers at school. Antonio, a sixteen-year-old sophomore, reported that students passed out flyers announcing the May 1 march without the school's approval; however, "some students got suspended for passing flyers . . . that weren't approved by the school, . . . but I wasn't one of those." Students were not the only ones passing out flyers or mobilizing students for the march. Antonio said that the day before the march, teachers "were making flyers and making posters. . . . I don't know how they did it. . . . The teachers [are not] Latinos or immigrants; they are white. We even got those teachers to the march that day." Similarly, sixteen-year-old Raul, a sophomore, stated that "one teacher gathered about four or five teachers from her department to come and help make signs, and then they told their class." One of Gabriel's teachers "actually told kids from her classes, 'If you guys want to come, meet me here, and we'll go together.' . . . So she . . . led them there. . . . It was a field trip. A lot of the teachers went."

Students also viewed teachers and staff who looked the other way as tacit supporters. Some teachers knew that students had attended the march but nevertheless permitted them to make up missed work. According to Anthony, a sixteen-year-old sophomore, "Some teachers were like, 'You went to march? So I can mark you excused.' . . . The principal was telling us if we were going to the march, we would be marked as truant for each class, but I don't think that happened. Most teachers didn't do it." Sixteen-year-old Samuel, also a sophomore, reported, "My teacher knew of my involvement and said that if I showed up I would be counted as present, but if I left, he wouldn't have anything to do with it. So basically he let me leave but still get credit." Most of Jocelyn's teachers "let me turn in the work I missed the next day; they were cool about it." Thus, teachers ignored school policy to avoid having students get in trouble.

Security guards were also complicit. At Jocelyn's school, "Usually there's one [security guard] in the main doors and the rest in the halls. One of my friends that went with me told me that a couple of security guards would play dumb and let them leave pretending not to see them."

The ultimate indicator of school support for the immigrant rights marches, however, was the principal's actions. At Samuel's school, "the principal was standing outside when students were leaving, and it was encouraging because he was not saying anything to the students walking out."

Conclusion

Most of the students who participated in the marches attended predominantly Latino schools. These demographics alone, however, do not explain how students missed school to participate in the marches without suffering any severe punishment, as was the case in some heavily Latino schools in Los Angeles and Houston. Why did Chicago educators react differently?

CPS students did not directly confront or challenge school policies, and many officials looked the other way. Students, administrators, and teachers found loopholes in specific school policies and practices that created a gray area in which what was permissible and what was possible blurred. Although Chicago Board of Education policies and state law prevented the CPS from granting students permission to miss school to attend the march, administrators, teachers, and other staff had a choice about whether to ignore or follow school policies.

Chicago's history of support for immigrant rights helps to explain why local and school authorities were lenient toward students. While this support is key for understanding the more benevolent outcomes in Chicago, it does not explain youth mobilization. Youth in Chicago and across the United States have played a central role in the immigrant rights movement. In most cases, students did not work in conjunction with adult leaders. Young people's leadership and participation are significant, particularly in light of the restrictive environment school officials created.

High school students' massive participation in the 2006 marches caused

CPS to change its official approach, at least in practical terms. The 2007–8 CPS calendar indicated that all schools were scheduled to have a half-day on May 1, 2007, and that students would be released at noon, but system officials did not send out a letter regarding the march, and there were rumors that not all schools implemented the half day. The following year, officials circulated a letter to the "CPS community," but it was distributed only to school administrators and merely instructed staff to tell students to come to school on May 1. Because the letter did not go directly to parents, they could claim ignorance of the policy. Further complicating the situation, CPS also announced that students who went to the marches as part of school field trips would receive service learning credit hours. Although Illinois state law dictates that missing school to participate in a non-school-sponsored protest, sit-in, or walkout is an unexcused absence, CPS was in effect recognizing the immigrant rights march as a legitimate form of civic and political engagement. Thus, student actions not only challenged but transformed institutional policies.

Since 2006, Chicago students have participated in increasing numbers in marches. The Immigrant Mobilization Project's 2006 and 2007 surveys found that the rates of high school age youth (eighteen years old and younger) participating in the marches increased. Chicago's students recognized the difference between the permissible and the possible and used their skills to broaden that gray area. In the end, students followed their hearts and marched, regardless of the formal policy, for the rights of their families, friends, and communities. Students ultimately needed not permission to march but recognition of their creative strategies for participating in a movement despite official disapproval.

Notes

The author thanks several undergraduate students at the University of Illinois at Chicago who helped conduct interviews.

1. For reasons of confidentiality, all names of interviewees are pseudonyms. By "predominantly Latino," I mean that more than 48 percent of the students at those schools are Latino. Five of the ten schools had Mexican student populations between 48.4 percent and 93.7 percent. The ten schools had Puerto Rican student populations of between 0.2 percent and 11.4 percent. Of the remaining three schools, one was racially mixed, another was 55 percent white, and one was 60.1 percent black.

References

Alvarez, Robert R., Jr. 1986. "The Lemon Grove Incident: The Nation's First Successful Desegregation Court Case." *Journal of San Diego History* 32 (2): 1–16.

Andolina, Molly, Krista Jenkins, Cliff Zukin, and Scott Keeter. 2003. "Habits from Home, Lessons from School: Influences on Youth Civic Engagement." *PSOnline*, April, 275–80.

Aronson, Leonard. 1973. "Pick Sites in Froebel Disput

Avila, Oscar. 2006. "Seeking to Aid Immigrants—Cook
tions on Residents' Status." *Chicago Tribune,* Septer

Barrera, B. James. 2004. "The 1968 Edcouch-Elsa Hig
dent Activism in a South Texas Community." *Aztl*

Billig, Shelly H. 2000. "Research on K–12 School-Bas
Builds." *Phi Delta Kappan* 81 (9): 658–64.

Chicago Public Schools. 2006. "Absenteeism and Truan
Public Schools Policy Manual. http://policy.cps.k12.il.us.
cessed February 1, 2007.

———. 2009. "Student Code of Conduct for the Chicago Public Schools for the 2009–
2010 School Year." In *Chicago Public Schools Policy Manual.* http://policy.cps.k12
.il.us/documents/705.5.pdf. Accessed September 25, 2009.

Chicago Public Schools, Office of High School Programs. 2007. *Service Learning.* http://
servicelearning.cps.k12.il.us/Guidelines.html. Accessed January 31, 2007.

Collins, Patricia Hill. 2000. *Black Feminist Thought: Knowledge, Consciousness, and the
Politics of Empowerment.* New York: Routledge.

Conzen, Michael P. 2005. "Chicago's Ethnic Mosaic in 1980." In *Encyclopedia of Chicago.*
http://www.encyclopedia.chicagohistory.org/pages/2989.html. Accessed August 10,
2008.

Donato, Ruben. 1997. *The Other Struggle for Equal Schools: Mexican Americans during
the Civil Rights Movement.* Albany: State University of New York Press.

Duncan, Arne. 2006. Letter to Chicago Public Schools Community. April 28.

Escobar, Edward J. 1993. "The Dialectics of Repression: The Los Angeles Police Department and the Chicano Movement, 1968–1971." *Journal of American History* 79 (4):
1483–1514.

Flores-González, Nilda, Amalia Pallares, Cedric Herring, and Maria Krysan. 2006. *UIC
Immigrant Mobilization Project General Survey Findings.* http://www.wilsoncenter
.org/news/docs/uicstudy.pdf. Accessed August 31, 2009.

Giroux, Henry A. 2003a. *The Abandoned Generation: Democracy beyond the Culture of
Fear.* New York: Palgrave Macmillan.

———. 2003b. "Racial Injustice and Disposable Youth in the Age of Zero-Tolerance."
International Journal of Qualitative Studies in Education 16 (4): 553–65.

Glassner, Barry. 1999. *The Culture of Fear: Why Americans Are Afraid of the Wrong
Things.* New York: Basic Books.

Herman, Edith. 1973. "Principals: New Victims of Protest." *Chicago Tribune,* February 11.

Johnson, Jannise. 2006. "School's Threats Led Teen to Commit Suicide." *Inland Valley
Daily Bulletin,* April 9. www.dailybulletin.com. Accessed July 25, 2006.

Konkol, Mark J., Annie Sweeny, Lucio Guerrero, and Eric Herman. 2006. "Massive
March: 'We Are Not a Plague': Up to 700,000 People Flood the City's Streets." *Chicago
Sun-Times,* May 2.

Maass, Alan. 2006. "Week of the Walkouts: Immigrant Rights Fight Comes to Schools
across the U.S." *Socialist Worker Online,* April 7. http://socialistworker.org/2006
–1/583/583_07_Walkouts.shtml. Accessed January 31, 2007.

A. 1999. *Framing Youth: Ten Myths about the Next Generation.* Monroe, mmon Courage.

, Sharon. 2006. "Inland Youth Mourned as 'Martyr': Immigrants: He Killed nself after Telling His Mother He'd Be Punished for Joining a Walkout." www pe.com, April 10. Accessed July 25, 2006.

Mora, Carlos. 2007. *Latinos in the West: The Student Movement and Academic Labor in Los Angeles.* Lanham, Md.: Rowman and Littlefield.

Mukherjee, Elora. 2007. *Criminalizing the Classroom: The Over-Policing of New York City Schools.* New York: New York Civil Liberties Union.

Muñoz, Carlos. 1989. *Youth, Identity, Power: The Chicano Movement.* New York: Verso.

Noguera, Pedro. 1995. "Preventing and Producing Violence: A Critical Analysis of Responses to School Violence." *Harvard Educational Review* 65 (2): 189–212.

Olivo, Antonio, and Oscar Avila. 2006. "We Have to Change the World." *Chicago Tribune,* May 2.

Police to Crack Down on Student Walkouts: Truants Could Face Fines, Community Service. 2006. http://www.nbc4.com, March 28. Accessed January 31, 2007.

Ready, Timothy, and Allert Brown-Gort. 2005. *The State of Latino Chicago: This Is Home Now.* Notre Dame, Ind.: University of Notre Dame Institute for Latino Studies.

Saavedra's Statement about Student Walkouts. 2006. http://www.click2houston.com/education/8323034/detail.html, March 28. Accessed January 31, 2007.

Saltman, Kenneth J., and David Gabbard, eds. 2003. *Education as Enforcement: The Militarization and Corporatization of Schools.* New York: Routledge Falmer.

Soll, Fredric, and Edith Herman. 1973. "Tuley Protesters Battle Police." *Chicago Tribune,* February 1.

Spring, Joel H. 1985. *American Education: An Introduction to Social and Political Aspects.* New York: Longman.

Torney-Purta, Judith. 2002. "The School's Role in Developing Civic Engagement: A Study of Adolescents in Twenty-eight Countries." *Applied Developmental Science* 6 (4): 203–12.

Valencia, Richard. 2002. *Chicano School Failure and Success: Past, Present, and Future.* New York: Routledge.

Youniss, James, Susan Bales, Verona Christmas-Best, Marcelo Diversi, Milbrey McLaughlin, and Rainer Sulbereisen. 2002. "Youth Civic Engagement in the Twenty-first Century." *Journal of Research on Adolescence* 12 (1): 121–48.

Zukin, Cliff, Scott Keeter, Krista Jenkins, and Michael X. Delli Carpini. 2006. *A New Engagement? Political Participation, Civic Life, and the Changing American Citizen.* New, York: Oxford University Press.

PART 4

Subjectivities

10

Minutemen and the Subject of Democracy

DAVID BLEEDEN,
CAROLINE GOTTSCHALK-DRUSCHKE,
AND RALPH CINTRÓN

While the majority of chapters in this volume focus on undocumented immigrants and pro-immigration community organizers, our work follows from our desire to seek out the perspectives of the opponents of illegal immigration who engage in political organizing and display a passion and commitment equal to those of the undocumented immigrants who have marched en masse through the streets of Chicago and other U.S. cities since the spring of 2006. The activities and opinions of the anti-illegal-immigration activists (the term they use to describe their political stance) with whom we spoke tell us quite a bit about American liberal democratic subjectivity. Between the spring of 2006 and the summer of 2007, we interviewed twelve male and female anti-illegal-immigration activists who were self-identified members of the Chicago and Illinois Minuteman Projects and an analogous group, the Twenty-first Century Paul Revere Riders. Most of our interviewees live in Illinois, but some do not, and almost all were American-born citizens of European descent. Our interviewees ranged in age from their early forties to late sixties. We also examined their numerous Web sites and others they recommended. We focus on three connected themes our interviewees discussed: consciousness-raising, a figure we call the hypercitizen, and the Constitution and the rule of law.

The rhetorical vocabulary on which we rely in this chapter may be unfamiliar to our readers. *Ethos* refers to credibility; *mythos* refers to the social imaginary (a shared set of beliefs and attitudes); and *topos* refers to a theme or commonplace. We address the nationalist under- and overtones of anti-illegal-immigration arguments rather than emphasizing issues of race and racism, and we criticize, perhaps surprisingly to many of our readers, American liberal democracy.

Consciousness-Raising

We have noticed a tendency among the academic and activist Left to collapse all anti-illegal-immigration activists—the Minuteman Project, the Minuteman Civil Defense Corps, independent activists, the Ku Klux Klan, neo-Nazis, and so on—into one general category and to dismiss all of these groups as racist. Such an approach prompted activists "asserting the right to a campus that is free of hate speech" to boycott Chris Simcox's May 2008 appearance at DePaul University on the grounds that he is the "racist co-founder of the Minutemen" (ChicagoMayDay 2008) and spurred a Santa Cruz Indy Media author to refer to the Minutemen as "a racist vigilante group" (Alejo 2005). It also incited students to mob the stage during Jim Gilchrist's October 2006 speech at Columbia University because "the Minutemen are not a legitimate voice in the debate on immigration. They are a racist, armed militia" (DePillis 2006). *All* anti-illegal-immigration activists, the story goes, are hateful racists who ought to be ousted from the public immigration debate.

Of course, beyond the charges of racism and hate speech, there are serious accusations of violence leveled against the Minutemen. While we have heard reports of violence emerging from the West Coast, the midwestern anti-illegal-immigration activists that we spoke with as we researched this project never alluded to any violent acts in which they were involved. We need to be clear, then, that the activists with whom we spoke for this project are loosely affiliated with the Chicago Minuteman Project and the currently inactive Illinois Minuteman Project, both of which are midwestern groups and, nationally speaking, are identified with Jim Gilchrist's Minuteman Project, not Chris Simcox's Minuteman Civil Defense Corps.

Simcox is known for his continued efforts to patrol the U.S.-Mexico border with a pair of binoculars and a rifle, attempting seriously to aid (and perhaps humiliate) the U.S. Border Patrol. Gilchrist in contrast, is a former U.S. Marine, a licensed certified public accountant, and a budding politician and is responsible for what he called the "dog-and-pony show" that drew a thousand people, including at least one of our informants, to the U.S.-Mexico border in April 2005 for what can best be described as guerrilla theater writ large. As Gilchrist explained, that event "was political activism. . . . Patrolling the border is only about 5 or 10 percent of what the Minuteman Project is about. The other 90 to 95 percent is driving this issue up through city councils, mayors, state legislatures, and governors into the halls of Congress to force change" (Thomas 2008). In other words, Gilchrist's Minuteman Project defines itself as a collection of political activists working to draw attention to what they see as the problem of illegal immigration.

We focus on this particular and timely form of political organizing in part because it is far too easy for the charges of racism and hate speech leveled against the Minutemen to obscure the significant implications of their nationalist rhetoric and their project as a whole. In their words, "The Chicago Minuteman Project is not a racist organization and welcomes participation from all citizens and legal residents of the United States of America. The 'racist' label is a tactic frequently used by our opponents in their attempts to end civil discussion of the dangers posed by illegal immigration" (Chicago Minuteman Project 2007). (While this defense may or may not be disingenuous, we find it telling that they retreat to legal citizenship as a protective measure.) In light of their public group statements, we do not attempt to engage in a debate about whether individual members of the Minutemen are racist; however, we do attempt to understand what the activities of the Minutemen and related anti-illegal-immigration activists tell us about American liberal democracy.

In March 2005, President George W. Bush called the Minutemen assembling at the U.S.-Mexico border "vigilantes," a label with which they take serious issue. The activists see themselves as active citizens working to return the United States to the rule of law. Indeed, the Minutemen's reliance on action reminds us of Aristotle's and later Kant's distinction between "active" and "passive" citizens (Aristotle 1985; Kant 1991). These notions have structured conventional and even normative notions of contemporary political order in which active, taxpaying, voting, property-owning, law-abiding citizens have rightful claims because they, more than others, shape the social order into what is interpreted as good and just. On its face, then, Minuteman discourse is not aberrant at all but is part of this long-standing tradition. As critics of the conventional political order, which includes democracy's distinction between active and passive citizens, we are skeptical of this tradition, and we are not surprised that Minuteman discourse is consistent with it.

Although anti-illegal-immigration activists present the duties of active citizenship as inherently moral and open to all (as a means of cultivating *ethos*), they see the performance of active citizenship as open only to documented American citizens. While many of the anti-illegal-immigration activists with whom we spoke presented home and business ownership, military service, and the exercise of the right to assemble as duties that attested to individuals' good moral character, these are precisely the performances that so enraged these same activists when performed by noncitizens. For example, our informants expressed disgust with banks that accepted the *matrícula consular* (an official, if controversial, identity card issued by the Mexican government) as means of obtaining home loans and with the undocumented immigrants who gathered for the May 1 marches across the country. (As recorded elsewhere in this volume, the majority of marchers were documented citizens, a point of which most initial observers, including the Minutemen, were unaware.) At any rate, from the perspective of the Minuteman Project, the duties of active citizenship can only be performed by—and are only worthy of merit when performed by—sanctioned citizens.

As sanctioned citizens, these anti-illegal-immigration activists see the performance of citizenship as something akin to Gilchrist's vision: "You have to educate the public, which is what I am trying to do" (Thomas 2008). Or, as one of the creators of the Twenty-first Century Paul Revere Ride, a motorcycle ride across the United States, put it, the event emerged out of a single question: "How can we bring awareness, bring education, to the American public?" The subject of this educational project is the cost—both material and psychic—of undocumented immigration to the United States.

All of our informants talked very specifically about both their "education" in the perils of undocumented migration and how they shared this education with others as an expression of their civic duty. Many of our informants, like Gilchrist, portrayed the events of September 11, 2001, as "a wake-up call" regarding the permeability of U.S. borders and the U.S. government's inability to protect average Americans from external terror. Once these activists became "informed" about undocumented migration—or, as one interviewee explained, once he "started to learn a lot of things about what was really going on"—other sociopolitical problems such as the "War on Terror," increased economic stratification, political corruption, increased outsourcing, and neighborhood crime became symptoms of *the* major problem: the U.S. government's failure to police the border and adequately enforce existing immigration laws.

September 11 became a central *topos* in the anti-illegal-immigration activists' argumentative tool kit. The terrorist attacks became a touchstone, a contextualized commonplace, with which to make the argument that average Americans must take back their country from internal and external threats. If these events provided a fissure through which the Minutemen's argument could flow, the massive immigration marches in the spring of 2006 opened a floodgate. By May 2006, "Main Street" conservative voices such as Rush Limbaugh, Lou Dobbs, and Pat Buchanan and an increasing number of national-level politicians quickly responded to the immigrants marching in the nation's streets. And so did the Minutemen. As one leader of the Minuteman Project explained, Chicago's enormous May 1 march "was the best thing that ever happened. . . . Because I'd go and tell somebody, 'There's a problem with illegal immigration' and they'd look at me like . . . they thought I was nuts—off on a tangent. Now, they know I ain't off on a tangent." The marches made the immigration question visible; the bodies in the streets could no longer be ignored. In short, after May 1, 2006, the Minutemen seemed to find many more sympathetic friends and neighbors than they had first imagined. At this moment, the line between the "extreme" Minutemen and the American mainstream began to collapse, aided, in part, by the Minutemen's aggressive outreach tactics. As one informant detailed, "All the Minuteman Project is representing is, to me, [for] the average everyday person [to] get up off of your ass, turn the TV off, and take back your country. You've been disassociated with the political process for so long; you have no idea who you're putting into office. Shame on you. America was never meant to run like this. Get up off your butt. Do your political duty. Be a patriot. And get involved. And quit complaining. That's what the Minuteman Project is really about." The Minutemen, then, argue that they are engaged in a sustained crusade to encourage American citizens (and only citizens) to enact their citizenship as the Minutemen do—through duty, vigilance, and action.

These anti-illegal-immigration activists perform their citizenship by gathering at local politicians' offices, hosting radio and television shows, appearing at city council meetings, maintaining immigration-related Web sites, and staying in touch with one another through a variety of well-maintained listservs. They maintain a balance between spectacular performance (like the Twenty-first Century Paul Revere Ride or the gathering at the U.S.-Mexico border) and plain-old activism. Their listserv emails are filled with invitations to political rallies at the offices of congressional representatives to "encourage elected public servants to uphold and preserve the United States Constitution through the enforcement of law" (Chicago Minuteman Project 2007). They are savvy political organizers and experienced rhetoricians; their language, often purposefully spectacular and hyperbolically denigrating, is intended to raise ordinary citizens' consciousness about the pernicious consequences of both unchecked "illegal" immigration and what they consider to be a pervasive disregard for the rule of law.

This Minuteman civic activism is significant in and of itself, but more is at stake in their efforts: these opponents of illegal immigration seek the construction and subsequent policing of a singular and stable American culture. The Minutemen attempt to act as gatekeepers at the American borders, and they do so as a means of safeguarding not just the geographical content of the United States but also, and more consequentially, the nation's ideological, social, and cultural content.

As Gilchrist explained, his Minutemen are "mined from the motherload [sic] of patriotism" (Gemma 2007), and this patriot army serves a dual purpose: to educate the American people about the threats of immigration and corruption and to spread the Minuteman *ethos,* their particularized version of American culture rooted in the American *mythos* or imaginary. As the Minutemen recruit other active citizens, members of the Minuteman Project borrow the *ethos* of America's Founding Fathers, inventing and then relying on a shared American heritage based in Revolutionary War history, the U.S. Constitution, and the rule of law. The Minutemen, then, have created a highly particularized version of Americanness culled from a precise reading of American history and wielded against an immigrant threat.

Rather than radically altering or dismissing the tenets of American democracy, the Minutemen represent the limit form of American democratic subjectivity; they take American democratic subjectivity to its logical extreme. The Minutemen do not actually misunderstand or fail to act on democratic principles (a charge leveled by pro-immigration activists who insist that the Minutemen's desire to arrest immigration flows and protest immigrant organizing is un-American and antidemocratic); instead, the Minutemen understand and act out democracy in a logical albeit hyperbolic way. If the Minutemen are legitimized by the Constitution's grounding in "We the People," the Minutemen's prime objective is the ideological battle for control over the content of that *We,* a *We* defined against a non-American, noncitizen *not-We.*

The Taxpayer and the Hypercitizen

One of the primary ways in which anti-illegal-immigration activists define this *We* is through an appeal to their status as taxpayers; this distinction between legal taxpayer and nontaxpayer structures many of their anti-illegal-immigration arguments. But the Minutemen are not alone in appealing to this figure. The *topos* of the beleaguered taxpayer complaining of wasteful government spending pervades the American imaginary, representing both left-leaning and right-leaning political philosophies. But why is the taxpayer even a topic? At its root, the strain of paying taxes may reflect an actual burden, particularly on working- and middle-class incomes. But this materialist answer seems insufficient partly because the *topos* of the strained taxpayer appears to cut across all classes. Moreover, most arguments based on this figure may be hyperbolic. This taxpayer argument may well exist less because it points to real conditions and more because it occupies an important niche in American populist discourse. When one group or another launches the *topos* of the taxpayer, judging whose set of facts best constitutes reality may be less interesting than paying attention to the *topos* itself, its abundant prevalence and power. It is evoked so much because it organizes broad segments of the American imaginary.[1]

We begin our inquiry by asking two questions: What is the democratic subject, and what consequences does it have for shaping subjectivities? Political theorist Barbara Cruikshank observes that since at least Tocqueville, political discourse has distinguished between the terms *subject* and *citizen* (1999). Whereas subjects are subject to a sovereign power, such as a monarch or dictator, citizens are sovereign over themselves, and democracy is the form of governance that guarantees this rule of the people over themselves. This distinction, for all practical purposes, constitutes the virtue and moral superiority of democracy.

But Cruikshank points out the fictive nature of this distinction. Following Michel Foucault, she argues that democracy operates as a form of power that produces subjects. That is, any political order, even the most "liberatory," is a form of power that both governs life and shapes it so that individuals become identifiable as particular social entities. For example, the Minutemen understand themselves as subject to the rule of law, but they also understand themselves as having rights and the ability to protest the possible loss of those rights. But these rights and freedoms are not inalienable, as democratic governance may claim; rather, they are profound projections of democracy, and they permanently mark the subjectivities of people. Indeed, only in the extent to which the general population believes these rights and freedoms to be inalienable (that is, naturalized as part of the universal condition of being human as contained in the concept of human rights) does democratic governance create itself as something more than a form of power—as innately virtuous, for example. In other words, subjugation does not disappear during the historical transformation from subject to citizen, from monarchical/totalitarian rule to democratic rule. And one reason why it does not disappear is that under democratic governance, the state's power to enable rights is the same power that can disable rights, which is particularly evident in times of emergency.

But even if we agree with Cruikshank that democracy indeed produces subjects, we repeat our question in the hope of locating a more succinct conclusion: What is this democratic subject? Democracy, as the political condition that we live in, produces democratic subjects—that is, individuals who believe that they are sovereign, that they are the state, and that the institutions of political order are at their behest. The extent to which such beliefs are taken at face value (that is, naturalized as opposed to being taken as projections or productions of the political order) is the extent to which the political order purchases the subjectivities of individuals—for example, the members of the Minuteman Project and like-minded Americans. So, given our definition, is the democratic subject identified with a specific kind of subjectivity? Our preliminary answer is that there is nothing definitive, no single specific subjectivity that gets made under the experience of democracy. One could be a democratic socialist, liberal democrat, Christian democrat, libertarian, and so on. In short, no specific ontological subject is native to democracy.

With this understanding of both the democratic subject and its many possible subjectivities, we turn to the figure of the taxpayer. The ordinary taxpayer is a *topos* that signals a specifically American subjectivity that can align itself with right-wing as well as left-wing causes. The *topos*, particularly when wielded by libertarians, often opposes the state's authority to tax. As such, it signals the rights and virtues of individual autonomy over and against the state. The Minutemen are not necessarily libertarian—indeed, one member told us that "libertarians are too radical." Hence, their evocations of the ordinary taxpayer do not necessarily signal, as such evocations often do among libertarians, a deep-seated animosity to the principle of taxation; rather, the Minutemen are concerned about the ways in which elites (both government and corporate) have dodged the sovereign will of the people to profit from and exploit undocumented workers, leaving ordinary Americans with fewer jobs and higher taxes.

That is, in the broad segment of the American imaginary to which the Minutemen adhere, the *topos* of the burdened ordinary taxpayer represents a certain unassailable moral standing. According to one interviewee, "As a taxpayer, I am heavily burdened to pay for social services that are given to anyone in America, legal or illegal. . . . As a taxpayer, I object to paying massive amounts of money to help them be born and educated, while American children . . . are being hurt by the lack of good schools, good teachers, and good medical facilities because we are spending that much more money on people who are here illegally." What we find most interesting is the hyperbole of this statement, the desire for moral unassailability, and the rhetorical mechanics that produce a position impervious to counterargument. This moral unassailability occurs despite the fact that the undocumented pay a variety of taxes that these sorts of statements ignore.

Their rhetorical mechanics have two starting points. The first is bound up with the psychic life of the monetary exchange. The payment of money functions metonymically, not metaphorically, in at least a few but certainly not all cases, as a payment of self. In this light, it becomes understandable why it is important for the self to seek comparable worth in the objects or person(s) sacrificed for. Second, the logic of the monetary exchange is extended by applying it to the idea of the ordinary taxpayer. The figure of the ordinary taxpayer functions as a kind of "authentic citizen"—the person who most deserves to belong to the nation—while those who are "non-taxpayers or individuals who pay little in taxes are 'free riders' on public goods in the sense that they benefit from a good they have not paid for" (Rector, Kim, and Watkins 2007). Free riders, then, have dodged their obligations.

The idea of free riders is insightful because it stages the classic American historical figure of a taxpayer burdened by government imposition on citizens' liberties and rights. But even if taxation constitutes government's most negative action (an idea that is not universally accepted), fulfilling their obligations bestows on ordinary taxpayers a moral positioning as authentic citizens. Ordinary taxpayers are model or authentic citizens because they do not incur a net fiscal deficit—that is, they pay their fair share of taxes, and what they receive in government benefits does not exceed their payments.

Thus far, we have argued two dimensions of a certain moral positioning regarding the *topos* of the taxpayer in the American imaginary: (1) Any payment, including taxes, represents to some extent a payment of self, and so we demand worth of those things for which we sacrifice; (2) those who pay taxes—as opposed to those who do not—not only have made a genuine sacrifice of self but also have a more rightful claim on the state because they are authentic, moral citizens. Our argument now makes one last turn: toward the notion of the hypercitizen.

Taxes historically are evidence of state power. But do taxes act differently in representative democracies? After all, the power of citizens to elect others to make decisions for them about taxation and other matters would suggest a fundamental difference between the functions of taxation under totalitarian and democratic regimes. And ultimately, the *topos* of the ordinary taxpayer crystallizes the distinction between totalitarian power and democratic power. Under democratic power, taxation becomes less of an odious imposition through which governments signify their sovereignty. That is, the figure of the ordinary taxpayer flips the relationship of power from subjects to citizens, and citizens thus become the owners of themselves and of the state, since to a significant degree they literally pay for the state.

This distinction between subject and citizen—and the figure of the taxpayer is only one of its elements—participates in the establishment of an essential messianism at the core of democracy, which is captured in the resonating metaphor of "the beacon of democracy" in reference to either democracy itself or the nation-state that supposedly best projects democracy. As one of our interviewees stated in nearly apocalyptic terms, the greatest loss that could befall humanity itself is the loss of democracy as embodied in the culture called America: "More importantly for humanity, you're gong to diminish the flame of what the Statue of Liberty means because we'll be drowning America in a couple hundred million extra people whom we have to provide the basic services for, which reduces the entire thing. So we're not going to find a cure for cancer, we're not going to find a cure for diabetes, we're not going to get [to] Alpha Centauri because you're providing what? Flush toilets and a school for all these extra two hundred million people who will come here in the next twenty-odd years if we do not take care of our illegal immigration problem and massive legal immigration."

What consequences, then, might we draw from our argument that within the messianism of democracy the ordinary taxpaying citizen transforms the imposition of taxation? By transforming the abuses of government with the action of voluntarily paying taxes, abuse itself does not disappear but moves into the hands of a now-abusive taxpayer, who demands accountability from all officeholders and those who have not paid their "fair" share. Accountability becomes the watchdog of such a citizenry intent on uncovering all forms of waste, fraud, and abuse. Here lie the origins of the democratic hypercitizen, the limit form of democratic subjectivity. Through such actions as the power of the vote and taxpaying, the hypercitizen is sanctioned constitutionally as the legitimate owner of government. In claiming this ownership, the hypercitizen performs one of the subjectivities that only democracy can grant, taking the democratic, messianic rhetorics of liberty, rights (including property rights), and freedom as granting legitimate ownership over oneself and one's affairs. When this segment of the American imaginary speaks, it says, "No one, much less the state, has the right to take from me what I have honestly earned from my own sweat." As suggested earlier, the hypercitizen is Kant's "active citizen" on steroids. He is hypervigilant regarding the duties of others to the body politic and wields accountability as if it were a virtue term against those in power and those on the margins, the free riders. The figure of the burdened, ordinary citizen performing civic duties (voting, paying taxes, repairing property, obeying the rule of law) acquires moral rectitude through civic engagement. Theoretically speaking, passive citizens might be worthy of civic charity, but democracy's dependence on an active rather than passive citizenry fabricates a common sense that hinders the realization of that counterbelief. After all, if what best shapes a good and just social order is an active citizenry, then it follows that we must resist, as if in perpetual war, our passive citizens.

Minuteman discourse, therefore, is not aberrant at all but part of this long-standing tradition. To the hypercitizen, the undocumented represent a particularly frightening future in which rightful ownership slips out of their hands and dislodges the messianic subjectivity that constitutes the hypercitizen. Underlying the anti-illegal-immigration activists' extensive rhetoric of impending, apocalyptic loss is precisely that sense of the United States being at a crossroads, fighting for its survival against other nation-states rising up as economic engines, against foreign militants taking down towers, but particularly against those nameless "illegal" (and legal) hordes that strain the U.S. infrastructure. Against this backdrop, the heroic, ordinary taxpayer watches in dismay as both U.S. corporations and government become complicit in this grand betrayal. As long as these fears remain in place, the Minutemen's arguments remain nearly impervious to counterargument. Ultimately—and here perhaps we depart from our immigrant rights colleagues—the undocumented and the activists that lead them cannot offer a radically alternative vision, for in their desires for citizenship they simply confirm the values, if not the intensity (at least not yet) of the hypercitizen. For the hypercitizen, in effect, is one of the structural consequences of the democratic subject and its confluence with the nation-state, both of which require the foundational premise that nation-states represent a unified "people"—in short, a unified culture.

The Constitution and the Rule of Law

This final section of our argument details what we see as the major forces binding the arguments made thus far: culture and specifically its entanglement with language as well as its relation to the U.S. Constitution. Our informants were extensively involved in supporting legislation to establish English as the official U.S. language. One group, ProEnglish, a Washington, D.C., political action committee, states its goals as "protecting our Nation's unity in the English language" and "defend[ing] English's historic role as America's common, unifying language" (ProEnglish 2009). The idea that language—English, in this case—unifies America is deeply revealing.

We see this emphasis on language as fulfilling a specific need, one described by Etienne Balibar (1993). Following Balibar, we contend that a socially unifying entity is necessary given that no nation-state has a naturally occurring ethnic foundation. Instead, the various populations that comprise the nation-state are ethnicized, and a representation is thus constructed that appears to form a natural, delimited social formation identifiable by its shared origins. Balibar calls the group of people brought into being by the nation-state "fictive ethnicity," a "fabrication" that enables the projection of a "pre-existing unity" (the nation) identifiable within and giving rise to the state (1993). Fictive ethnicity allows the projection of the image of the universal unity of the people so that each individual is assigned an ethnic identity. This identification then idealizes politics so that the state is thought to be the result of the nation.

Language, Balibar argues, is the primary means by which fictive ethnicity is produced. Given its omnipresence, language produces fictive ethnicity in such a way that it appears natural, imparting the sense that a "national character" that transcends both individuals and institutions is inherent in the people (see also Anderson 2006; Gellner 1983; Hobsbawm 2000; Smith 2002). In the act of connecting and reconnecting through various forms of communication, nationals form a "language community" that continually reproduces itself as an interconnected, dynamic "uninterrupted chain of intermediate discourses" (Balibar 1993, 97). The act of these exchanges within a given natural language presupposes a common code or set of norms. Thus, legislating English as the official language is not aberrant, as many left-leaning activists assume; rather, it manifests a deep concern about the construction of the American nation, which is to say that anti-undocumented-immigration activists are deeply concerned about American fictive ethnicity itself.

They see American culture as under attack and believe themselves to be engaged in a "culture war."[2] For these people, undocumented immigrants bringing their own (non-American) culture represents a horrifying attack against a culture born, in large part, through language. These activists seek to preserve what they see as a singular, exceptional "American culture," defined by one informant as "the sum total of the customs, beliefs, artistic creations, attitudes, goals, and norms that make a society what it is. It is passed down, as a treasure, from grandparent to parent to child. In other words, culture is what gives us our identity." American culture, then, defines Americanness. For these activists, American culture is the definitive content of American fictive ethnicity, expressed by a set of symbols representing these universally cognizable virtues authentically transmitted by American English. This culture war thus constitutes an effort to protect a hyperorthodox, exceptionalist version of American fictive ethnicity, to eviscerate the potential destruction of American culture and protect its byproducts—freedom, liberty, prosperity, equality, rule of law, and so forth—and, thereby, the American nation.

One nontrivial feature of American fictive ethnicity is that America is a nation of immigrants—the melting pot narrative. This fact suggests that the production of the American nation is an ongoing project; hence, the question "Who is an American?" remains open, and fictive ethnicity is never completed. For anti-illegal-immigration activists, this incompleteness opens the possibility for what they consider to be the corruption of authentic American culture from within. To fight this possibility, they contend, aspiring nationals must "assimilate" themselves into American culture. One activist summarized this position: "Genuine American culture . . . is under constant assault. Some of our country's detractors vilify all that is traditionally American, while others would reduce our traditions to one more example of quaint folklore beside those of other nations. . . . Where can one find American culture? Only in a place where Americans treasure it and lovingly transmit it from generation to generation. Immigration laws should ensure that those who seek to live permanently on American territory be willing to adopt and preserve its culture." On this reading, adopting American culture means that those who wish to inhabit the United States must actively embrace and "preserve" American culture as extraordinary truth. Hence, the Minutemen and like-minded Americans fear that those who do not embrace American culture and fail to assimilate are subverting the nation.

The Minutemen thus represent a particular strand of hyperculturalism. Here is the active citizen pressuring passive citizens into performing their citizenship and, fortified by the virtuous rule of law, telling undocumented people to leave. The Minutemen believe that American culture is uniquely exceptional and that all other cultures are not only inferior but should aspire to emulate the example set by America and Americans. One activist insisted that "we are the lighthouse, we are the beacon for so many things that are good in the world. . . . America is still seen as the beacon of liberty, the beacon of freedom, the beacon of opportunity." This is clearly no simple exceptionalism; this brand of messianism maintains that only American culture has actualized freedom, liberty, justice, equality, and prosperity. Exceptional culture requires similarly exceptional protection—the task of the hypercitizen. All of the factors constituent of this culture, all of the components of American fictive ethnicity, must be guarded against attack, and these activists have taken on this task.

This hyperculturalism leads us to conclude that the Minuteman Project furthers a form of American fictive ethnicity characterized by the limitation of Americanness to only a select few. The key to understanding this argument is an understanding of the protective measures these activists advocate. The activists believe that the state, as *nation*-state, is responsible not only for the protection of citizens' bodies but also for the furtherance of American culture and therefore the protection of the liberal universals that American culture has actualized. The U.S. Constitution details the means of accomplishing these protections. According to one activist, "When they put the Constitution together, they wanted to guard against tyranny 'cause they knew, from experience, what happens with man. We're human beings, and we have a tendency to get greedy, cheat, lie, steal, so they put all these safeguards in our Constitution." The Constitution thus serves as the exemplar of the social contract. By adhering to the Constitution, Americans have freed themselves from the excesses of human nature and the bondage of tyranny. In short, engaged in a world historical process, they have actualized the promise of the Enlightenment.

This connection between the Constitution and American culture is central for anti-illegal-immigration activists. They imply that the Constitution is profoundly embedded within "genuine American culture." If the Constitution represents a codified instantiation of cultural norms, customs, beliefs, attitudes, and goals, then it is the means by which American culture is not only reproduced—or passed from one generation to another—but also deeply integrated into American culture itself. This originary Constitution, belonging to and yet transcendent of all Americans, is the purest instantiation of the exceptionality of American culture; for the Minutemen, the Constitution summarizes American culture's identity and provides the mechanism for the culture's continual protection and reproduction.

Given this view of the Constitution, those who violate the rule of law—corrupt politicians, corporations, undocumented migrants, and so forth—attack the transcendent fundaments of American culture itself; their actions threaten the well-being of all Americans, the "people," the owners of America from whom the Constitution emerged. Given this threat, the Minuteman Project pursues its goal of protecting American culture by proffering a definition of "the people." In the terms of the Constitution, these activists seek to define and delimit the *We* who form "a more perfect Union." But defining this *We* is no simple matter, particularly given that the Constitution is not at all specific about citizenship, which is what juridically defines who is a member of "the people." These anti-illegal-immigration activists object to all of the legislation that specifies the details about both citizenship and naturalization. Moreover, they are convinced that none of this legislation is being enforced.[3]

Most important, this legislation concerning citizenship and naturalization poses a quandary for these anti-illegal-immigration activists. The idea that America is a country of immigrants is the bedrock of American fictive ethnicity; as such, these activists must embrace this open aspect of both "American culture" and the Constitution. But these activists also contend that U.S. freedom is not guaranteed and that those who want to destroy American culture will do so from within, through cultural difference. On the one hand, then, these activists must embrace the openness of American culture; on the other hand, they must protect the citizenry from this openness. One activist echoed Abraham Lincoln: "America will never be destroyed from the outside. If we falter and lose freedoms, it will be because we destroyed ourselves." The best way to fend off this possibility is to dramatically limit migration, for immigrants represent a difference that might shatter the unity of "We the People." Thus, American fictive ethnicity, geographic borders, and the Constitution appear to require both openness and closedness.

These co-present necessities—by which we mean the simultaneous demands on anti-illegal-immigration activists both to embrace the openness on which the country is founded and to work tirelessly to close off this openness by guarding American culture from dilution by immigrants—seem to be an artifact not just of American democracy but of "democratic" nation-states in general. If such is the case, anti-illegal-immigration activists would appear to be responding to imperatives that structure all "democratic" nation-states. Closing this openness, then, is a structural feature of democratic nation-states. Closure through both legal and more informal means represents an imperative that liberal democratic nations cannot dodge. For the activists we interviewed and for many other Americans, this making of a coherent people, of a shared culture or fictive ethnicity, becomes obsessive when coupled with the belief that the culture itself is innately (naturally) exceptional, even superior. Closure, then, protects America and assures the continuation of America's exceptionalism—and provides these activists with a specific rationale for extreme juridical limitations on citizenship and residency. The enactment of this closure, both in juridical and nonjuridical terms, is the defining characteristic of these activists' singular form of American fictive ethnicity.

In understanding the Constitution in this way and in marshaling related weapons such as legislation to make English the official language, these activists not only seek to combat the danger they perceive but also identify and exclude the would-be disintegrators of their culture. That is, this limit form of American fictive ethnicity also functions as a mechanism for the creation and identification of the Other by defining those who fall outside of "the people." This move reveals something significant about these activists' understanding of both American democracy and democracy itself: it functions not only by way of an identifiable "We the People" but also by an outside that is, therefore, constitutive (see also Honig 2003). Positively stated, "the people" must simultaneously be both the *We* and the not Other. The power (*kratos*) of "the people" (*demos*), democracy, thus has two facets: one in which the people defines itself via a constitutive outside and one in which this defined people exercises sovereignty over itself.

The Minutemen's propensity for spectacle, wild rhetorical flourishes, and hypercitizenship make them appear to be radical extremists. However, the Minutemen's entire project emerges directly from their conception of the rule of law and their understanding of the Constitution. This conception emanates directly from the Minutemen's singular, culturalist understanding of what it means to be American.

Conclusion: The Minutemen as Liberal-Democratic Subjects

The views of anti-illegal-immigrant activists are coherent extensions of certain aspects of liberal democracy. For example, the Minutemen value the same activism that has been a historical backbone linking together today's progressive Left belief in participatory democracy (including, ironically, the beliefs of immigrant rights organizers), liberal democracy, different varieties of ancient republicanism, and finally the polis of classical Greek elites. Within this tradition, activism is a moral *topos* waiting to be seized so that today's vigilant hypercitizens (who are, in effect, sanctioned by democracy's central tenet of rule of the people) can mobilize activism and claim legitimacy and authority over free riders, both citizen and noncitizen. For these hypercitizens, the U.S. Constitution and the rule of law function as prized cultural artifacts that have enabled the United States to realize Enlightenment principles and to become the hope for humanity's future.

These appropriations of a kind of messianic democracy are not merely manifestations of nationalism or American nativism. They are essential elements of democracy itself. Hence, certain language policies and the sanctioning of a "We the People" via a *not-We* are necessary consequences of a democratic nation-state. We do not believe immigrant rights marchers, or those on the Left in general, when they say that these consequences can be rectified by advocating the "true spirit" of democracy—that is, a more tolerant democracy. Democracy as an organization of sociopolitical relations is also a fund of *topoi* (a collection of premises) that at times can be wielded to dissolve some power differentials while at other times can reinforce other differentials. Thus, democracy has no "true spirit" but bows to the material imperatives of the day; hence, the Minutemen are consistently democratic and wield the same overtones of democratic virtue as their opponents. The two sides of immigrant activism thus share a common structure of public argument in which opponents are hinged together by similar premises, mirror to each other similar values and virtues, and run the risk of becoming another frozen debate between two camps of idealists, settled not so much by "justice" (for how do we separate "the just" from the wielding of justice as virtue?) but by the exertion of power in the form of conservative legislation or liberal legislation, depending on who wins.

Race is one essential issue in this frozen debate. Immigration supporters commonly brand anti-illegal-immigration activists as racists. But opponents of illegal immigration deplore such accusations: "We're out there to enforce the law, and they're calling us racist. It doesn't matter if we have Mexican Americans on our side or not." In fact, the Chicago Minutemen like to discuss the coalitions they have formed with individual Mexican Americans and self-identified black organizations: "My experience is that the main reason people use the term 'They're all a bunch of racists' is because that is used as a strategy to cut off any debate or discussion. . . . They shut off debate by saying that 'You're all a bunch of racists, fascist, xenophobic, KKK racists.' And that's how they approach it because they have absolutely no argument on the issue of illegal entry, so they shut off the debate."

This activist rightly notes the phenomenon of the trump argument, which evokes some ultimate authority (God, the Bible or Koran, the parental or teacherly "because I say so," George W. Bush's "I am the decider"). Trump arguments are useful because they settle the confusions of the immediate by summoning a transcendent or an inviolable that is hard to counter. Because racism has come to represent an ultimate sin associated with ethnic cleansing, fascism, or the suppression of civil rights, it is one of *the* ultimate condemnations. Hence, there is no reply except denial. Accusations of racism thus shove all other points, including potentially relevant ones, off the argumentative stage. In other words, because of its power, the charge of racism can be both extraordinarily tempting and very thin.

We do not know whether the specific Minutemen we interviewed are racists. We are more convinced that they are hypercitizens and hyperculturalists—or, more accurately, that our use of these terms has more explanatory power than the charge of racism insofar as it reveals consequences that the democratic nation-state instigates. We do not argue that race is not an issue in the United States—it surely is. We are not saying that racism does not intersect with the sorts of cultural nationalisms to which we have pointed—of course it does, and it has done so structurally via quota systems as in the U.S. historical preference for European immigrants. We are not saying that racism has been determinately negated, despite the Minutemen's claims to the contrary. An indispensable part of post–civil rights movement American fictive ethnicity is indeed that the United States is moving beyond its racist past, and these anti-illegal-immigration activists are deeply committed to this progress narrative, so much so that several of them accused undocumented migrants of reactionary racism. But to reduce the Minutemen to racists is to miss the point.

The Minutemen's arguments cannot be interpreted solely as racist or as working-class responses to the loss of jobs. Their arguments need to be placed in a more global context that includes South African black responses to "illegal" black Zimbabweans; Mexican responses to "illegal" Guatemalans on the Mexican-Guatemalan border; Russian responses to "illegal" Tajiks, Uzbeks, and others from the former Soviet Union; the responses of black Dominican Republicans to "illegal" black Haitians; and initiatives currently being discussed in the European Parliament that would tighten the rules against its estimated eight million undocumented immigrants, the bulk of whom come from the former Soviet Union and Central and Eastern Europe and only secondarily from the Middle East, Central Asia, China, and the Indian subcontinent (see Wines 2007; Kramer 2007; Vucheva 2008; Salt 2005). One conclusion to be drawn from the European Union data is that these immigrants are significantly white. The European Union proposals are distinctly nonracist, and the black-on-black violence in South Africa would also seem not related to race.

Obviously, we do not have the space here to look into the details of the global examples just presented. But if we did, might that inquiry further deconstruct the Left's critique of the Minuteman Project as racist and thicken our own analysis of Minutemen as hypercitizens/hyperculturalists emerging from the American experience of liberal democracy? The Minutemen are but a special case within a more global wave of anti-undocumented-immigrant sentiment inflected differently in different regions. In these varied contexts, the roles of racism, class, nationalism, and the structures of liberal democracy might have different weights. A single constant, however, may be organizing these many responses: the Westphalian nation-state form is under strain because its current logic cannot accommodate emerging social realities.

After centuries of tinkering, the Westphalian state is now thought to be an outgrowth of a limited "people," an assimilated, legal citizenry—fictively imagined—that through democratic elections legitimizes a leadership that declares allegiance to a constitution and the rule of law. The coupling of a particular people to a particular state is reified through geographic, linguistic, and symbolic borders and ultimately made real by the power of international law. One of the pillars of the contractual relation between a people and their state is a functioning economy. But when the economy or some other aspect of the contract seems insufficient, the people move—as they are now doing with increasing frequency. But the Westphalian nation-state is not premised on this hypermobility; rather, for all practical purposes, it is premised on its opposite—that is, the stability of a people practicing their rightful will through deliberative politics. From within this ideology, then, what seems natural is a continuous, coherent people, a closed *We*. Hence, hypercitizenship and hyperculturalism are always waiting to emerge from the deep structures of the democratically legitimized nation-state form.

Because the premises and legal structures of the nation-state do not easily adapt to the realities of hypermobility, many of these nationalist groups counter these new instabilities with their own icons. Russians evoking "Mother Russia," for example, are relying on a kind of hypernationalism without further rationalization borrowed from democratic principles. The Minutemen we interviewed are also fervently nationalist, but because they and many other Americans view democracy as one more nationalist icon, they fashion themselves into ultimate democratic subjects who are thus ultimately legitimate. In this sense, democracy does not do away with but rather helps to produce the Minuteman Project.

Notes

1. We have analyzed the empirical data provided by parties on both sides of the ideological divide on whether the undocumented pay taxes and whether public services have deteriorated as a consequence of nontaxpaying immigrants, issues that are central to the Minuteman Project. We conclude that the undocumented pay more taxes than immigration opponents imagine, positively contribute to certain labor sectors but not others, and burden public services less than anti-illegal-immigration activists claim.

2. This talk of a culture war or a "clash of civilizations" may well remind readers of Huntington 1993, 1996.

3. For a detailed explanation of the Minuteman Project's arguments regarding the lack of enforcement of existing immigration law, see Mortensen 2009.

References

Alejo, Tomas. 2005. "The People Confront Racist Minutemen in Sacramento." *Santa Cruz Indy Media,* October 30. http://santacruz.indymedia.org/newswire/display/18890/index.php. Accessed May 13, 2009.

Anderson, Benedict. 2006. *Imagined Communities: Reflections on the Origin and Spread of Nationalism.* London: Verso.

Aristotle. 1985. *The Politics.* Ed. Carnes Lord. Chicago: University of Chicago Press.

Balibar, Etienne. 1993. "The Nation Form: History and Ideology." In *Race, Nation and Class: Ambiguous Identities,* ed. Etienne Balibar and Immanuel Wallerstein, 86–106. London: Verso.

ChicagoMayDay Google Group. 2008. Email, May 13.

Chicago Minuteman Project. 2007. Email, May 29.

Cruikshank, Barbara. 1999. *The Will to Empower: Democratic Citizens and Other ⌣ jects.* Ithaca: Cornell University Press.

DePillis, Lydia. 2006. "Read This Now: Minuteman Mobbed." *The Bwog,* October 4. http://www.bwog.net/index.php?page=post&article_id=2265. Accessed May 13, 2009.

Gellner, Ernest. 1983. *Nations and Nationalism.* Ithaca: Cornell University Press.

Gemma, Peter B. 2007. "Looking Up from the Grass Roots: Minutemen Project Represents 'Middle American Radicals' in Action." *Social Contract Quarterly* 17 (3). http://www.thesocialcontract.com/artman2/publish/tsc1703/tsc_17_3_gemma.shtml. Accessed August 10, 2009.

Hobsbawm, E. J. 2000. *Nations and Nationalism since 1780: Programme, Myth, Reality.* Cambridge: Cambridge University Press.

Honig, Bonnie. 2003. *Democracy and the Foreigner.* Princeton: Princeton University Press.

Huntington, Samuel P. 1993. "The Clash of Civilizations?" *Foreign Affairs.* http://www.foreignaffairs.com/articles/48950/samuel-p-huntington/the-clash-of-civilizations. Accessed August 10, 2009.

———. 1996. *The Clash of Civilizations and the Remaking of the World Order.* New York: Simon and Schuster.

Kant, Immanuel. 1991. *Political Writings.* Ed. Hans Reiss. Trans. H. B. Nisbet. 2nd ed. Cambridge: Cambridge University Press.

Kramer, Andrew. 2007. "Markets Suffer after Russia Bans Immigrant Vendors." *New York Times,* April 14.

Mortensen, Ronald W. 2009. *Illegal, but Not Undocumented: Identity Theft, Document Fraud, and Illegal Employment.* June. http://minutemanproject.com/newsmanager/templates/mmp.asp?articleid=723&zoneid=24.

ProEnglish: English Language Advocates. 2009. http://www.proenglish.org. Accessed November 13, 2009.

Rector, Robert, Christine Kim, and Shanea Watkins. 2007. *The Fiscal Cost of Low-Skill Households to the U.S. Taxpayer.* www.heritage.org. Accessed May 13, 2009.

Salt, John. 2005. *Current Trends in International Migration in Europe.* Strasbourg, France: Council of Europe.

Smith, Anthony D. 2002. *Nations and Nationalism in a Global Era.* Cambridge: Polity.

Thomas, Steven M. 2008. "The Minuteman Reconsidered." *Orange Coast,* January 28.

Vucheva, Elitsa. 2008. "EU to Toughen Rules against Illegal Migrants." *EU-Digest,* May 23. http://www.eu-digest.com/2008/05/euobservercom-eu-to-toughen-rules.html. Accessed November 13, 2009.

Wines, Michael. 2007. "Influx from Zimbabwe to South Africa Tests Both." *New York Times,* June 23.

11

Immigrants, Citizens, or Both?

The Second Generation in the Immigrant Rights Marches

NILDA FLORES-GONZÁLEZ

Some U.S.-born Latino youth who attended the immigrant rights marches claimed to have received puzzled looks and at times harsh comments when they told non-Latinos they would be taking the day off to attend an immigrant march. For example, Jorge, a twenty-two-year-old Mexican,[1] said, "They don't see why I should care [about the immigrant marches] since I was born in the United States and nobody is undocumented in my family and just stuff like that so they really kind of looked at me odd for being so politically active." These non-Latinos could not understand why fellow "Americans" would bother with an issue that did not seem to affect them directly. These comments reflect a popular yet limited assimilationist view that assumes that national (i.e., American) identification supersedes ethnic (in this case, Mexican) identification. This view is based on a presumed pattern of incorporation of early European immigrants, who for the most part assimilated and became "American" by the third generation. Any residues of ethnic identity among the descendants of European immigrants are considered purely symbolic, playing only a minimal role in their daily lives. That is, ethnic whites choose when and where to summon their ethnic identity, and when they do so, it is usually relegated to special occasions such as ethnic holidays (Waters 1990). This view assumes that people identify primarily as Americans, leaving ethnic identity secondary. In contrast, for nonwhites, including the Latino youth in this study, ethnic identification is not optional as a result of racial markers such as phenotype (skin color) and cultural markers such as language and religion (Waters 1990). Their ethnicity can overshadow their national identity. Immigrant rights march participants such as Jorge and other U.S.-born Latinos challenge the notion that these identities are dichotomous and incompatible.

This chapter calls for a different understanding of the incorporation of U.S.-born Latinos that goes beyond the European immigrant-based assimilation model. Based on new transnational theories, I offer an alternative explanation for U.S.-born Latinos' dual identification as immigrants and as citizens, and the participation of members of the second generation in the immigrant rights marches as an expression of this dual subjectivity. Furthermore, these identities are interconnected yet have different meanings and functions for second-generation Latinos, illustrating the complexities of living in a transnational context. The chapter first examines old and new theoretical approaches to the analysis of second-generation identification before turning to the second generation's dual identities and concluding with a discussion of how second-generation Latino youth are simultaneously asserting their status as both immigrants and citizens.

This chapter is based on interviews with sixty U.S.-born Latino youth between the ages of fourteen and twenty-nine who participated in any of the five immigrant rights marches that took place in Chicago in 2006 and 2007. Forty-nine of the interviewees were members of the second generation, and eleven were members of the third generation. Forty-eight were Mexican, nine were Puerto Rican, and three were from other Latino groups.

Assimilation or Transnationalism?

According to the traditional model, immigrants follow a straight-line assimilation, with each generation becoming more assimilated than the last and descendants usually being absorbed into the mainstream by the third generation. This assimilation model is based on the supposed rapid incorporation of European immigrants at the turn of the twentieth century. Some researchers believe that new immigrants will follow the same pattern as earlier European groups, eventually giving new shape to America's middle class as they "melt" into it (Alba and Nee 2003). Taking into account structural barriers faced by new immigrants, others propose a segmented assimilation model, arguing that new immigrants are assimilating into different racial sectors within U.S. society (Portes and Zhou 1993; Zhou 1997; Portes and Rumbaut 2001). This theory assumes that some will assimilate into the white middle class, others will assimilate into a middle-class ethnic enclave, and the rest will assimilate into a native minority group such as blacks, with the particular sector determined by structural factors such as race, class, and the reception of the host country (Zhou 1997). Given most Mexicans' nonwhite race, low socioeconomic status, and subjection to discrimination in the United States, Portes and others predict assimilation mainly into native minority groups.

Recent research challenges these assimilationist approaches by demonstrating how second-generation incorporation is much more complex than previously assumed.[2] New transnational approaches critique assimilationist models for failing to take into account the effect of transnational patterns of living on the assimilation process. Transnationalism, they argue, coexists with, overlaps, or complements the assimilation process (Jones-Correa 2006). Researchers have recently begun to emphasize how transnational lives may not involve the kind of practices that involve direct transactions described by earlier scholarship on transnational migration. (For new transnational perspectives, see Basch, Schiller, and Szanton Blanc 1994; Kasinitz 2004; Levitt 2001; Waters and Jiménez 2005.) Using a basic definition of *transnationalism,* only 10 percent of the members of the second generation can be considered transnational in the sense that they participate socially, economically, and/or politically in both the sending and receiving countries (Rumbaut 2006; Kasinitz et al. 2008). Instead, many individuals move between societies but do so in temporary and irregular ways, such as when they travel to their "homeland" for funerals, for vacations, or to live temporarily with relatives (Foner 2006; Jones-Correa 2006; Kasinitz et al. 2008; Levitt 2001; Levitt and Waters 2006; Smith 2006).

However, even though most second-generation youth cannot be called trans-nationals, they can be thought of as leading transnational lives. While the U.S.-born children of immigrants may not engage in tangible transnational activities such as sending remittances, their lives still take place in a transnational context. Levitt and Schiller (2004) suggest that the members of the second generation live in transnational social fields in which social relationships involve both the sending and receiving communities.[3] Thus, incorporation is not limited to their experiences in the United States but also includes their experiences, direct and indirect, with the sending community.

Levitt and Schiller (2004) use the concepts of "ways of being" and "ways of belonging" to explain the transnational lives and subjectivities of the members of the second generation. "Transnational ways of being" refers to relationships with people, organizations, and institutions that are transnational. The members of the second generation are embedded in transnational families and communities where contact with the sending country is part of everyday life, if not directly, then through the actions of other members of the family or community (Smith 2005). Levitt and Schiller caution that these transnational ways of being or relationships with transnationals do not automatically make the second generation transnational but may lead to what Aranda calls "emotional embeddedness" (2006, 84). Aranda explains that although the physical lives of the first- and second-generation Puerto Ricans she interviewed took place in the United States, their emotional lives remained connected to Puerto Rico. Aranda identifies two factors that lead to emotional belonging: ties to family and community and racialization in the United States. Family and community ties are formed through ongoing migration flows that replenish the community, keep the second and third generations in close contact with immigrants, and form multigenerational families and communities, particularly as people from different generations intermarry and live next to each other (Waters and Jiménez 2005). Furthermore, most of the members of the second generation live in highly segregated communities, or "traditional gateways," where the presence of coethnics and immigrant institutions and organizations are a large part of their lives and help connect them to their roots (Levitt and Waters 2006; Waters and Jiménez 2005).

In addition to these social ties, the emotional belonging of the members of the second generation is triggered by dual racialization in the United States (Smith 2006; Fouron and Schiller 2006). On the one hand, U.S.-born Latinos are racialized as native minorities. Smith (2006) finds that second-generation Mexican Americans in New York identified as immigrants to avoid the negative connotations of being a Mexican American or of being identified with other stigmatized native minorities, such as Puerto Ricans. Others have found similar processes among second-generation West Indians who respond to being stigmatized as black by emphasizing their immigrant roots (Waters 1999; Butterfield 2004; Fourer and Schiller 2006). On the other hand, Latinos are also racialized as immigrants and thus perceived as foreigners and as illegals (Oboler 1995; Rosaldo 1987; Rosaldo and Flores 1997). "Illegal immigrant" has also been equated with "Mexican" and is often applied to anyone who looks Mexican regardless of legal status or ethnic/national origin (Chávez 2001; DeGenova 2005; Santa Ana 2002). Aranda (2006) concludes that this racialization (and its accompanying discrimination) erodes second-generation youths' emotional attachment to the United States and intensifies their feelings of emotional belonging to their immigrant families and communities.

While Aranda's transnational ways of being speak to why the second generation emotionally connects with immigrants, the transnational ways of belonging show how this emotion is expressed (Levitt and Schiller 2004). Ways of belonging describes the specific practices that show the members of the second generation's emotional connection to or identification with their parents' country of origin, such as displaying markers of identity on their clothing, participating in ethnically marked events such as parades and festivals, and, I argue here, marching for immigrant rights.

As compelling as Aranda's argument is, however, it still reproduces the existing dichotomy between attachment to the country of descent and to the United States, a dichotomy that seems to suggest that leaning toward one distances oneself from the other. This idea has been problematized in other contexts, such as recent scholarship on hometown associations, which shows patterns of belonging to and participating in both country of origin and the United States (see chap. 8). Itzigsohn (2009) argues that subscribing to more than one ethnic identity—such as Dominican and Latino—is not contradictory. He asserts that the relationship between national origin and panethnicity "is not an either-or one but one of complementarities" (127). He adds that while the former is imbued with emotional meaning, the latter has a political end. My research on the second generation's participation in the immigrant marches suggests the coexistence of ways of being and ways of belonging that reflect identification with both immigrant communities and the United States as a national imagined community. Hence, participation by members of the second generation in the immigrant marches exemplifies their ways of belonging both to immigrant families and communities and to the United States. That is, marching is simultaneously an outward expression of their subjectivity as immigrants and as U.S. citizens. By marching, the members of the second generation performed citizenship in ways that established their rights within the polity as well as increased their connection to immigrant communities.

"We Are All Immigrants"

Our interviewees commonly used such phrases as "Immigration affects everybody," "Everyone knows an immigrant," and "We are all immigrants." Victoria, a seventeen-year-old Puerto Rican, said, "I was there in support, coming to stand up for my people because we are all immigrants. . . . Everybody is an immigrant." For Eloisa, a twenty-three-year-old Venezuelan, dealing with immigration was simply "part of what it is to be a Latina." And Carmen, a fourteen-year-old Mexican, reported, "Not only do I live in an area where there's a lot of immigrants, but I come from an immigrant family." Immigration touches the everyday lives of many second-generation youth not only through interactions with family and community members but also through encounters with outsiders who racialize these youth as immigrants.

Most of the second-generation youth in this study consider themselves immigrants even though they were born in the United States. In Levitt and Schiller's terminology, theirs is a transnational way of being that mostly involves identifying with immigrants from their parents' homeland but not necessarily involving themselves in the social, political, or economic life of that homeland. According to sixteen-year-old Andrea, who described herself as a light-skinned Latina whom people often mistake for white, "I haven't really been to Mexico or anything like that. It just feels weird growing up because I knew I was Mexican or from Mexican descent, and I [have] never been there. I don't speak Spanish, although everyone that I was around in Chicago and Indiana [did]. There were a lot of Mexicans. . . . You could say that I'm Latina. I don't know Spanish, [and

I'm not] familiar with the culture, but I still kind of go back to my identity." The emotional connection that Andrea and others discuss does not necessarily require formal ties to the homeland or even speaking Spanish or knowledge of cultural practices. This connection is not rooted in a homeland but encompasses a more panethnic dimension that ties together Mexicans, Mexican Americans, and other Latinos as immigrants (see chap. 13).

These narratives convey a transnational way of being that is nurtured in the immigrant family. These families are multigenerational and mixed-status, including members of the first and second generations and at least one undocumented person. Forty-five percent of the youth we surveyed in May 2007 live in mixed-status families. Parents and older children usually are undocumented or legal residents, while younger children are U.S.-born citizens.

Relations beyond the nuclear family also nurture the second generation's transnational ways of being. As the family circle expands, mixed-status becomes more common; youth often referred to blood, in-law, and fictive relatives who are undocumented. Diana, a twenty-six-year-old Mexican, asserted, "It hit home personally because I am a natural-born citizen, [but] my husband is not. Unfortunately, he is illegal. We have two children, and they are natural-born U.S. citizens, but because of these laws that the federal government is passing, my family is affected." In some cases, the family connection to the undocumented is more distant. Lissette, a twenty-year-old Puerto Rican, said, "This is an issue not just for immigrants. This is an issue for everyone. . . . Personally, I have family who are married to undocumented immigrants. They're documented now, but they weren't before. . . . One of my cousins, her husband is *Mexicano*. He's documented now, but a few times he had to cross the border [illegally] to go see his mom before she died." This statement reflects the social complexities of the Latino community, where intermarriage brings together people from different Latin American nationalities and legal status. (For Puerto Ricans' connections to immigrants, see Flores-González 2008.)

Living in immigrant communities further nurtures these transnational ways of being among the members of the second generation, who come into daily contact with people who are directly involved in transnational activities. The majority of the youth interviewed live in Latino neighborhoods—generally but not exclusively Pilsen, Little Village, and Back of the Yards. They come into daily contact with immigrants, both legal residents and the undocumented, who compose a significant portion of these communities. Hence, even those who do not have undocumented immigrants in their immediate or extended families have undocumented friends.

Lucia, a twenty-one-year-old Mexican, watched her best friend suffer when her father was facing deportation: "It was terrible. I hated seeing what my friend was going through. And her whole family was just getting separated just like that, and it was not good because her dad is the one that brings in all the money, and if they took him away, my friend has to go, too, because they can't survive without him." This connection to immigrants is also reinforced by ethnic identification. According to Kimberly, a sixteen-year-old Cuban, "It was important for me to stay united with my people. Not only with my family and community, but my people as a whole." The second generation often used *my people* to include coethnics, other U.S.-born Latinos, and immigrants of any legal status.

Transnational ways of being are also stimulated by the racialization youth experience outside their communities. Interviewees spoke of the indiscriminate categorization of Latinos as immigrants and of their experiences with discrimination and criminalization. In their view, "Americans" (by which they mean whites) do not differentiate Latinos by country of origin or legal status, viewing all Latinos as immigrants. Lori, a twenty-year-old Mexican, stated, "They like to categorize people regardless of their race. If you look Mexican, you are automatically an immigrant, no matter if you were born here or not." This conflation cuts across linguistic, economic, and social status, and few Latinos can avoid being categorized as immigrants. Markers such as speaking Spanish, which is fairly common among members of the second and third generations, often and sometimes erroneously signify to others an immigrant status. In Lissette's words, "The stereotype is always all about Mexican and Latino. [In reality,] it's not always that way. And people discriminate against anyone who's Spanish speaking. It's not just undocumented workers. You could be a well-to-do person with lots of money, [but] if you speak Spanish, you might be looked down upon." Being labeled an immigrant is highly stigmatizing, particularly because of the lack of distinction made between legal and undocumented arrivals (see DeGenova 2005). Explains Jessica, a twenty-four-year-old Puerto Rican, "To be an undocumented immigrant is something deemed as inferior, as something that's lower than the lower class, because at least the lower class has the right to vote, at least the lower class has access to all kinds of benefits and things like that. Someone who is undocumented doesn't, so there is this negative association with particularly Mexican immigrants that the undocumented status has given them." The members of the second generation also feel that they face discrimination and treatment as second-class citizens, partly because of their color and partly because of their immigrant background. José, a twenty-two-year-old Mexican, said, "Some of the injustices are just the way our people—Latinos, minorities in general—are being treated. You know they are not treated as human beings but basically as second-class citizens . . . just like even in factories the mistreatment of employees. . . . People are tired of the way they're being treated. We all want the same human rights. We don't want to be discriminated [against] because we're darker." Our second-generation interviewees commonly used *we* when speaking about immigrants or, like José, first referred to immigrants as *them* before shifting to *we*. Thus, statements such as "We are immigrants" or "We are not criminals" are quite common among the members of the second generation. This phenomenon indicates a certain internalization of the conflation of U.S.-born Latinos with immigrants, both legal and undocumented.

In the past decade, the racialization of Latinos has taken on pernicious aspects as undocumented immigrants have increasingly been viewed as criminals and as threats to national security, especially after September 11, 2001. This trend has brought these young people's self-identification as immigrants front and center, as they also felt targeted. Juan, a twenty-year-old Mexican, stated, "The government is making it seem that Latinos are terrorists when in fact we are not. They make it seem like we do not contribute anything to society and that we are all criminals." Another Mexican, nineteen-year-old Henry, similarly countered the association between immigrants and terrorism: "We're not a violent hate group. We're not. We're here to work. . . . We have to look at what unites us, and what unites us is that we're being exploited as workers, as immigrant workers." Both of these young men repeatedly used *we,* thereby including themselves as part of the targeted group.

The Sensenbrenner Bill further conflated immigrants with criminals, seeking to turn undocumented immigrants and anyone (including parents, siblings, friends, coworkers, and clients) who assists them into felons. Abigail, a sixteen-year-old Mexican, felt compelled to act: "I wanted to go and fight for what's right, I guess. Like how they are trying to pass that law, and it wasn't right how it affects actually me and everybody. 'Cause if you know somebody that's an immigrant, you'll get put in jail, too. I didn't want that to happen to" her parents.

This reaction is not surprising given that the Sensenbrenner Bill threatened the families and communities of members of the second generation as well as them personally. Although citizenship had previously protected them, the measure would have made them direct targets of anti-immigrant policies. And as the political became personal, acting became a matter of family and community preservation.

This sense of urgency compelled these youth to march and to think of ways in which they could utilize their status as U.S. citizens to stop these policies. In this way, the Sensenbrenner Bill simultaneously rendered the second generation's immigrant identification more salient and made its members realize the political value of their citizenship. Participation in the marches taught them that being a citizen allowed them to serve as a public voice for undocumented immigrants. This process reinforced their identification with immigrants.

Becoming Political

For most members of the second generation, participation in the immigrant rights marches was strongly linked to their dual identities as immigrants and as citizens. Their enactment of citizenship articulated ways of belonging to the immigrant community. That is, citizenship allowed them to act in ways that expressed and further cemented their identification as immigrants. Paradoxically, while their status as citizens set them apart from immigrants, it also made them tangibly demonstrate that they were part of this community. Rosa, a twenty-year-old Mexican, felt "that it is my duty as a Mexican American to help others with the benefits of my citizenship. . . . As a citizen, I thought it was important to support those who seem to have no voice in this country. I wanted to march for those who couldn't or wouldn't. I was marching for my family and friends." Furthermore, while members of the second generation may have shown their ways of belonging to the immigrant community in more individual ways in daily life, the immigrant rights marches were a crucial moment that helped make public their sense of belonging to the immigrant community. In other words, the immigrant rights marches transformed them from passive members of the immigrant community into active representatives of that community.

Youth aged between fourteen and twenty-eight comprised 51 percent of the participants in the May 1, 2006, immigrant rights march, a figure that rose to 54 percent for the May 1, 2007, demonstration. In 2006, 72 percent of these participating youth were citizens; this number reached an overwhelming 93 percent a year later. And for many U.S.-born Latino youth, the marches provided an initiation into political action as well as into protest as a form of political expression. Delia, a twenty-five-year-old Mexican, was typical. Before the immigrant rights marches, she had given little thought to what it meant to be a citizen, much less to exerting her citizenship through political action. Among those who had some prior political participation, much of it had been limited to voting. Michael, a fifteen-year-old Mexican, had "never done anything like this before." Another Mexican, Juan, aged twenty, explained the reasons that he and others had not participated: "I have never really gotten into volunteering. It was never asked of me in high school or grammar school. . . . I wasn't really involved because I never really thought about it and the effects that some immigrants go through. . . . I kept to myself and stayed away from any sort of politics. I often feel like doing something, but it's hard . . . Nowadays I am a full-time student and full-time worker, so I have [almost] no free time, and my free time is spent doing homework or . . . with family and church." This lack of political and civic engagement often results from a lack of opportunity. Second-generation youth seem to want to participate but lack the know-how or the connections to organizations that provide such opportunities. In addition, as Juan pointed out, schools do little to engage students politically (see also chap. 9).

Our findings are consistent with those of other research that shows that today's youth, especially urban youth of color from lower socioeconomic backgrounds (like most of the youth interviewed for this project), have fewer opportunities to learn, practice, and exercise their political rights (Andolina et al. 2003;

Atkins and Hart 2003; Camino and Zeldin 2002; Ginwright, Cammarota, and Noguera 2005; Hart and Atkins 2002; Sanchez-Jankowski 2002; Sherrod 2003; Youniss et al. 2002; Zukin at al. 2006). Our findings also support studies that report low levels of political participation among Latino youth. López (2003) finds that Latinos between the ages of eighteen and thirty have lower rates of voter registration and turnout than do whites and African Americans of that cohort. Other studies find that although 67 percent of young Latinos are disengaged from politics (Marcelo, López, and Kirby 2007), they are twice as likely to engage in protests (25 percent) than any other group (López et al. 2006). Similar patterns in the late 1960s, a period of turmoil and protests, shaped Latino youth's political activism. Demonstrations such as the 1968 Los Angeles walkouts, the Chicano Moratorium, and the anti-immigrant propositions that swept California in the 1990s initiated thousands of Latino youth into politics (Muñoz 2007; Mora 2007; Oropeza 2005). Although protests provided Latino youth with their introduction to politics during the 1960s and 1970s, many of these people later assumed more conventional political identities (Muñoz 2007). Today, a large number of Latino youth are again following that path.

For a significant portion of the second generation, however, the marches constituted an extension of previous political activity. Some of these young people come from families in which politics formed a part of everyday life. Eloisa, a twenty-three-year-old Venezuelan, explained, "Immigration [activism] has always been something that I kind of grew up to. I grew up thinking pro-immigration, pro . . . human rights . . . so, it didn't take much for me to [think], 'Okay, let me go and march'. . . . It's not something out of the ordinary. It's natural." Similarly, Laura, a sixteen-year-old Mexican who assumed a leadership role by organizing and mobilizing at her school and through a youth organization, Zócalo Urbano, comes from a family of activists. She participated in the marches "because my family, with them it's a must. . . . My family influenced me, but now it's my own thing. Now I know that's what I should be fighting for, that's the struggle of my people."

Laura and many other young people who had impressive political résumés were members of youth-led organizations focusing on social justice. Two sister organizations, Batey Urbano and Zócalo Urbano, played a central role in organizing and mobilizing youth for the immigrant rights marches.[4] Batey and Zócalo are the youth components of the Puerto Rican Cultural Center and Centro sin Fronteras, respectively (see chap. 13). Both groups use Latino youth culture, especially hip-hop, to engage youth in social justice (Flores-González, Rodríguez, and Rodríguez Muñiz 2006). Most members of these organizations are second- and third-generation, but they live in the Latino and immigrant communities that host the organizations (Batey in Humboldt Park and Zócalo in Pilsen). In addition to participating in the marches, these youth groups organized and mobilized other youth to attend demonstrations by visiting schools and speaking at other youth spaces. They also conducted fund-raising events to defray the costs associated with their immigrant activism.[5] Because of Zócalo's affiliation with Centro sin Fronteras, most of the group's activism focuses on immigration, and its members regularly volunteer at citizenship workshops and many other events sponsored by Centro sin Fronteras. Zócalo members also participated in the July 1, 2005, Back of the Yards march (see chap. 2). According to Armando, a twenty-five-year-old Mexican, "I've been involved in the movement for immigration reforms since the very beginning with Centro sin Fronteras. . . . The first big giant march was July 1, 2005, and prior to that we had smaller marches, and in between we had other marches. I had the privilege of traveling with Emma Lozano [director of Centro sin Fronteras] to Mexico City and talking with different dignitaries and community representatives in Mexico to get support. . . . I [previously went on] different trips to Washington to support the Familia Latina Unida." Involvement in organizations such as Batey Urbano and Zócalo Urbano gave members of the second generation the opportunity to learn, practice, and exercise their political rights. Community organizations are crucial for the political socialization of young activists (Andolina et al. 2003; Torres 2006). Peer interaction also plays a critical role in the process, as second-generation youth often learn political knowledge and behaviors from each other and act on these behaviors collectively. For the most part, peer groups organized, mobilized, and attended the march together (see chap. 9).

Citizenship and Responsibility

Whatever their levels of political experience, for all members of the second generation, activism is linked to immigrant rights. Many interviewees echoed a comment by Francisco, an eighteen-year-old Mexican, that "even though I am a citizen, I wanted to support [family members] and join in on the cause because so many will be affected by the outcome." Many second-generation youth believed that their status as U.S. citizens gave them a special, protected position from which to advocate on behalf of immigrants. Armando "grew up amongst immigrants [and] can represent them without the fear of being deported. I don't see it as doing anyone a favor. I see it as a responsibility." Most of those interviewed shared this view of themselves as "the voice of the voiceless," as Victoria said: "We are voices for the people who are unheard. We are the voices for the people who can't speak English very well. We are the voices for the Latinos."

The members of the second generation were aware of the precarious situation faced by immigrants who might feel too vulnerable to speak up. Prior to the May 1, 2007, march, Veronica, a twenty-two-year-old Mexican, wondered about the turnout "because people are scared with the recent raid on the [Little Village] Discount Mall. I mean I am extremely skeptical about the timing of the raids, I am very suspicious of it . . . because I think it's a way to terrorize [people] to not participate in the march." In such a climate, the members of the second generation saw their citizenship as requiring them to step up to the plate and go to bat for immigrants. Said Rosa, "I feel that it is my duty as a Mexican American to help others with the benefits of my citizenship. . . . As a citizen, I thought it was important to support those who seem to have no voice in this country. I wanted to march for those who couldn't or wouldn't. I was marching for my family and friends." This point of view contrasts with studies that show that most young people view political participation as a "choice" rather than as a "duty," "responsibility," or "right" (López 2003; Zukin et al. 2006). Despite what they consider to be their marginal status, many youth reflected on the advantage that came with their birth. Antonio, a nineteen-year-old Puerto Rican, said, "I am nobody but what I have. I'm a U.S. citizen, and I have a responsibility. I have a right that I can do [sic]. I can be the voice for the voiceless."

Among many second-generation youth, the immigrant marches mark the beginning of a new self-understanding as political subjects with the right and the power to demand changes. They believe that massive displays such as the megamarches send an important message to the public and to Congress. According to Antonio, "The rally accomplished letting the government know that we're standing up, we are making a stand and [making] a statement that we're demanding—we're not asking, but we're demanding legalization." They also learned, however, that these expressions need to be supported by ongoing action and intense political pressure.

These young people remain willing to march, but they are maturing politically and in the process considering additional options for engagement. Many say that marching is just part of the equation and that if they want to effect change, they must engage in other political spheres. Most mentioned voting, but others suggested strategies such as canvassing or "walking door to door" and speaking to their peers about the immigration issue. Irma, an eighteen-year-old Mexican, stated, "The march can only do so much, so I think that the next step is to write to congressmen to take another perspective of this movement. Because doing constant marches is only going to do so much. I think that our generation, the young generation, should step up and voice. . . . Writing to Congress or writing to powerful people, that should be another step." Regardless of the forms of political engagement they envision, the Latino youth in this study have begun to see and assert themselves as political actors and to see hope for the future if they become more engaged.

Conclusion

The immigrant rights marches profoundly touched the members of the second generation, unleashing a rush of emotion. Jorge said, "The March 10 march was actually really intense. I remember that it was intense in many different ways. And there's personal factors that came into play why it was a very emotionally intense day. [When I] came to realize how many people were actually there, I cried, because I couldn't really believe that there was that many. I'd been to previous amnesty marches, and I've gone with various different organizations from the past few years, but this is the first time I've seen so many people together for one cause, and I really did cry. I couldn't even describe the intensity I felt. . . . It was just amazing to be part of it." This intensity led Jorge and other second-generation youth to feel pride in being Latino and immigrant. Armando described it as "a beautiful day to be Mexican." Even youth with high levels of political participation were awed at the unprecedented rally. The marches fueled hopes that change is possible through political involvement. The marches also provided the members of the second generation with an outlet for expressing and reaffirming their connection to the immigrant community while establishing and asserting their location in the polity as U.S. citizens. The marches also showed them the meaning of substantive citizenship, evidencing the impact of political action and the difference that active citizens can make. Hence, the marches became a transformative experience for second-generation youth, changing their views on the meaning of citizenship and helping them to envision their political role among the immigrant community.

The second generation also transformed the immigrant rights struggle. What until then had primarily been a movement of longtime immigrant activists became a broad-based struggle that included other sectors (see chaps. 1, 2). The involvement of second-generation youth challenged the rigid and assimilationist notions that create false dichotomies about who does or does not belong to the nation as well as the view that these youth are anomalies for their dual identification as immigrants and citizens. Their participation demonstrates their dual subjectivity as immigrants and as U.S. citizens and shows that those simultaneously living in transnational fields and racialized communities have a complicated identity.

Notes

1. I use the term *Mexican,* and not *Mexican American* or *Chicano,* to identify the ethnic background of the second- and third-generation youth because that is the term that is generally used in Chicago and among the youth who participated in the study. All names of interviewees in this chapter are pseudonyms.

2. Research on the educational achievement of Latinos shows that many students manage dual identities at home and at school without major educational or social consequences (Flores-González 2002; Mehan et al. 1996). Telles and Ortiz (2008) find that Mexican Americans show an inconsistent pattern of assimilation well into the fourth generation, with nonlinear as well as uneven assimilation along different dimensions. For example, economic assimilation stagnates after the second generation, and cultural, social, and political assimilation unfold unevenly and slowly. Although acquisition of the English language is fairly quick, it does not eliminate the use of Spanish until at least the fourth generation. Moreover, ethnic identification as Mexican and racial identification as nonwhite, as well as support for the legalization of immigrants, persist past the fourth generation. Furthermore, the retention of these ethnic markers does not necessarily depend on exposure or contact with immigrants, since Mexican Americans who live in segregated nonimmigrant communities show similarly low rates of assimilation as those living in immigrant communities. Telles and Ortiz point to the partial role of racialization coupled with intergenerational transmission of ethnic and racial notions in the persistence of Mexican American identity through the generations.

3. Levitt and Schiller define social fields as "a set of multiple interlocking networks of social relationships thought which ideas, practices, and resources are exchanged, organized, and transformed" (2004, 7).

4. Batey Urbano was founded in the Puerto Rican community as an outlet for Latino hip-hop and activism. Its success led to the formation of Zócalo Urbano in the Mexican community.

5. Batey Urbano hosted a fund-raiser featuring local youth performing hip-hop that generated enough money to pay for a charter bus to an immigrant rights mobilization in Washington, D.C., in September 2007. Most of Batey's activism focuses on fighting gentrification to preserve their community, however. For more on participation by the Puerto Rican Cultural Center (and Batey) in the immigrant cause, see chap. 13. Batey members' support for immigrant rights is connected to their identification with immigrants as a consequence of the Puerto Rican experience on the mainland (Flores-González 2008).

References

Alba, Richard, and Victor Nee. 2003. *Remaking the American Mainstream: Assimilation and Contemporary Immigration.* Cambridge: Harvard University Press.

Andolina, Molly W., Krista Jenkins, Cliff Zukin, and Scott Keeter. 2003. "Habits from the Home, Lessons from School: Influences on Youth Civic Engagement." *PSOnline,* April, 275–80.

Aranda, Elizabeth M. 2006 *Emotional Bridges to Puerto Rico: Migration, Return Migration, and the Struggles of Incorporation.* Lanham, Md.: Rowman and Littlefield.

Atkins, Robert, and Daniel Hart. 2003. "Neighborhoods, Adults, and the Development of Civic Identity in Urban Youth." *Applied Developmental Science* 7 (3): 156–64.

Basch, Linda, Nina Glick Schiller, and Cristina Szanton Blanc. 1994. *Nations Unbound: Transnational Projects, Postcolonial Predicaments, and Deterritorialized Nation-States.* London: Routledge.

Butterfield, Sherri-Ann. 2004. "'We're Just Black': The Racial and Ethnic Identities of Second-Generation West Indians in New York." In *Becoming New Yorkers: Ethnographies of the New Second Generation,* ed. P. Kasinitz, J. H. Mollenkopf, and M. C. Waters, 288–312. New York: Sage.

Camino, Linda, and Sheperd Zeldin. 2002. "From Periphery to Center: Pathways for Youth Civic Engagement in Day-to-Day Life of Communities." *Applied Developmental Science* 6 (4): 213–20.

Chávez, Leo. 2001. *Uncovering Immigration.* Berkeley: University of California Press.

DeGenova, Nicholas. 2005. *Working the Boundaries: Race, Space, and Illegality in Mexican Chicago.* Durham: Duke University Press.

Flores-González, Nilda. 1999. "Puerto Rican High Achievers: An Example of Ethnic and Academic Identity Compatibility." *Anthropology and Education Quarterly* 30 (3): 342–62.

———. 2002. *School Kids, Street Kids: Identity Development in Latino Students.* New York: Teachers College Press.

———. 2005. "Popularity vs. Respect: School Structure, Peer Groups, and Latino Academic Achievement." *International Journal of Qualitative Studies in Education* 18 (5): 625–42.

———. 2008. "'We Have Similar Struggles': Puerto Rican Youth in the Immigrant Marches." Paper presented at the meetings of the Puerto Rican Studies Association, San Juan.

Flores-González, Nilda, Matthew Rodríguez, and Michael Rodríguez Muñiz. 2006. "From Hip-Hop to Humanization: Batey Urbano as a Space for Latino Youth Culture and Community Action." In *Beyond Resistance: Youth Activism and Community Change,* ed. Shawn Ginwright, Pedro Noguera, and Julio Cammarota, 175–96. New York: Routledge.

Foner, Nancy. 2006. "Second-Generation Transnationalism." In *The Changing Face of Home: The Transnational Lives of the Second Generation,* ed. P. Levitt and M. C. Waters, 242–54. New York: Sage.

Fouron, Georges E., and Nina Glick Schiller. 2006. "The Generation of Identity: Redefining the Second Generation within a Transnational Social Field." In *The Changing Face of Home: The Transnational Lives of the Second Generation,* ed. P. Levitt and M. C. Waters, 168–210. New York: Sage.

Ginwright, Shawn, Julio Cammarota, and Pedro Noguera. 2005. "Youth, Social Justice, and Communities: Toward a Theory of Urban Youth Policy." *Social Justice* 32 (3): 24–40.

Hart, Daniel, and Robert Atkins. 2002. "Civic Competence in Urban Youth." *Applied Developmental Science* 6 (4): 227–36.

Itzigsohn, José. 2009. *Encountering American Faultlines: Race, Class, and the Dominican Experience in Providence.* New York: Sage.

Jones-Correa, Michael. 2006. "The Study of Transnationalism among the Children of Immigrants: Where We Are and Where We Should Be Headed." In *The Changing Face of Home: The Transnational Lives of the Second Generation,* ed. P. Levitt and M. C. Waters, 221–41. New York: Sage.

Kasinitz, P. 1992. *Caribbean New York: Black Immigrants and the Politics of Race.* Ithaca: Cornell University Press.

———. 2004. "Race, Assimilation, and 'Second Generations,' Past and Present." In *Not Just Black and White: Historical and Contemporary Perspectives on Immigration, Race, and Ethnicity in the United States,* ed. Nancy Foner and George Fredrickson, 278–300. New York: Sage.

Kasinitz, P., John H. Mollenkopf, Mary C. Waters, and Jennifer Holdaway. 2008. *Inheriting the City: The Children of Immigrants Come of Age.* New York: Sage; Cambridge: Harvard University Press.

Levitt, Peggy. 2001. "Transnational Migration: Taking Stock and Future Directions." *Global Networks* 1 (13): 195–216.

Levitt, Peggy, and Nina Glick Schiller. 2004. "Transnational Perspectives on Migration: Conceptualizing Simultaneity." *International Migration Review* 38 (145): 595–629.

Levitt, Peggy, and Mary C. Waters. 2006. Introduction to *The Changing Face of Home: The Transnational Lives of the Second Generation,* ed. P. Levitt and M. C. Waters, 1–30. New York: Sage.

López, Marc Hugo. 2003. *Electoral Engagement among Latino Youth.* College Park, Md.: Center for Information and Research on Civic Learning and Engagement.

López, Marc Hugo, Peter Levine, Deborah Both, Abby Kiesa, Emily Kirby, and Karlo Marcelo. 2006. *The 2006 Civic and Political Health of the Nation: A Detailed Look at How Youth Participate in Politics and Communities.* College Park, Md.: Center for Information and Research on Civic Learning and Engagement.

Marcelo, Karlo Barrios, Marc Hugo López, and Emily Hoban Kirby. 2007. *Civic Engagement among Minority Youth.* College Park, Md.: Center for Information and Research on Civic Learning and Engagement.

Mehan, Hugh, Irene Villanueva, Lea Hubbard, Angela Lintz, and Dina Okamoto. 1996. *Constructing School Success: The Consequences of Untracking Low Achieving Students.* Cambridge: Cambridge University Press.

Mora, Carlos. 2007. *Latinos in the West: The Student Movement and Academic Labor in Los Angeles.* Lanham, Md.: Rowman and Littlefield.

Muñoz, Carlos. 2007. *Youth, Identity and Power: The Chicano Movement.* New York: Verso.

Oboler, Suzanne. 1995. *Ethnic Labels, Latino Lives.* Minneapolis: University of Minnesota Press.

Omi, Michael, and Howard Winant. 1994. *Racial Formation in the United States: From the 1960s to the 1980s.* New York: Routledge.

Portes, Alejandro, and Ruben Rumbaut. 2001. *Legacies: The Story of the New Second Generation.* Berkeley: University of California Press.

Portes, Alejandro, and Mia Zhou. 1993. "The New Second Generation: Segmented Assimilation and Its Variants." *Annals of the American Academy of Political and Social Sciences* 530 (November): 74–96.

Oropeza, Lorena. 2005. *¡Raza Sí! ¡Guerra No! Chicano Protest and Patriotism during the Viet Nam War Era.* Berkeley: University of California Press.

Rosaldo, Renato. 1987. "Cultural Citizenship, Inequality, and Multiculturalism." In *La-

tino Cultural Citizenship: Claiming Identity, Space, and Rights, ed. William V. Flores and Rina Benmayor, 27–38. Boston: Beacon.

Rosaldo, Renato, and William V. Flores. 1997. "Identity, Conflict, and Evolving Latino Communities: Cultural Citizenship in San José, California." In *Latino Cultural Citizenship: Claiming Identity, Space, and Rights,* ed. William V. Flores and Rina Benmayor, 57–96. Boston: Beacon.

Rumbaut, Ruben. 2006. "Severed or Sustained Attachments? Language, Identity, and Imagined Communities in the Post-Immigrant Generation." In *The Changing Face of Home: The Transnational Lives of the Second Generation,* ed. P. Levitt and M. C. Waters, 43–95. New York: Sage.

Sanchez-Jankowski, Martin. 2002. "Minority Youth and Civic Engagement: The Impact of Group Relations." *Applied Developmental Science* 6 (4): 237–45.

Santa Ana, Otto. 2002. *Brown Tide Rising.* Austin: University of Texas Press.

Sherrod, Lonnie. 2003. "Promoting the Development of Citizenship in Diverse Youth." *PSOnline,* April, 287–92.

Shibutaki, Tomatsu, and Kian Kwan. 1965. *Ethnic Stratification.* New York: Macmillan.

Smith, Robert C. 2005. *Mexican New York: Transnational Lives of New Immigrants.* Berkeley, California: University of California Press.

———. 2006. "Life Course, Generation, and Social Location as Factors in Shaping Second-Generation Transnational Life." In *The Changing Face of Home: The Transnational Lives of the Second Generation,* ed. P. Levitt and M. C. Waters, 145–67. New York: Sage.

Telles, Edward E., and Vilma Ortiz. 2008. *Generations of Exclusion: Mexican Americans, Assimilation, and Race.* New York: Sage.

Torres, Maria De Los Angeles. 2006. *Youth Activists in the Age of Postmodern Globalization: Notes from an Ongoing Project.* Chicago: Chapin Hall Center for Children.

Waters, Mary C. 1990. *Ethnic Options: Choosing Identities in America.* Berkeley: University of California Press.

———. 1999. *Black Identities: West Indian Immigrant Dreams and American Realities.* New York: Sage and Harvard University Press.

Waters, Mary C., and Tomas R. Jiménez. 2005. "Assessing Immigrant Assimilation: New Empirical and Theoretical Challenges." *Annual Review of Sociology* 31:105–25.

Youniss, James, Susan Bales, Verona Christmas-Best, Marcelo Diversi, Milbrey McLaughlin, and Rainer Silbereisen. 2002. "Youth Civic Engagement in the Twenty-first Century." *Journal of Research on Adolescence* 12 (1): 121–48.

Zhou, Mia. 1997. "Segmented Assimilation: Issues, Controversies, and Recent Research on the New Second Generation." *International Migration Review* 31 (4): 825–58.

Zukin, Cliff, Scott Keeter, Molly Andolina, and Krista Jenkins. 2006. *A New Engagement? Political Participation, Civic Life, and the Changing American Citizen.* New York: Oxford University Press.

Representing "La Familia

Family Separation and Immigrant Activism

AMALIA PALLARES

Deportation of an undocumented immigrant affects not only the deportee but also the U.S. citizens and legal residents who are members of the deportee's nuclear family. The term *mixed-status family* refers specifically to families that include at least one undocumented member and one legal resident or citizen. The legal changes implemented since 1997 have led to increased deportations, increased family separations, and the increased visibility of these separations, both among immigrant communities and the general population. One immediate consequence of these state-led processes is that the family has become politicized in new ways and has acquired political meaning for undocumented immigrants and their families, legal immigrants, and the wider Latino communities in which they reside. This chapter examines one group of families' struggles to prevent deportation and ensure legalization.

According to a Pew Hispanic Report, in 2005, the United States had between 11.5 million and 12 million undocumented immigrants and 6.6 million families in which either the head of the family or the spouse was undocumented or unauthorized. In addition, nearly two-thirds of children living in families headed by an unauthorized person (an estimated 3.1 million children) are U.S. citizens by birth and thus face separation from their families if their parents are deported. Another 1.8 million unauthorized children also risk losing at least one parent through deportation (Passel 2006). Moreover, legal residents convicted of certain crimes can now be deported, affecting even children whose parents are documented.[1] Human Rights Watch estimates that since 1997, at least 1.56 million people, many of them U.S. citizens or lawful residents, have been separated from their husbands, wives, sons, and daughters by deportation (Parker 2007). According to several recent reports, deportation causes child trauma rreparable damage to family structure, personal relationships, and the ousehold economy (Capps et al. 2007).

The possibility or experience of deportation has led many members of mixed-status families to become active in different facets of the immigrant rights movement. At the May 1, 2007, march, 47 percent of participants were members of mixed-status families (figure 12.1). In addition, participants from mixed-status families were less likely to be first-time marchers, slightly more likely to be occasional or frequent marchers, and more concerned with legalization. However, they were less likely to participate in more standard civic activities and significantly less likely to vote when eligible to do so (figures 12.2, 12.3, 12.4, and 12.5).

Members of mixed-status families have also relied on other political strategies. Chicago and the rest of the country have recently seen various campaigns and organizations, including Chicago's La Familia Latina Unida (LFLU), Families for Freedom in New York, and Homies Unidos in Los Angeles, calling attention to the effect of deportation on families.[2] Differing from social service models, in which organizations are designed to assist immigrants, this activism increasingly relies on the direct participation of undocumented immigrants and their family members. The political work of these groups played a central role in placing deportation and related family-separation issues on the immigrant rights agenda during the 2006 and 2007 marches.

Figure 12.1. Family Status of Marchers, 2007

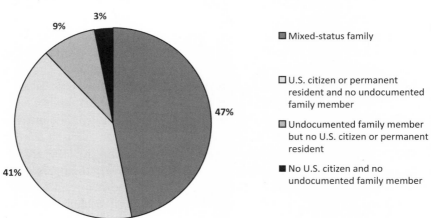

Data for figures in this chapter are from Amalia Pallares, 2007, "Family Matters: Strategizing Immigrant Activism in Chicago," Woodrow Wilson International Center for Scholars, available at http://www.wilsoncenter.org/news/docs/Chicago%20Pallares.pdf.

Figure 12.2. Important Reasons for Marching, 2007

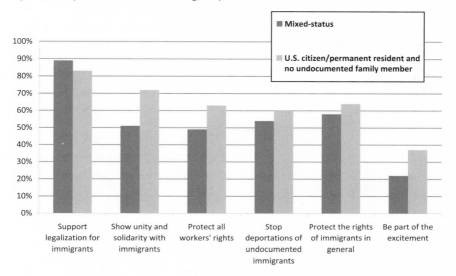

Figure 12.3. Frequency of Participation of Marchers, 2007

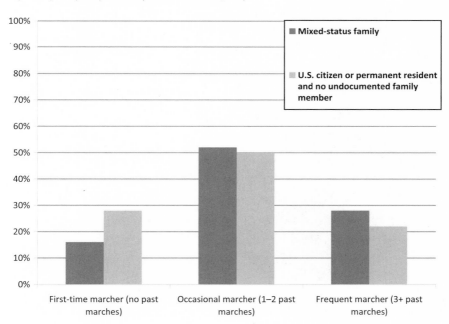

Figure 12.4: Civic Participation of Marchers, 2007

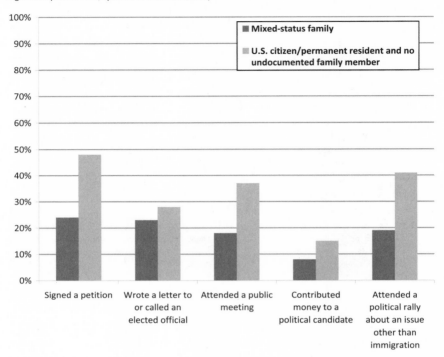

Figure 12.5. Family Status of Eligible Marchers Who Voted in an Election

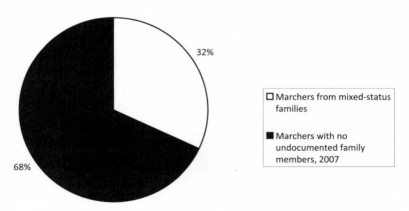

This chapter relies on a case study of LFLU, a campaign affiliated with the Centro sin Fronteras, to explore the relationship between experiences of family separation and recent immigrant activism against more restrictive immigration laws. Many immigrants threatened by deportation and their family members have not only made their cases public but become activists themselves, working to help not only themselves but also other families in similar situations. These activists rely on prevalent values of family preservation, continuity, and unity, arguing that these moral goals should supersede immigration laws. These activists also challenge a liberal political framework based primarily on the notion of individual rights, arguing that the deportation of parents violates the right of citizen children to be raised by their parents in their country of birth. This type of activism clearly presents particular difficulties not only because the activists are noncitizens whose presence the state considers unlawful but also because they are viewed as the excludable Others who help to define and delimit the nation (see De Genova 2005; Ngai 2005; Honig 2003). The study of this type of activism thus requires a new model of citizenship as participation that incorporates as well as transcends models based on the experience of minority and civil rights activism in the United States.[3]

Activists have organized despite these impediments, but doing so is not an easy task and presents its own particular challenges. How does one represent an alternative story or vision that fights the dominant discourse of undocumented immigrants as unlawful and therefore morally suspect? What kinds of political mechanisms, strategies, and discourses are deployed in these struggles? This chapter focuses particularly on the ways in which antideportation activists represent themselves and their families, offering some preliminary observations about how these efforts may help or hinder their political goals.

Background

The notion of family and its preservation, unity, and continuity has become a common referent for immigrants and their descendants as well as for a broader supporting community. The prioritizing of family unity is neither new nor an immigrant invention and has been reinforced by post-1965 family reunification policies and laws. However, the more recent politicization of family and family unity can be traced to the early and mid-1990s. The religious Right's political platform of family values made family sacrosanct, elevating the importance of its preservation and placing it in direct opposition to abortion and the rights of homosexuals, bisexuals, and the transgendered. The effectiveness of this discourse is visible not only in local and national public policies designed to curb reproductive freedom and gay civil and social rights but also in the Democratic and the Republican Party's adoption and appropriation of much of the language and goals of the family values movement (see Gillis 1997). The politicization of family unity among immigrants gained relevance in the mid-1990s with California's Proposition 187 and other local initiatives and finally the federal Illegal Immigration Reform and Responsibility Act of 1996 and the Personal Responsibility and Work Opportunity Reconciliation Act of 1996. It continued and became exacerbated after September 11, 2001, when national security became a new justification for further immigration enforcement and border control.

These changes in immigration and national security laws have led to increased deportations (from 189,026 in 2001 to 319,832 in 2007), stricter border enforcement, and the creation of expedited removals and thereby increased family separations (U.S. Department of Homeland Security, Office of Immigration Statistics 2008).[4] These changes have also severely restricted the individual legal options available to undocumented immigrants. For example, immigration judges now have less discretion, section 245 (i) has been eliminated, and suspensions of deportation have been terminated.[5]

LFLU focuses on stopping deportations and reunifying families separated through deportation. The campaign is housed in the Pueblo sin Fronteras organization, based in Pilsen, a primarily Mexican neighborhood on Chicago's Near West Side, and its former president is Elvira Arellano, an undocumented immigrant who was initially detained in 2002 and was deported in August 2007, after five years of activism, including a year in sanctuary.[6] Since her deportation, LFLU has focused on lobbying for a private bill, sponsored by congressional representatives from Illinois, that would benefit thirty-five mixed-status families who have been separated or are facing imminent separation as a consequence of the deportation of one member.[7] In most of these cases, people left the United States to visit a very sick or dying relative and were detained and deported upon their return and banned from attempting to enter for ten years. All of them subsequently returned again to reunite with their children and spouses. Some were detained yet again (and banned from attempting to return for twenty years) but nonetheless returned. Many of these individuals had formal reunification requests in process.[8]

Since 2003, parents as well as children from these families have traveled several times to Washington, D.C., to meet with members of Congress. They raised awareness as well as funds for their trips by outing themselves, making the details of their cases known to community members, religious congregations, and local, state, and national politicians. These families saw themselves as assuming a national cause, bringing publicity not only for themselves but also for thousands of similar cases.[9]

The LFLU has also participated in rallies to stop deportations. As the national movement for immigration reform intensified in 2006, LFLU members worked to mobilize people, underscoring the importance of stopping the raids and deportations, particularly at the July 19 march. LFLU members saw this facet of mobilization as fundamental in assuring the inclusion of people who had previously been deported and who would not necessarily be included in any comprehensive immigration reform.

The private bill's failure to make headway in Congress and the increasingly politicized national environment led LFLU activists to pursue more radical strategies. They adopted the cause of the IFCO workers arrested in April 2006, many of whom had resident or citizen family members (see chaps. 1, 2).

In May 2006, Elvira Arellano joined Flor Crisóstomo, one of the detained IFCO workers, in a hunger strike in Pilsen that lasted 40 days and was designed to pressure for a fair hearing of the IFCO workers in court. Once the judge who heard the cases granted them several months to prepare their case, Arellano and others ended the hunger strike. And the following August, Arellano, facing an order to report to the local immigration office for deportation, sought sanctuary in the Adalberto Unido Church. She invoked not only an ancient tradition of churches harboring those seeking a safe haven but the more recent U.S. political experience of churches providing sanctuary to Central American refugees fleeing persecution during the 1980s, in which the Chicago Religious Task Force on Central America played an important role as national coordinator (see Golden and McConnell 1986; Crittenden 1988). Arellano's actions attracted great national and international attention from immigrant rights advocates as well as restrictionist activists and led to renewed efforts to pursue the private bill as well as more recent joint efforts by Mexican and American legislators to address the question of immigration reform. Arellano became a national symbol, adopted and supported by some pro-immigrant organizations and movements throughout the country and vilified by restrictionist groups. However, some immigrant rights groups questioned Arellano's strategy, viewing it as excessively personal and disconnected from the broader struggle and fearing that it would incite a backlash. Others claimed that Arellano's case carried great symbolism and motivated people in the same situation and that her struggle helped, rather than hurt the movement.

Lawyers for Arellano's seven-year-old son, Saul, pursued but lost a case in which they claimed that in deporting Arellano, the federal government was denying his rights as a citizen. In addition to lobbying in Washington, Saul and other children have traveled throughout the United States and Mexico to call attention to his cause. They have testified before the Cook County Board and the United Nations and have joined other children in filing a class-action lawsuit to protect the rights of citizen children. The Centro sin Fronteras has also worked closely with Congressman José Serrano to promote the Citizen Child Protection Act, which would return more discretion to judges in cases of possible family separation. And in April 2007, the Adalberto Unido Church and Centro sin Fronteras joined other churches and organizations to launch the New Sanctuary Movement, which has enabled more than twenty other people to enter sanctuary in different churches across the United States.[10]

Who Represents?

The undocumented have always faced the fundamental question of whether they can be represented, much less represent themselves, given their lack of legal standing. Some legal gains have been made in this respect. For example, the U.S. Equal Employment Opportunity Commission, which enforces U.S. laws that prohibit discrimination in employment, has represented undocumented workers in issues having to do with discrimination and nonpayment of wages. Likewise, unions such as the Service Employees International Union and Latinos United have stood for the rights of undocumented workers. Legal status clearly has not prevented undocumented people from participating in marches and rallies and engaging in specific political struggles. However, in their previous political activity in unions, community organizations, schools, and political parties, undocumented immigrants worked through the available channels without necessarily disclosing or politicizing their status. Fewer institutional protections or mechanisms are available when the undocumented are organizing to protest their own deportation. (For undocumented immigrants' political activism in Los Angeles, see Varsanyi 2006.) Hence, they become much more vulnerable to public scrutiny.

In addition to the challenges of self-representation in the political sphere, undocumented immigrants' ability to represent themselves in their individual cases of deportation and legalization has diminished as a consequence of the end to suspensions of deportation; thus, others must represent or stand in for the undocumented. In cases of suspension of deportation, an individual had to show that leaving the United States would mean an extreme hardship. After legislators who saw the suspensions as a loophole that allowed too many undocumented people to stay eliminated the procedure in 1996, however, the undocumented could avoid deportation only through a cancellation of removal, in which it is necessary to prove not only extreme and unusual hardship but also that this hardship would affect citizen or legal resident relatives, not the person facing deportation (Coutin 2003). As a consequence, judges may no longer consider the hardships faced by potential deportees. Not only is this standard far more difficult to meet, but it essentially means that the conditions and rights of others serve as stand-ins for the conditions and rights of the potential deportee.

This problem of representation also appears in LFLU's activism. One of the group's key strategies for gaining public support has been to highlight children, who have become local, national, and international spokespersons for the cause. This strategy is tied to the reality that the children are citizens and future potential voters who have a deeply personal stake on the issue. However, this emphasis on children tends to displace the bodies and voices of undocumented parents.

This process was evident in September 2006, when Cook County Board member Roberto Maldonado held hearings on the issue of declaring the county a sanctuary for undocumented immigrants, meaning that no county official or police officer would be required to collect information on a person's legal status unless that person was charged with a felony.[11] Several representatives of immigrant organizations, community organizations, and churches spoke, most of them in favor of the proposal. Raquel Jiménez, an LFLU member, undocumented immigrant, and mother of three who was almost deported while pregnant, explained her situation in fluent if slightly accented English. Her twelve-year-old son then spoke, describing briefly and eloquently in non-accented English why it was important for him to have his mother remain in the country. Jiménez remained in the background and did not speak again. Several members of the press immediately sought to interview the boy, and news programs on both of Chicago's Spanish-language television stations subsequently showed the boy as the primary spokesperson on behalf of the immigrants. The boy's media appeal was clear, but something might have been lost when Jiménez herself was not featured, and there may be political consequences of having a stand-in representation of Jiménez and others like her.

This is not a problem entirely of immigrant activists' own making, however. Their reliance on children may be seen as an understandable response to the obstacles encountered when the undocumented attempt to represent themselves, publicly speak for themselves, and actively resist. Nowhere is this more evident than in Arellano's case. The controversy surrounding her decision to seek sanctuary to avoid deportation included comments by columnist Mary Mitchell of the *Chicago Sun-Times* and Eric Zorn of the *Chicago Tribune* suggesting that it was not Arellano's place to resist deportation.

Mitchell (2006) opposed Arellano's right to use Rosa Parks as a model of activism. While Mitchell's column was clearly informed by African Americans' complicated and ambivalent relationship to the immigration issue, the author argued that Arellano had no right to resist because her actions were out-of-bounds legally, morally, and historically. As an undocumented immigrant, Arellano had broken the law, whereas Parks—technically at least—had not.[12] Mitchell implied that as a recent immigrant, Arellano had no links or relationship to the historical oppression of African Americans and their inferior place in the labor market. Erasing the labor history of Mexicans and Mexican Americans in the United States, Mitchell's argument also erased the illegality of the acts of many nineteenth-century abolitionists and 1960s civil rights activists. In a narrative that places Arellano outside of history, outside of exploitation, and outside of the law, there is no figurative or real space in which she can claim any rights from the state.

Zorn argued that Arellano was not the ideal poster child for this cause because she had broken the law by reentering after a prior deportation and by using false documents: "Our leaders can't summon the political will to secure our borders and enforce our laws. But Arellano's not helping things. She's not a particularly good cause celebre, as these things go. She has twice entered the country illegally, has been convicted of carrying a false Social Security card, speaks very poor English for someone who has been in this country nine years, and she plays her so-called 'anchor baby,' a 7-year old son who is a U.S. citizen because he was born here[,] as her trump card" (Zorn 2006a).

Restrictionists usually use the term *anchor baby* to describe children supposedly being used to sponsor undocumented parents for citizenship. While current U.S. law does not permit children to sponsor their parents, restrictionists often use the idea as an example of how undocumented immigrants are cheating the system. While Zorn (2006b) later apologized for his use of the term (in response to two letters of outrage) and acknowledged that it was not a neutral term a journalist should use, he never expanded further on the question of Arellano's worthiness as a poster child. Indeed, his silence on this issue is most telling: there is no ideal poster child because there is no place for these people or their cause.

Arellano is only atypical in that she did not passively accept deportation. Zorn developed his position by explaining that her defiance "drips with a sense of entitlement that many Americans find off-putting." This act of resistance, in and of itself, ultimately makes her an inadequate cause célèbre and justifies the refusal to allow her voice legitimately to represent herself or others.

Martin Barrios, a member of LFLU and the father of two children, was deported after proceedings during which he received inadequate legal representation that made him unable to appeal. Unlike Arellano, Barrios did not seek sanctuary while his new lawyers fought his removal but continued his regular family life at home. The *Chicago Sun-Times* (Cepeda 2006) ran a column sympathetic to Barrios, contrasting him with Arellano: "Martin Barrios stuck his neck out on this issue and is paying the price for his activism. You have to respect him for that. But the longer Arellano is allowed to flout the law, the more intolerant people will become about immigration reform." Left unstated is the precise nature of the difference between Barrios and Arellano, both of whom were undocumented LFLU activists. Is the difference that he complied when immigration agents arrived to carry him away? That he is a conventional family man, not a single mother? That he waited in the privacy of his home? Barrios's illegal entry into the United States was not mentioned, while Arellano's was emphasized. Moreover, she receives sole blame for increasing opposition to immigrant legalization. The column suggests that while the likes of Barrios will make Americans more tolerant, the likes of Arellano test American benevolence.

These columns raise the question of whether the issue at hand is only or primarily illegal entry or what is increasingly viewed as illegal and immoral political agency? The logical extension of the *Sun-Times's* message is that the only meritorious undocumented immigrant, the only one who will be tolerated, is the one who avoids being caught or who, if caught, accepts his or her fate and goes away quietly, unseen. The price is deportation, and anything less is unacceptable and immoral.

This view is not limited to Arellano's case, although she made it more evident. During the May 1, 2006, march, *Chicago Tribune* reporters asked several people their opinions on the rallies. One man stated that he was sympathetic to the plight of undocumented immigrants but that they should not have shown themselves (Secter and Zuckman 2006). This statement reproduces the mistaken assumption that all marchers were undocumented and confirms the prevailing view that the undocumented can be withstood or tacitly accepted if they physically remain in hiding. In this context, it is quite ironic that to make her case politically visible, to appear publicly, Arellano had to isolate herself physically. Undocumented immigrants both resemble and differ from racial and ethnic minorities seeking civil rights; the undocumented also resemble gay rights groups, which must deal with the particular complications of coming out to make their cause known and understood and face sanctions from a "Don't ask, don't tell" society.

An Alternative Representation

A more complicated reading of Raquel Jiménez's brief appearance before the Cook County Board is possible. Although she barely spoke, she did appear, establishing her legal status, her role as a mother, and her relationship to her son, the spokesperson. Her son could have appeared without her. However, this approach would have defeated the point. Her son was not merely a stand-in but a continuation of her, intrinsically connected to her, a member of her family. She, her citizen husband, and her citizen children (including one who was testifying the same week before the United Nations) constituted a family as political subject. This image sits at the center of strategic political identity formation deployed by members of LFLU as well as other antideportation activist groups.

The displacement of representation as well as the reality of family separation increasingly means a focus on the collective and relational and specifically on the family rather than on the individual as political subject. As it is not possible to not be seen and not be heard and become a political subject, undocumented immigrants resisting deportation will continue to step outside of the bounds, outside of their place. However, the immigrant movement's challenge does not merely involve tactics alone but also incorporates the formation of a political identity that can inform activists' ideas, strategies, and positions.

The problem of representation remains, and we must understand the rise of the family as a political subject in relationship to this basic problem. Not only have antideportation groups gambled on the appeal of the family, using its unity, continuity, and reproduction as their primary axis of political identity, but they are also firm believers in its importance (however differently they may construct it), and these deeply held beliefs and the need to create an alternative political subject that goes beyond the individual subject constantly inform and reinforce each other.

Three themes dominate the framework for immigration activists' political subjectivity: one focuses on individual rights and responsibilities, whereas the other two are based on different ways of conceptualizing, understanding, and arguing for family. These themes are not mutually exclusive. The immigrants I interviewed often raised more than one of these themes and frequently interspersed them. However, these themes inform their actions in different ways.

Individual Subjectivity

The immigrants interviewed frequently described themselves as model citizens. They emphasized that they were law-abiding, paid their taxes, worked to support their families, did not receive welfare, and were not a burden on the state. This discourse of morality and responsibility is characterized by two main themes. First, the illegality of their unlawful entry is outweighed (and at times outright questioned) not only by their moral standing and law-abiding behavior but by their social responsibility as workers who support society: "They call us delinquents, terrorists. I ask those people who think we are that: Who is paying your social security check right now? They can come tell me. I have worked twenty years in this country, and I have not received a penny split in half of social security. But social security benefits go to those people who hate me, who want to see my family separated."[13]

Interviewees frequently underscored their responsibility in light of the concomitant irresponsibility of those who need workers to clean their houses, park their cars, care for their lawns, and work in their factories as well as of those who benefit from immigrants' private consumption and public contributions. The people interviewed also mentioned the state's lack of responsibility and contradictory position, accepting contributions from immigrants while threatening to expel them. (For a compelling discussion of the question of deportability, see De Genova 2005.)

A second common theme is the rejection of criminalization. Interviewees claimed accurately that people who enter illegally are not breaking a criminal law and should therefore not be criminalized. While civil violators of immigration law can become criminal offenders if they are found guilty of social security fraud, most family members equate criminality with far graver acts. LFLU members frequently commented that they were not criminals because they had not robbed or killed. Others share this aversion to the equation of illegal entry with criminalization, as the marches in response to the Sensenbrenner Bill illustrate.

This reliance on individual political subjectivity maintains the spotlight on individuals' acts and is therefore more vulnerable to counterarguments about legality/illegality, responsibility, and individual criminality at a time when the far Right frequently levels accusations against individual immigrants. Simultaneously, because they are stigmatized as a group, undocumented immigrants' self-representation as morally exemplary individuals is not particularly effective as long as other members of the group are not exemplary. Arellano and others may contend that they are not criminals, but anti-immigrant groups and the state itself have done a good job of wedding the terms *criminal* and *alien* by focusing on those few undocumented immigrants who have committed serious crimes.

Fighting for the Children

The first family-based subjectivity focuses specifically on the rights of children as citizens and frames their struggle as worth pursuing. Undocumented immigrants fight to stay here because they want better lives, better opportunities, and a better future for their children.

This perspective emphasizes the rights of children as birthright citizens: if they have to leave the country with their deported parents, children are denied the privileges of their citizenship. The children's educational accomplishments and strong feelings of belonging in the United States are often emphasized, and their departure is expected to lead to a decline in their well-being, a possible loss of accomplishment, and a denial of opportunity. Fernando, the undocumented father of three children who is facing deportation, stated, "I have friends [in Mexico] who say, 'Come over here. There is work.' But the future is here with my children because they were born here. I believe that because this country is so great and its economy is so strong, there are more opportunities for them here." Emphasizing the personal welfare of the child leads, however, to strategies that underscore the child's unique situation rather than the more general negative effects of separating children from their mothers. According to one attorney, a hardship must be beyond the normal hardship of child-family separation, which is already assumed. Judges and politicians may consider waiving deportation when children have life-threatening illnesses or other disorders that would be more difficult to address in Mexico. Arellano received an extension of her deportation based on the claim that Saul had attention deficit hyperactivity disorder and would not have access to adequate treatment in Mexico. The limits of these strategies became evident, however, when her request for a further extension was denied based on the state's assessment that Saul had improved considerably and that his condition was not serious enough to require that he remain in the United States.

LFLU parents often define themselves as struggling primarily on behalf of their children, stating that were it not for the children, they would have given up long ago and somehow gotten by in Mexico. Benjamin, a citizen and the father of three children who are also citizens, explained his reasons for fighting his undocumented wife's deportation:

> The easiest thing to do would be to say, "We are going to Mexico." [But] what are we going to do in Mexico? I have no riches over there. We don't have land or a house, I don't have a job and would have to look for one, but that is not the issue. I would be betraying the rights of my children in this country. And I can betray many people, but not my children. And they have the right to be here and to be here as a family. My wife is asking absolutely nothing of anybody—only that they let her remain here with her family. That is all. And they need to respect my rights. [speaking in English: I am an American citizen and I do have rights. That's what I want and my kids want, to be heard.] . . . My children, as American citizens, their rights have been violated.

LFLU activists argue that children are placed in the impossible situation of having to choose between their country and their family. Remaining in the United States without their parents would also mean a decline in accomplishments, opportunity, and well-being since they would suffer the emotional, physical, and financial effects of separation. LFLU parents also stress the trauma that a previous deportation or its possibility places on children. Such threats have negative effects on children's performance in school, temperament, relationship to parents, and feelings about justice and democracy in the United States. As Benjamin put it, "The children that are growing up in this hell are developing a very negative opinion of the country in which they were born instead of saying 'I love my country.' It is not the country it says it is. My children cannot accept the Pledge of Allegiance's mention of justice and liberty for all. [His daughter] can explain better to you. She says, 'What justice?' This is their experience, what they have lived in the past two years." The girl then continued, "When I am in school, I don't say [liberty and justice for all], and my teachers get angry. They say they will send me to the office if I don't say it. I don't believe in what it says, because there is no justice for my mother, and they are saying that there is justice. It's a lie. I don't want to say it on any day. Sometimes I don't say it when my teachers aren't looking." The parents argue that these experiences have not only victimized but also politicized children. Several parents reported having initially tried to guard their children from these issues and exclude them from their activism; the children insisted on participating, however, because they felt they had to do something. While the public activities of these children, particularly Saul Arellano, have generated debate about whether they are being used by their parents, we need to think critically not only about children's potential to engage in meaningful political action and participation but also about the extent to which these children's lives have already been profoundly altered by acts of the state. As one undocumented mother, Vanessa, explained, "Sometimes I question whether I am giving my child a good life, as I spend my time between work, rallies, and political meetings, often bringing him with me. But who am I kidding? It's not like we would be spending Sundays with friends and family at a barbeque. We already don't have that life." This subjectivity, "We are fighting for the children," has taken central stage in the LFLU's activism. In addition to the various legal challenges brought by Saul Arellano and other children and lobbying efforts that feature children, the Centro sin Fronteras has supported Serrano's Citizen Child Protection Bill. The Centro sin Fronteras and LFLU hope that these efforts will result in the legalization of undocumented immigrants who are parents and have previous deportations, even if future legalization measures exclude people with prior deportations. While this strategy garners public sympathy and may seem in some instances to be the most effective political route, it does have its limits. It does not fully represent the rights, needs, and desires of all family members, and it excludes individuals and families without minor children who are citizens. It can also expose activists to the criticism that children are being improperly used and made to feel unduly responsible for their parents' plight.

This approach also runs into the same obstacles as other children's rights issues, since most polities recognize children not as full citizens but as proto-citizens with limited rights and responsibilities. An attorney for the Centro sin Fronteras told me that immigration judges were more likely to rule that deportation of a parent would be an extreme hardship in the cases of older children, when there is a stronger argument that their lives are in the United States and that the disruptions of leaving would be severe. Younger children are considered more adaptable.

Fighting for the Family

For the LFLU, the unity and continuity of family is in and of itself a value that must be preserved and pursued above the laws of the state. This discourse has its foundations not only in cultural and religious understandings immigrants bring from Mexico but in U.S. ideologies that have historically privileged the idea family unity. These ideologies are apparent in family law, family reunification in immigration policy, and more recently in arguments made by Christian conservatives deploying a discourse about the importance of preserving and exalting family values. In the past two decades, this discourse has permeated both the Republican and Democratic platforms (Gillis 1997, 48).

The people I interviewed measured their contributions to U.S. society not only in terms of their work and their financial weight but in their family values. They frequently used this commitment to the idea of family, however idealized, to distinguish themselves from others and to explain why they had to break U.S. law by leaving the country to visit ailing relatives. Several interviewees understood caretaking as form of social citizenship that benefits not only one's children but society as a whole. They often argued that by caring for their children in low-income urban neighborhoods, undocumented mothers were ensuring that these children would not be involved in gangs or become criminals. By being both hard workers and constant presences in their children's lives, undocumented fathers keep their children motivated and off the streets. By seeking to deport these parents, LFLU members claim, the state is disrupting not only their families but also society and is promoting future social disorder. This view is intimately connected to these undocumented parents' more individual self-presentation as morally ideal individuals. It represents an extension of this ideal protocitizen as a model parent, building family and community, attending church, and setting an example for children. Men represent themselves as hardworking breadwinners, women as ideal homemakers. Arellano and other single parents represent themselves as both. They believe that this fulfillment of their duties to their communities and to the nation, not only as individuals but as parents, should outweigh the illegality of their crossing.

This discourse bears some resemblance to the dominant family values discourse that regularly draws a relationship between the decline of family and social disorder (Gillis 1997, 48). LFLU parents frequently referred to dominant political discourse on family values to point out the inconsistency between that discourse and the separation of their families. They questioned not the discourse but the fact that deportation threatened their ability to reproduce family values. This glaring contradiction frequently became the basis for a radical critique of American democracy. Regarding Jiménez, who was detained when she was four months pregnant, Arellano stated, "They speak of family values but when they shackled her and chained her pregnant stomach, where were their family values? Are not our families worth as much as theirs? What were they thinking, that the baby inside her stomach was also going to run away?" Awaiting a deportation notice, Fernando reflected, "This country views itself as democratic and plays with the lives of people. I don't understand how the United States is in a war with other countries for peace and democracy, speaking of family unity, and over here the first thing you see is that there is no democracy and there is no family unity. In the debate on immigration reform in the Senate, they talked a lot about the family. But one goes out on the street with fear, thinking that you will be seized and separated from your family." Benjamin also referred to family values: "When they took my wife, here I was, knocking on doors to see who could take care of my kids. It was ridiculous and stupid. However, they speak of family values in Washington, they speak of human rights, they speak of so many things that sound so good, but in reality they are completely opposed to what they say. Let them explain to my children why they cannot have their mother here." This family subjectivity that focuses on the preservation of family for the sake of the family (as opposed to for the sake or for the rights of the children) is simultaneously inclusive and exclusionary. It incorporates the rights, needs, and desires of adults—citizen, resident, and undocumented parents and grandparents—and most supporters of the movement refer to this subjectivity when they state that they believe families "should not be separated." It refers to the survival and continuity of the interpersonal relationships that have historically sustained marginal populations through racial, social, and economic oppression. But it also relies on a conventional model of the traditional family, reproducing both the moral ideals of the Christian Right in a competition of sorts over who has more family values and traditional gender norms that are not only informed by prevalent cultural beliefs but also encouraged by a legal system that has historically rewarded those who display the most conventional morality and represent themselves as ideal and indispensable caretakers (mothers) and irreplaceable breadwinners (fathers). Those who do not fit this conventional model are subject to questioning, frequently from within immigrant circles but also, and more important, by border agents, lawyers, judges, and opponents of immigration reform. It is in this context that we should understand the restrictionist group of Arizona mothers who repeatedly asked, "Where is the father of Elvira Arellano's son?"

Arellano does not necessarily fit this notion of conventional morality. A single mother who is estranged from her son's father, she represents a gendered hybridity, both caretaker and breadwinner. She has turned down multiple marriage proposals from men drawn to her cause, a conventional if at this point suspect solution to her plight. Her work as an organizer has been fraught with difficulties, as working with fathers of families has at times instigated the suspicions and jealousy of their spouses. As an adult, she has never been supported by any man: she has worked since she was a teenager, first in Mexico and then in Aurora and Chicago, and most recently in this country was supported by the congregation of Adalberto Unido and activists from the Centro sin Fronteras. Some observers have understood her act of seeking sanctuary in the church as gender crossing: said one older Mexican woman in October 2006, "We are with you, my child. You have your pants on right."

Conclusions

The family as political subject plays an increasingly important role in shaping the forms of self-representation that undocumented immigrants create in response to the decline in their opportunities for legal self-representation and the questioning of their right to political agency. As a plural that groups undocumented parents and citizen children and spouses, this subjectivity emphasizes the indissoluble ties among family members, countering dominant representations of the undocumented as illegal individuals and questioning a liberal political model that posits the polity as an aggregate of individuals.

As their legal options have diminished, the state has tightened its noose, and social opposition to undocumented immigrants has increased, undocumented immigrants have become more organized. Prior to 1996, when suspension of deportation was a possibility and judges had more discretion, undocumented immigrants' efforts and energy were devoted exclusively to demonstrating that they were model individuals and were more American than not. This approach represented an individual or at best familial strategy, deployed only with the assistance of a lawyer. No collective organizing was required. But in the face of disempowerment and the almost impossibility of self-representation as individuals, they have pursued stand-in representation through the focus on children. They have also pursued collective representation by deploying the family as political subject and by organically linking themselves to the broader immigrant movement (both as mobilizers and as symbols), allowing the details of their pain to be made public and thus rendering the private public in novel ways.

Arellano's August 2007 arrest and deportation brought more attention and salience to the question of the representation and self-representation of undocumented immigrants and mixed-status families. Immigration and Customs Enforcement deported her within hours of her arrest, probably to avoid giving the matter any further publicity given its symbolic value. Restrictionist activists considered her deportation a victory, confirming their assertions that she had no right to be in the country, much less to represent herself and her case. With few exceptions, throughout her sanctuary year, the mainstream press focused on her as an individual rather than as a political activist linked to a grassroots organization and to regional and national networks of immigrant rights advocates. Her deportation and the support of activists who staged mobilizations throughout the country at which participants chanted, "We are all Elvira Arellano," forced many members of the press to address her case as one of many as well as to ask whom she represented. For immigrant rights supporters who were not vocal Arellano supporters, the case raised a series of questions: Does Arellano represent us? Who represents the undocumented? Does the focus on an individual hide or erase the plurality of cases and voices, help or hurt the cause? Would other strategies or alternatives of representation be more viable and politically effective? Supporters, critics, and the mainstream press have agreed only that at the very minimum, Arellano took great personal risks to call attention to the issue.

The ultimate outcome of the strategies of representation employed by the LFLU and similar organizations remains a political work in progress. While scholars of citizenship have begun to point to the need critically to examine the exclusionary aspects of citizenship that shape the experience of undocumented residents as the "present absents" in the U.S. polity, scholars of social movements must now focus on the specific agency of the undocumented—that is, on the relationship between exclusion from citizenship and the forms of political representation, strategies, and identities that undocumented people can deploy and on the impact of these movements on formal and substantive practices of liberal citizenship.

Notes

1. Individuals can be deported even if they were convicted of felonies before 1996, when the law was enacted, and if they have already served their time for the conviction.

2. Homies Unidos and Families for Freedom work for the rights of families of deportees who have committed felonies and have criminal records, whereas LFLU does not.

3. As Ngai (2005) has shown, Asians and Latinos have faced consistent historical marginalization as Others and exclusion as unlawful. As D. Gutiérrez (1995) has analyzed, the question of lawfulness has divided Mexican immigrants, as lawful Mexican immigrants and organizations have opted to exclude undocumented immigrants and oppose undocumented migration.

4. Expedited removal involves the processing and immediate deportation of people caught at the border without a hearing in front of a judge.

5. Expedited removal has effectively increased the power of border patrol agents. Judges are now limited by statute in their final determination when a prior deportation order has been issued. The end to the suspension of deportation hearings (at which immigrants could go before a judge and argue that their deportation would lead to extreme hardship) removed that (limited) avenue for appeal (Coutin 2003). Section 245 (i) prevented family separations by allowing immigrants seeking permanent residency to apply to remain in the United States while doing so instead of returning to their country of origin and applying through the U.S. consulate.

6. With the exceptions of Arellano and her son, Saul, all names of LFLU members interviewed in this chapter are pseudonyms.

7. A private bill is introduced on behalf of specific individuals and affects only those individuals.

8. The law makes no provisions for emergency visits home by persons whose family members are formally requesting that they be admitted to the United States. Their only option is to seek pardons if they are stopped while trying to return, but such pardons are rarely granted.

9. Some immigrant rights groups have not supported this strategy because the bill would help only a few families and would not change the legal conditions of the millions of other undocumented immigrants.

10. In distinction from the sanctuary movement of the 1980s, which was more effective at providing sanctuary for immigrants, the New Sanctuary Movement has focused on addressing raids, detentions, conditions in detention centers, and fairness in legal procedures and has joined with many other immigrant advocacy groups to call for a moratorium on deportations.

11. The board passed the measure in June 2007, making Cook the nation's first sanctuary county.

12. While Montgomery, Alabama, had a 1900 municipal ordinance that allowed bus drivers to segregate riders by race, it also stated that no passengers would be required to stand up or give up their seats if no more seats were available. However, bus drivers' standard practice was to order blacks to give up their seats when the bus was full to allow whites to sit down. Parks thus technically did not break Alabama law, although she did break with custom (Hawken 2007, 79).

13. Most interviews were conducted in Spanish and translated by the author.

References

Arellano, Elvira. 2006. Interview by Amalia Pallares. June, Chicago. Tape recording and transcript on file at the University of Illinois at Chicago.
———. 2007. Interview by Amalia Pallares. October, Chicago. Tape recording and transcript on file at the University of Illinois at Chicago.
Ávila, Oscar. 2007. "Church Standoff Stirs Immigrant's Hometown." *Chicago Tribune,* February 19. http://archives.chicagotribune.com/2007/feb/19/news/chi-0702190181feb19. Accessed May 14, 2009.
Ayala, Vanessa. 2006. Interview by Amalia Pallares. June, Chicago. Tape recording and transcript on file at the University of Illinois at Chicago.
Begin, Christopher. 2007. Interview by Amalia Pallares. February, Chicago. Tape recording on file at the University of Illinois at Chicago.
Capps, Randy, Rosa Maria Castañeda, Ajay Chaudry, and Robert Santos. 2007. *Paying the Price: The Impact of Immigration Raids on America's Children: A Report by the Urban Institute for the National Council of La Raza.* http://www.urban.org/UploadedPDF/411566_immigration_raids.pdf. Accessed May 14, 2009.
Cepeda, Esther. 2006. "Immigrant Mother Hurts Her Cause with Standoff." *Chicago Sun-Times,* December 19.
Coutin, Susan Bibler. 2000. *Legalizing Moves: Salvadoran Immigrants' Struggle for U.S. Residency.* Ann Arbor: University of Michigan Press.
———. 2003. "Suspension of Deportation Hearings and Measures of Americanness." *Journal of Latin American Anthropology* 8 (2): 58–95.

Crittenden, Ann. 1988. *Sanctuary: A Story of American Conscience a* *lision.* New York: Weidenfeld and Nicolson.

De Genova, Nicholas. 2005. *Working the Boundaries: Race, Space* *Mexican Chicago.* Durham: Duke University Press.

Gillis, John R. 1997. *A World of Their Own Making: Myth, Ritual,* *Family Values.* Cambridge: Harvard University Press.

Golden, Renny, and Michael McConnell. 1986. *Sanctuary: The New Underground Railroad.* Maryknoll, N.Y.: Orbis.

Gutiérrez, David. 1995. *Walls and Mirrors: Mexican Americans, Mexican Immigrants, and the Politics of Ethnicity.* Berkeley: University of California Press.

Gutiérrez, Fernando. 2006. Interview by Melissa Rivera-Santana. June, Chicago. Tape recording and transcript on file at the University of Illinois at Chicago.

Hawken, Paul. 2007. *Blessed Unrest: How the Largest Movement in the World Came into Being, and Why No One Saw it Coming.* New York: Viking.

Honig, Bonnie. 2003. *Democracy and the Foreigner.* Princeton: Princeton University Press.

López, Roberto. 2007. Interview by Amalia Pallares. January, Chicago. Tape recording on file at the University of Illinois at Chicago.

Mitchell, Mary. 2006. "Blacks Know Rosa Parks and You, Arellano, Are No Rosa Parks." *Chicago Sun Times,* August 22.

Ngai, Mae. 2005. *Impossible Subjects: Illegal Aliens and the Making of Modern America.* 2nd ed. Princeton: Princeton University Press.

Parker, Alison. 2007. *Forced Apart: Families Separated and Immigrants Harmed by United States Deportation Policy.* http://www.hrw.org/reports/2007/us0707. Accessed May 14, 2009.

Passel, Jeffrey S. 2006. *The Size and Characteristics of the Unauthorized Migrant Population in the U.S.: Estimates Based on the March 2005 Current Population Survey.* March 7. http://pewhispanic.org/files/reports/61.pdf. Accessed May 14, 2009.

Quintana, Dora. 2006. Interview by Melissa Rivera-Santana. June, Chicago. Tape recording and transcript on file at the University of Illinois at Chicago.

Ramírez, Benjamin. 2006. Interview by Melissa Rivera-Santana. July, Chicago. Tape recording and transcript on file at the University of Illinois at Chicago.

Ramírez, Cristina. 2006. Interview by Melissa Rivera-Santana. July, Chicago. Tape recording and transcript on file at the University of Illinois at Chicago.

Secter, Bob, and Jill Zuckman. 2006. "Will Marches Help or Hurt Cause? Bystanders Divided on Whether Protests Can Sway Washington." *Chicago Tribune,* May 2.

Seif, Heidi. 2004. "'Wise Up!' Undocumented Latino Youth, Mexican-American Legislators, and the Struggle for Higher Education Access." *Latino Studies Journal* 2 (2): 210–30.

U.S. Department of Homeland Security, Office of Immigration Statistics. 2008. *Immigration Enforcement Actions: 2007.* December. http://www.dhs.gov/xlibrary/assets/statistics/publications/enforcement_ar_07.pdf. Accessed August 17, 2009.

Varsanyi, Monica. 2006. "Getting Out the Vote in Los Angeles: The Mobilization of Undocumented Immigrants in Electoral Politics." In *Latinos and Citizenship: The*

Dilemma of Belonging, ed. Suzanne Oboler, 219–46. New York: Palgrave McMillan, 2006.

Zorn, Eric. 2006a. "Deportation Standoff Not Helping Cause." *Chicago Tribune,* August 17.

———. 2006b. *Sinking "Anchor Babies."* August 18. http://blogs.chicagotribune.com/news_columnists_ezorn/2006/08/sinking_anchor_.html. Accessed August 17, 2009.

Grappling with *Latinidad*

Puerto Rican Activism in Chicago's Pro–Immigrant Rights Movement

MICHAEL RODRÍGUEZ MUÑIZ

Passionately chanting "¡Boricua y Mexicano, luchando mano a mano!" (Puerto Rican and Mexican, struggling hand in hand!), the demonstrators marched down the narrow, empty halls of the Rayburn Building in Washington, D.C., on September 12, 2007. The chant, led by youth, echoed powerfully, suggesting a crowd much larger than the two hundred people present. They were visiting the country's capital to reenergize the immigrant rights movement, all but proclaimed dead by mainstream press after the arrest and expeditious deportation of undocumented activist Elvira Arellano (see chaps. 2, 12).

Confused congressional aids and staff peered out of offices, puzzled by the vocal mélange of immigrant rights activists and supporters. In an attempt to gain control of the boisterous grouping, several U.S. Capitol Police officers formed a wedge that divided the crowd in half. Undeterred by the move, the front line of the group pushed forward, making its way to the office of the speaker of the House, Democratic Congresswoman Nancy Pelosi. After hearing that Pelosi was "unavailable" to speak to them, activists began to tape a poster-sized letter to her office door. The letter demanded an immediate moratorium on family separations and Immigration and Customs Enforcement raids.

Suddenly, a congressional staffer, presumably bothered by the commotion, slammed a nearby door. Perceiving the door slamming as an affront, the diverse group, which included veteran community leaders, activists, and organizers as well as immigrant children and youth, responded by aggressively and defiantly chanting "¡Sí Se Puede!" (Yes, we can!). In that explosive instant, a comment by Puerto Rican New York assemblyman Joel Rivera during a press conference earlier that day seemed to become a reality: "We are one Latino nation, we are one. . . . We are family."

As the mood intensified and chants reached a thunderous volume, the Capitol Police, now visibly unsure about how to deal with the situation, exercised their power by detaining two young Puerto Rican activists. After remaining in custody at a nearby police station for nearly five hours, they returned to their bus and received a hero's welcome. In the midst of applause and cheers, they playfully proclaimed their pride at having become "political prisoners," albeit temporarily.

The detained youth were members of Café Teatro Batey Urbano, a Puerto Rican/Latino-focused youth center located in Humboldt Park, in northwestern Chicago (Flores-González, Rodríguez, and Rodríguez Muñiz 2006). They formed part of a contingent of more than fifty supporters from Batey Urbano's parent organization, the Juan Antonio Corretjer Puerto Rican Cultural Center (PRCC). The PRCC, a grassroots institution noted for its long history of radical political activism, was one of only a handful of organizations to heed Arellano's call to mobilize. The PRCC has participated in the struggle for legalization as a steadfast ally of Pueblo sin Fronteras (PSF), a prominent Chicago-based Mexican immigrant rights organization (see chap. 2).

As this scene illustrates, the diverse participants, organizations, and political figures involved in the immigrant rights movement include a committed sector of the Puerto Rican community. Grassroots organizations, activists, religious leaders, and Puerto Rican elected officials have consistently advocated progressive immigration reform and stood in defense of the human rights of their undocumented "brothers and sisters." As individuals, Puerto Ricans numerically account for only a small percentage of the overall number of mega-march participants. We should not, however, underestimate their presence as an organized group within demonstrations or the political value and influence of their support.[1]

In this chapter, I focus on the particular nature of PRCC activism in the immigrant rights movement, using in-depth interviews with PRCC activists. I pay specific attention to the invocation of the pan-ethnoracial category/identity of *Latinidad* (see Aparicio and Chávez-Silverman 1997; Flores 2000; Lao-Montes 2001). More than superficial appeals tagged onto protest signs and banners, the PRCC's call for "Latino unity" was at once strategic and ethical, collective as well as personal. What emerges here is a localized political manifestation of *Latinidad,* fashioned by activists in such a way as to manage its homogenizing properties while retaining its potential for political advancement.

This grassroots engagement did not emerge in a vacuum. *Latinidad* is rooted in a long history of social engineering and quite possibly in an even longer experience of interactional germination among Latin American migrants and their descendants. Furthermore, it cannot be separated from the recent popularization and proliferation of the labels *Hispanic* and *Latino,* which are regularly mobilized, in diverse ways, by dominant institutions (state, media, corporations) for political or economic objectives (Davila 2001; Oboler 1995). PRCC activists exist within a cultural milieu in which they regularly encounter, confront, and negotiate with countless manifestations of *Latinidad* in policy reports, song lyrics, religious sermons, billboards, store windows, and fast-food chains (to name just a few of the places where it has spread). These activists are lucidly aware and critical of the fact that the mainstream invocation of *Latinidad* is predicated on some degree of homogenization, whereby diverse populations are brought under one canopy, often on the basis of some admixture of presumed ethnoracial sameness.

In light of this far-reaching and seemingly inescapable invocation, it is quite possible that U.S. society has entered an era in which there is little room to simply avoid or ignore *Latinidad,* especially for members of Latinized populations. This chapter contributes to recent empirical research that interrogates the interplay between dominant constructions of *Latinidad* and those emerging from below (see, e.g., Davila 2004; García and Rúa 2007; Itzigsohn and Dore-Cabral 2000). Far from a one-way process, *Latinidad* is a dynamic site of meaning construction, emerging from contradictory social locations and resulting in unpredictable creations. Focusing on the immigrant rights movement as a site of construction, this analysis explores the ways in which PRCC activists grapple with *Latinidad* and the perceived problem of homogeneity/social invisibility. Through this deliberate and historically specific engagement, they work to elaborate an oppositional vision of *Latinidad* that promotes Puerto Rican cultural and political distinctiveness while simultaneously establishing the grounds for movement-oriented Latino solidarity.

Latinidad and the Search for Meaning(s)

More than twenty years ago, sociologist Felix Padilla published the first monograph-length analysis of Latina/o identity formation. In his seminal *Latino Ethnic Consciousness,* Padilla examined the emergence of a panethnic political identity among Chicago's Puerto Rican and Mexican community leaders and organizations. A strategic response to post–civil rights affirmative action opportunities, "Latinismo," as he termed it, is a "manipulative device for the pursuit of collective political, economic and social interests in society" (1985, 165). One of Padilla's respondents commented, "We cannot get [Mexican] South Chicago to get mad at [Puerto Rican] Westtown if Westtown doesn't support their immigration situation. That is a Mexican problem that cannot be resolved through a Latino effort. But we can get them to come and talk to Westtown about jobs, about things that are hitting everybody" (62–63). Based on such responses, Padilla concluded that Latina/o group solidarity was largely confined to temporary "situations" where the interests of Latina/o groups converged and that shared, local socioeconomic conditions served as the basis of "Latinismo." As conceptualized here, Latina/o panethnicity is thus preeminently a matter of structural commonality and political expedience. This structural emphasis, pursued further by López and Espiritu (1990), remains central to the sociological study of panethnic phenomena (see Okamoto 2003). In the absence of shared social conditions, largely produced by racialization and racial subordination, scholars remain skeptical about the potential for panethnic collaboration. López and Espiritu conclude that structural heterogeneity leaves Latino/a groups with "little common ground on which to co-operate" (207). Though this assertion about Latinas/os is questionable, the objective existence of common structural conditions (and thus common material interests) is expected to translate into panethnic identity and political mobilization.

Current panethnic scholars and their predecessors have challenged the assumed primordial foundation of panethnicity. These analysts locate the emergence of panethnic identity within contemporary political and economic conditions (Okamoto 2003; Padilla 1985) rather than within presumed kinship ties and shared cultural practices. But empirical reality is never quite so straightforward. As recent studies have demonstrated, social differences within panethnic formations complicate the terrain on which these expressions supposedly rest (Davila 2004; Espiritu 1992; Itzigsohn and Doré-Cabral 2000; Okamoto 2006; Pérez 2003; Rivera 2001). For this reason, scholars have begun to move away from the "search for latinidad in consensus" to a recognition of the inherent "tensions" involved in its construction (Rúa 2001, 118).

In certain respects, however, this recognition is limited by a problematic emphasis on "difference." Some scholars have failed genuinely to examine the tension between "commonality" and "difference" as co-constitutive elements of identity formation (Hall 1990). The important focus on difference is only a temporary corrective insofar as it is assumed objectively to impede panethnicity. De Genova and Ramos-Zayas's otherwise important work, *Latino Crossings,* exhibits this slippage, as its authors argue that the uneven application of U.S. citizenship to Puerto Ricans and Mexicans prevents the popular development of a durable pan-Latina/o identity. In this way, some treatments of "difference" only reverse the objectivist assumptions embedded in early panethnic scholarship, suggesting that difference objectively prevents or limits the possibility of collaborative mobilization or identity formation. I seek a greater appreciation of the perceptions, ideologies, and narratives that inform and organize distinct expressions of oppositional *Latinidad.* At base, this analysis recognizes that "commonalities" and "differences" are socially generated and cannot be assumed to exist a priori or to affect a social context in a predetermined way. The question then shifts toward how commonality and difference are constructed and mobilized for particular ends within a historically specific context.

A nonobjectivist approach might take sociological theorizing on panethnicity in new and exciting directions. One possible line of inquiry I pursue is the widely accepted proposition that politicized panethnic formations are essentially temporary and self-interested vehicles for the attainment of political and economic resources. The first step is recognizing that material interests must be perceived as such and that what is considered a group interest is always subject to reformulation (Cornell 1996, 281). Furthermore, we must begin to explore moments where political solidarity is not explicitly organized around immediately discernable "shared" interests.

In the specific case of *Latinidad,* a different orientation might help elucidate how, as Jones-Correa notes, identities strengthen and gain "a certain inertia" over time (1998, 111). This lack of attention to temporality is a key weakness of existing approaches to panethnic identity formation (Yashar 2005). Since the passage of time does not automatically produce durable identities, we need to identify what social repertoires (cultural practices and discourses) make particular readings of history meaningful (Flores 2000; Trouillot 1995). Without reifying "time," another potential question, also explored here, is how the historicity of ongoing interactions might nurture intimate relationships among activists or organizations.

If we propose to study this phenomenon from a nonobjectivist position, we must begin with the view that *Latinidad* is a contested and contradictory site of "discursive formations" (Lao-Montes 2001). This is not to say that expressions of *Latinidad* are socially insignificant and merely ideas. I recognize that this potent construction emerges from ongoing social interactions that are embedded in historically rooted and contemporarily manifested power relations, themselves situated in particular political, cultural, economic, and spatial arrangements. However, the sociohistorical and material bases of *Latinidad*—like all spheres of "reality"—are made meaningful and otherwise intelligible only through discourse. As Hall insightfully states, "Events, relations, structures do have conditions of existence and real effects, outside the sphere of the discursive; but . . . it is only with the discursive, and subject to its specific conditions, limits and modalities, do they have meaning" (2003, 91).

In this vein, Itzigsohn insists that our research agenda must "investigate whether and in what ways people adopt a Latino and Latina identity, the meanings they attribute to it, the political projects constructed around it, and the sites in which these identities and projects are constructed" (2004, 197). My analysis thus concentrates on the ways in which a local group of Puerto Rican activists makes sense of, shapes, and grapples with the category Latina/o and transforms it into a meaningful identity and mode for progressive social action within the immigrant rights movement.

Methodology

In the wake of the 2006–7 megamarches, I conducted twenty-two interviews (along with several follow-up interviews) with Puerto Rican activists and elected officials as well as a smaller sample of Mexican activists. This chapter is based on ten interviews with Puerto Rican activists and PRCC supporters. I have used pseudonyms for all participants except for recognized public figures.

The PRCC respondents ranged from organizational elders to youth supporters and are divided roughly equally by gender. As with most activist organizations, the PRCC leadership is rather educated, and many members are students and professionals. However, most of the group's leaders come from poor and working-class backgrounds. As with much of the social movement scholarship, this study centers on the perspectives of lead activists. While I interviewed some rank-and-file participants, I intentionally chose to focus on the workings of the PRCC's dominant organizational discourses in its specific construction of *Latinidad*. Similar to Taylor and Rupp's (1993) study of lesbian feminist communities, this chapter is informed by qualitative research and my participation in the PRCC.

The PRCC: An Overview

Founded amid intense urban political struggles during the mid-1970s by a group of disaffected teachers, progressive religious leaders, community organizers, and radical activists,[2] the PRCC has become the reputed center of Chicago's Puerto Rican nationalist politics (Ramos-Zayas 2003). Its thirty-five-year organizational history is far too complicated to adequately describe here, but a brief summary provides a context for a better appreciation of the PRCC's involvement in the immigrant rights movement and the nuanced ways it engages *Latinidad*.

Named after Juan Antonio Corretjer, a Puerto Rican revolutionary leader and poet, the PRCC is built on "a philosophy of self-determination, a methodology of self-actualization and critical thought, and an ethics of self-reliance" (PRCC 2004). These concepts have been activated through a form of anticolonial Puerto Rican nationalism adapted to the urban realities of life in the diaspora (Ramos-Zayas 2003).

An umbrella organization, the PRCC hosts and houses various projects and affiliate programs that address such community needs as education, health, culture, teen pregnancy, AIDS/HIV, and youth engagement.[3] As a result of its three decades of hard political work in community building, the PRCC enjoys a great deal of respect from local Puerto Rican community leaders and elected officials. Its presence is quite influential, as its pivotal involvement in a host of community-based initiatives evidences.

Because of the organization's progressive political agenda, a number of PRCC leaders have been imprisoned for refusing to testify before federal grand juries investigating the Puerto Rican independence movement. PRCC activists have been slandered by local media and by people with ties to the Federal Bureau of Investigation (FBI). In 1983, the FBI raided the PRCC headquarters, confiscating computers and ransacking the child-care room. The FBI became interested in the PRCC and its leaders as a consequence of the group's alleged links to Las Fuerzas Armadas de Liberación Nacional, a clandestine armed Puerto Rican revolutionary organization (Ramos-Zayas 2003). However, these attempts at repression failed either to prove any connections or to neutralize the PRCC's political potency.

The PRCC has led and contributed to many of the major political causes on the island and in the Puerto Rican diaspora. These struggles include the international campaigns to release two generations of Puerto Rican political prisoners and to end the U.S. military's bombardment of the island of Vieques.[4] In the local context, PRCC activists are among the most active in the struggle to prevent (or at least slow) the spread of gentrification in Humboldt Park (Flores-González, Rodríguez, and Rodríguez Muñiz 2006; Rinaldo 2002). Working with the local alderman and other community groups, the PRCC helped to create the Paseo Boricua cultural/commercial corridor along Division Street, which is marked by two massive steel monuments of the Puerto Rican flag. This community-based effort to demarcate Humboldt Park as a "Puerto Rican" space (Flores-Gonzalez 2001; Ramos-Zayas 2003; Rinaldo 2002) has taken place alongside PRCC articulations of Latino unity.[5] Paseo Boricua is now the home of Flor Crisóstomo, who in January 2008 became the second undocumented immigrant to take sanctuary at the Adalberto Unido Church.

Though focused on Puerto Rican cultural affirmation and national self-determination, the PRCC considers "solidarity" a core political value. As such, the center has a legacy of providing political support for non–Puerto Rican social movements. This support represents an outgrowth of relationships with radical and progressive sectors of the black, Mexican/Chicano, and white communities. In many ways, this development parallels the collaboration described in Pulido's (2006) recent study of Third World activism in Los Angeles during the 1970s. Throughout its history, the PRCC's closest allies, both locally and throughout the United States, have been Mexican activists.

In Chicago, the PRCC shares its most intimate bond with the PSF. PRCC activists have long collaborated with the PSF to establish a national "Latino agenda." Beginning in 2000, this initiative sought the unification of two seemingly disparate social causes: the legalization of undocumented workers and the removal of the U.S. Navy from Vieques. Since then, the two groups have organized joint marches, vigils, lobbying efforts, and acts of civil disobedience and have supported each other on local issues. The PRCC's participation in the immigrant rights movement is not a new occurrence but rather a long-standing practice.

The PRCC and the Immigration Movement

For PRCC activists, attending a demonstration or vigil in favor of immigrant legalization is not particularly noteworthy. While personally meaningful, efforts to build a Latino agenda exist on the level of organizational common sense, and these activists perceive nonparticipation as unthinkable. The dramatic Washington, D.C., rally is just one of many examples of PRCC support for immigrant rights.[6]

On March 10, 2006, the PRCC and its affiliate programs mobilized two small contingents for the initial megamarch. The first group, a van full of students from the Dr. Pedro Albizu Campos Puerto Rican High School, never reached the historic demonstration after becoming caught up in a massive traffic jam.[7] The second PRCC contingent, comprised mainly of Batey Urbano youth, participated, proudly carrying Puerto Rican flags and joining Mexican youth activists from the PSF youth project, El Zócalo Urbano. As in all events, the PRCC's participation was contingent on the presence and leadership of the PSF, which politically links the PRCC to the broader Mexican community.

For the follow-up May 1 rally, the PRCC organized a feeder march from Humboldt Park, while PSF organized a parallel march on the South Side to symbolize the unity between the Puerto Ricans and Mexicans. More than 250 people marched down Paseo Boricua toward Union Park. Participants included community activists, college students, students from Albizu Campos, and dozens of young parents from a satellite program, the Lolita Lebrón Family Learning Center. The march was led by an impressive image of *Latinidad,* with several PSF members carrying a small statue of La Virgen de Guadalupe flanked by large Mexican and Puerto Rican flags. Similar feeder marches have been organized to support every subsequent major demonstration.

The PRCC participates in megamarches to symbolize Puerto Rican support for undocumented immigrants. But this is only part of the purpose. The decision, for example, to organize feeder marches from Paseo Boricua was also informed by the perceived need to generate popular Puerto Rican awareness and support for the issue. The PRCC operates within a broader social environment in which Puerto Ricans and Mexicans have been imagined (and imagine themselves) as rivals, even though this perceived antagonism disregards long-standing social and familial ties between these populations. To challenge this view, PRCC activists have sought creative ways to challenge other Puerto

Ricans to support the immigrant rights movement. In some cases, PRCC leaders have publicly criticized local opposition. Despite some intracommunity controversy over its support for immigrant rights, the PRCC refuses to end its involvement.

Arellano's controversial August 2006 decision to seek sanctuary in the Adalberto Unido Church almost immediately prompted several core activists to organize a twenty-four-hour-a-day vigil that ultimately lasted more than two weeks. This effort sought to contradict the talk of a small but vocal group of Puerto Ricans who disapproved of Arellano's decision to seek sanctuary in the "Puerto Rican" rather than "Mexican" community. Others more vehemently invoked narratives of illegality and called for Arellano's immediate arrest and deportation. During the vigil, at least one PRCC supporter stood outside the church with a Puerto Rican flag in hand, attempting to symbolize and in the process realize Puerto Rican support. More than twenty people took two- to four-hour shifts at the vigil, unfazed by rainstorms and video camera lights.

The following summer, the PRCC made another dramatic gesture in favor of Latina/o solidarity by naming Arellano and her son, Saul, honorary marshals of the twenty-ninth Puerto Rican People's Day Parade. Saul walked with Cook County commissioner Roberto Maldonado and a contingent of PSF activists, while his mother waved a small Puerto Rican flag from within the church. In 2008, the PRCC named another undocumented activist, Flor Crisóstomo, its honorary marshal.

In addition to participating in marches and these symbolic acts, the PRCC has also challenged local and out-of-state Puerto Rican community leaders and elected officials to embrace the Latino agenda. The PRCC's executive director and political anchor, José López, has been particularly effective in persuading Puerto Rican elected officials to take on immigration as a social issue. He asserts that the Puerto Rican community can embrace *Latinidad* without sacrificing distinctiveness. In the weeks following Arellano's deportation in August 2007, the PRCC drew on these contacts to help arrange a speaking tour for Saul that included New York, Philadelphia, Boston, and Cleveland. Since the fall of 2008, the PRCC has concentrated its efforts in the ¡Ya Basta! campaign, which is being spearheaded by Puerto Rican religious leaders, Congressman Luis Gutiérrez, and several local pro-immigrant organizations, including the PSF.

The PRCC's effort to spread a politicized vision of *Latinidad* requires an investment of a considerable amount of political, economic, social, and symbolic capital. PRCC leaders remain deeply committed to the group's relationship with the PSF and to their shared goal of building a national Latino agenda. The fact that PRCC activists must plan and execute deliberate expressions of solidarity within the Puerto Rican community suggests that Latino unity has not yet become an automatic practice for the rest of the community, however. This is not to say that

other organizations or even individual Puerto Ricans do not support or participate in the movement—some do—but rather that such involvement remains the
exception and not the rule. Accordingly, one of the PRCC's primary objectives
is generating mass Puerto Rican support for undocumented immigrants and in
so doing laying the groundwork for a unified Latina/o political agenda.

Historical Narratives of Collaboration

In conversations about their involvement in the immigrant rights movement,
PRCC activists regularly called on a long history of Latina/o collaboration. An
established organizational narrative describes historical intersections and intimacies among Latina/o populations. According to some activists, this history
began with Simon Bolivar's nineteenth-century "Bolivarian Dream," and a sense
of history and historical purpose informs their collective actions, practices of
solidarity, and commitment to building a Latino agenda.

Scholars recently have begun to examine the role of historical narratives in
identity construction (Cornell 2000). Scholarship indicates that "history" and
"historical memory" do not objectively exist in the past; rather, they are selectively summoned and refashioned for present purposes (Trouillot 1995). As
French historian Le Goff writes, "Memory, on which history draws and which
it nourishes in return, seeks to save the past in order serve the present and future" (1992, 99).

Although PRCC activists argue that collaboration among Latin American
peoples has occurred for centuries, more recent local encounters appear most
consistently in their movement narrative. Movement elders, who participated in
the first wave of "Latino" political activism, served as the key transmitters of collective memory (Olick 1999). The late 1960s and 1970s were regarded as pivotal
moments in which Chicago's Puerto Ricans and Mexicans as well as other "op-
pressed nationalities" joined the worldwide clamor for self-determination and
national liberation. Echoing Padilla's (1985) study, PRCC activists maintain that
Latino politics emerged during this era. For José López, a veteran of the Puerto
Rican independence movement and many local causes, little is novel about present-day expressions of Latino unity: "You can't talk about Proyecto Pa'Lante at
[Northeastern Illinois University], bilingual education, we can't talk about Mexican and Puerto Rican and Latino studies or recruitment programs anywhere in
Chicago, without talking about the linking and the solidarity of Puerto Ricans
and Mexicans. . . . Anything that we can talk about has always been Mexicans
and Puerto Ricans and other Latinos working together for those things."

Since most of the PRCC's core activists are too young to have participated
in earlier campaigns, they rely heavily on the recollections of their elders. A
number of activists first learned about previous struggles while participating

in university-based Puerto Rican student organizations, such as the Union for Puerto Rican Students. These student organizations also depict (and thus imagine) their current campaigns for tenure for Latino faculty members and for Latino cultural centers as continuations of 1970s' Latina/o student activism. These depictions consistently occur alongside mention of activist figures such as Puerto Rican political prisoner Oscar López Rivera and slain Mexicano labor organizer Rudy Lozano and landmark events such as the 1973 Latina/o student takeover of University Hall at the University of Illinois at Chicago. These images are important within movement mythology, often chosen to exemplify the history of Puerto Rican and Mexican solidarity and specifically the long-standing relationship between the PRCC and the PSF.

Though the past was universally summoned, it was not uniformly available to all activists. The narrative did not constitute a cohesive or detailed whole and was in some cases rather fragmented. In addition, as with any historical account, the PRCC's collective memory is marked by "silences" (Trouillot 1995). Missing from stories were moments of discord or contention between Puerto Rican and Mexican activists. In a related way, respondents went to great lengths to either downplay community-level tension or dismiss any reference to conflict as signs of ignorance of shared sociohistorical conditions. This phenomenon is not at all surprising given that this organizational narrative seeks to legitimate pan-Latina/o collaboration and to destabilize the widely accepted view of Puerto Rican and Mexican animosity. This narrative of collaboration, fused with an encompassing radical frame, provides a powerful ideological foundation for the PRCC's oppositional expression of *Latinidad*.

Latinidad and the Frame of Colonialism

Scholars argue that similar histories of colonialism, conquest, and racial domination are potential sources of Latino unity and collective identity formation (Alcoff 2005; Aparicio 2003; Flores 2000). This potential often is not realized, as these factors do not automatically generate intra-Latina/o bonds. These experiences must be subjectively perceived as commonalities if they are to stimulate activism or identity formation. Social movement scholars have argued that such a development requires a unifying interpretative frame that problematizes existing realities and focuses on the need and possibility for social change (Polletta and Jasper 2001; Snow and Benford 1992). Within the PRCC, the dominant "collective action frame" is colonialism (Benford and Snow 2000; Snow et al. 1986).

PRCC activists understand the historical and contemporary political and social status of Puerto Ricans, both on the mainland and in the diaspora, preeminently through the lens of colonialism (Ramos-Zayas 2003; Rinaldo 2002). Problems facing the Puerto Rican barrio of Humboldt Park, such as gentrification, high rates of drug use, violence, and disproportionate incidences of asthma, HIV/AIDS, and obesity were regularly cited as proof of a "colonized" reality. As Claudia, a member of the National Boricua Human Rights Network, asserted, the concept of colonialism has provided the "vocabulary, the consciousness to be able to talk about . . . all of the things we have experienced but never [knew] what they were or why they were."

Though largely focused on the particular experience of Puerto Ricans, the colonial frame developed and elaborated at the PRCC is not limited to this population. In actuality, it shapes how activists understand the social position of other groups, especially those viewed as racial minorities. The PRCC's long-standing solidarity with Mexican and black activists stems in part from this colonial worldview. PRCC leaders contend that any human-rights-based movement that arises from these "marginalized" communities contributes to the broader—and shared—project of decolonization. For PRCC activists, the view that Puerto Ricans and Mexicans share a colonial past and present works to make sense of present-day pan-Latina/o collaboration.

According to Melba, a Batey Urbano youth activist in her early twenties, Puerto Ricans and Mexicans share very little in terms of dialect, food, dance, and tradition. She believes, however, that Puerto Ricans and Mexicans share particular colonial experiences such as migration and racism: "We are forced to come here. It's a bigger issue than 'We are here now and now there is racism.' There are centuries of colonialism, . . . and Mexico and Puerto Rico are prime victims of that. So before we were even here, our families have had to deal with that in our respective countries. We relate on that level when we are able to talk about those things and to cope with the things we have to go through because of the color of our skin." In contrast to dominant discourses found in media productions, Melba does not locate *Latinidad* in a presumed cultural heritage but instead stresses shared sociohistorical conditions. Though not all PRCC activists summarily dismissed the existence of shared Latina/o cultural practices, all echoed Melba's structuralist assertion. In this way, they view the plight of undocumented immigrants as a manifestation of colonialism (or, in the case of Mexico, of neocolonialism). Similarly, anti-immigrant rhetoric was interpreted less as an assault on immigrants and more as a racist attack against Latinos.

Together, the frame of colonialism and the narrative collaboration contribute to a transnational view of *Latinidad*. José López places immigration within a broader colonial context: "The iceberg obviously is deeper, and the iceberg is colonialism and racism in the world and how these define the relationship between the U.S. and Latin America. So fundamentally, the basic issues of Latin America and Latinos will not be resolved until you take colonialism and racism head-on. And that can only happen with a real process of mutual developments that are based on the dignity of Latin America and as equal partners, rather than subordinates."

Most PRCC activists demonstrated little interest in separating the politics of Latinas/os from Latin America. They viewed the building of a Latino agenda as a liberatory project for the entire hemisphere. Within this vision, Puerto Rico's national independence is considered a top priority. This perceived realization generates a sense that the future of Puerto Ricans and Puerto Rico is linked to other Latinos. The interviewees doubted that independence could be achieved without the active participation of Latinas/os residing in the United States. While these activists have always considered outside support an important factor, they now believe that the decolonization of Puerto Rico is contingent on Latina/o comrades. According to Jasmine, a former member of Batey Urbano and a staff member of at the Albizu Campos High School, "There is too much of [Puerto Ricans' and Mexicans'] histories and our future tied. I honestly believe the independence of Puerto Rico lies in a lot of these struggles here." This could be seen as merely an emotive expression of self-interest, but such an interpretation would simplify a more complex phenomenon. Instead, the assertion by Jasmine and other PRCC activists demonstrates a profound shift in political consciousness. She does not describe other Latinas/os as merely momentary or peripheral supporters but rather as a community intimately bound by history and future prospects. Puerto Rico's freedom—the paramount objective of PRCC activists—is now imagined within the broader framework of *Latinidad*.

The frame of colonialism helps these Puerto Rican activists imagine themselves as similar to their Mexican counterparts and supplies them with their radical critique of U.S. domination in the Americas as well as a way to understand their urban conditions. Clearly invested in the creation of a Latina/o social movement, the PRCC's practice and conceptualization of *Latinidad* does not emerge in a discursive vacuum.

Grappling with *Latinidad:* Homogeneity and Distinction

When the PRCC mobilizes supporters to an immigrant rights rally, it does so in part to challenge and delegitimate the pervasive idea of Puerto Rican/Mexican animosity. At first glance, this idea, popularly exemplified by national boxing rivalries, would seem to demonstrate the weakness or limits of *Latinidad*. Yet upon closer examination, an underlying assumption becomes apparent: these two groups *should* get along. Not all ethnic or racial group relations are subjected to such expectations. They are directed only at those groups imagined as comprising a homogenous pan-ethnoracial community. Perceived homogeneity, often on the basis of language and culture, informs this assumption. Precisely for this reason, the supposed conflict between Puerto Ricans and Mexicans intrigues many journalists and scholars.

Even when unrecognized, as in this case, homogeneity operates as an intrinsic feature of all expressions of *Latinidad*. The PRCC and its activists exist within a social context in which *Latinidad* is already to some extent "common sense." Ironically, the PRCC is an inadvertent recipient of the constructive work of dominant institutions, whose racializing practices have been instrumental in the creation of pan-ethnoracial imaginaries (Espiritu 1992; Flores-Gonzalez 1999; Itzigsohn 2004; López and Espiritu 1990; Oboler 1995; Omi 2001). Simply put, PRCC members do not need to start at ground zero to convince each other and their constituents of the need to support their "Mexican brothers and sisters." Their rearticulation of *Latinidad,* therefore, inevitably mobilizes a preexisting and taken-for-granted sense of "groupness" (Brubaker and Cooper 2000).

Of course, PRCC activists do not readily view themselves as participants in or beneficiaries of the homogenization of diverse Latina/o populations. In fact, these activists criticize the ascendant view that all Latina/o groups are essentially the "same" (Lugo-Lugo 2008). Critical of what López and Espiritu (1990) call "racial lumping," Naomi commented, "To a white person, to the government, however you want to put [it], there is no difference between a Puerto Rican, Mexican, Guatemalan; we are all the same. We are people of color, minorities. Many Americans don't even know that Puerto Ricans are citizens; they view us as undocumented immigrants."

As scholars have noted, this racialized sameness homogenizes considerable diversity, washing away distinctive features and social differences across and among groups (Lugo-Lugo 2008; Oboler 1995). PRCC activists increasingly confront a social totality that makes sense of Puerto Rican culture and political needs by reference to a generic "Latino" abstract, particularly in an urban context in which Mexicans account for the overwhelming majority of the city's Latina/o population and in neighborhoods formerly considered "Puerto Rican" (De Genova and Ramos-Zayas 2003a). This imposed homogeneity, activists worry, may silence Puerto Rican cultural distinctiveness and render invisible specific political realities facing the Puerto Rican community.[8] This concern is clearly related to the fact that PRCC's political projects are primarily geared toward the Puerto Rican community and are anchored in nationalist discourses (Ramos-Zayas 2003). This anxiety about remaining distinct is not solely a PRCC phenomenon and might very well become an important dimension of the study of *Latinidad*. In her study on Peruvian immigrants, Paerregaard writes, "Rather than merely adopting the status of Hispanics and assimilating into the existing communities, they create symbols and imaginaries that make them visible as a national minority" (2005, 93). Despite recent research that illustrates the ways in which nationalism and panethnicity are not necessary antithetical (e.g., Okamoto 2003; García and Rúa 2007), other scholars (Pallares 2005) have shown how people may draw on nationalism to resist imputed homogeneity. Within the immigrant rights movement, however, the PRCC's politics of national distinction take place alongside and are in some ways complementary to articulations of commonality.

As participants within the immigrant rights movement, PRCC activists emphasize their Puerto Ricanness. No act of solidarity is complete without at least one Puerto Rican flag hoisted high. This symbolism not only is viewed as a necessary corrective to the view of Puerto Rican/Mexican antagonism but also communicates to the broader social field that Puerto Ricans are present as a distinctive Latina/o group. In a way, they carefully try to navigate the Latino empowerment discourse while remaining a distinct entity within it (Itzigsohn 2004). As José López comments, "There is a Puerto Rican identity and a Mexican identity, and those two identities must be preserved, must be nurtured, must be perpetuated." This belief in national cultural affirmation greatly informs the PRCC's practice of distinction, best captured by the refrain "¡Boricua y Mexicano, luchando mano a mano!"

The tension between the poles of homogeneity and distinction has helped to generate a particular vision of *Latinidad* among PRCC activists. They posit that Latinas/os are similar but not identical. Puerto Ricans and Mexicans resemble each other in terms of sociohistorical realities but remain distinct in terms of cultural identity and certain political conditions—that is, direct colonialism. This claim of similarity (instead of sameness) seeks to generate and rationalize collective pan-Latina/o political action without obscuring Puerto Rican particularity, a delicate move best demonstrated by the ways in which PRCC activists manage the difference of citizenship.

De Genova and Ramos-Zayas (2003a, 2003b) have argued that unequal access to U.S. citizenship hinders the development of a pan-Latina/o identity. As a result, they suggest, *Latinidad* is "haunted by the politics of citizenship" (2003b, 44). The PRCC case suggests that the "problem" of citizenship depends substantially on how citizenship is perceived. Unlike the everyday barrio residents interviewed by De Genova and Ramos-Zayas, PRCC activists argue that U.S. citizenship should serve as an impetus for rather than an impediment to Latina/o politics. This active pronouncement seeks to contradict Puerto Ricans' popular invocation of U.S. citizenship to distance themselves from the suspicion of racialized Latino "illegality." In efforts to challenge this local practice and construct the basis for joint Latino activism, these politicized actors posit U.S. citizenship as a space for both distinction and similarity.

PRCC activists manage the legal status difference between Puerto Ricans and other Latinas/os first by problematizing the Puerto Rican experience of U.S. citizenship. They believe that Puerto Ricans are second-class citizens, granted citizenship solely for the benefit of U.S. colonial interests. According to Melba, "Just because we are U.S. citizens doesn't mean we benefit from being U.S. citizens. Not all U.S. citizens are treated the same way. White U.S. citizens unfortunately have a lot more benefits, privileges, and opportunities than we do as Latinos, as Puerto Ricans. It's not like we are citizens . . . because the U.S. wants us to be citizens. We are citizens or we have imposed citizenship because it's beneficial for the U.S. to have extra bodies to take bullets in the war or to have extra hands in working in the U.S. that they necessarily would not have without us here, or to be able to experiment on us in our country." Melba echoed Ramos-Zayas's claim that the Puerto Rican experience and those of other racialized populations demonstrate "the existence of multiple and inherently unequal citizenships" (2004, 41).

Although they critique the "benefits" of U.S. citizenship, PRCC activists do not equate their status with that of undocumented immigrants. They recognize that they are somewhat privileged relative to noncitizens but view themselves as much less privileged than whites. This perception of second-class U.S. citizenship not only acknowledges the status difference between Puerto Ricans and other Latinas/os but also positions Puerto Ricans closer to the social status of undocumented Latina/o immigrants. The PRCC's experiences with political repression, as part of which the group has been labeled "anti-American" and even "terrorist," weighs heavily on its members' position on U.S. citizenship (see Ramos-Zayas 2004).

This management of difference involves not only questioning or critiquing the value of Puerto Rican U.S. citizenship but also transforming this "fact" of citizenship into an opportunity to act ethically. PRCC leaders believe that as U.S. citizens (albeit colonial citizens), Puerto Ricans have a moral obligation to advocate on behalf of other Latinas/os. Activists consistently described their work as providing a "voice for the voiceless." (For further discussion of this issue with regard to youth, see chap. 11.) Daniel, a member of Batey Urbano in his early twenties, elaborated, "We can try to be a voice. . . . We are U.S. citizens but Latinos who have the same experience as other Latinos of racism, displacement, so again we are able challenge the power structure that has forced other Latinos into being displaced again through deportations." As a Puerto Rican, Daniel believes, he has unquestioned access to citizenship but shares in a host of oppressive experiences. Naomi agreed: "We have a voice that other Latino groups don't have. . . . It was imposed on us, but we have it, and we need to do something with [it]." Turning citizenship into a responsibility to act, then, provides Puerto Rican activists with a source of public distinction through which to practice their politicized *Latinidad*. This call for Puerto Ricans to use their political "voice" exists alongside perceived anxieties regarding the social invisibility imposed on Puerto Ricans by dominant expressions of *Latinidad*.

The assertion that all Latinas/os are similar but not identical emerges with the interaction between preexisting ideological frameworks and perceptions about the implications of Latina/o homogenization as well as the demographic transformations under way in local communities. Despite the potential for *Latinidad* to erase Puerto Rican cultural, political, and social distinctions, PRCC activists refuse to abandon the cause in favor of building a progressive Latino agenda. This refusal to reject the politics of *Latinidad*—even when they are acutely aware of its potential pitfalls—signifies the present-day power exercised by this pan-ethnoracial construct.

Conclusion

Social movements, including the immigrant rights movement, are chief sites of "struggle over the production of ideas and meanings" (Snow and Benford 1992, 136). In the immigrant rights movement, PRCC activists have engaged in a stubborn effort to create a liberatory vision of *Latinidad*. Expressed most symbolically during demonstrations and rallies, their vision permeates the PRCC's institutional framework. Albizu Campos High School teachers facilitate discussions of immigration and Latino solidarity in their classrooms. Batey Urbano youth organizers host events with Mexican youth activists to create a space for politicized Latina/o encounters. Leaders of community tours of Paseo Boricua mention the "sanctuary" at Adalberto Unido Church and highlight Puerto Ricans' support for Elvira Arellano. Speeches weave present-day PRCC activism into a legacy of pan-Latina/o collaboration dating back to the nineteenth century. This oppositional discourse also interacts with life histories, some which are already deeply marked by familial and romantic relationships with members of other Latina/o groups (Pérez 2003; Rúa 2001) and interacts with dominant, homogenizing readings of *Latinidad*.

This exploratory look inside one manifestation of pan-Latina/o political collaboration focuses on local activists' subjective orientations (perspectives, narratives, and ideologies), thereby overcoming the objectivist limitations of much of the sociological scholarship on pan-ethnoracial formation. As Taylor and Whittier insist, "Collective political actors do not exist de facto by virtue of individuals sharing a common structural location; they are created in the course of social movement activity" (1992, 110). The subjective dimensions of identity formation remain undertheorized within panethnic movement scholarship, and insufficient energy consequently has been dedicated to analyzing the dynamic interactions among dominant, popular, and political expressions of *Latinidad*. This chapter explores one such interaction by way of a case of self-conscious, highly political actors who are wrestling with *Latinidad* and the perceived implications of homogeneity and its corollary, social invisibility. Future research must elaborate analytic frameworks to help us better understand the interplay between the manifold invocations of *Latinidad* and the processes by which individuals, organizations, and groups develop distinct manifestations.

In Latina/o Chicago, a group of Puerto Rican activists perceive a need to remain distinct in particular and nonnegotiable ways. This sentiment intriguingly exists alongside organizational intimacies and the desire to harness the intended (and unintended) political potential arguably embedded within the most significant pan-ethnoracial formation in contemporary U.S. society. For these activists, the national immigrant rights movement is a necessary site in which to express their particular conception of *Latinidad*. It is impossible to predict the long-term effect that these practices and discourses will have on the local political landscape or on the prospects for national collaboration among Latina/o groups. In much the same manner, it is difficult to anticipate how Puerto Rican activists in other regions will ultimately decide to engage the burgeoning immigrant rights movement or Latino politics more broadly. It is certain, however, that within Chicago's diverse immigrant rights movement, PRCC activists have searched for and carved out an "alternative ethos" on which to ground the "Latino imaginary" (Flores 2000, 189).

Notes

1. PRCC activism is deeply intertwined with the outspoken involvement of local Puerto Rican elected officials, particularly Congressman Luis Gutiérrez, former Cook County commissioner Roberto Maldonado, former state senator and city clerk Miguel Del Valle, and former alderman Billy Ocasio. I have conducted interviews with some of these officials and will pursue the analysis of their involvement in the immigration movement in future work.

2. Historically, while the majority of the PRCC's activists have been Puerto Rican, the organization has counted on the involvement and, in several cases, the leadership of Mexicans and other Latinas/os. This phenomenon points to an interesting dynamic (though it is not the focus of this chapter) of non–Puerto Ricans committing themselves to a Puerto Rican nationalist project rather than participating in their "own" movement.

3. The PRCC has attracted considerable academic attention throughout its history. Recent publications include Rinaldo 2002; Antrop-González 2003; Ramos-Zayas 2003; Rodríguez Muñiz 2005.

4. For more than sixty years, the U.S. Navy used the island of Vieques, located several miles off the southeastern coast of Puerto Rico, as a bombing range and training ground. Opposition to the navy's presence was a constant feature of local politics and gained mass support after the accidental death of civilian David Sanes on April 19, 1999. In Chicago, the PRCC was deeply involved in the issue and received much support from the PSF.

5. These practices may offer empirical support for García and Rúa's (2007) suggestion that scholars move away from positioning national identities in contradistinction to a pan-Latina/o identity. Instead, these authors challenge analysts to explore the intersections between these non-mutually-exclusive modes of identification.

6. I focus on the period between 2006 and 2008, but PRCC participation neither began nor ended with the megamarches.

7. Unlike most Chicago public schools, this alternative high school not only encouraged students to participate but also transported interested students to the march. See chap. 9.

8. This concern parallels Lugo-Lugo's discussion of the current "invisibility of Puerto Rico's colonial status" (2006, 125). Moreover, Flores (2000) insists that the exceptionality of the Puerto Rican colonial condition is the greatest challenge *Latinidad* faces.

References

Alcoff, Linda Martín. 2005. "Latino vs. Hispanic: The Politics of Ethnic Names." *Philosophy and Social Criticism* 31 (4): 395–407.

Antrop-González, Rene. 2003. "This School Is My Sanctuary: The Dr. Pedro Albizu Campos Alternative High School." *Centro Journal* 15 (2): 233–55.

Aparicio, Frances R. 2003. "Jennifer as Selena: Rethinking Latinidad in Media and Popular Culture." *Latino Studies* 1 (1): 90–105.

Aparicio, Frances R., and Susana Chávez-Silverman. 1997. Introduction to *Tropicalizations: Transcultural Representations of Latinidad,* ed. Frances R. Aparicio and Susana Chávez-Silverman, 1–20. Hanover: University Press of New England.

Benford, Robert D., and David A. Snow. 2000. "Framing Processes and Social Movements: An Overview and Assessment." *Annual Review of Sociology* 26:611–39.

Brubaker, Rogers, and Frederick Cooper. 2000. "Beyond 'Identity.'" *Theory and Society* 29 (1): 1–47.

Cornell, Stephen. 1996. "The Variable Ties That Bind: Content and Circumstance in Ethnic Processes." *Ethnic and Racial Studies* 19 (2): 265–89.

———. 2000. "That's the Story of Our Life." In *We Are a People: Narrative and Multiplicity in Constructing Ethnic Identity,* ed. P. Spickard and W. J. Burroughs, 41–56. Philadelphia: Temple University Press.

Davila, Arlene. 2001. *Latinos Inc.: The Marketing and Making of a People.* Berkeley: University of California Press.

———. 2004. *Barrio Dreams: Puerto Ricans, Latinos, and the Neoliberal City.* Berkeley: University of California Press.

De Genova, Nicholas, and Ana Y. Ramos-Zayas. 2003a. *Latino Crossings: Mexicans, Puerto Ricans, and the Politics of Race and Citizenship.* New York: Routledge.

———. 2003b. "Latino Rehearsals: Racialization and the Politics of Citizenship between Mexicans and Puerto Ricans in Chicago." *Journal of Latin American Anthropology* 8 (2): 18–57.

Espiritu, Yen Le. 1992. *Asian American Panethnicity: Bridging Institutions and Identities.* Philadelphia: Temple University Press.

Flores, Juan. 2000. *From Bomba to Hip-Hop: Puerto Rican Culture and Latino Identity.* New York: Columbia University Press.

Flores-González, Nilda. 1999. "The Racialization of Latinos: The Meaning of Latino Identity for the Second Generation." *Latino Studies* 10 (3): 3–31.

———. 2001. "Paseo Boricua: Claiming a Puerto Rican Space in Chicago." *Centro Journal* 13 (2): 7–23.

Flores-González, Nilda, Matthew Rodríguez, and Michael Rodríguez Muñiz. 2006. "From Hip-Hop to Humanization: Batey Urbano as a Space for Latino Youth Culture and Community Action." In *Beyond Resistance! Youth Activism and Community Change: New Democratic Possibilities for Practice and Policy for America's Youth,* ed. S. Ginwright, P. Noguera, and J. Cammarota, 175–96. New York: Routledge.

García, Lorena, and Merída Rúa. 2007. "Processing Latinidad: Mapping Latino Urban Landscapes through Chicago Ethnic Festivals." *Latino Studies* 5 (3): 317–39.

Hall, Stuart. 1990. "Cultural Identity and Diaspora." In *Identity: Community, Culture, Difference,* ed. J. Rutherford, 222–37. London: Lawrence and Wishart.

———. 2003. "New Ethnicities." In *Identities: Race, Class, Gender, and Nationality,* ed. L. Alcoff Martín and E. Mendieta, 90–95. Malden, Mass.: Blackwell.

Itzigsohn, José. 2004. "The Formation of Latino and Latina Panethnic Identities." In *Not Just Black and White: Historical and Contemporary Perspectives on Immigration, Race, and Ethnicity in the United States,* ed. N. Foner and G. M. Fredrickson, 197–218. New York: Sage Foundation.

Itzigsohn, José, and Carlos Dore-Cabral. 2000. "Competing Identities? Race, Ethnicity and Panethnicity among Dominicans." *Sociological Forum* 15 (2): 225–47.

Jones-Correa, Michael. 1998. *Between Two Nations: The Political Predicament of Latinos.* Ithaca: Cornell University Press.

Lao-Montes, Agustin. 2001. Introduction to *Mambo Montage: The Latinization of New York,* ed. A. Lao-Montes and A. Davila, 1–52. New York: Columbia University Press.

Le Goff, Jacques. 1992. *History and Memory.* New York: Columbia University Press.

López, David, and Yen Espiritu. 1990. "Panethnicity in the United States: A Theoretical Framework." *Ethnic and Racial Studies* 13 (2): 198–224.

Lugo-Lugo, Carmen R. 2006. "U.S. Congress and the Invisibility of Coloniality: The Case of Puerto Rico's Political Status Revisited." *Centro Journal* 18 (2): 125–45.

———. 2008. "'So You Are a Mestiza': Exploring the Consequences of Ethnic and Racial Clumping in the U.S. Academy." *Ethnic and Racial Studies* 31 (3): 611–28.

Oboler, Suzanne. 1995. *Ethnic Labels, Latino Lives: Identity and the Politics of (Re)Presentation in the United States.* Minneapolis: University of Minnesota Press.

Okamoto, Dina. 2003. "Toward a Theory of Panethnicity: Explaining Asian American Collective Action." *American Sociological Review* 68 (6): 811–42.

———. 2006. "Institutional Panethnicity: Boundary Formation in Asian-American Organizing." *Social Forces* 85 (1): 1–25.

Olick, Jeffrey K. 1999. "Collective Memory: The Two Cultures." *Sociological Theory* 17 (3): 333–48.

Omi, Michael. 2001. "The Changing Meaning of Race." In *America Becoming: Racial*

Trends and Their Consequences, ed. N. J. Smelser, W. J. Wilson, and F. Mitchell, 1:243–63. Washington, D.C.: National Academy Press.

Omi, Michael, and Howard Winant. 1986. *Racial Formation in the United States: From the 1960s to the 1980s.* Ed. M. Apple. New York: Routledge.

Padilla, Felix M. 1985. *Latino Ethnic Consciousness.* Notre Dame, Ind.: University of Notre Dame.

Paerregaard, Karsten. 2005. "Inside the Hispanic Melting Pot: Negotiating National and Multicultural Identities among Peruvians in the United States." *Latino Studies* 3 (1): 76–96.

Pallares, Amalia. 2005. "Ecuadorian Immigrants and Symbolic Nationalism in Chicago." *Latino Studies* 3 (3): 347–71.

Pérez, Gina. 2003. "'Puertorriqueñas Rencorosas y Mejicanas Sufridas': Gendered Ethnic Identity Formation in Chicago's Latino Communities." *Journal of Latin American Anthropology* 8 (2): 96–124.

Polletta, Francesca, and James M. Jasper. 2001. "Collective Identity and Social Movements." *Annual Review of Sociology* 27:283–305.

Puerto Rican Cultural Center Juan Antonio Corretjer. 2004. *PRCC Mission Statement.* http://prcc-chgo.org/mission. Accessed May 14, 2009.

Pulido, Laura. 2006. *Black, Brown, Yellow, and Left: Radical Activism in Southern California.* Berkeley: University of California Press.

Ramos-Zayas, Ana Y. 2003. *National Performances: The Politics of Class, Race, and Space in Puerto Rican Chicago.* Chicago: University of Chicago Press.

———. 2004. "Delinquent Citizenship, National Performances: Racialization, Surveillance, and the Politics of 'Worthiness' in Puerto Rican Chicago." *Latino Studies* 2 (1): 26–44.

Rinaldo, Rachel. 2002. "Space of Resistance: The Puerto Rican Cultural Center and Humboldt Park." *Cultural Critique* 50:135–74.

Rivera, Raquel Z. 2001. "Hip-Hop, Puerto Ricans, and Ethnoracial Identities in New York." In *Mambo Montage: The Latinization of New York,* ed. A. Lao-Montes and A. Davila, 235–62. New York: Columbia University Press.

Rodríguez Muñiz, Michael. 2005. "Exercises in Puerto Rican Self-Determination: The Humboldt Park Participatory Democracy Project." *Diálogo* 9:8–11

Rúa, Merida. 2001. "Colao Subjectivities: PortoMex and MexiRican Perspectives on Language and Identity." *Centro Journal* 13 (2): 117–33.

Snow, David A., and Robert D. Benford. 1992. "Master Frames and Cycles of Protest." In *Frontiers in Social Movement Theory,* ed. A. D. Morris and C. McClurg Mueller, 133–55. New Haven: Yale University Press.

Snow, David A., E. B. Rochford, S. K. Worden, and Robert D. Benford. 1986. "Frame Alignment Processes, Micromobilization and Movement Participation." *American Sociological Review* 51 (4): 464–81.

Taylor, Verta, and Leila J. Rupp. 1993. "Women's Culture and Lesbian Feminist Activism: A Reconsideration of Cultural Feminism." *Signs: Journal of Women in Culture and Society* 19 (1): 32–61.

Taylor, Verta, and Nancy E. Whittier. 1992. "Collective Identity in Social Movement Communities: Lesbian Feminist Mobilization." In *Frontiers in Social Movement Theory*, ed. A. D. Morris and C. McClurg Mueller, 104–31. New Haven: Yale University Press.

Trouillot, Michel-Rolph. 1995. *Silencing the Past: Power and the Production of History*. Boston: Beacon.

Yashar, Deborah J. 2005. *Contesting Citizenship in Latin America: The Rise of Indigenous Movements and the Postliberal Challenge*. New York: Cambridge University Press.

Contributors

FRANCES R. APARICIO is a professor of Latin American and Latino studies and a University Scholar at the University of Illinois at Chicago. She has written extensively on Latino/a cultural studies, literature, popular music, language, and identity and on teaching Spanish as a heritage language. She is author of *Listening to Salsa* (1998) and coeditor of *Tropicalizations* (1997), *Musical Migrations* (2003), and *Hibridismos Culturales* (2006). Her English translation of *El Libro de la Salsa* by César Miguel Rondón was published in 2008.

JOSÉ ANTONIO ARELLANO is a doctoral student at the University of Chicago. His research interests focus on twentieth-century American literature, literary theory, and the relation between aesthetic form and the structure of American society.

XÓCHITL BADA is an assistant professor of Latin American and Latino studies at the University of Illinois at Chicago. Her research interests focus on transnational communities, race relations, migration and development, absentee voting rights for migrants, labor rights of undocumented workers, and migrant-led grassroots organizations. She has contributed several chapters to edited volumes and coauthored a report on Mexican migrant civic participation published by the Woodrow Wilson International Center for Scholars and the University of California, Santa Cruz.

DAVID BLEEDEN is a doctoral student in philosophy at DePaul University. His primary fields of research are political and legal philosophy and the rhetoric of the nation-state and nature.

RALPH CINTRÓN is an associate professor in English and Latino and Latin American studies at the University of Illinois at Chicago. His research and teaching interests are in rhetorical studies; ethnography, particularly urban ethnography; urban theory; theories of globalization; political theory, particularly the anthropology of democracy; and social theory. His publications include *Angels' Town: Chero Ways, Gang Life, and Rhetorics of the Everyday* (1998), which won honorable mention for the Victor Turner Prize for Ethnographic Writing from the American Anthropological Association.

STEPHEN P. DAVIS is a graduate student in anthropology at the University of Illinois at Chicago. His research interests include immigration, faith-based leadership in social movements, the geography of religion, and Latinos in the United States. He is currently conducting an ethnographic study of the Priests for Justice for Immigrants and activist parishes in Chicago.

LEON FINK is a distinguished professor of history at the University of Illinois at Chicago, where he edits *Labor: Studies in Working Class History of the Americas* and contributes to the doctoral concentration in the history of work, race, and gender in the urban world. A specialist in labor and immigration history, he is the author or editor of seven books, including *The Maya of Morganton: Work and Community in the Nuevo New South* (2003), *Progressive Intellectuals and the Dilemmas of Democratic Commitment* (1998), and *In Search of the Working Class: Essays in American Labor History and Political Culture* (1994). He is currently at work on *Sweatshops at Sea: Governing Labor in a Globalized Industry, 1800–2010*.

NILDA FLORES-GONZÁLEZ is an associate professor in sociology and Latin American and Latino studies at the University of Illinois at Chicago. Her work focuses on race and ethnicity, identity, and education among Latino youth. She is the author of *School Kids, Street Kids: Identity Development in Latino Students* (2002) and has published several articles. She is currently working on a book examining the development of ethnic, racial, and political identities among Latino youth.

CAROLINE GOTTSCHALK-DRUSCHKE is a doctoral candidate in rhetoric and a National Science Foundation IGERT fellow in the Landscape, Ecological, and Anthropogenic Processes Program at the University of Illinois at Chicago. Her research and teaching interests include rhetorical ethnography, agroecology, political theory, and community-based pedagogy.

ELENA R. GUTIÉRREZ is an associate professor in Latin American and Latino studies and gender and women's studies at the University of Illinois at Chicago. She is a scholar of Latino health, reproductive politics, Chicana feminism, Chicano history, and social activism. Her publications include *Undivided Rights: Women of Color Organizing for Reproductive Justice* (coauthored with Jael Silliman, Marlene Gerber Fried, and Loretta Ross, 2004) and *Fertile Matters: The Racial Politics of Mexican-Origin Women's Reproduction* (2008).

JUAN R. MARTINEZ is a doctoral candidate in sociology at the University of Illinois at Chicago. His interests are in racial and ethnic relations, immigration, racialization, religion, and Latinos in the United States. He is currently conducting an ethnographic study of white-Mexican relations in a suburban community.

SONIA OLIVA is a doctoral candidate in sociology at the University of Illinois at Chicago. Her dissertation is on Latino and black race relations at a Chicago public high school. Her research interests include race and ethnic relations, Latinos and schooling, Mexicans in Chicago, and media representations of Latino youth.

IRMA M. OLMEDO is an associate professor emeritus of education at the University of Illinois at Chicago. She conducts research in teacher education, bilingualism, and oral histories of Latinas. Her work has been published in *Anthropology and Education Quarterly* and *Linguistics and Education*. She has taught courses on bilingualism and curriculum as well as on social studies for prospective teachers.

AMALIA PALLARES is an associate professor of political science and Latin American and Latino studies at the University of Illinois at Chicago. Her research focuses on comparative social movements in Latin America and the United States as well as on Latino immigrants and political identity formation in the United States. She is the author of *From Peasant Struggles to Indian Resistance: The Ecuadorian Andes in the Late Twentieth Century* (2002) as well as several articles and is currently working on a book on undocumented immigrant activism and family separation.

JOSÉ PERALES-RAMOS is director of operations in the Office of Institutional Diversity and Equity at DePaul University. He serves on the boards of the Diversifying Higher Education Faculty in Illinois Program and the Illinois Latino Council on Higher Education.

LEONARD G. RAMÍREZ is the director of the Latin American Recruitment and Educational Services Program at the University of Illinois at Chicago. He has been active in Chicago's Latino community affairs for more than twenty-five years. He is past board president of the Instituto del Progreso Latino, an adult education center serving primarily immigrant Mexicans from Chicago's Pilsen and Little Village communities. He is presently a member of the Illinois Latino Council on Higher Education and a board member of the Diversifying Higher Education Faculty in Illinois Program.

MICHAEL RODRÍGUEZ MUÑIZ received a master's degree in sociology at the University of Illinois and is currently a doctoral student at Brown University. He has contributed chapters to two edited volumes, and his research interests include identity formation, Latino social movements, and racial categorization.

R. STEPHEN WARNER is a professor of sociology emeritus at the University of Illinois at Chicago. He studies sociology of religion, focusing on immigration and youth. He is the author of *New Wine in Old Wineskins: Evangelicals and Liberals in a Small-Town Church* (1988) and *A Church of Our Own: Disestablishment and Diversity in American Religion* (2005) and coedited *Gatherings in Diaspora: Religious Communities and the New Immigration* (1998) and *Korean Americans and their Religions: Pilgrims and Missionaries From a Different Shore* (2001). He is a past president of the Society for the Scientific Study of Religion.

Index

accountability, 187–88

ACORN (Association of Community Organizations for Reform Now), xxviiin4, 44–45, 155, 157

Adalberto United Methodist Church: and Arellano, 50, 221, 231–32, 245; and Crisóstomo, 243; map, 39; and New Sanctuary Movement, 222; Puerto Rican support for sanctuary, 253

AFL-CIO Solidarity International, 153; and undocumented workers, 13, 15, 17, 45, 110–11, 127

African Americans: civil rights struggle, 141n6, 223, 234n12; demographic information, 37, 156; march participation of, xvii, 137–38, 157; and movement, 51, 116, 154, 156–57, 223; voter registration rates, 207

Aguilar, Rudy, 133

Albany Park Community Center, 43

Alinsky, Saul, 88, 132

American Federation of State, County, and Municipal Employees, 116

American Friends Service Committee, xxviiin4, 14

Americanness, 183–93; vs. ethnic identity, 198; exceptionalism, 191–92; melting pot narrative, 190, 192; Mexican activist emphasis on, xxii; and Minutemen,

183–84; and racism/racialization, 195, 204; and taxpaying, 184, 185–88

Americans for Legal Immigration Political Action Committee, 20

Amezcua, Salome, 48, 130, 131, 139

amnesty, 15; AFL-CIO support for, 111; and Catholic Church, 90; hometown associations, 148; marches for, 45; 1986, 134. See also Dignity and Amnesty; legalization

Amnesty-Vieques Human Chain, 45

anchor baby. See citizen children; representation

anti-illegal immigration rhetoric, as racist, 3, 72, 180, 181, 194–95, 248. See also Minutemen; restrictionism/restrictionist movement

Anti-Terrorism and Effective Death Penalty Act (1996), 11

Antrop-González, R., 103–4

Aparicio, Frances R., xxiv–xxv

Aranda, Elizabeth M., 200–201

Arango, Carlos, 14, 44

Arellano, Elvira, 231–32: activist strategies, xi, 49, 50, 220, 221; criminalization, 227; deportation, xii, 50, 220–21, 224, 228, 232–33, 237, 245; family values discourse, xxvii, 230; in print media, 70, 71, 223–25; Puerto Rican support for, 245,

253; as representative of undocumented immigrants, 56

Arellano, José Antonio, xxv–xxvi

Arellano, Saul, 221, 228, 229, 245

Arreola, Artemio, 47–48, 112–15, 118, 130, 131; on heterogeneity of movement, 52; organizational affiliations, 53

Ashcroft, John, 19

Asian immigrants. *See* Chinese immigrants; Filipino immigrants; Korean immigrants

Asociación Tepeyac, 15

assimilation, xxii, xxvii, 97, 190, 198, 199–200, 211n2. *See also* Americanness; second generation

Association of American Geographers, 80

Association of Community Organizations for Reform Now (ACORN), xxviiin4, 44–45, 155, 157

asylum, 11, 12–13, 21

Avila, Oscar, 70–71, 75

Back of the Yards march (2005), 47, 114, 155; in print media, 71–72, 123; size estimates, xi, 47; youth participation in, 208. *See also* participation in marches

Back of the Yards neighborhood, 39, 91, 126, 203

Bada, Xóchitl, xxvi

Badillo, David, 38

Balanoff, Tom, 109, 113, 115–16, 118. *See also* Service Employees International Union

Balibar, Etienne, 189–93

Ballvé, Marcelo, 68

Barrios, Martin, 224–25

Bartosic, Mark, 83

Batey Urbano: focus of, 211n4, 211n5; Latino/a panethnicity, xxvii–xxviii, 238, 253; map, 39; March 10, 2006 march, 244; and political education, 46, 207–8. *See also* Centro sin Fronteras; youth and youth activism

Benito Juárez High School, 6, 39, 168

Berg, Richard, 118

Bernardin, Joseph, 91

Beyerlein, Kraig, 87–88, 94n6

Bilbray, Brian, 21

bilingual education, 154

binational civic engagement, 146–58; defined, 159n1; as new system, 146–47. *See also* hometown associations; transnationalism

Binational Forum of Michoacano Migrants Living Abroad, 148

bishops. *See* Catholic Church

Blagojevic, Rod: immigrant descent, 43; and immigrant rights marches, 48, 167–68; Mexican support for, 151–52; New Americans Order, 43, 135, 152

Bleeden, David, xxvi–xxvii

Block, F., 142n14

Boehm, Michael, 81, 89

Bolivar, Simon, 246

border enforcement/patrol: after September 11 attacks, 18–19, 182; expedited removal, 9, 11, 19, 220, 233n4, 233n5; fences, 9, 21, 22; funds for, 7; and Green Party, 137; increase in, 8–9, 23, 220; vigilantism, 8, 28, 180, 181

Border Protection, Anti-Terrorism, and Illegal Immigration Control Act. *See* Sensenbrenner Bill

Bordertown (2006 film), 74

boycotts, xii, 6, 13, 48

Bracero program, 23, 110

Brown Tide Rising (Santa Ana), 65

Building Democracy Initiative of 2007, 21

Bush, George W., 20

Café Teatro Batey Urbano. *See* Batey Urbano

California: Los Angeles marches, 6, 166; Proposition 187 (1994), 9–10, 147, 165, 220

canvassing, 209

Cárdenas, Marco, 47, 155

Carpentersville, Illinois, 50, 157–58

Carrasco, Rosie, 53

Casa Aztlán: advocacy, xxviiin4, 12, 38, 43, 126; Back of the Yards march, 47; Coordinadora '96, 44

Casa Michoacán, 39, 47–48, 113, 130–31, 153

Casa Romero, 43

Catholic Bishops, U.S. Conference of, 94n7

Catholic Church, role of, in immigrant rights movement, xxv, 79–93; and amnesty, 15; Catholic school, 105; Coordinadora '96, 44; encouragement to participate in marches, 79–80, 82–83, 83–84, 86–87, 94n6; history, 90–91; increase of, 46; priest activism, 83, 85–86, 92–93, 127, 155; sanctuary, 221, 222; and substantive citizenship, 87–90

Católico (Spanish-language Catholic periodical), 92

Center for Community Change (national organization), 57

Centro de Acción Social Autónomo (CASA), 38, 40, 59n2

Centro de la Causa, 38, 126

Centro de Trabajadores Latinos, 15

Centro sin Fronteras: advocacy, xxviiin4, 43, 46; and Arellano, 231; Back of the Yards march, 47; citizen children, 221–22, 229; Coordinadora '96, 44; and elected officials, 136; leadership models, 132; March 10 Coalition, 47–48, 58, 131; in marches, 50, 51–52, 131, 142n17; mobilizations before and after marches, xi, xii, 44–45, 155; physical location, 220; and PRCC, 238, 243–44; in print media, 70; and STRIVE Act, 57–58; Vieques, 254n4. *See also* La Familia Latina Unida; Lozano, Emma; Zócalo Urbano

Cepeda, Esther, 75, 123

Chacón, Oscar, 54–55, 55–56, 56–57

Chavez, Cesar, 110

Chicago, 37–55; coalitions prior to megamarches, 44–47; and immigrant rights, xii, xxi–xxii, 52–55, 57–58, 167–68, 173; and immigration, 37–38, 43, 111, 125, 167; Latino activist history of, 38–44, 46–47, 125–27; machine politics, 41, 42–43, 57, 59n3; post-megamarch mobilizations, 49–52; as sanctuary city, xi, 41, 167. *See also* Daley, Richard M.; May 1, 2006 march; megamarches; schools; *and individual marches*

Chicago Federation of Labor (CFL), 109, 112, 118

Chicago Minuteman Project. *See* Minutemen

Chicago Sun-Times, 66; and Arellano, 223–25; immigration-related content, 71, 75; Latinos as sources in, 69–70; May 1, 2006 march, 73; on movement leadership, 123

Chicago Tribune, 66, 67; and Arellano, 223, 224; clergy activism, 83; immigration-related content, 70–71, 74–75; Latinos as sources in, 69–70; marches in, 72–73, 79, 225; on role of *Hoy,* 68

Chicago Workers' Collaborative, 114

children. *See* citizen children; second generation; youth and youth activism

Chinese immigrants, xxiii, 38, 105–6, 110

Christians. *See* Catholic Church

churches. *See* Adalberto United Methodist Church; Catholic Church; sanctuaries; *and names of specific churches/parishes*

Cicero, town of, 83, 85

Cintrón, Ralph, xxvi–xxvii

Citizen Child Protection Act, 221–22, 229

citizen children, rights of, 86, 103, 221–22, 227–29, 232, 245

citizenship: active, 181–82, 183, 206; and colonialism, 251–52; and Constitution, 191–92; defined, 184–85; dual, 128; and education, 100, 102–3, 106; as goal, 53–54, 157; hyper-, 187–88, 193, 194, 196; and march participation, xvi, 181–82, 202, 210; in movement leadership, 125; as participation, 219; routes to, 134–35; sponsorship for, 224; vs. subjects, 187; substantive, xxv, 87–90, 94n7, 210; and taxpaying, 186–87; as tool, xxiii, xxviii, 205–8, 208–9, 252; unequal application of, 240; and voting, 181, 188, 204. *See also* mixed-status families; Puerto Rican Cultural Center; second generation

vs.Citizenship and Immigration Services, U.S., 19

civic engagement: and churches, 87, 88–89, 94n7; patterns of, xviii, xx, xxi, 150–51, 159n2, 216, 218; political participation, 42, 207; and schools, 164–66, 174; of second generation, 206; voting, 146, 206, 209. *See also* binational civic engagement

civil rights struggle, African American, 141n6, 223, 234n12

class, xviii, 149, 199

clergy. *See* Catholic Church; *and names of specific clergymen*

cloture, 23–24, 30n18, 31n21

Cloward, Richard, 124, 133

Club la Purísima, 157–58

Coalition of African, Arab, Asian, European, and Latino Immigrants of Illinois, 45

coalitions: among churches, 88, 127; benefits/problems of, 12, 130–31, 133–34, 136; and hometown associations, 128–29; in 1970s–1980s activism, 40; pride in, 94n2; in print media, 73; prior to megamarches, 13–17, 44–47; Puerto Rican, 243–44; services to immigrants, 29n3. *See also* Illinois Coalition for Immigrant and Refugee Rights; March 10 Coalition

Cockcroft, James, 157–58

colonialism, 211n5, 247–49, 251–52, 255n8

Comité de Immigrantes en Acción, 15

Comité Patriótico Mexicano, 44

Commission of Latino Affairs (Chicago), 41

community growth, 125–27, 139

community service organizations, 7–8, 12, 43. *See also* hometown associations

comprehensive immigration reform: and congressional strategies, 136; and Democratic party, 50; as goal, 53–54, 124, 125, 130, 139, 140; and Gutiérrez, 41–42; vs. local policies, 27; and Obama, xiii; and prior deportees, 221; proposed bills, 20–22, 22–26; restrictionist view, 20; and September 11 attacks, 18; stepwise path to, 135. *See also* policy/legislation (national)

Comprehensive Immigration Reform Act of 2007. *See* Secure Borders, Economic Opportunity, and Immigration Reform Act

Confederation of Mexican Clubs, 112

Confederation of Mexican Federations in the Midwest (CONFEMEX), 129, 154, 155, 158

Congressional Hispanic Caucus, xii, 14, 24

Congress of Spanish-Speaking Peoples, xxii

Constitution, U.S., 184, 191–93

Cook County, Illinois as sanctuary county, xii, 49, 167, 223, 234n11

Coordinadora '96, 13–14, 44

Cornelius, Wayne, 151

Coronado, Linda, 40

Corretjer, Juan Antonio, 242

criminalization: of assistance to undocumented immigrants, 21, 205; and division within immigrant movement, 233n3; of hiring undocumented workers, 7, 110; opposition to, xxii, 47, 48, 141n12, 227; restrictionist views, 72; and second generation immigrant identification, 204–5; of undocumented immigrants, 76n5, 135, 204–5, 219, 227; of youth, xxvi, 166. *See also* deportations; employers and employment; raids; Sensenbrenner Bill

Crisóstomo, Flor, xi, xii, xiii, 71, 221, 243, 245

Cruikshank, Barbara, 184–85

Cuban immigrants, 38, 66, 68

culture war, 189–93

Curran, Brendan, 80, 86

curriculum: citizenship, 100; in civic education, 164; funds of knowledge concept, 98, 102, 106; immigration patterns, 97–98, 101, 105–6; relevance to students, 98–99, 101–2. *See also* schools; teachers

Customs and Border Protection Agency, U.S., 19. *See also* border enforcement/patrol

Dahm, Charles, 84, 85–86, 88, 94n4

Daley, Richard J., 59n3

Daley, Richard M.: immigrant descent, 43; and machine politics, 42; march support, 48, 52, 167–68; minimum wage veto, 112; and sanctuary laws, 41

D'Amezcua, Maria, 48, 53, 128

danzantes aztecas, 52, 59n11

Dávila, Arlene, 67

Davis, Stephen P., xxv, 80

De Genova, Nicholas, 240, 251

dehumanization of immigrants, 65

Del Valle, Miguel, 254n1

democracy, liberal, 192–93, 193–94

democratic leadership structures, xxv–xxvi, 130–31, 132–33, 142n18

Democratic Party: control of Congress by, 21, 23, 49–50; family values discourse, 219–20, 230; limitations of, 57–58; movement attitude toward, 49–50, 135–37

democratic subjectivity, 184–85, 193–94

demographic/statistical information: hometown association membership, 150; immigrant populations, 37–38; Latino civic/political engagement, xx–xxi, 42, 207; Latino/Mexican populations, 37–38, 42, 44, 125–26, 139, 156; of marchers, xvi–xxi, 80–82, 216–18; media and Latino content, 66; mixed-status families, 203, 215–16, 218; support for immigrant rights, xxii–xxiii; union membership, 111; voting rates, xix, 42, 157, 207, 216, 218. *See also* Immigrant Mobilization Project; participation in marches; Pew Hispanic Center surveys

Department of Homeland Security (DHS), 18–19, 27

deportations: of Arellano, xii, 50, 220–21, 224, 228, 232–33, 237, 245; and declining Mexican populations, 125; as disruptive to family, 230; increase in, 3, 11–12, 18, 26, 51, 220; judicial discretion, 29n9, 220, 222, 227–28, 232, 233n5; Latino concern about, xxii–xxiii; and moratorium demands, xiii, 24, 85–86, 220–21, 234n10, 237; and moratorium in Chicago, xii, 58; and national security, 18–19; and offenders, 11, 16, 25, 29n9, 215, 233n1, 233n2; in print media, 69, 71; as reason for marching, xviii–xix, xxi, 217; reentry after, 27, 224, 229; response in 1950s and 1960s, 126; as threat to labor organizing, 86, 111. *See also* expedited removal; mixed-status families; second generation

Development, Relief, and Education for Alien Minors (DREAM) Act, xiii, 21, 25, 30n18

Día de la Raza, 16

Dignity and Amnesty, 15–17, 29n11, 44–45

discrimination. *See* racialization; racism

Domínguez, Alejandro, 20

DREAM Act, xiii, 21, 25, 30n18

Dugan, Bill, 115–16

Duncan, Arne, 168–69

Durazo, María Elena, 115

Durbin, Richard, 21, 48, 167–68

Earle, Peter, 40

Echevarria, Ignacio and Santiago, 3

economies and immigration, 106, 195–96, 226

electoral politics and elected officials: cloture, 23–24, 30n18, 31n21; machine politics, 41, 42–43, 57, 59n3; march participation, 14, 47, 48, 52, 142n16, 167; in Mexico, 128, 156, 155, 159n3; as motivation to obtain citizenship, 157; movement attitude toward, 57–58, 135–37; political action committees, 151–52; and Puerto Rican activism, 254n1. *See also* Daley, Richard M.; Gutiérrez, Luis; voter registration drives; voting

emotional embeddedness, 200–201

Employee, Family Unity, and Legalization Act, 16

employers and employment: cooperation with marchers, 84; employment verification, 7, 25, 27, 28; fear of joblessness, 114; raid threats, 86, 111, 116. *See also* labor involvement in immigrant rights movement; raids

enforcement: coupled with legalization, 21, 22–23, 26; coupled with some reunification measures, 25; expansions in, 26–28, 219–20; local police involvement in, xii, 9, 19–20, 51. *See also* border enforcement/patrol; deportations; raids

English as official language, 28, 189, 192

Enhanced Border Security and Visa Entry Reform Act (2002), 18

Erie Neighborhood House, 43

Espinosa, Leticia, 67

Espiritu, Yen Le, 240, 250

ethnic identity: and assimilation, 211n2; dual, 202–3, 211n2; fictive ethnicity, 189–93, 195; formation, 240, 246; and march participation, xvii; as means of defining solidarity, 204; vs. national

identity, 198; subjective dimensions, 253–54. *See also* Latino/a panethnicity
ethos defined, 179
European immigrants. *See* Irish immigrants; Italian immigrants; Polish immigrants
expedited removal: defined, 9, 11, 233n4; expanded eligibility conditions, 19; increase in, 9, 220; loss of judicial hearing, 11, 233n5

Familia Latina Unida, La. *See* La Familia Latina Unida
Familias Unidas Campaign (United Families), xii, 24
families: funds of knowledge concept, 98, 102, 106; march participation, 5, 172, 207; as political subjects, 225–26, 229–32; role in transnational contexts, 200–201. *See also* mixed-status families
Families for Freedom, 216, 233n2
family reunification, 8, 17, 25
family values discourse, xvii, 219–20, 229–32
Farm Labor Organizing Committee, 12, 15, 38
Farragut High School, 168
Federation of American Immigration Reform (FAIR), 8, 20, 21
fictive ethnicity, 189–93, 192–93, 195
Filipino immigrants, 6, 38, 49
Fink, Leon, xxv
Flake, Jeff, xii, 15, 22–23
Flores-González, Nilda, xvi, xxiv, xxvii
Freedom Act (Dignity and Amnesty's proposal), 15, 16
Freedom Rides (2003), 29–30n11
free riders, 186–87, 193
free trade, 137
Freire, Paulo, 132
funds of knowledge concept, 98, 102, 106

Gaete, Claudio, 128, 134
García, Jesús, 40, 41
García, Lorena, 255n5
Garza, Laura, 115
George, Francis, 83, 90, 91

German immigrants, 91, 118
Gilchrist, Jim, 180, 182, 183
Gingrich, Newt, 65
globalization, 134, 140, 195–96
Gottschalk-Druschke, Caroline, xxvi–xxvii
Graf, Gary, 83
grassroots-institutional divide, 57–58
Green Party, 137
guest worker programs, 20, 23, 30n17
Gutiérrez, David, xxii, 233n3
Gutiérrez, Elena R., xxiv
Gutiérrez, José Luis, 43–44
Gutiérrez, Juan José, 13, 14
Gutiérrez, Luis: on community self-representation/leadership, 136; Freedom Act, 16; on hometown associations, 128–29; immigration proposals, xiii, 25, 46, 134–35; Latino Immigrants Rights March (1996), 14; march support, 45, 47, 48, 167; political career, 41–42, 137; and PRCC, 254n1; SOLVE Act, 21; STRIVE Act, xii, 22–23, 57, 158; ¡Ya Basta! campaign, xii, 24, 245

Hadden, Jeffrey, 92
Haitian immigrants, 12–13, 14, 45
Haitian Refugee Immigration Fairness Act (1998), 12–13
Hall, Stuart, 69, 241
Hastert, Dennis, 83, 142n15
hate crimes, xii, 28
hate speech, 180, 181
Heartland Alliance for Human Needs and Human Rights, 45, 59n7
Heredia, Carlos, 130
Hernández, Edwin, 87–88, 94n6
heterogeneity within immigrant rights movement, 51, 52–55, 55–57, 57–58
Hibbing, John R., 151
Hispanic Caucus, Congressional, xii, 14, 24
Hispanic Democratic Organization (HDO), 42, 59n6
Hispanic term, 238–39
history of immigrant rights movement: Catholic Church, 90–91; in Chicago, 38–44, 46–47, 125–27; contemporary movement's characteristics, xxii–xxiv;

hometown associations, 146–47, 148, 152–53; national, 7–8, 10, 12–18, 44–46, 134; Puerto Rican Cultural Center, 242–44; youth activism, 126, 165. *See also* immigration patterns, historical

Hoffman Plastic Compounds, Inc. v. National Labor Relations Board (2002), 114

Holzer, Claudio, 89

Homeland Security Act (2002), 18–19

homeownership, 87, 88, 181

hometown associations, xxvi, 146–59; Back of the Yards march, 47, 155; march participation of, 5, 47, 155; March 10 Coalition, 47–48, 133, 156; as resource for leadership development, 112, 128–29; significance of, 149, 150; U.S. political engagement, 151–52, 153, 154, 155–58, 201–2; work toward binational agenda, 45–46, 158–59

Homies Unidos, 216, 233n2

homogenization. *See* Latino/a panethnicity

Horton, Myles, 132

Hotel Employees and Restaurant Employees International Union. *See* UNITE HERE

household income and march participation, xviii

House's Immigration Reform Caucus (HIRC), 21, 23, 30n20

Hoy: immigration-related content, 68, 69, 71–72; Latinos as sources in, 66, 68–70; May 1, 2006 march, 74; Minutemen article, 47, 72; responsibility to Spanish-speaking community, 67

Hoyt, Joshua, 70

Human Rights Watch, 215

Humboldt Park neighborhood: gentrification, 243, 247; map, 39; youth organizing in, 46, 207, 238

Huntington, Samuel, 151

hypercitizenship, 187–88, 193, 194, 196

hyperculturalism, 189–93, 196

identification: banned for undocumented immigrants, 22, 28; consular, 45, 154; counterfeit, xii, 59n10, 70

IFCO Systems raid, xi, 5–6, 26, 49, 221

IIRIRA (Illegal Immigration Reform and Immigrant Responsibility Act, 1996), xii, 10–12, 19–20, 51, 220

illegal immigrant term, 73, 103, 201

Illegal Immigration Reform and Immigrant Responsibility Act (IIRIRA, 1996), xii, 10–12, 19–20, 51, 220

Illinois Coalition for Immigrant and Refugee Rights (ICIRR), 8; as advocacy organization, 43; and Arreola, 53; Back of the Yards march, 47; in immigrant rights movement, xxviiin4; pre-megamarch initiatives, 44–45, 46–47; Sept. 2000 march for immigrant rights, 155; as source for print media, 70. *See also* Tsao, Fred

Illinois Labor History Society, 109

Illinois Minuteman Project. *See* Minutemen

imagined community, 66, 185–88. *See also* fictive ethnicity

immigrant civil society, 159n1

Immigrant Mobilization Project (IMP): origin of, xv–xvi; survey of marchers, xvi–xxi, xxviiin2, 80–82, 168, 174

Immigrant Workers Freedom Ride (2003), 17, 112

Immigration and Customs Enforcement (ICE), xii, 19, 25, 26–27, 116. *See also* deportations; enforcement; raids

Immigration and Nationality Act (1990, 1994), 8, 12, 110

Immigration PAC, 58

immigration patterns, historical: curricular attention to, 97–98, 101, 105–6; labor movement relationship, 110; Mexican immigration, 38, 111, 125–26, 127; and policy/legislation, 134

Immigration Reform and Control Act (IRCA, 1986), 7–8, 19, 29n2, 110, 134, 148

Independent Political Organization of Little Village, 40

Industrial Areas Foundation, 132

Institute for Mexicans Abroad. *See* Instituto de los Mexicanos en el Exterior

Instituto de los Mexicanos en el Exterior: and Arreola, 112, 115; elections for, 149; role in expanding immigrant networks,

45–46, 128, 129, 141n11; as site for data collection, 148

Instituto del Progreso Latino, 40, 43, 126–27

International Ladies' Garment Workers Union (ILGWU), 40, 110

International Union of Electrical, Salaried Machine, and Furniture Workers, 13–14

International Workers' Day, 16, 25, 94n2, 114–15, 117, 118

invisibility of undocumented immigrants, 73, 225

IRCA (Immigration Reform and Control Act, 1986), 7–8, 19, 29n2, 110, 134, 148

Irish immigrants, xxiii, 43, 91

Italian immigrants, 43, 91

Itzigsohn, José, 202, 241

Jackson, Jesse, 156–57

Jiménez, José "Cha-Cha," 40

Jiménez, Maria, 14, 15, 17

Jiménez, Raquel, 223, 225, 230

joblessness, fear of, 114, 116

Jobs with Justice coalition, 115

Jones-Correa, Michael, 241

journalistic objectivity, 68–69

Juan Antonio Corretjer Puerto Rican Cultural Center. *See* Puerto Rican Cultural Center

Katolik (Polish-language Catholic periodical), 92

Kennedy, Edward, 15, 21, 27, 46, 47

Klein, Margarita, 115

Kolbe, Jim, 15

Korean immigrants, xxiii, 6, 14, 49

Ku Klux Klan, 28

labor antagonism with immigrants, 126

Labor Council for Latin American Advancement, xii, 118

labor involvement in immigrant rights movement, xxv, 12, 109–18, 133; as advantageous move, 117–18, 137–38; boycott resistance, 6; Coordinadora '96, 13–14, 44; financial support, 48, 109, 138; guest worker programs, 23; home-town associations, 147, 152, 153; May Day significance, 16, 25, 94n2, 114–15, 117, 118; and movement independence, 138; and movement leadership, 110, 127, 137–38; on national level, 17–18, 45; representation of undocumented workers, 222; undocumented status and labor organizing, 15, 86, 111, 116. *See also* AFL-CIO Solidarity International; raids; *and names of individual unions*

labor/workers' rights as reason for marching, xviii

La Familia Latina Unida (LFLU), xxvii, 215–33; activist strategies, 208, 220–21; Arellano's deportation, 50; case study, 219; citizen children, 221–22, 227–29, 232; family as political subject, 225–26, 229–32; family values discourse, 229–32; individual subjectivity, 226–27, 231–32; political strategies, 216–18, 220–21; and representation, 222–25, 232

language: assimilation and, 211n2; of church services, 85, 88, 91; English as official, 28, 189, 192; and ethnic identification, 198, 202–3; and fictive ethnicity, 189–90; and perceived homogeneity, 249; Spanish as marker of immigrant identity, 67, 204; Spanish as second, 154

La Raza, 66, 76n2, 123

Las Fuerzas Armadas de Liberación Nacional, 243

Latin American Community Migrant Summit, 158

Latinidad. See Latino/a panethnicity

Latino and Immigrants' Rights March (1996), 13–14

Latino/a panethnicity, xxiii, xxvii–xxviii, 239–42; and colonialism, 211n5, 247–49; homogeneity vs. difference, 249–53, 254; immigrant identification, 202–3; megamarches and, 244; vs. nationalism, 255n5; in 1970s–1980s activism, 40; Puerto Rican solidarity with immigrant rights movement, xxvii–xxviii, 238–39, 239–40, 246–47, 249–53, 254; and racialization, 239–40, 247–49, 250; subjective dimensions, 253–54

Latino Crossings (De Genova and Ramos-Zayas), 240
Latino Ethnic Consciousness (Padilla), 239–40
Latino invisibility, 73
Latino Mobilization Summit Conference (2005), 129–30
Latino Policy Forum (formerly Latinos United), 43, 222
Latino populations, 37–38, 125–26, 139, 156
Latinos Progresando, 126–27
Latino term, 238–39
Latino USA, 13
Latino Youth Alternative High School, 38, 126
leaders, types of, 141n1
leadership in immigrant rights movement, 123–40; democratic structures, xxv–xxvi, 130–31, 132–33, 142n18; and electoral strategies, 135–37; heterogeneity of, 133–35; home country political background, 155; hometown associations, 112, 128–29; as indigenous resource, 125–27, 138–39; and Instituto de los Mexicanos en el Exterior, 141n11; labor movement role, 110, 127, 137–38; March 10 Coalition, 129–32; and multiple organizational memberships, 53, 149, 152; roles of, 123–24, 139–40, 142n14
League of United Latin American Citizens, 12, 14
Leal, David, 151
Legal Immigration Family Equity Act (2000), 12
legalization: and assimilation, 211n2; causes for opposition, 224–25; clergy support for, 83; coupled with stricter enforcement, 21, 22–23, 26; and immigrant rights movement, xxiii, 51, 53–54, 58, 141n12; incomplete application of, 134, 136; labor support for, xxv, 17, 109–10, 112; Mexico-U.S. negotiations, 18; and migration of relatives, 8; and mixed-status families, 216; and Obama, 25; in print media, 71, 73; and prior deportation, 229; rallies demanding, 109–10,

155, 209; as reason for marching, xviii–xix, xxi, 217; of refugees, 12; and travel, 148; for undocumented students, 21. *See also* amnesty
legislation. *See* policy/legislation (national); policy/legislation (state/local)
Le Goff, Jacques, 246
Levitt, Peggy, 200–201, 202, 211n3
liberal democracy, 192–93, 193–94
libertarians, 185–86
Librería Nuestro Continente, 141n8
Little Village neighborhood: growth/success of, 126; Independent Political Organization of, 40; map, 39; raid in discount mall, xii, 50, 59n10, 209; and second generation, 203; voter registration drives in, 88, 94n8
lobbying, 50, 55, 57, 220
local ordinances, 28, 50, 157–58
local police: and immigration laws, xii, 19–20, 51; local sanctuaries, 28, 223; reporting requirements of, 9
Lolita Lebrón Family Learning Center, 244
López, David, 240, 250
López, José, 245, 246, 248–49, 251
López, Marc Hugo, 207
López, Omar, 112, 131; dual citizenship campaign, 128; election bid of, 137; on gains, 135; March 10 Coalition, 48, 130
López Rivera, Oscar, 247
López-Vigil, Nativo, 115
Los Angeles marches, 6, 166
Lott, Trent, 65
Lovato, Robert, 25
Lozano, Emma: Back of the Yards march, 114; on elected officials, 136; and Freedom Act, 16; on labor involvement in movement, 138; March 10 Coalition, 47–48, 129–30; multiple organizational memberships, 53; organizing trip to Mexico, 208; and print media, 70. *See also* Centro sin Fronteras
Lozano, Rudy, 40, 247
Lugo-Lugo, Carmen R., 255n8

machine politics, 41, 42–43, 57, 59n3
Maldonado, Roberto, 49, 223, 245, 254n1

Manjarrez, Timoteo "Alex," 148–49
map, 39
marches. *See* megamarches; *and specific marches*
March of Immigrants, Indigenous, and the Poor (1997), 14
March 10, 2006, march, xi, xv, 113, 139; and Catholic Church, 79–80, 90; Chicago's success, 5, 48; and labor, 109; and plans for further actions, 130; in print media, 71, 79; Puerto Rican participation, 244; youth participation, 168. *See also* March 10 Coalition; megamarches
March 10 Coalition, xi, 129–34, 135–40; and comprehensive immigration reform, 139; democratic leadership structures, 132–33, 142n18; on elected officials/ electoral politics, 57–58, 136–37, 142n16; funding, 131, 138; and hometown associations, 47–48, 133, 156; and labor movement, 113, 114–15, 116–17, 137–38; megamarch organizing, 47–49, 113, 129–32; national outreach, xii, 17, 156–57; role of, 53, 135, 139–40, 142n13; as site for data collection, 148; 2007 march, 50; 2008 march, 51–52, 142n17
Martinez, Juan R., xxv, 79
Maya, Beatriz, 15
May Day, 16, 25, 94n2, 114–15, 117, 118
May 1, 2006, march, xi, xv, xvi–xxi, 7, 49; African American participation, 157; and Catholic church, 90; decision to organize, 48–49; labor and, 109–10, 116–17, 137–38; outside views of, 225; in print media, 72–74, 225; Puerto Rican participation, 244; and schools, 163, 168. *See also* March 10 Coalition; megamarches; participation in marches
May 1, 2007, march, xii, xvi–xxi, 24, 50, 168, 216–18; mixed-status families, 216; organization of, 142n17; and schools, 174; youth participation, 168, 206
May 1, 2008, march, xii, 24; Centro sin Fronteras, 51–52, 131; danzante groups, 52, 59n11; in print media, 75–76
May 1, 2009 march, xiii; 25
May 1 Youth Network, 46

McCain, John, 15, 21
McCann, James A., 151
McNulty, Timothy J., 71
media, xxiv–xxv, 65–76; anti-immigrant sentiment in, 47, 72, 75, 123; immigration issues in, 46, 67, 70–72, 75–76, 139; Latino underrepresentation, 66, 69–70; march coverage, 5, 48, 52, 66, 72–76, 123; objectivity, 68, 69; as public information source, 65; youth, 164. *See also Chicago Sun-Times*; *Chicago Tribune*; media, Spanish-language
media, Spanish-language: advocate for immigrant rights, 67, 68; children as spokespeople, 223; immigration issues in, 69, 71–72, 75–76, 139; Latino representation in, 66, 68–70; march coverage, 74, 123; march support, 66, 72, 167; proactive role in immigrant rights, 46; radio, 47, 50, 70–71, 72, 114, 155, 167; struggle for mainstream respectability, 66–67. *See also Hoy*; *La Raza*; media
Medina, Eliseo, 113
megamarches, xv, 4, 6, 7, 49; citizen participation, 181–82; community political education, 5, 138–39, 206–7; Daley's support for, 167; demographic information, xvi–xxi, 80–82, 216–18, 238; as evidence of Chicago's activism, 37; historical precedents, 44–47; and hometown associations, 151–52; Latino invisibility, 73; legal status and, 221, 222; and media, 71–72, 75–76; and Minutemen, 182–83; movement invigoration, 54, 138–39, 151; political capital, 56, 58, 133, 135; and representation, 56; and second generation, 198, 205–6, 210. *See also* March 10 Coalition; participation in marches; *and individual marches*
Melrose Park village, 44, 83, 84, 85
melting pot narrative, 190, 192. *See also* assimilation
Menendez, Robert, 27
Menjivar, Cecilia, 87–88
Mexican American Council, 126
Mexican American Legal Defense and Education Fund, 10, 12, 38, 41, 59n5

Mexican Civic Committee, 126
Mexican civil rights movements of 1970s, xxii–xxiv, 40
Mexicans, 38, 125–26, 139; assumed to be immigrants, 43, 201; church customs, 85; civic participation, 150, 159n1; historic divisions between, 131, 140; immigration patterns, 38, 111, 125–26, 127; as major participants in megamarches, 6
Mexicans for Blagojevich, 151–52
Mexicans for Political Progress, 151
Mexico: Chicago consulate, 117; elections, 128, 156, 155, 159n3; and hometown associations, 147, 155; migrants' involvement in home politics, xii, 153, 155, 156, 158–59; in print media, 74, 75; and United States, 18, 44, 134
Miami Herald, 66, 69
Michoacán Federation, 112, 115
Michoacán hometown associations, 152–53, 157–58
migration dangers, 9
minimum wage measures, 112
Minutemen, xxvi–xxvii, 179–96; and active citizenship, 181–82, 183; consciousness-raising activities, 180–84; as democratic subjects, 193–94; as hypercitizens, 187–88, 194; hyperculturalism, 189–93, 196; immigration laws as "broken system," 20; and megamarches, 182–83; nationalism, 196; perceived as racist, 180, 181, 194–95; political influence, 21; in print media, 47, 69, 72, 74; role in motivating Back of the Yards march, 47, 114, 155; and U.S. Constitution, 191–93; use of taxpayer *topos,* 186–87. *See also* anti-illegal immigration rhetoric; restrictionism/restrictionist movement
Mitchell, Mary, 223–24
mixed-status families, xxvii, 215–33; activist focus on, 46–47; and anti-deportation activism, 24–25, 220–22, 232; citizen children, 86, 103, 221–22, 227–29, 232, 245; and deportation threat, 24–25, 86, 103, 215–16, 219, 227–29; family as political subject, 225–26, 229–32; individual subjectivity, 226–27, 231–32; and

second generation immigrant identification, 203–4; support for immigration reform, xxiii; taxpayer *topos,* 226. *See also* families
mobility and strain on nation-state, 195–96
mobilization vs. organization, 54–55, 123–24
Molina Guzmán, Isabel, 66–67, 68, 69
Morales, Fabian, 131
Morales, Jorge, 40
Morris, A. D., 141n6, 141n11, 142n13
Mujeres Latinas en Acción, 38, 126, 141n8
Mujica, Jorge: activist career of, 113–14; on democratic leadership structures, 132; on Democratic Party, 136; on history of immigrant rights movement, 7, 134; on labor's role, 137; on marches' lack of lasting effect, 50, 56; on May Day significance, 115; megamarch organization, 48, 109, 118, 132; on political experience of new immigrants, 127; in print media, 70
Mundelein, George, 91
Muslim immigrants, xxiii, 19, 30n13
mutual aid societies, 38, 126
mythos, defined, 179

Napolitano, Janet, xiii, 27
National Alliance of Latin American and Caribbean Communities (NALACC), 16, 46, 55–56, 154
National Coalition for Dignity and Amnesty for Undocumented Immigrants, 15–17, 29n11, 44–45
National Conference of Catholic Bishops, 84, 90
National Council of La Raza, xxiii, 12
National Hispanic Encuentro (1972), 84
National Immigrant Rights Strategy Convention (2006), 17
nationalism, 196, 250–51, 255n5
nationality and march participation, xvii
National Network for Immigrant and Refugee Rights, 12, 14, 16, 29n3
national security: immigration's association with, 44, 54, 155, 205, 220; increased immigration enforcement, 18–19; permeability of borders, 182

nation-states: globalization's strain on, 195–96; imagined culture/fictive ethnicity, 66, 188, 189–93; liberal democratic requirement of closure, 192–93, 193–94

nativism, 29n4; effect on Democratic Party, 57; growth of, 8, 91, 129; and hate crimes, 28. *See also* restrictionism/restrictionist movement

naturalization. *See* citizenship

Navarro, Armando, 129

Near West Side, as port of entry, 126, 141n7. *See also* Pilsen neighborhood

New Americans Executive Order (Illinois), 43–44, 135, 152

New Americans Vote program, 46

New Majority Coalition, 142n17

New Sanctuary Movement, 222, 234n10

newspapers. *See* media; media, Spanish-language; *and names of specific papers*

New York Times Magazine, 157–58

Ngai, Mae, 233n3

Nicaraguan Adjustment and Central American Relief Act (1997), 12–13

No Child Left Behind Act, 99, 101

nonobjectivism, 241, 253

Nuevo Herald, 66–67

Numbers USA, 20

Obama, Barack, xiii, 24, 25, 48

Ocasio, Billy, 254n1

October 12 symbolism, 16

Oklahoma City bombings, 11

Oklahoma Taxpayer and Citizen Protection Act (2007), 28

Oliva, Sonia, xxvi

Olmedo, Irma M., xxv

Operating Engineers Local 150, 115–16

Operation Gatekeeper (California border), 9

Operation Hold the Line (Texas border), 9

Operation PUSH (People United to Serve Humanity), 51

Operation Safeguard (Arizona border), 9

organization, vs. mobilization, 54–55, 123–24

Organization of Latin American Students, 38, 126

Ortiz, Vilma, 211n2

Our Lady of Guadalupe parish, 91

Padilla, Felix, 239–40

Paerregaard, Karsten, 250

Pallares, Amalia, xvi, xxiv, xxvii

Parks, Rosa, 223, 234n12

participant observation, 147–48

participation in marches: African American, xvii, 137–38, 157; and Catholic Church, 79–80, 82–83, 83–84, 86–87, 94n6; and citizenship, xvi, 181–82, 202, 210; elected officials, 14, 47, 48, 52, 142n16, 167; families, 5, 172, 207; hometown associations, 5, 47, 155; and household income, xviii; non-Mexican immigrants, xxiii, 6, 14, 49, 118; and patriotism, xix–xx, 4; Puerto Rican, 238, 244; and religion, 80–82; whites, xvii, xx, 72–73, 80, 172; youth, xvii, 51, 97, 104, 168, 173–74, 206, 208, 244. *See also* demographic/statistical information; *and individual marches*

participatory democracy, 193

Paseo Boricua, 243, 253

Pastor, Ed, 14

Patriot Act (2001), 18, 19

patriotism, among march participants, xix–xx, 4

Pelosi, Nancy, 24, 237

Perales-Ramos, José, xxv–xxvi

Perlman, Selig, 110

Personal Responsibility and Work Opportunity Reconciliation Act (PRWORA, 1996), 10, 220

Pew Hispanic Center surveys, 65; Catholic Church role in march participation, 86–87, 94n6; Latino concern for immigrant rights, xxii–xxiii; rates of civic participation, xxi, 150, 159n2; undocumented populations, 215

Pilsen neighborhood: Catholic Church in, 91, 127; map, 39; as Mexican/immigrant community, 91, 126, 141n7, 153, 207, 220; as port-of-entry community, 80, 84, 153; Resurrection Project, 88, 127; and second-generation immigrants, 203; voter registration drives in, 88, 94n8;

youth organizing in, 46. *See also* Casa Michoacán; Catholic Church

Piven, Frances Fox, 124, 133

police. *See* local police

police treatment of protesters, 165–66, 237–38

policy/legislation (national), 4–26, 30n16, 50; activist decisions about, 53–54, 134–35; comprehensive immigration reform efforts, 20–22, 22–26; decreased options for undocumented immigrants, 220, 232; Democratic Party control of Congress, 49–50; escalated enforcement, 26–28, 219–20; family reunification, 8; immigrant rights victories in, 12–13; and immigration patterns, 134; and labor organizing, 114; Latino concern about, xxiii; private bills, 220, 233n7; restrictive, 7–12, 20, 23; view as flawed, 20, 89, 134, 191–92. *See also* Sensenbrenner Bill; *and names of individual bills*

policy/legislation (state/local), 50; restrictive, 27–28, 157–58, 165; supportive, xi, 28, 41, 43–44, 46, 154, 223

Polish immigrants: church accommodation, 85, 91, 92; holiday parades, 43; immigration patterns, 38, 105–6, 111; march participation, xxiii, 6, 14, 49, 118

political engagement. *See* civic engagement; hometown associations

politics. *See* electoral politics and elected officials

populations. *See* demographic/statistical information

Portes, Alejandro, 199

port-of-entry communities, 80, 84, 125–26, 153, 201

PRCC. *See* Puerto Rican Cultural Center

priests. *See* Catholic Church; *and names of specific priests*

Priests for Justice for Immigrants, 85–86, 92

ProEnglish, 189

Proposition 187 (California, 1994), 9–10, 147, 165, 220

Protect Citizens and Residents from Unlawful Raids and Detention Act (2008), 27

Protestant church. *See* Adalberto United Methodist Church

Protestant church and transnationalism, 87–88

Pueblo sin Fronteras. *See* Centro sin Fronteras

Puerto Rican Cultural Center (PRCC), 43, 237–54; colonialism, 247–49; demonstrations/protests, 237–38; and elected officials, 254n1; and immigrant rights movement, xxvii–xxviii, xxviiin4, 237–38, 243–44, 244–46, 246–47; independence movement, 243, 249; Latino/a panethnicity, xxvii–xxviii, 238–39, 239–40, 246–47, 249–53, 254; map, 39; Mexican leadership in, 254n2; nationalist discourses, 250–51; and Vieques, 243–44, 254n4. *See also* Batey Urbano

Puerto Ricans: activism of 1970s–1980s, 40; Chicago populations, 38; transnational context, 200–201

Pulido, Laura, 243

Pulido, Rafael "El Pistolero," 47, 50, 70–71, 114, 155

Pulido, Rosanna, 47, 69, 71–72, 114

Quigley, James, 91

quinceañeras, 85

racialization: and assimilation, 97, 199, 211n2; and discrimination, 204; and ethnic identification, 198; and exclusion from body politic, 66; and labor movement, 126; and Latino/a panethnicity, 239–40, 247–49, 250; racial profiling by immigration authorities, 92, 137; and schools, 166; and second-generation immigrant identification, 56, 200–201, 202, 204–5, 211n2; vs. substantive citizenship, 94n7; white spaces, 73

racism: and access to churches, 91; and access to citizenship benefits, 252; and anti-immigration activists, 3, 72, 180, 181, 194–95, 248; hate crimes, xii, 28; hate speech, 180, 181; labor movement as unifying, 137–38

raids, xxii; Chicago city moratorium on,

xii, 58; escalation in, 3, 26–27, 85–86; IFCO Systems, xi, 5–6, 26, 49, 221; Little Village Discount Mall, xii, 50, 59n10, 209; and moratorium demands, xiii, 24, 85–86, 234n10, 237; PRCC, 243; in print media, 71; role in growth of immigrant rights movement, 5–6, 38, 50; as threat to labor organizing, 86, 111, 116

RainbowPUSH Coalition, 139, 154

Ramírez, Leonard G., xxv–xxvi

Ramos-Zayas, Ana Y., 240, 251, 252

Reagan Revolution, 135

Real ID Act (2005), 21

redistricting, 59n5

refugees, 8, 10, 11, 12–13, 21, 84, 95n10

religion: and ethnic identification, 198; and march participation, 80–82

remittances, 150, 151, 200

representation: Catholic Church and, 105; family as political subject, 225–26; grassroots organizations, 56–57; immigrants' self-, 55–56, 222–23, 227, 232; from within Mexican community, 136; mixed-status families, 222–25, 227, 232; as responsibility of citizenship, xxiii, xxviii, 205–8, 208–9, 252; teachers and, 106. *See also names of specific politicians*

Republican Party: Contract with America (1994), 135; control of House by, 21; decline of power of, 49–50; family values discourse, 220, 230

research methods: activist interviews, xxviiin2, 124–25, 238, 242; case studies, 219; clergy interviews, 80, 94n1; Minuteman interviews, 179; multistage block sampling technique, xxviiin2; participant observation, 147–48; print media/journalist interviews, 66; qualitative, 141n4; subjective, 253; teacher interviews, 99–100; youth interviews, 163–64, 199. *See also* demographic/statistical information; Immigrant Mobilization Project; Pew Hispanic Center surveys

restrictionism/restrictionist movement, 8, 29n4; anchor baby term, 224; and Arellano, 221, 231, 232; backlash against megamarches, 50; effect on Democratic Party, 57; effect on immigrant rights

movement, 30n15; and hate crimes, 28; in House of Representatives, 21; and policy, 7–12, 20, 23, 27–28, 157–58, 165; in print media, 69, 72, 74; and September 11 attacks, 182. *See also* anti-illegal immigration rhetoric; Minutemen; nativism

Resurrection Project, 88, 127

Rivera, Geraldo, 14

Rivera, Joel (New York assemblyman), 237

RJR Nabisco, boycott of, 13

Rodríguez, América, 68, 76n3

Rodríguez, Cynthia, 130

Rodríguez Muñiz, Michael, xxvii

Rosaldo, Renato, 94n7

Rúa, Merída, 255n5

Rush, Bobby, 48

Safe, Orderly, Legal Visas and Enforcement Act (SOLVE), 21

Salgado, Juan, 131, 135, 136

Sánchez, Linda, 157

sanctuaries: churches as, 95n10, 221, 222, 243; Cook County, Illinois, xii, 49, 167, 223, 234n11; laws creating, xi, 28, 41, 223; New Sanctuary Movement, 222, 234n10; Puerto Rican support for, 253. *See also* Adalberto United Methodist Church; Arellano, Elvira; Chicago: as sanctuary city

Santa Ana, Otto, 65

Schiller, Nina Glick, 200–201, 202, 211n3

schools, 163–74; alternative, 255n6; bilingual education, 154; exclusion of student political engagement, 166, 206; lessons in Latino/a panethnicity, 253; and march absences, 105, 168, 171–73, 173–74; negative responses to youth protest, 163, 165–67, 167–71; policy change resulting from youth activism, 173–74; as safe environments, 103, 164. *See also* curriculum; teachers

Schubert, W. H., 99

Schumer, Charles, xiii, 25

second generation, xxvii, 198–210; assimilation models, 199–200; and Catholic Church, 88, 89; dual identities, 199, 202, 205–6, 211n2; immigrant identification

of, 201–2, 202–5, 205–6, 210; as representatives of undocumented immigrants, 56, 205–8, 208–9, 222–23, 225, 227–29; rights of citizen children, 86, 103, 221–22, 227–29, 232, 245; and transnational life context, 200–206; trauma of deportation threat on, 228. *See also* mixed-status families; youth and youth activism
Secure American and Orderly Immigration Act (2005), 21
Secure America through Verification and Enforcement Act (2008), 24
Secure Borders, Economic Opportunity, and Immigration Reform Act (2007), xii, xxi, 23–24, 50
Secure Fence Act (2006), 21
Security through Regularized Immigration and a Vibrant Economy Act (STRIVE), xii, 22–23, 57–58, 135, 158
segmented assimilation model, 199
Sensenbrenner Bill (2006): clergy protest of, 83; criminalization of assistance to undocumented immigrants, 21, 205; criminalization of immigrants, 5, 125, 205; House passage of, 20–21; Latino Mobilization Summit Conference, 129–30; marches' role in defeating, xv, 7, 49; as mobilizing force in immigrant rights movement, 5, 47, 113, 146, 156; in print media, 71
September 11 terrorist attacks: and immigrant rights movement, 16, 44; immigration enforcement after, 18–20; restrictionist portrayal of, 182. *See also* terrorism
Sepúlveda, Orlando, 137
Serrano, José, 14, 221–22, 229
Service Employees International Union (SEIU): deportation effect on organizing efforts, 111; megamarch support, 47–48, 109, 112–13, 115, 116; outreach to Mexicans, 127; support for immigrant rights, 13, 44–45, 155; and undocumented workers, 222
service learning, 164, 174
Seven Points of Unity, 130
Sikkink, David, 87–88, 94n6

Simcox, Chris, 180
Sin Fronteras. *See* Centro sin Fronteras
¡Sí! Se Puede! (Cohn), 104–5
¡Sí! Se Puede (Yes We Can) chant, 24, 237
Skerry, Peter, 88
sleeping giant metaphor, xv, xxviii, 4
Smith, Robert C., 201
social movements defined, 52–53
social studies curriculum, 98–99, 101
Soliz, Juan, 40
Soltero, Anthony, 103, 167
SOLVE Act (Safe, Orderly, Legal Visas and Enforcement Act), 21
Soto, Marcia, 47–48, 129–30
Spanish language. *See* language; media, Spanish-language
Spring, Joel H., 164
statistical information. *See* demographic/statistical information
St. Francis of Assisi parish, 91
St. Pious V Catholic Church, 44, 84, 85, 91
STRIVE Act, xii, 22–23, 57–58, 135, 158
Student/Tenant Organizing Project, 157
subjectivity, 184–85, 187, 193–94, 225–27, 229–32
substantive citizenship. *See under* citizenship
surveys. *See* demographic/statistical information; Immigrant Mobilization Project; Pew Hispanic Center surveys
Swedish immigrants, 105–6
Sweeney, John, 110

Tancredo, Tom, 30n20
taxpayer *topos,* 86, 89, 184, 185–88, 196n1, 226
Taylor, Verta, 253
teachers, 97–107; interviews of, 99–100; negative response to student activism, 170–71; roles of, 101–7; support for student activism, xxv, 100, 163, 171, 172–73, 174
Teachers for Social Justice, 98
Teamsters Local 743, 118
Telemundo, 66
Telles, Edward E., 211n2
Temporada de Caza (Echevarria), 3
Ten Points of Unity, 130, 141n11

Tepeyac Association (New York), 12
terrorism, associated with immigration, 54, 155, 205, 220. *See* Homeland Security Act; national security; September 11 terrorist attacks
Theiss-Morse, Elizabeth, 151
topos, defined, 179
Torres, Maria de los Angeles, 42
Torrez, Yolanda, 20
transnationalism: and globalization, 140; and Latino/a panethnicity, 248–49; and length of residence in U.S., 150; and religion, 87–88; and second generation, 200–206; ways of being, 200–201, 202–5; ways of belonging, 201, 205–6; zero-sum hypothesis, 151
trump arguments, 194
Tsao, Fred, 17, 24–25, 46, 53–54, 57
Twenty-first Century Paul Revere Riders, 179, 182

Union for Puerto Rican Students, 246–47
Union of Needletrades, Industrial, and Textile Employees. *See* UNITE HERE
unions. *See* labor involvement in immigrant rights movement; *and names of specific unions*
United Auto Workers, 13
United Electrical, Radio, and Machine Workers of America, 115
United Farm Workers, 13, 110
United Food and Commercial Workers (UFCW), 111, 115, 116
United States: and hometown associations, 147; and Mexico, 18, 44, 134
UNITE HERE, 44–45, 111, 112, 115, 127
University of Illinois at Chicago, 39, 40, 247. *See also* Immigrant Mobilization Project
Univisión, 66
Unzueta, Martin, 114, 117
U.S. Border Patrol. *See* border enforcement/patrol
U.S. Citizenship and Immigration Services, 19
U.S. Conference of Catholic Bishops, 94n7
U.S. Constitution, 184, 191–93

U.S. Customs and Border Protection Agency, 19. *See also* border enforcement/patrol

Valenzuela, Angela, 104
Vargas, Lucilla, 69
Vásquez, Art, 40
Velazquez, Nydia, 14
Victims of Trafficking and Violence Protection Act (2000), 13
Vieques, Puerto Rico, 45, 243–44, 254n4
voter registration drives: as consequence of megamarches, 152; of immigrants prior to 2008 elections, 58; in local political organizing, 157; in Pilsen and Little Village, 88, 94n8; in response to restrictive legislation, 46, 51
voting: church support for, 89; and citizenship, 181, 188, 204; in city elections, 40; as civic participation, 146, 206, 209; and family status, 216, 218; and Latino support for immigrant rights, xxiii; in Mexican elections, 128, 155, 156, 159n3; rates of, xix, 42, 157, 207, 216, 218; school lessons, 100, 164

Walls and Mirrors (Gutiérrez), xxii
Walt Disney, boycott of, 13
Warner, R. Stephen, xxv, 79
Washington, Harold, 40–41
Waukegan, Illinois, xii, 51
Weber, Max, 141n1
welfare reform, 10, 220
West Town Coalition of Concerned Citizens, 40
whites: and Americanness, 204; demographic information, 37; and ethnic identity, 198; and immigrant descent, 43; march participation, xvii, xx, 72–73, 80, 172; and print media, 69–70, 74–75; voter registration rates, 207
Whittier, Nancy E., 253
Wilson, Pete (California governor), 10

¡Ya Basta! campaign, xii, 24, 245
Young Lords Organization, 40
youth and youth activism, 163–74; and

church, 88; citizen children, 86, 103, 221–22, 227–29, 232, 245; coalition involvement, 46, 133; criminalization of, xxvi, 166; fear of mobilizations, 169; history, 126, 165; march participation, xvii, 51, 97, 104, 168, 173–74, 206, 208, 244; narratives from elders, 246–47; protests, 237–38; and representation, 56, 106; and schools, 6, 103–4, 165–67, 171–73, 173–74; and teachers, xxv, 100, 104–5, 163, 171, 172–73, 174. *See also* Batey Urbano; mixed-status families; schools; second generation; Zócalo Urbano

Zavala, Moises, 116–17, 129
zero-sum hypothesis of transnational incorporation, 151
Zócalo Urbano, 39, 46, 207–8, 211n4, 244
Zorn, Eric, 223, 224

LATINOS IN CHICAGO AND THE MIDWEST

Pots of Promise: Mexicans and Pottery at Hull-House, 1920–40
Edited by Cheryl R. Ganz and Margaret Strobel
Moving Beyond Borders: Julian Samora and the Establishment of Latino Studies
Edited by Alberto López Pulido, Barbara Driscoll de Alvarado, and Carmen Samora
¡Marcha! Latino Chicago and the Immigrant Rights Movement
Edited by Amalia Pallares and Nilda Flores-González
Bringing Aztlán to Chicago: My Life, My Work, My Art   *José Gamaliel González,
edited and with an Introduction by Marc Zimmerman*

The University of Illinois Press
is a founding member of the
Association of American University Presses.

Composed in 10.5/13 Minion Pro
with Meta display
by Jim Proefrock
at the University of Illinois Press
Manufactured by Thomson-Shore, Inc.

University of Illinois Press
1325 South Oak Street
Champaign, IL 61820-6903
www.press.uillinois.edu